The Education of Booker T. Washington

From Hollis Reed, *The Negro Problem Solved* (1864). Courtesy New York Public Library's Digital Image Gallery.

Michael Rudolph West

THE EDUCATION OF

BOOKER T. WASHINGTON,

American Democracy and the Idea of Race Relations

COLUMBIA UNIVERSITY PRESS
NEW YORK

Columbia University Press

Publishers Since 1893

New York, Chichester, West Sussex

Copyright © 2006 Columbia University Press

All rights Reserved

Library of Congress Cataloging-in-Publication Data

West, Michael Rudolph, 1962-

The education of Booker T. Washington : American
democracy and the idea of race relations / Michael
Rudolph West.

   p. cm.

Includes bibliographical references and index.

ISBN 0–231–13048–1 (cloth : alk. paper) —

ISBN 0–231–50382–2 (electronic)

1. Washington, Booker T., 1856–1915—Political and
social views. 2. United States—Race relations—
Philosophy. 3. Racism—United States. 4. United
States—Race relations—Political aspects.
5. Racism—Political aspects—United States.
6. African Americans—Civil rights—History.
7. Civil rights movements—United States—
History. 8. Democracy—United States. 9. United
States—Politics and government—Philosophy.
I. Title. E185.97.W4W47   2006

370.92—dc22   2005054750

Columbia University Press books are printed
on permanent and durable acid-free paper

Printed in the United States of America

c 10 9 8 7 6 5 4 3 2 1

References to Internet Web Sites (URLs) were accurate at the time of writing. Neither the author nor
Columbia University Press is responsible for Web
sites that may have expired or changed since the articles in this book were prepared.

To Patty
For when words fail
providing reasons to think thoughts of long dreams

Contents

Preface

THIS WORK seeks simultaneously to explain Booker T. Washington—his life and what he meant to the nation—and his part in the history of "the Negro problem," a term that has since the early 1960s fallen out of use. It once was a rubric encompassing the complex of problems ascribed to African Americans themselves ("the problem with Negroes"); to their anomalous presence in America as slaves and, later, as free people; to the antipathetic attitudes of other Americans; to the legacy of the past; or to some other cause. Washington's life is rather the more known commodity: the conservative who founded Tuskegee Institute, a pragmatist in an age of hard reality for African Americans. But many of his supporters called him a visionary who offered a means of solving "the Negro problem." My argument is that Washington's solution was an idea, a theory here called "race relations," that opened a way for the ideological reconciliation of two opposites: racist proscription and democracy.

Judged by the esteem of his contemporaries, Washington's idea was a great success. Judged by the sorry fate of many millions of African Americans, Washington's leadership was a failure. As a biography, this work seeks to reveal the personal and political dimensions of Washington's journey up from slavery: what he thought about Southern and Northern white people, about the legacy of slavery and the capabilities, needs, and possibilities of the former slaves. As a history of an idea, it sets his thought within the context of that of other racial pundits who likewise sought a solution to "the Negro problem," among them Thomas Jefferson, Samuel C. Armstrong (Washington's mentor), and the social scientist Gunnar Myrdal.

Additionally, I set Washington's portrayal of his rise within the context of that of other self-made men, while suggesting that, in fact, what most helped Washington to realize his ambitions was the democratic promise that was the Reconstruction era and the efforts of those African American men and women who struggled to define freedom and leadership to their own ends. Last, *The Education of Booker T. Washington* poses questions about the continuing prevalence of the idea of race relations down to the time of the modern civil rights movement.

The power of Washington's idea—the race relations idea—is the key to understanding the successful progress of Jim Crow America and the shape of the civil rights movement that sought to dismantle Jim Crow. Thus, Washington's thinking is the key to understanding the form of that movement and its greatest leader. In the introduction that follows, I argue that Martin King's genius did not rest on the innovation of nonviolence, as it is commonly supposed. For decades, Africans Americans had protested and demonstrated nonviolently. As well, the goals sought by the civil rights movement did not require violent methods to be achieved. Instead, and within the context of a coordinated and systematic protest movement, King's advocacy of passive resistance caused a sufficient number of Americans—hundreds of new activists, scores of politicians, perhaps millions of private individuals—to see that justice required not racial reconciliation and the false peace of segregation, but the productive sowing of conflict, the disruption of racial harmony, to serve black people's ends. King's accomplishment, then, was to call into question as an ideological matter the race relations idea that had prevailed since Washington's time. His doing so, if incompletely and only temporarily, paved the way for the movement's success in the fight against the forces of segregation during the early 1960s.

Professor Barbara Jeanne Fields was present at the conception of this study, and her work on Southern history and the potent idea of race, and, most especially, her faith in democracy are in many ways at its heart. I owe her a very great debt. Her example as scholar, friend, and adamant intellectual is a continuing inspiration as well as a challenge to me, and it is among my fondest hopes that this work meets her expectations.

The late James Shenton, as well as Alan Brinkley, Winston James, and Eric Foner, each once or at present of the Columbia University Department of History, made an important contribution to this work. Professor Brinkley, though he has likely long ago forgotten it, made a detailed analysis of an earlier approach to this subject that caused me to think much more deeply about what it was I was after. Professor James shared with me his wide knowledge and his numerous insights into the nature of the African American as well as Afro-Caribbean struggles. In addition to his teaching and advising, Professor Foner, through his work, early on inspired an ambition that, while now somewhat chastened, remains as a desire to master understanding of the past.

Pete Daniel of the Smithsonian Institution, formerly an editor with the Washington papers, responded to a call for help in the graceful and exemplary fashion for which he is well known, and, shared his own insights into Washington's life and its meaning. Adolph Reed Jr., professor of political science at the New School for Social Research, and I have long been engaged in conversation about politics, ideology, and the Negro problem. This is true even despite the fact that the dialogue was mainly one-sided and carried on by myself as I learned from his work.

A debt is owed to the Ford Foundation for the support provided me by it dissertation fellowship program for minorities, and to Henry Louis Gates Jr. and the late Richard Newman for welcoming me to the Du Bois Institute at Harvard University, where I spent an interesting year. I wish to thank as well Professors John Anderson, Ross Beales, Karen Turner, Noel Cary, and the other members of the Department of History at the College of the Holy Cross, whose provision of a warm and collegial environment, cheers, and some prodding were all quite welcome. Professor Eugene McCarthy of the Department of English at Holy Cross helped me find the courage of my convictions on a crucial matter of interpretation. My students, especially Erin O'Connell and Daniel McGinn-Shapiro, were receptive participants in an ongoing series of after-class seminars that helped me to work out the means of bridging the distance between the certain truths we insist upon in America about race and nation and the past and the more difficult and often contrary truths about which I was and am quite certain. Ms. O'Connell also greatly assisted me in correcting the book's notes.

Peter Dimock of Columbia University Press is the editor of this book. It came his way, as it were, over the transom. He read it, for which I thank him, and responded to it in such a timely way, and with such sensitive understanding for the involved purposes that went into it, that I cannot thank him enough.

Two friends contributed greatly to this work and to my spirits during the course of its being written. Marion K. Manneker was with me during much of the original conception, encouraged me with good humor, and shared with me the insights of his broad and free-ranging intelligence. Tony Kaye, taking time away from his own very important work on slave politics in Mississippi, shared with me his deep thinking on the interplay of politics and ideology, past and present, and helped me mightily by participating in hours-long telephone conversations on Washington and the idea of race relations and other assorted topics. I hope I am owed as much as I owe these good comrades.

I thank Rudolph and Linda West for all the time standing against falsity in human affairs, and inspiring me to seek after the truth in human nature. And I thank Marlees R., Phoebe C., and Malcolm R. West both for manifesting an appropriate appreciation of stories from the life and times of Booker T. Washington and, often enough, for insisting upon forays outside that life and those times and into their own.

From the beginning, the person to whom this work is dedicated, Patricia Moon West, patiently listened to my thoughts on Washington, rivers, and long dreams, read thoughtfully every word I wrote on those subjects, demanded clarification when it was sometimes needed, and gave great succor when it was almost always necessary. It would not have been done without her.

The Education of Booker T. Washington

Introduction

B EFORE THE present hawking of iconic images of the latest flavor
in perishable celebrity; before the virtues of nonviolent passivity
were uncoupled from the obligations of nonviolent resistance in the
rush to enshrine Martin Luther King as an abstraction that all Americans
are presumed to worship; before the letter "X" was transformed from the
mysteriousness of that which is long gone into just another bit of merchan-
dise; before culture and lifestyle and politics became synonymous, each
and all commodities neatly organized and readily available for convenient
browsing; before all that, a similarly conceived artifact from the dawn of
mass-market selling enjoyed its own extended vogue. This was a piece of
business called *The Booker T. Washington Calendar*. Years and decades after
Washington's death, the scattering to the winds of the lesser parts of his
great Tuskegee Machine, and the falling out of favor of his educational phi-

losophy even at the school he founded, a symbolic Washington lived on in America as an image pregnant with meaning: an inspiration and a portrait of what might be, a constant scold against what ought not be, a watchful warder over the people's fate.

Today, one hears occasionally of Washington's name being held up for praise of one sort or another, not only from the black-people-should-stop-complaining-and-start-their-own-businesses phalange of contemporary controversialists, but also from Jim Crow nostalgists, who say things like, "We had vibrant communities back then, with our own doctors and lawyers and . . ." Generally, the potent, symbolic Washington has all but passed from the scene, a casualty of the civil rights movement and the resonant meaning of its own symbols and icons. Nevertheless, individuals who grew up in the Jim Crow South can yet remember Washington's eyes upon them: hung up in kitchens and barber shops, on the walls of schoolhouses and over the desks of studious strivers, as well as next to the till at pool halls and juke joints, where striving of another sort took place. The slogan of one such calendar read "Onward and Upward," Langston Hughes recalled in 1965, and the whole of the presentation looked like this: "A glowing photograph of Dr. Washington adorned the top center crowning a pathway to the sunup [to] which freed Negroes marched with the humble tools of agriculture and simple industry in hand—hoes, mallets, axes, and hammers—while amiable and approving whites looked on from the sidelines." "Everybody seemed happy," Hughes wrote. And emblazoned across the top was the word "Progress."[1]

Washington, the prophet of progress, eventually appears in an ironic way to some of those who are closest to his shadow, as with the students who made a joke of the monument to Washington on the Tuskegee Institute campus he built up from the seeming inhospitality of the Deep South countryside. One of them, Ralph Ellison, would leave it to a character in a novel to describe it: "the cold Father symbol, his hands outstretched in the breathtaking gesture of lifting a veil that flutters in hard, metallic folds above the face of a kneeling slave; and I am standing puzzled, unable to decide whether the veil is really being lifted, or lowered more firmly in place; whether I am witnessing a revelation or a more efficient blinding."[2]

Time preys upon the past, tarnishing its statues, soiling its symbols, and making monuments to departed heroes appear, in the best light, as instances, now ironic, of obsolete grandeur. The solemnity of statues, the meaning of icons, can be lost, buried beneath the accumulated graffiti of both ill-informed and well-informed Kilroys. But what of time's effect on dreams and the memories of dreams?

%%%

THE SPECIFIC purpose of *The Education of Booker T. Washington* is neither to restore Washington to a place of honor nor to judge him an atavism. Rather, its aim is, first, to recount how he came to be associated with progress, a panacea in his person, word, and deed to all the pain and troublesome anxiety Americans like to associate with the black presence in America; second, to analyze the persuasiveness of his ideas; and third, to place those ideas in the events of his life down to the time of his ascension to the stage at Atlanta, Georgia, in 1895 to give the speech that would make his name.

My broader purpose in writing *The Education of Booker T. Washington* is to establish a groundwork for understanding the ideological origins of the civil rights movement, without, one hopes, prejudicing the account of Washington in his own time. I was once told, disapprovingly, by one of the most important contributors to the legal fight against segregation, whom I had apprised of my subject, "We weren't very ideological." Because of this, I should say just what I mean by "ideological" as against other kinds of origins. Historians and others have put down a solid foundation for our understanding a good part of the story of whence the civil rights movement came. They do so by establishing that long before Rosa Parks refused to give up her seat on a bus in Montgomery, Alabama, and the boycott and the emergence of Martin King that followed, launching the modern freedom struggle, African Americans and a few allies and helpers protested against segregation and disfranchisement and otherwise worked, with only limited success, to break the bonds of racist proscription; that by December 1, 1955, black people in Montgomery and new, more prosperous black communities elsewhere in the South were experienced in mobilization such that it was a matter of "organizing the organized" rather than discovering the secret of fire or first inventing the wheel.[3]

These origins, this history of the activist precursors to the movement, show demonstrations, voter registration efforts, and boycotts that were more sporadic and less systematic than what was to come after 1955, and particularly after the onset of the student-led sit-in movement in early 1960. Where the early efforts do not differ from the modern movement, however, is in their nature as nonviolent efforts to bring pressure to bear on Jim Crow. Because they were nonviolent, the question emerges: What is the significance to the unfolding of the movement of King's espousal of nonviolence? The answer lies in ideology, by which I mean the nature of the ideas or premises with which Americans conceived of the African American situation and reckoned with the legitimacy of means through which change in the situation might take place. These ideas, along with the political and social reality of segregation and disfranchisement, formed the environment within which King and the movement took shape, the context for their defeat of segregation and disfranchisement, and their less success-ful struggle to inaugurate the reign of a thoroughgoing justice in America. What I have sought here is to show how Booker T. Washington and ideas that he gave voice to three-quarters of a century earlier lie back of the civil rights era's dramatic unfolding and ambiguous result.[4]

A special report, interrupting some television show or other, to announce the death of Martin King is one of my first memories. Worried and con-fused, but sure of the ill tidings his murder represented, I was moved to ask my parents if we were going to have to leave the country. I was five then, living in Lansing, Michigan, and so perhaps it was what had come before—news and vivid images of protests and marches and riots and troop movements within American cities—that led me to this dramatic moment in my brief life. Or, perhaps my memory is faulty, and I asked the question as a result of the terrible riot that had taken place an hour's drive away in Detroit the year before or the general unease evoked in me by George Wal-lace's running frighteningly well—it seemed to me—for the presidency. I do feel sure that, in this time or just after, I was carried along to at least a few marches—in Lansing, or later in Ann Arbor, and, certainly, some in Ithaca, New York, where my family moved in the immediate aftermath of a brief but somewhat storied takeover of the Cornell University student union. And I can clearly recall the wholly promiscuous manner in which my sister and I flashed peace signs to passing motorists and each other, and a button we sometimes wore that read, "I'm for One Race—the Human Race!"

I do not offer this sketchy résumé with any hope that the reader will be overawed by my special status as observer-participant in the struggles of the late 1960s and early 1970s. Or to set myself up to claim some broad-bore perspective—black or white or some mixture thereof, as these things are sometimes construed. Instead, I am trying, in a preliminary and tenta-tive way, to describe the destiny of common dreams, and I mean only to offer my own example as a fair representative of that of the large number of Americans who, with the death of Jim Crow and legalized forms of dis-crimination, were moved to dream of new and better possibilities in that time; those who could, through the light cast by King and the civil rights movement, see or imagine seeing a land of justice on a near horizon. How many? Decidedly less than a majority of Americans, but that is no belittle-ment of a movement, the best part of which—like the 1960s sit-in begun by four North Carolina A&T freshmen in Greensboro, North Carolina—chal-lenged existing consensus rather than sought its embrace.

Then the light, like the sun in relative eclipse, dimmed. And the movement, the rush at what was supposed to be the end of the long river of black struggle, delivered us and with us, our fondest hopes, not to the promised land but out to sea, and buffeted ever onward toward farther shores. And if it can be said that we are, in these matters, adrift, whose voice calls out? Do we indeed hear the echo of King's call for earnest, democratic struggle? Or do we hear the more distant reverberations of a voice of "progress," the siren song of a century past?

The promise of democracy in tension with the forces seeking to retard that promise constitutes the first main theme of this work. In memory, the advancement of democracy—struggles dared, challenges met, leaders emergent, victories and defeats—can be confused with the powerful idea of progress. I mean to show progress as offered up by Washington and his advocates, to be a false substitute for democracy. And I mean to suggest that words like *progress*, conventionally defined as unmitigated goods, play a profound role in that substitution.[5]

%%%

I AM perfectly prepared to stipulate that not all agree on this matter of being adrift; as I have said, I am only trying to describe a kind of feeling of disappointment that the best hopes of the civil rights movement were not realized and to establish a grounding with those still drawn to the river and the warm waters of a sustaining faith that "the People" might make their world a better place. Surely, some would deny this, asserting that what was done was all that could be done, and that now that legal equality exists, it is time for black people to pull up bootstraps and sink or swim like other Americans with their noses pressed to grindstones. One can insist (as my students often do at the beginning of the semester) that nothing has changed and all is tragedy. Likewise, one can insist that King was "all about" rendering "race" a dead letter, and then squint with steely-eyed precision at this or that passage or part of a sentence from King in order to assert the crusade he described is accomplished; that now is the time for the assessing of individual character (and who among us is afraid to stand shorn of our trivialities and submit to society's scrutiny?). And, in response, one might proclaim that what King stood for was a long haul against racism and discrimination and poverty and militarism.

These debates (such as they are) about King and the legacy of the era for black people and the nation go on, their endurance and continuing interest signs not of a coming eventual enlightenment, I think, but of ambivalence about what has been achieved, and with the appearance of being an endless game, a loop leading nowhere. "There's wrong on both sides," one sometimes hears, as though there were only two, when in fact there are many more than two, multiple sides amounting to a piled-high diversity that is capped by those words spoken on certified occasions, the clichés of annual King breakfasts, the scripts enacted before concluding the program with another arms-interlocked chorus of "We Shall Overcome."

Absurdities abound, as one would expect when good faith and bad faith, glibness and solemnity, claim equal footing.[6] Thus we see and hear certain savants describing dreams, claiming an hour upon the stage of what talking heads, cultural players and pretenders both, call "our national conversation on race": assistant professors of diverse topics, who find their mettle as crack shots aiming at the heart of just what is wrong with black people; deconstructors of "blackness," openers of windows, unlockers of doors, promising they, finally, will be the one to reveal the secret truths African Americans stubbornly conceal; ministers to indeterminate congregations, small streams pretending at being large rivers, promising a national salvation if only for a price; latter-day heads of civil rights organizations who congregate behind microphones—just like Martin and Ralph did—but now to hand out another image award to this or that semi-sympathetic celebrity; artisans of hip-hop and their streetwise academic advocates who would supplant the fogies of established groups and institutions by way of their hard-edged authenticity and greater marketability; other scientists of sound who undertake experiments to prove that it is possible that four or six or eight or ten hundred thousand black men may be brought in and out of the nation's capital without any tangible effect but that it is better to be a healer than a divider; and on and on and on.

In chapter 1 I pay further attention to this queer habit of mind, this problematizing of black people's lives, and sketch some of its history. It is my second main theme, here, for if, as I believe, scrutinizing African Americans is a national pastime, Washington is our home-run king (our Henry Aaron to an earlier time's Babe Ruth). The story I tell involves how Washington came to run the field, out-arguing (with some of the people who counted most) proponents of what he himself called "the various and conflicting opinions as to what is to be [the Negro race's] final phase in our economic and political life."[7] His personal victory, through a mixture of ideas and earnestness, pandering, and dissembling, came at a cost: he became not a leader of black men and women, but a creature of the power of white politicians, editors, and influential educators; he became Negro leader, beholden not to the democratic consent of those who ostensibly raised him upon their shoulders, but to the favors of white public opinion makers.

One encounters the free-form scrutinizing of the nature and future of African America, the gypsy intuitions of fortunetellers divining black people's errors and best interests, on amateur stages as well as on professional ones. Some years ago, in New York, a former college classmate of my wife approached me at a party, meandered around it a bit before asking me a question about a particular black figure who had captured her fancy, an essayist and acerbic social commentator on black misbehaving—crime and drugs and sex—and the foibles of black public figures who seemed unwilling or unable to clean up this mess. "Why," she wondered, was he not "more of a black leader?" (That is, why did blacks not accept him as their leader?) "You like him," I replied (without, I hope, any rancor, but cryptically), "so maybe he should just be a white leader."

Left there, one plays the game, bats the ball back over the net of our national conversation. For every puff of rock cocaine there are six or seven or eight snorts of the powdered variety; if this group of men and women, as it is often said, have failed since the 1960s to constitute themselves into proper family units, one takes note of the concurrent dramatic increase in the rending of American families, generally, and cracks back with something snappy about glass houses and stones. "Yes, but can't they least afford these bad habits?" Out to sea, do you ask the crest of a wave to stop its crashing?

It has been my experience that such encounters sometimes begin in indirect ways: as snippets of half-heard conversation, at parties or on public transportation. Often (though not always) the voices are loud enough that one might plausibly deny one's eavesdropping: "They segregate themselves." "They enslave themselves all the time in Africa." "They all think that he didn't kill his wife." "They should do like we do" (or the Jews, the Asians, or the Jamaicans do). "What do they want?" Although, in these voices, there is an inevitable aspect of challenge, an invitation to join the joust, the tone varies: sometimes aggressive, hostile even; other times striking a note of sincere and sympathetic questioning.

In the case of my wife's friend, she and I both knew that African Americans were now able to participate in elections and otherwise ratify their support for this political figure or that social commentator. But the period in question was a tumultuous time in New York, a time of "street militants" marching, but also significant success for political figures like David Dinkins and, especially, Jesse Jackson; a time when the notion of "a black misleadership" gained a certain currency, calling in question, it seemed to me, the success of those in the vicinity of the corridors of power rather as much as the ambiguous results of those stuck marching out in the street.[8] To my interlocutor, an obvious solution to the problem was for black New Yorkers to rally behind her particular pet (a witty raconteur and one of that type of old-school intellectual hipster that derives great pleasure from always referring to "Negroes," no matter the context or currently popular term). At the same time, she was checking me out, too, reconnoitering to see if I was the sensible type, not blinded or biased or embittered, not a part of what, by her lights, was a problem of race relations.

Thus framed, two roles were available to me. I might have denied what I knew in order to confirm her in her definition of the problem, been her reassuring guide leading her along the way to the conclusion that both of us have our hearts in the right place on these matters. Or I might have said that she did not understand the black perspective. There is seductive but false satisfaction to be found in playing out either script. In the first, the satisfaction is of reconciliation, but one attributing to simple human verities a depth they do not deserve; a kind of self-deluding exaggeration that if we two can traverse the racial divide, then perhaps there is hope that all Americans might be so reconciled. In the second, there is satisfaction in the confirmation of the problem, a concrete enactment of racial division in the irreconcilable disagreement of two individuals.

Many Americans find amusement in witnessing or participating in such verbal jousting, the small-scale version of our national conversation, and are inclined toward self-congratulation either for their toleration of diverse perspectives or for their articulation of their group perspective or defense of their culture, or—another approach—for chiming in with still another perspective to prove that the divide is not all black and white. And so the table grows larger, the numbers of players increase; "race cards" are dealt and trumped in turn. Writers, like adventuresome archaeologists, like big-game hunters, journey to colleges and traverse campuses, heedless as they pass colorful groupings of hooked-up couples and roommates and friends, in search of the school cafeterias where they have been assured they will find their prey. There, their gazes flit over the thirty or forty long tables with a smattering here or there of black students to fix on the one table where five or eight or ten have gathered their trays. Noting this, the rise of black studies and "identity politics," a doyen of vital-center liberalism expresses his fears of "balkanization" in America (even as, in the actual Balkans, a massacre is taking place).[9] One month newspaper editors will print headlines reading "Racial Progress Seen," when an African American becomes the first to accomplish something or other, and the next month, "Enduring Racial Division," based on what some pollster has said the evidence means if two-thirds of African Americans support affirmative action policies and two-thirds of European Americans are against them, or if African Americans are four times more likely to say that black people receive less than fair treatment in the workplace and in public accommodations, or, even, five times more likely to believe that a football player's guilt had not been proved in his murder trial. And those who adhere to the national conversation figure they have arrived at something like the sad truth: they line up over there, we line up over here, and never the twain shall meet.

On the other hand, for those whose faith rests not in racial reconciliation but in democratic struggle and whose hope is for justice, what is perhaps most useful is the evidence of that which is not seen in those numbers as they are conventionally interpreted, those things concealed by the common equation. Turn down the chatter of the national conversation, step outside the game, re-do the math with real numbers rather than the misleading black-and-white of percentages, and we see that a greater number of European Americans than African Americans take the nominally "black position" (even, on some questions, a greater number of white people than there are black people).[10]

The relative merit of these positions is not the point. Nor is the point the glib academic ritual known as "complicating" matters. Nor is it my point to state the obvious: that a majority of Americans can or need to come together for change to take place. Leave the imagined debate, and it is possible to recognize that what needs to be explained—what really poses such an ideological problem to Americans that we must conceal it from ourselves—is not what most black people think. That can be represented as embitterment, lack of balance, the embrace of victimhood, or, if the denizens of talk radio shows are correct, unsuitability to fulfill the responsibility of a juror; accounted for, in other words, to just such an extent that they may be easily sloughed off. But what of that substantial minority of white Americans who also take the "black" position? Are they an aggregation of especially fervent football fans huddled up with knee-jerking, bleeding hearts of the maligned "P.C." crowd? Or are they persons who have paid attention in the same way many African Americans have to a long history of governmental misconduct as well as to more recent developments since the 1960s? Are they persons who have seen through the racial-conversation game and opted not to play, who refuse to concede that the struggle for justice—not "racial justice"—was over a generation ago? If so, then their concealment, the obliteration of their voices, within the dark recesses of our national conversation suggests that the game is not so much about "inclusion" or "diversity"—value-neutral terms that are inevitably mistaken for politics—as it is about policing the margins of the political and intellectual mainstream. And further, that the game's endpoint, the framework of racial reconciliation in which the racial perspectives of black America and white America will be made one, is but the means and rhetoric of evasion, the charade obscuring real problems and forestalling the coming together of specific groupings of Americans in purposeful action.

The preceding has been my effort to chart our present waters, as well as an invitation to the reader to think about the course of the nation since the King era. My intention in the pages that follow is to begin the process of evacuating the origins of our conventional rhetoric, to scrutinize it persuasiveness, and to analyze its logic.

%%%

IN APPROACHING this subject, I have limited myself to a relatively narrow field of primary material along with Washington's published work, including, especially, his autobiography.[11] In doing so, I have sought to take Washington seriously as if not an intellectual, then at least a thinking man, someone who expounded what seemed to many Americans of his time and later to be a comprehensive program addressing the needs of black people and the nation. It is in his capacity as philosopher of a social problem and his molding of the opinion of a most influential part of the public that Washington, his telling of his life, and his telling of the story of African Americans "up from slavery" are most important, and it is his ideas and the way they formed a part of an enduring American consensus that have been most neglected.

This emphasis in my interpretation of Washington proceeds, first and foremost, from the continuing, if not generally acknowledged influence of Washington's ideas on our own time. Moreover, I believe that certain errors have led two different bodies of historical literature—that on Washington and other African American leaders and that on Southern history—to miss the cardinal significance of what Washington and his message symbolized for his own time. My critique of the historiography is developed further in the body of the study. For the moment I want to offer a few introductory comments on these errors and their consequences.

Biographical studies of Washington and accounts of African American leadership at the turn of the century interpret Washington in various ways. In one interpretation, Washington is a black conservative emphasizing the creation of economic enterprises and stressing black people's responsibility for their own fate over and above the defense of civil rights and the attack on racism he might have stressed. Another interpretation sees Washington as merely a puppet or tool of powerful white persons, a "white man's black man," as one historian calls him, although whether this controlling white person is of the South or the North or both is not all the time clear.[12] What these interpretations share are two assumptions: first, that Washington was simply a pragmatist, and second, that there is such a thing as an authentic black leader, a pure product of African America from which he organically emerges. The interpretations divide merely on the question of whether Washington is such a leader.

The second literature is that of Southern history, and that discipline's study of the post-Reconstruction period and the stirrings of progressivism in the South. Generally speaking, historians of Southern progressivism distinguish what they consider to be the good and beneficial aspects of turn-of-the-century reform—increased funding for education being outstanding—from those not to their taste like segregation and other aspects of racist proscription (including a relative decrease in educational funding for black children and the deliberate retarding of secondary education for African American children).[13] From a moral perspective this distinction is all to the good, but it is not a distinction most progressives, South and North, made in any consistent way. My argument is that Washington's leadership had much to do with the tying together of both these strands, and with convincing his followers and supporters that the total result was indeed progress.[14]

If that is so, the notions of Washington as simply a tool of white power—an "Uncle Tom"—as a "black conservative," and, generally, the question of whether he was an authentic leader of African Americans rather miss the point.[15] There were African Americans willing to go much farther than Washington in appealing to the prejudices of white bigots. Take, for an example, William Hannibal Thomas, whose racist screed was no different from that of contemporary white racists.[16] But Thomas was not renowned like Washington for the simple reason that saying what he said had no appeal to optimists looking for a hopeful, progressive way out of the seemingly intractable situation in which America somehow found itself in the 1890s.

Equally, there were, in the age of Washington, African Americans like Alexander Crummell who were actual philosophical conservatives. However, the forces that elevated Washington after his 1895 address at the Cotton States and International Exposition in Atlanta were not looking for any type of conservative. Rather, they sought and found a visionary who could help them see their way through an essentially ideological process of reconciling the innovations of systematic segregation and disfranchisement with their faith in America as a land of fairness, decency, equality of opportunity, and justice for all. Washington's accomplishment, in short, is to tie together in one idea the dangling strands of many ideas about the meaning of both reality (brutal oppression) and humanitarian concern (brutal oppression is wrong, the Negro is not receiving a fair deal) and tie them together so that the bundled strands will appear as a plausible and optimistic way for Americans and the Negro to climb out of the hole into which fate has placed them. In this light, Washington's project and his importance do not lie solely within African American history, but within a broader history of American thinking (and wrangling) on social questions going back to colonial times.

Toilers within this tradition, embodied by Thomas Jefferson as well as by Washington, were ever seeking a solution to the problem they supposed to come about from the presence of black people in America. The means they proposed to accomplish this resolution might be fantastical as practical matters, flights of fancy that only dreamers could believe in—like the notion that segregation and disfranchisement together were consistent with democracy and means of bettering the situation of African Americans. But the real significance of these plans and other sorts of final solutions lies in their accomplishment of an ideological peace of one sort or another between potentially warring forces and ideals. In the rise of Jim Crow, Washington played a crucial role in the domestication of an iniquitous system. He took up this long American dream and, through his vision, solved it, casting his dream for America and the Negro out into the world and down through the ages. This, he said, was his aim; this, his supporters said, was his accomplishment. Washington's words at the Cotton States and International Exposition were much ballyhooed; the next year, in 1896, the Supreme Court's decision in *Plessy v. Ferguson* was met "mainly with apathy" in the nation's newspapers.[17] The explanation for these different reactions is not complicated: Americans judged that when it came a favorable evaluation of what was a manifest denial of equal protection and fundamental fairness, there was greater value in Washington's words—those of a black man and former slave—than those of an elevated panel of white judges. And this was so because Washington's words and the example of his person were sufficient to sustain a pretense of democratic process—a compromise between two large polities, Negro America and America, "separate but equal"—upon wholly antidemocratic proceedings, with the lone man, Washington, somehow empowered to give consent for the whole of African America in the dispossession of their rights as American citizens.

Today, we do not suppose that the America of Washington's time had, in a progressive way, solved the problem of racism and poverty or otherwise established a regime of justice. It had not, and the means embraced by Washington and his supporters could not, but the move did help replace the idea of justice with the dogma of racial peace; and, in doing so, this innovation did serve some interests and their ends.

Even morally right thinking about these matters may be blinded by the very innovations of the time under scrutiny. In his famous "Atlanta Compromise" address of 1895, Washington used as a central metaphor the figure, symbolized by his own upraised hand, that "In all things that are purely social we can be as separate as the fingers, yet one as the hand in all things essential to mutual progress."[18] Following him, Americans say that segregation created two societies, one black and one white. It did not, and all the notions that flow from this mistaken impression are likewise untrue. One is the idea of "the Negro leader" who is supposed to function as the counterpart to regular social, political, and business leaders, not "white leaders," and whose power and authority are expressed and employed through the institutions of America, not those of "white" society. That is to say, the genuine leaders preside over the institutions of governance, justice, and the police power to which African Americans are subject, just like those citizens who are allowed to vote and move about freely where they will. Because segregation did not create two societies or nations, disfranchisement cannot have created a democracy for those (most, though not all white men) who were protected in their right to vote. That is to say, the notion of a partial (or "*Herrenvolk*") democracy is specious, an effective, if transparent self-delusion Americans maintained through the six decades of the twentieth century—as the world's bastion of democracy—that we need not tarry long over.[19] Democracy is at an end if it is once extended on the basis of universal manhood suffrage, and then, by hook and by crook both, it is denied to half of the polity in Mississippi and South Carolina and at least one out of three voters throughout the South. Even though the Fifteenth Amendment may remain on the books, it is rendered a dead letter for the whole of the nation. Thus, the American system that endured from the age of Washington to the late 1960s no more merits the name "democracy" than "National Socialism" merits identification with the promise or premises of socialism. And it does not much matter what is called the hook and what is called the crook: there is on one hand terrorism and corruption, and on the other hand the Compromise of 1877 and the antidemocratic, legally sanctioned devices invented with the Mississippi Plan of 1890 and copied for deployment by the other Southern states thereafter.

In the twenty years after his performance at Atlanta catapulted him to national prominence, his supporters and adherents called Washington many favorable things. In the American tradition holding that politics is the art of the possible, perhaps the most laudatory of these characterizations is that he was realistic or pragmatic, a quality attributed to him by both his friends and those who were more grudging admirers.[20] In a different way, these characterizations, too, miss the point. For what type of pragmatism must he be practicing if, at the end of his two decades of leadership, African Americans have more dramatically foreshortened horizons than at the beginning? Is it realism to suggest that black people can advance relative to white people when their abilities to participate in the polity, in civil society, and in economic affairs have been systematically extirpated?[21]

Washington's importance, in my view, derives from what he said to cause influential white persons to crown him *the* Negro leader, not from what he did as a leader of black people. It is Washington the visionary shaper of public opinion as opposed to Washington the conservative, "Uncle Tom," or realist who succeeded smashingly in apprehending and satisfying the demand from white reformers, New South publicists, Northern liberals, and nascent Progressives for a rhetorical way out of a moral and political conundrum, as distinct from an actual and democratic way out of a nasty antidemocratic situation. His were marching orders of the mind, rather than those directing real troops to hasten themselves hither and yon. One element of this means of ideological egress is the promise of progress he offered the nation. A second is that the first principle of Negro leadership, embodied by Washington, is responsibility to white persons. This is not a new idea in the age of Washington, but one that had a particular meaning when the African American leadership cadre was liquidated by the disfranchisement policies and widely proclaimed goal of "white supremacy" in the Southern politics of the 1890s

Escape from difficult problems through a turn of mind, affirmations of progress despite evidence of crisis in the Southern economy, and a Negro leadership selected by white persons are the components of what in this book I call Washingtonianism. However, Washingtonianism's most important and longest enduring element is an idea and a theory in one. This idea is "race relations." I do not mean that he had an idea about race relations but rather that his idea was race relations. Washington developed an analysis about African America's strengths and weaknesses, about segregation, racism, the forces arrayed against black people, and the forces that might potentially ally with black people. The product of that analysis was a solution that ought to be called race relations: how African Americans and white persons relate to one another purporting to be both cause and cure of black backwardness and white hostility; race relations as an analysis generating race relations as a cure for the complex of difficulties Americans used to group as "the Negro problem." Washingtonianism is not a notion about race relations. Rather, Washingtonianism advanced race relations as a notion about Jim Crow, an idealist rendering of the Jim Crow reality conforming to positive convictions about its fairness and benevolence, and the fairness and benevolence of the United States and its freedom- and justice-loving citizenry.

In attributing this meaning to "race relations," it is not my intention to manipulate the meaning of terms or to wrangle with rhetoric. Quite the contrary, I believe I am being true to the historical invention and deployment of the term in Washington's time as popularized especially by him. Its current use in the popular vernacular and by specialists is a product of Washington's success, and, it seems to me, suffers from the same or an even greater problem than when it was newly minted. Americans take "race relations" as a normative term, with little mindfulness of either its historical derivation or its obscurantism. In the conventional wisdom, African Americans have race relations, but white Americans, in the absence of black people and other "minorities," except in instances that rather tend to highlight the black rule, do not. Or, the term is bandied about as a synonym for racism faced by black people.[22] Most commonly, "race relations" is employed as if it were an analytic tool in itself endowed with the power to measure our strivings for the right and good: here are the rules of solitaire, these are the suits, this is the game described; we all win if the hearts and diamonds and clubs and spades are properly arranged. My position is that the term is of no such usefulness. Historically, we know some of the cards were marked and the deck stacked; as a view of history, race relations is simply not a full deck.

One way of illustrating this inadequacy comes from a consideration of romantic and marriage relationships between black and white persons—so-called miscegenation. What does the increase in the incidence of such relations indicate in the judgment of Washington's time but bad race relations? By the light of our own time, the same facts are taken to mean good (or at least improving) race relations. Rather than divorce ourselves from the logic of the past (a private matter made political), we remain married to it. A wiser course would be to recognize race relations for what it is: a term reflecting the specific self-understanding of those complicit in the manufacture of inequity and racism.

The race relations idea is the means by which segregation and racist proscription are assimilated by American ideology such that Americans in the age of segregation may persist in calling the American scheme of things democratic despite manifest legal and other proofs to the contrary. Moreover, the formulation, ritualizing race and casting every situation in terms of race, obscures a wider reality by isolating and coloring the experience of African Americans. It also enables Americans to see both Washington's time and the subsequent history of the civil rights movement's assault on the edifice of Jim Crow, not as a difficult and heroic victory for the movement and for black people or as an indictment of the whole of America's treatment of African Americans, but as progress, the realization of the American dream, and a gift to Negroes (as in the commonplace: black people were "granted" or "given" their rights in the 1960s). And to see black advancement in isolation from the broader and more rapid advancement of other Americans, including those white Southerners and others whose prosperity was directly attributable to their exploitation of the disadvantage under which African Americans, especially, but not exclusively, were made to struggle.

My point here is easily illustrated. In the age of Jim Crow, if a sharecropper who can trace a part of his ancestry back to Africa prospers against the odds to purchase his own land, this is evidence of good race relations even if the landowner and his creditors have lined their pockets with the greater part of his productivity. If ten or twenty thousand sharecroppers who can trace a part of their ancestry back to Africa live like peons in constant, miserable poverty we readily attribute their fate to bad race relations, an answer that presumably would provide little succor to ten or twenty thousand poor white people suffering a similar fate, Joads and Ewells and "lint-heads" all gray bits of trash blown along by the wind. The one is disfranchised and segregated; the other has little political voice. There are differences, one supposes, but the nature of that difference cannot be captured in race relations. To explain the plight of the latter upon terms different from the former is merely to fall prey to the obscurantism an unjust order throws up in its defense. The idea of race relations is a form of analytic segregation.

The great import of the race relations idea lies not only in what it helps clarify for many Americans in the Age of Washington, but also because it survives Washington, remaining in force down to the time of the civil rights movement as the main ideological buttress sustaining antidemocratic practices and proscription in a nation elsewhere aggressively proclaiming its democratic creed and institutions. The endurance of this oppression was made ideologically secure, but not by racism as such. Americans, as a general matter, have hesitated to embrace in a straightforward way the idea of racist oppression (so that, for example, once Americans might speak of a putative "race oppression," and today the preferred term is "racial oppression"). The constitutional doctrine upholding segregation might have been summed up as "separate and equal" or "separate yet equal," but became "separate but equal," the phrase pronouncing itself—voice rising—almost as if questioning its own validity.

Those closest to and most directly involved in the oppression of black people, the minority of Americans who gained the most from this iniquity in exploiting sharecroppers and industrial laborers, as well as those who bled extortionate rents from captives of big city ghettoes may not have required any such rhetorical scruple, no matter what they might have instructed their legal and political hirelings who carried their interests before judicial and legislative bodies. But "not separate and not equal" is hardly a basis for a national consensus, even though that phrase is precisely accurate. It is the process by which the vastly more numerous majority of Americans who are not involved in bending backs and sweating workers come to make a choice either to philosophize disgrace or call it by its name and, perhaps, struggle for its undoing that is the key to understanding the success of Jim Crow. Judicial phrase-making was not sufficient. The prevalence of Washington's idea enabled Americans to isolate African America's just claims from those democratic values they elsewhere proudly proclaimed. Its beauty lies in the way it allows an evasion of the question of costs: the consequences of this injustice visited upon these Americans; the large margin separating these Americans from what they deserved and had earned; the consequences for the nation's political and economic and social development that were the result of the acceptance of the new system of segregation, the invigorated discrimination and finely tuned exploitation; the political and intellectual consequences of the triumph of a double standard fettering not African Americans alone, but tying down workers, as well, hindering the formation of solidarities, and liberating those who might otherwise have given serious scrutiny to the fate of their fellow Americans to believe themselves free persons in an innocent American democracy.

All efforts to press black people's claims to justice, equality, and freedom were evaluated, North and South, on this basis of whether they would upset good race relations, racial harmony, and so on and on. Thus was the African American movement's ability to build alliances limited. And so, too, were black people's efforts at moral suasion as even sympathetic friends, bowing before conforming notions of what white people would bear, limited their advocacy to improving race relations. This was the invisibility about which Ralph Ellison wrote so powerfully fifty years ago. An invisibility that was result of black people's interests and claims being distorted through the lens of relativism such that in 1950 W. E. B. Du Bois, even at the very dawning of the civil rights movement, was moved to comment, "I am forced to remember that relativity applies to the Negro problem here, and not simply to the sun and the stars."[23]

The race relations idea, the relativism condoning "the Negro's place," the damping down of the people's possibilities, and the fettering of democracy, was what the modern black movement, emergent after 1954, was forced to fight right alongside their battling bigots in the streets and courthouses: the consensus that made meaningful such statements as "our negroes were happy 'til . . ." the Communists or the NAACP or Martin King or SNCC came to town, meddling with thriving racial harmony. The movement and, especially, King's insistence that in the fomenting of creative conflict a higher justice, far superior to the false peace of good race relations, could be obtained was a direct challenge to the race relations idea.[24]

Illustration of the race relations idea functioning as a national consensus can be found in a brief comparison of two of the movement's major engagements: the 1962 failure in Albany, Georgia, and the 1963 success in Birmingham, Alabama. In the former instance, King was "branded a loser," not as Taylor Branch would have it, "because segregation still stood," but rather because Sheriff Laurie Pritchett's tactic of nonviolently handling demonstrators (publicly, at least) caused the national press and the Kennedy administration to understand King and the movement as the instigators of conflict (racial strife, the fomenting of racial animus) and thus unworthy of sympathetic intervention. In Birmingham, Police Commissioner Bull Connor's brutal tactics yielded the opposite response. Segregation in both cities was equally unjust; the movement in both cities sought confrontation and crisis. But it was only in Birmingham that the movement won national attention and both popular and strategically situated support because there Connor and his minions were seen as the cause of the problem. King's "Letter from a Birmingham City Jail" represents the greatest expression of his efforts to convince Americans that the present racial harmony is "an obnoxious negative peace," and that good intentions and a belief in democracy require movement off the fence of putative moderation and good race relations to a position of partisanship with black people's aspirations for freedom, citizenship, and justice.[25] This was what drew together some considerable number of Americans to form the modern civil rights movement: not the wearing pull of guilt; not Schwerner and Goodman, but Schwerners and Goodmans and, most of all, many Cheneys; not the motive of perfecting race relations, but that of instituting democracy, its promise and its challenge to act in concert with others to work their will on the institutions of American life; a democratic resolve manifest in sit-ins and marches and voter registration drives, and sympathy pickets and boycotts and letters to Congress, or mere quiet sympathy realized in some less profound way, then or later or perhaps not at all.

The prevalence of the antidemocratic thrust of the Negro problem, the relativism to which Du Bois referred, runs throughout American history.

The history of the Negro problem is the history of an enduring American resolve to naturalize and domesticate treatment that otherwise would be recognized as antithetical to our foundational beliefs. The race relations idea, Washington's contribution, is the answer to that phase of the Negro problem manifest in the segregation era.

Writing a half century ago, an earlier biographer went to the heart of what Washington represented to the nation even years after his death: "Greater by far than the sum of all Booker Washington's functional achievements was the man himself."[26] There is a key to understanding the larger history of the Negro problem and the black struggle buried within this perspective on Washington as the embodiment of his own vision, his very existence was evidence of peaceful, national progress.

The challenge I have undertaken is not an attempt at a definitive biography of a man but an exploration of the race relations idea at its genesis in the mind of a man at a specific moment in the history of the American nation; to tell the intertwined history of an idea and a man, and of a time in America that brought forth both. For Washington's life story, I have sought to grapple with the mythos surrounding him, especially with his telling of his life story and the reality often concealed by his shaping of that story to comport better with his notion of the problems of black people and their solution. This has been done, not to debunk Washington and refute his advocates, but to restore to him the full measure of his humanity, recognizing him choices and complexities—aspects of that humanity denied him by Washington the autobiographer as well as most of the other writers of his life: a product of slavery but a child of emancipation; an exceptional example born of some exceptional mentors, but also a son of specific parents and of an African American community seeking to define their freedom within the democratic politics of the Reconstruction era; and, generally, as a man whose ambition to lead black people became entangled in the treacherous shoals of the post–Reconstruction era Negro problem.

I have also sought to demonstrate the seductiveness, then and now, of Washington's words as Negro leader sui generis, as singular Negro leader or "Head Negro in Charge" (as it is sometimes termed). His enthronement as such endowed his words with a particular authority. It is this influence, the power of Washingtonianism, that requires analysis as well: of Washington's special persuasiveness, as historian as well as pundit, and his extraordinary ability to enchant, enthrall and seduce an eager audience motivated by an odd mix of idealism and bad faith, racism and wishful thinking.

With the exception of parts of the first chapter, *The Education of Booker T. Washington* is an account of the first, formative phase of his life, from his birth in 1856 to 1881, when he set off to build his school at Tuskegee. My special concern is with the influences on him in that period and an analysis of his telling of his life story that seeks to illuminate Washington's reasons for stressing, in the years of his ascendance, certain influences and relationships and not others. It is my belief that his appeal, or, more to the point, the appeal of his portrayal of his life has much to do with why many Americans in his time and later believed he held the key to solving the Negro problem. At the same time, my interest is in revealing the reasons—psychological as well as social and political—for what Washington came to believe.

Many would say it is impossible to know that, that Washington showed many different faces to the world, and, anyway, one can never reach to the heart of a pragmatist, especially one who employed ghostwriters to put out a constant stream of publicity materials—including some "autobiographical" writings. Needless to say, I am not convinced that this is true. Instead, I have tried to take seriously what Washington said and what was said about him, to take his ideas—even his platitudes and unctuous homilies about himself and black people, generally—seriously, to put what he said he thought about himself and others into play and see if it is possible to come up with a complex, but psychologically honest and politically revealing portrait of a complicated man.

Chapter 1 involves the setting up of the problem of the Negro problem: its usefulness as an ideological rubric encompassing the complex of problems having to do with racism and racial incapacity, subordination and equality before the law, and, generally, the place and future fate of African Americans in American society in Washington's time. It explores some of the thinking and the place within the history of the Negro problem of such figures as Thomas Jefferson and Frederick Douglass before Washington, and, subsequent to Washington's time, especially in the person of Gunnar Myrdal. It argues that Jefferson's thinking on race and democracy ought to be seen as an effort to solve the Negro problem in the period of its founding, when slavery caused African Americans to be presented as a radical exception to the rule of a general American freedom; that the consequences of the Civil War and Reconstruction meant, for a time, the overthrow of the Negro problem by virtue of slavery's demise, the rise of real democracy, violent and vibrant at once, and equality before the law; that the Negro problem reasserted itself as a consequence of events in and after the Reconstruction era having little to do with how black and white people felt about each other, but with decisive consequences in terms of the subordination of African Americans; and, finally, that Washington's significance lies in his solving of the Negro problem with his formulation of a theory, race relations, that allows democracy to coexist with Jim Crow, the negation of democracy.

Chapter 2 concerns Washington's life as a slave and the way Washington invokes the idea of good race relations in slavery, while at the same time his own experience suggests a recognition of the limits of the theory as it applies to his own later ideas about Negro progress. It makes note, as well, of evidence that even as a slave Washington had large aspirations for greatness, that early on it was his aim to be a leader of the people, and one who would offer something particular in line with the separate and particular needs and interests of black people, and not simply as an instrument for the imposition of good order.

Chapter 3 examines how Washington, serving his own later purposes, writes about his life amid the first blush of freedom to make it comport with the race relations idea: the freedpeople are a child race not up to the task of freedom, squandering their opportunities and alienating white people, all with the result of making Reconstruction a tragic chapter in the nation's and the Negro's history. This, too, is a personal story for Washington (as well as an occasion for examining the way his appeal tended to set his example against the general African American rule). In his telling, his stepfather personifies the debilities of black people, setting up Washington's rescue through the care and guidance of white sponsors and mentors. Washington's life has often been seen as a quintessential American success story. In chapter 3, I explore this tradition and Washington's place in it by comparing the components of his story with Horatio Alger's fantasies of boys escaping from exigent circumstances.

Chapter 4 argues that another and more accurate view of Washington's life points to a much larger engagement on his part in what was only later on seen by him as a negative experiment in black political participation in Reconstruction. This alternate view suggests the likelihood that at the time, as opposed to in his maturity, Washington was of a divided mind about the meaning of Reconstruction and the role of politics in helping him to achieve greatness; that is to say, that what occurred to him was manifest not so much a political problem, alone, but, for him, a problem with personal and psychological as well as political dimensions. In this latter aspect, there are questions relating to Washington's personal identity and his "race" that are examined in some detail here and in the final chapter.

Chapter 5 explores Washington's career at the Hampton Institute and the influences of his mentor Samuel C. Armstrong, as well as of political currents in the later stages of Reconstruction. These influences lead Washington toward making resolutions both psychological, having to do with his sense of his place in the world, and political, having to do with administering or managing African Americans in an educational and therapeutic context, rather than leading them in a democratic one. He was not alone in the conclusions he reached; indeed, Rutherford B. Hayes's contribution to the history of the Negro problem came to Washington in the form of a gift of one of Washington's most potent metaphors. But it was Washington's task and conception of his role as Negro leader in the absence of black political mobilization to transform the race relations idea into a new paradigm. He did this amid the pressures, briefly glimpsed in this chapter, of building a school in the Deep South.

As this work is very much concerned with the power of Washington's ideas, his vision and persuasive power, chapter 5 begins and ends with my own chancing to describe in metaphorical terms a larger meaning of the age of Washington; to speak of rivers where Washington spoke of separated fingers and ships lost at sea. In so doing I can claim no more credit for being the originator of those terms than Washington was of his.

All that night he did not close his eyes and now and then his restless body gave a slight shudder as the images of his waking dream whirled tensely in their too-tight orbits. He peered out of his window and saw vast, wheeling populations of ruled stars, swarming in the convened congresses of the skies anchored amidst nations of space and he prayed wordlessly that a bright, bursting tyrant of living sun would soon lay down its golden laws to loosen the locked legions of his heart and cast the shadow of his dream athwart the stretches of time.

—RICHARD WRIGHT, *THE LONG DREAM*

Chapter 1

"The Great and Intricate Problem"

Democracy, the Negro Problem, and the Idea
of Race Relations

WHEN HE died, they spoke not so much of his tangible accomplishments as of the effect his ideas and example had on them personally, and on the nation. Amid the grief of friends and supporters gathered to mourn his passing and to pay homage to his life's work, there were a few harsh words for his opponents and enemies. But those who had reviled him or otherwise sought to traduce his leadership and philosophy were mainly ignored, consigned, for that day at least, to the long shadow he cast. He was a paragon, they said, an inspiration, and the embodiment of "the true Christian spirit." He "stood in the most delicate position of any man on the American Continent, be he black or white," one speaker said, seeking ever to maintain "peace and unity and friendship between the two races." He gained a hearing with presidents and other powerful men, not chasing down spoils or other partisan advantage, but on the march for harmony and progress for all: "Not some men down," one speaker said, quoting Lowell, "but all men up." The final speaker best captured the sentiments of the day and the audience's sense of their fallen leader: "he has given us a vision which we may have with us every day," a vision of a new America of racial harmony as brilliant as "the setting sun shining through a circle of clouds" at "the very tip top" of a mountain.[1]

That the year was 1915 and the person thus memorialized was Booker T. Washington will no doubt come as something of a surprise to those accustomed to the association of Martin Luther King Jr. with mountaintops and visions of racial justice and peace. The odd ring of familiarity in the eulogists' portrait of Washington, bringing to mind as it inevitably does memories of King's own words, might be understood as nothing more than a curious artifact of a bygone era—a testament, perhaps, to African American progress, significant only in the fact that over the long distance traveled by black people since the age of Washington, Americans have developed a more rigorous criterion for judging who is (and who is surely not) a visionary leader. A decidedly more prosaic Washington is preserved in the accumulated writing of more than three-quarters of a century. Ignoring or rejecting out of hand the man as described by those who laid him to rest in 1915, Washington is remembered as simply a conservative among radicals, a realist uneasily situated in a pantheon of prophetic black leadership. Four decades distant from King's mountaintop, Washington's "vision"—if it can at all be said to merit that honorific—seems rather like that of someone standing atop a molehill.

It is possible, likely even, that Washington would not have objected too strongly to such a view of his life and his, perhaps, incongruous place in the African American pantheon, whether or not stripped of its invidiousness. It was a part of his style to stress his heterodoxy and (like contemporary black conservatives who rail against "the civil rights establishment") the considerable jeopardy into which he was placed by breaking with conventional black wisdom. A fair guess is that Washington would have relished his modern image for its neat comportment with the image he himself advertised in writings and speeches. Being all the time right, and for all of time (or in any other abstracted, philosophical sense), was never his primary object. Instead, the work was the thing: what could, not what should, be done based on the determination, he would write in his autobiography, "to face the situation just as it was."[2] Washington's biographer agrees, finding that he "simply met each day as it came, pragmatically."[3] It is in this sense that Columbia University president Seth Low was paying Washington what to Low and other of his contemporaries was a very great compliment when he called him "one of the most simple-minded men I ever met."[4] Joel E. Spingarn, early on a patron of Washington's and later one of a handful of the most important leaders of the National Association for the Advancement of Colored People, echoed Low and went beyond him as well, comparing Washington to Spingarn's friend and colleague, W. E. B. Du Bois. In a 1938 address which proved to be his valedictory on twenty-five years of service to the NAACP, Spingarn spoke of the perfect and "profound gulf that separates men of action from men of thought," statesmen from intellectuals. While Du Bois, "the intellectual thinker," was a theoretician, Spingarn said, Washington was "a man of action."[5]

Spingarn expresses something, in the process of explaining Washington and Du Bois, about the nature of liberal reform in its comprehension of what Spingarn would call the problem of "the welfare of the American negro."[6] That is not, however, to suggest that he offers any great or significant insight into the nature of their disagreement or their times. The form of that disagreement itself, as Spingarn helped crystallize it, is important and has endured as an apparatus of analysis. This is especially so precisely because Spingarn was a committed racial liberal and an intelligent man; his understanding of the contours of the difference hold more significance than, for example, that of H. G. Wells, who three decades earlier glimpsed briefly the color line in America and said essentially the same superficial thing: "Du Bois is more of the artist, less of the statesman. He conceals his passionate resentment all too thinly." Washington is the statesman, on the other hand, a usage Wells meant to be taken "in the highest sense."[7] The notion of a fundamental idealist-realist split has endured and, indeed, flourished to such an extent that no one would even think to investigate as an epistemological matter this odd, dichotomizing, feature of our approach to the historical experience of the African American people.[8] Instead of a serious consideration of what might otherwise be understood as metaphysical questions about the nature of that experience and the destiny of those people, and political questions about what those people might do to forge a destiny different from that set out for them by America, those matters are reduced to a series of oppositions—servility and resistance, accommodation and protest, integration and separation or nationalism, middle-class uplift and working-class insurgency, and so on. In their turn, these tend to reduce the past to a series of prefigurings of the post-1954 era, a "Whig history in black face," as Adolph Reed Jr. has called it.[9] The "sides" of these inexact and misleading categories are embodied in the persons of two Negro or black or African American "leaders"—they need not be leaders in any conventional sense—who together represent for their time the system of antinomies that is recapitulated throughout African American history from the house servant and the field slave to King and Malcolm X. And the greatest of these duos is Washington and Du Bois.[10]

In the seminal, turn of the century split between action and ideal, realism and radicalism, Washington and "Washingtonian accommodators" carried the day, dominating the agenda of black America over a small band of "Du Boisian protesters," and forging a working relationship with the powerful forces surrounding black people.[11] The pragmatic program of "interracial diplomacy" Washington spelled out in his 1895 "Atlanta Compromise" speech, the "wheeling and dealing" and "accommodationist tricks" that went along with it, made him, according to one student of the period, "the most powerful black leader of his time and perhaps of all time."[12] But Washington was also "the last black leader born in slavery," his modern biographer writes, "out of place in the age that would follow."[13] It was the idealists' necessary break with Washington's realism and their eventual superseding of it as early as Washington's death in 1915, but certainly by the time of the cultural renaissance of the 1920s and the rise of the NAACP and the Garvey Movement, that signaled the death knell of accommodationism. There began efforts that reached their ultimate destination after four decades of a "protest era" and in a civil rights movement motivated by idealism and the destruction of the edifice of white supremacy with which Washington and, by inference, the people of African America whom he ostensibly led, had reached an accommodation. August Meier provides a clear statement of this formulation. In the age of Washington, "Du Boisian protesters" were able to make only "a pathetic appeal to the shreds of benevolence and attachment to the Constitution that still existed in the dominant white majority." But it was precisely that type of appeal, manifest especially in "the NAACP's increasingly successful attempt . . . to capitalize upon this sentiment among whites," Meier writes, "that did so much to pave the way for the Negro revolt of our own times."[14]

Measuring the distance from a funeral in one Alabama city in 1915 to an arrest in another Alabama city in 1955 as a straight line of progress—up from Washington and up to idealism—may seem a rather presentist reading of the origins of the civil rights movement. Its main defect is what it fails to take into account: that upon the level of ideology—how Americans understood the African American situation—little had in fact changed over the whole course of time. Racist utterances and attitudes may have become marginally less popular in parlor, public, and politics, but such evidence might be more accurately understood as proof of the completeness of segregation's triumph: "racial tensions" were nonexistent, and lynching had all but disappeared; thus, the black and the white got along by being separate. Such silences are indicative not only of the extent to which Jim Crow's reign was virtually uncontested (beyond what the resistance a relatively small number of radicals, lawyers, and other, generally unsung individuals could muster), but also of the prevalence of what King and the civil rights movement exposed as a negative or false and "obnoxious" peace: the unroiled waters at the surface, seen in the absence of strife and the white South's oft-repeated declaration that "our Negroes" are happy, hiding a monstrous injustice just below.[15]

Nevertheless, the notion of a simple and straightforward course from Washington to the King-led movement has, in some quarters at least, a certain attraction and usefulness insofar as it fits with the prevailing sense of what is called America's racial past; that view locates all the ideological complexity, all the difficult, very complicated questions of equity and morality, as emerging only with the achievement of the civil rights movement's successes. In this view, a prelapsarian Negro history represented a record of slow, but steady advance toward the achievement of civil rights, freedom, and equality, a story not unlike that of other ethnic groups. After the break up of ideological consensus around 1965 or so, the American nation was forced from the garden by the combined clamor of the "ghetto black,"[16] the mau-mauing activist charlatan, their barely more seemly academic adjuncts, and other rabid critics of the Moynihan Report, and the white backlash these all engendered with quite negative consequences for liberalism and the New Deal consensus that was its buttress.[17]

Scholars have challenged the perspective on Washington that consigns him to the prehistory of the movement, a remnant of the ancien regime and a repository for that which we would now reject about his time. In one case his covert support of legal challenges to segregation and disfranchisement has been emphasized as a measure of his liberal outlook. Harlan documents Washington's efforts to challenge the raft of discriminatory legislation in the 1890s and afterward by covertly funding legal suits and lobbying efforts. Washington, he argues, "addressed many of the civil rights questions" the NAACP did, but attempted to "ameliorate" rather than "challenge racial injustice." While this may be, it is not clear how an effort taken in secret can constitute an element of his leadership of black people, the vast majority of whom had to be kept in the dark about such efforts for the sake of preserving Washington's relationship with the white South. Elsewhere, the conclusion Harlan comes to—"If his methods did not work, the same could be said of theirs"—is more rationalization than interpretation.[18] An earlier biographer, writing without the advantage of hindsight on the civil rights era, goes farther still, attributing to Washington's vision and accomplishments nearly all the good that had come to the Negro by 1948; he holds that it was the genius of Washington's program, combined with the beneficence of the American nation, that granted black people their homes and businesses and educations and bright midcentury prospects (rather than the hard effort of black noses to grindstones and hands upon bootstraps).[19] In a more recent study, the unfolding of "the civil rights movement in Tuskegee" is viewed as a testament to his prescience. But the arguments made in behalf of a posthumously more "relevant" Washington cannot stand strict scrutiny and tend, moreover, only to confirm the validity of the judgment of his leadership by the lights of how things turned out in the 1960s, with Washington serving as antithesis to King's thesis.[20]

There is an undoubted simplicity, if not intellectual power, in this version of the early origins of the civil rights movement: after Washington, a break with the past, followed by forty years flowing of "the river of black struggle," rolling along inexorably toward Montgomery and Martin King.[21] If it is true that Washington's leadership merits placement of him outside the pattern of protest, struggle, resistance, and the other concerns and commitments that came on in the flood in the 1950s—if he represents the realistic antithesis of the twentieth century idealistic rule—then the age of his ascendance may be understood as merely a respite from the surging of the main stream of the black struggle. The basic integrity of the river, its strong central current a direct reflection of black peoples' aspirations for freedom, is preserved; the logic of its steady course, between unvarying shores of democracy and equality, remains the same.

The question arises, however, if something is not missing in this type of narrative of the course of the river in and out of the age of Washington, which was, after all, also the age of segregation and disfranchisement, of lynch law and the elision of democracy. How can we account for such seeming backsliding in an age of progress? Certainly these developments cannot all be marked against Washington's name. But, just as certainly, an element of mystery has inevitably to attach itself to the person of an African American somehow able during the period called by the historian Rayford W. Logan the nadir of Negro history to become so powerful and so much in the good graces of white people that influential leaders in education, politics, and business, North and South, spoke of him upon the occasion of his death almost with a single voice of acclaim.[22] Casting backward eyes made jaundiced by distrust of that sort of popularity, some, with William Monroe Trotter, might indict Washington as "the Benedict Arnold of the Negro race."[23] However, even as it seeks to sweep Washington to the ash heap of history, such a conclusion confirms him as a man of action, one like Arnold, who disavowed his oath and betrayed his responsibilities.

But what manner of a man of action wins his reputation not in deed, but by the word? The mystery presented by "the Wizard of Tuskegee" runs deep, for the eulogists' estimation of him as a visionary was not in any simple way merely a laurel given in gratitude for two decades of good works teaching children and young adults at his school in Tuskegee (for, of course, there were other such men and women similarly devoted to education).[24] Those who memorialized Washington in 1915 only reiterated a two-decades-old benediction upon the new "Negro Moses" for a little more than ten-minute speech in which he had sought, he wrote, "to say something that would cement the friendship of the races."[25] "For twenty years," Theodore Roosevelt would write, Washington "had been the most useful, as well as the most distinguished, member of his race in the world."[26] This usefulness and the role Washington had created for himself was learned over the course of his experience in slavery and afterward in freedom, first within the promising developments of Reconstruction and, then later, outside that bright, democratic promise, and into the dark night of Reconstruction's aftermath, where Washington was caused to dream different dreams.

Unraveling the mystery to understand the peculiar alchemy through which an obscure educator's word is transmuted into the man of action's deed requires removal outward and upward from the mundanity of the river where black people live: outward to banks of the river and the surrounding terrain, and upward to the heights of theoretical exposition on black people's place within the American democracy. It is there, where the real and the ideal each float freely, and what is—the materiality of economic, political and social forces—need have no more reality than what might be imagined, that Washington the visionary described by his contemporaries leaves his mark: upon the long dream of a solution to the Negro problem.

%%%

AT SOME far remove from the age of Washington, and a not inconsiderable social distance from a time when Americans were at liberty to call black people out of their names with impunity, invocation of "the Negro problem" seems more than a little unsavory. The term and its close cognate, "the Negro Question," have lost the currency they once had as a way of naming matters relating to the fit and future of African Americans within the American nation.[27] Where once would be found "inquiries into the Negro problem" by domestic scholars and the stray foreign intellectual let loose in America, and "approaches to the Negro problem" from writers and controversialist, and various sorts of "answers to the Negro question" from agitators, legislators, political parties, social welfare organizations, and voluntary associations, since the civil rights era the rubric that made perfect sense to reasonably well-informed Americans before the 1960s has disappeared, been broken down. The Negro problem has been in a way disaggregated into component parts and shuffled out into categories of labor and thought. The problem (if there is a problem) is the problem of race as decoy or blind, a diversion or a place to hide from what is really the matter, the bad casting of a bad American drama originally authored by white persons but taken out on tour by black actors using "agency" to redraw their own roles. Or the problem is racism acting as cudgel or excuse, a shibboleth in both mainstream and radical politics to bar the door to certain contrary claims. Or it is the problem of "race relations." This latter was a term seldom used before the age of Washington, understood as unfortunate failure of intercultural understanding or inevitable result of immutable law, but maybe, hopefully, susceptible to solution through the accumulation of instances of progressive social intercourse between diverse individuals. Elsewhere, "race" (as social construction), culture, and psychology, the apparatus of postmodernists, replace politics, history, and race (as nature) as organizing principles of critical social inquiry.[28]

At least in regard to present-day concerns, the reasons for discarding the Negro problem are readily discernible. The establishment of de jure equality, the greater social equity relative to any previous period in American history, and the more decorous nature of the talk of our times, which is partly a product of those other developments, make use of the term seem, at best, an exercise in anachronism and, at worst, a deliberate insult and a gratuitous bit of rhetorical ugliness. Such revulsion is understandable. The term has within it, certainly, the general, though by no means universal, tendency toward a pejorative pronunciation—that is, as if to say "the problem (or problems) with Negroes"—in the same way white Southerners of a particular vintage would tend to growl out the word "Negro" to make it sound like "nigger." Following this line of reasoning one might be inclined to deconstruct historical usage of the term as merely a thin disguise of racism, a history of "how whites viewed the black presence as a 'problem'—a menace."[29] Such a view has in its favor the fact that when the Negro problem first came into common currency in the nineteenth century most Americans—indeed, the vast majority of Americans—held attitudes and opinions that were biased, prejudiced, and hateful, racist, in short. And racist not just by modern standards, but recognized as calumny by black contemporaries and a few others and as a human disaster manifest through the normal workings of American institutions.

In support of the notion that the Negro problem is simply racism written down, there are those works, like the 1877 effusion from the pen of someone called J. R. Ralls, *The Negro Problem*, filled up with pointed commentary on "the natural depravity of the negro," and "the bad impulses that flow from a low state of morals."[30] On the other hand, there are other, less vitriolic, less racist in the strictest sense of the word—one supposes—contributions to the solving of the Negro problem. If these perhaps do not appear so frequently as to be tit for tat for every tract such as Ralls's, then they appear at least in numbers too significant to be dismissed. The Rev. Hollis Reed's *The Negro Problem Solved*, appearing as the Civil War was coming to an end, is an example of this type, filled up with dismay "at the deep-rooted prejudice" against black people, and seeking "the deliverance of an unfortunate race from an untold series of wrongs and degradations." Such deliverance would come, the good reverend was sure, when the Negro was delivered back to his home in Africa. This done, a heaven on earth would be achieved in both Africa and America; lions would lie down with lambs, a scene depicted on the frontispiece of *The Negro Problem Solved*, but properly sorted so as not to mix up black lions and white lambs (or vice versa) but white lions and lambs and black lions and lambs each in their home place.[31]

What unites these two different works and makes them a piece with other contributions to the genre is their idealist framework joined with an escapist impulse. Both erase the role and contribution made by African Americans to the nation's growth (in Reed's terms, the warm wool on the backs of Americans who were able to fleece slaves, the dining on veal). Put another way: in each there is the almost inevitably unstated premise that it is possible to escape thorny problems of justice and equity, even basic matters of right and wrong, with the neat formulation, the mental adjustment, the new perspective (though often actually only the recycling of old saws). Give the magic eight-ball another shake, and black culture causes poverty. The poverty professional turned polemicist turned prophet looks into his crystal ball, and welfare causes poverty; he looks again and innate inferiority is the problem.[32]

There is something about this problematizing that marks the Negro problem as a characteristically American habit of mind, a combination of American can-doism with malign or benign objectification of black people. An aspect of this matter is the tradition in this country of what might be called racial punditry. Examples of the type abound: the Negro expert or race relations savant who makes the crude—even if seemingly sympathetic—totalizing statement that announces itself as a crucial, new insight into the true character of the Negro, "his" past and present and future, the mildly optimistic or wildly apocalyptic prospectus on what will be his future fate if he acts as he ought or as he ought not to behave.

Du Bois referred to this urge to racial punditry when he wrote sardonically of those who "gain now and then by singular accident and the exigencies of the book market, respectful hearing and wide advertisement."[33] Du Bois's efforts to deflate gadflying Negro experts proceeded from his recognition that their musings—professionally accredited or amateurish—took up serious questions. But whence does the impulse to problematize the Negro come?

In answering the question, the first misstep to be made is too readily to equate the ugliness of the Negro problem as an idea with the ugly historical reality that was African America's lot in this country. It is sometimes said that American history in relation to black people is the working out of an effort to maintain white supremacy. Slavery and segregation, poverty and deprivation, and, perhaps, even the mixed-bag state of things as they exist today, then, are but variations on the theme of America's doing ill to black people. Likewise, one sometimes hears that the "tragedy of race" issues from "America's original sin," the enshrinement of slavery at the nation's founding. This is a special favorite of politicians and commentators announcing their intention to make a powerful statement on "race matters." Among historians, a very good—because so seemingly powerful—example of the tragic pose comes from Winthrop Jordan: "It was a strange and eventually tragic happenstance of nature that the Negro's homeland was the habitat of the animal which in appearance most resembles man." To understand this as tragic it is necessary to conflate the project that first brought Europeans to Africa, when these first impressions (and others) were made, and where they would treat and trade and fight with and against, not Negroes, but various tribes and nations, with the later project that caused other Europeans, with the help of some Africans, to bring out of Africa some other Africans, now christened "Negroes," for the very specific purpose of providing productive labor in the New World. The conflation gives a very curious impression of inadvertency—"tragic happenstance"—and inevitability—"nature"—to the deliberate and intentional crime that was slavery.[34] With sins subsequent to 1787 explained as but shadows of the first big one, the black experience can be accounted for either as an echo of sin, "that shadow which lies athwart our national life," as Jsames Baldwin indicated, or as a record of slow, but sure, upward progress toward the achievement of those American values of democracy, freedom, and equality unfairly denied them at the outset.[35]

But, if this be tragedy, it is of a rather un-Shakespearean sort, an empty drama ending with the gesture of brief tears and barely damp hankies. Thus does a patina of deep feeling replace real thought and the rhetorical flourish of the grandstand play replace analysis.[36]

There is, within both this rhetoric of racial tragedy and the original sin idea, the implied and unreflected-upon supposition that present or ongoing evils are but the later links in a chain of events begun by posterity. An era's portion of that chain then loses its particular reason for forming (causes that might include the perfectly reasonable motivations of money, politics, jockeying by the whites for social position, or even entertainment). Assuming this shape, moral scrutiny fixes not on the victimizers of black people (for are they not controlled by the chain's reeling out?) but attaches itself to the black victim, the unwanted child as heir to the redounding sin, and the child's child and so on down through the ages.

White supremacy and original sin; however well such slogans and platitudes serve the proponent's ends, their sufficiency as models of historical interpretation is severely limited. The former has inevitably to neglect the sense of possibility that enabled African Americans, mostly ineffectually, but not always so, to struggle against the system oppressing them in slavery and thereafter, or to make that sense a virtue of some qualities of black people derived externally from the United States. As well, they can obscure differences between, for example, antiblack Southern yeomen and antiblack Northern free-soilers that, as a practical matter in the Civil War, are the margin of hope animating the invigoration of that sense of possibility.

As concerns the notion of "racial progress" in the general sweep of American history, such can only be maintained by erasing the promise of freedom in the Reconstruction enactments and ignoring the way the freedpeople's victory was snatched from them in the movement for disfranchisement and for segregation being made systematic; that is to say, if that was progress, then progress's advocates, Booker Washington among them, have much for which to be held to account.[37]

On the other hand, the sense in which the term "the Negro problem" is used in this study, the sense in which it would seem to be most useful and consistent with its historical usage, is that it was not merely a cover for racism, a racist rubric or a rubric for racists. Examination of the Negro problem's history is especially suited to drawing out and addressing difficult matters of American ideology because it operated simultaneously in the realms of politics and theory where race punditry finds its home. As such, it is a more accurate rubric encompassing the forces bedeviling black people than simply reducing them to matters of the abrogation of citizens' civil rights—a convention that too often has the consequence of assuming some-thing about the black struggle that may or may not be amenable to proof.

Beginning in slavery and continuing down to the time of the modern civil rights movement, the Negro problem functioned as an organizing principle for Americans engaged in controversy over the nature and des-tiny of African Americans, and implicitly or explicitly over the nature and destiny of the American nation and the grand experiment of democracy. As such, the Negro problem presupposes the existence of contention among Americans, especially including, in the nineteenth century at least, white Americans. It does so because it engrosses the thinking of African Ameri-cans, as well as their stated enemies and a not insignificant number of their friends. The Negro problem then was an umbrella, and an ideological for-mulation in and of itself: an idealist rendering of the problem posed by the exception the status of black Americans formed to the rule of freedom and equality in the American democracy. As ideology, it was also a means of escaping that contradiction.

%%%

THE CHARACTERISTIC of American society that invariably made the deep-est impression upon foreign visitors to the United States is the great extent of freedom enjoyed by the citizenry. Notwithstanding the fact that their favorable comments, those of Alexis de Tocqueville, in particular, are often deployed as if they were intended to be civic booster shots, the con-tent on this point found in their letters, travelogues and other writings should not diminished, nor the quality of insight in what struck strangers to these shores as something unique about America be dismissed because of its later usage. They found noteworthy the radical exposition on the idea of human equality contained in the Declaration of Independence, and, equally so, the care taken in crafting a written Constitution with its enumeration of the rights and liberties of the people. And they pondered the relative underdevelopment of American bureaucratic structures, par-ticularly westward of civilization on the frontier, as aspects of democracy's restless promise, as well as its dangers. But what democratic sense is to be made of the Negro?

In the twentieth century the Swedish economist and diplomat Gunnar Myrdal would conflate symbol—the Negro problem—with substance—the incongruous treatment of black people—to posit, not merely a contradic-tion in action, but "a moral dilemma," a kind of psychic pain or dissonance, in white people's minds. Holding that the source of and the solution to the

Negro problem lay "in the hearts of the American" (by which he surely meant "white Americans") who were at once committed to an "American Creed," antithetical to injustice, and guilty of mistreating black people, Myrdal insisted that this moral heartache was amenable to amelioration through a program of educational enlightenment. Once able to see their way beyond the dilemma, Myrdal believed, Americans would reach out across sectional and racial lines to solve the Negro problem as a matter of "economic, social, and political race relations."[38]

White Americans, unaware they suffered such a malady, might be excused for feeling Myrdal's diagnosis laughable and his prescription of a program of educational enlightenment insulting. Myrdal had not meant to give offense. Rather, it was his endeavor to solve the problem by creating a portrait of the Negro as victim without making white persons feel indicted as victimizers, but rather as the embodiment of all the American virtues.[39] Thus, the Negro, he argues, is an exaggerated American, denied a "balanced and integrated world view," and placed in a pathological situation from which there is no internal means of escape. Stymied by his failure to develop "articulate, systematized and stable opinions," the Negro appears from nowhere, prostrate before white America, the embodiment of "a moral lag in the development of the nation," and in need of salvation through a liberal application of the American creed.[40]

The problem with Myrdal's finessing of the new Negro problem in this way is that Southern defenders of the status quo could reply that black incapacity, rather than being an argument for ending segregation, was precisely the reason why segregation was good for both black and white people. Good race relations already were in existence, most white Southerners would say, with, on one hand, Negroes content in their place, and, on the other hand, white people going about the business of ruling in the best interests of two peoples not in need of racial adjustment—which would only bring about the stirring up of discontent in a settled situation. W. T. Couch made just such a point in an especially vehement but, on its own racist terms, quite coherent rejoinder to Myrdal.[41] Similarly, the state of Virginia, responding to the Supreme Court's initial *Brown v. Board of Education* decision in 1954, argued that the court itself had provided a rationale for segregation in insisting, citing Myrdal's work and others, that black children were damaged goods, "maladjusted" and lacking initiative.[42]

Hailed after its publication in 1944 as a beacon showing America a way out of its racial difficulties, Myrdal's moral dilemma argument has been understood by historians as constituting the moral and intellectual core of a gathering consensus after World War II that paved the way for the King-led civil rights movement of the late 1950s and early 1960s. Certainly, it was championed by liberals, who might have done better to realize that it was their own good convictions that brought them to Myrdal's thesis, rather than the reverse. And certainly, it was invoked by men like Martin King, but its greater efficacy is wholly another matter.[43]

Myrdal came to the United States with the working hypothesis initially that improving the Southern economy would ameliorate the worst aspects of the Negro problem. In accord with this idea, he describes in compelling detail the devastation of African American sharecroppers brought about by "the combination of world agricultural trends and federal agricultural policy initiated during the 'thirties." The consequent "revolutionizing" of the rural South, the uprooting of the black (and the white) peasantry, and the newfound ability of Southern landholders to use federal dollars to mechanize production make up perhaps the greatest scandal of the New Deal, but even Myrdal's remedy (anticipation of a postwar economic crisis to provoke a new federal intervention to help small holders and farm workers) hardly matches the scale of the problem he diagnoses.[44]

Soon, however, he played down economic planning, in preference for emphasis on the American creed. Perhaps this was because he was instructed to do so by those at the Carnegie Corporation who had hired him. "The whole question had been for nearly one hundred years so charged with emotion," Myrdal's employer, Carnegie President Frederick P. Keppel, wrote in explanation for Myrdal's importation to forage through the groves of Jim Crow, that "a fresh mind" was required to give the matter a new look.[45] However it happened, Myrdal soon learned to speak the language of the American Negro problem. His task was not to upset the New Deal coalition with its strong solid-South component, but to finesse the problem so that whatever change needed to take place would only be a matter of tinkering on the margins of the American system, and thereby domesticating the Negro problem within the framework of the new liberal state. The result was a moral clarion call either ignored or honored only on ceremonial occasions by liberals who might have been expected to know better, and an obscuring of fundamental matters of power, domination, and inequity behind a mask of consensus. For instance, liberal intellectuals who did invoke the contradiction Myrdal delineated did so in a manner more descriptive than proscriptive, mere recognition of "the dilemma" serving, as in Henry Steele Commager's *The American Mind*, to confirm the democratic essence of American society, and to do this without suggesting—as Myrdal had not suggested—or recognizing the need for a mechanism for making democracy a reality for African Americans.[46]

And then there is the matter of its rendering of African Americans in relation to an actual, living American system of values. The question Ralph Ellison asked in response to Myrdal's depiction of a pathological black culture—can black people have lived so long "simply by *reacting*?"—has a kind of corollary relevant to the history of the Negro problem.[47] Can a nation of free and equal citizens tolerate in its midst the presence of a people made conspicuous by their inequality without reacting, without some alteration in its beliefs and institutions? The fact that Myrdal, in 1944, could trot out a pristine American creed of democracy, liberty, and equality need hardly deter the obvious conclusion that it could not and did not. It is in consequence of that reacting that the Negro problem takes on the form—a problem in race relations—in which it was handed down to Myrdal; it is in consequence of that reacting that it appears as an abstract problem of psychology and interpersonal relations, rather than as a concrete problem of exploitation, subordination, and other deliberately manufactured inequities. The materiality of this injustice and the definite deliberateness behind its creation are what Myrdal and his liberal followers obscure. Thus it becomes a simple matter to be fixed once the minds of white persons are fixed. One thinks of the continuing popularity, even today, of such statements as "racism is caused by ignorance" and the plaintive "Can't we all just get along?" passed off as deep and morally profound wisdom. The fact that we hold these particular "truths" to be self-evident, rather than nonsensical and obscurantist, is, itself, indicative of an adulteration of the American creed. Establishing this point requires real attention to the vexingly interrelated history of the Negro problem and American democracy promised by the subtitle of *An American Dilemma* (*The Negro Problem and Modern Democracy*) but fumbled by Myrdal.

Myrdal would not be the last person to be taken in by the endlessly confusing riddle of the Negro problem, nor was he the first foreigner so misused. Alexis de Tocqueville, in *Democracy in America*, would speak of "the presence of a black population upon its territory" as "the most formidable of all the ills which threaten the future existence of the Union . . . and in contemplating the cause of the present embarrassments or of the future dangers of the United States, the observer is invariably led to consider this as a primary."[48] What were these dangers about which de Tocqueville was warning?

There are at least two ways of fumbling this question. The first is simply to treat de Tocqueville as a seer, a racial pundit who can foretell circumstances about which he has no knowledge. George M. Fredrickson does this, rightly insisting that Tocqueville came to believe that the Negro problem was "insoluble and certain to result in disaster," but then taking de Tocqueville's words as a prediction of the world of troubles of the twentieth century.[49] However, de Tocqueville, unlike Myrdal, makes no claims to racial punditry, and one might be inclined to give him the benefit of the doubt by substituting the word "slaves" or, better yet, "slavery" for "a black population"—so that the danger to the Union, as it would appear to most students of history today, is posed by emerging conflict between the divergent civilizations of the free North and the slave South. Doing so, however, is also erroneous and misses the extent to which he was not so much evaluating from the outside as he was accurately reflecting the outlook of the group of slaveholders and colonizationists within whose culture he immersed himself. The Negro was the sign of their pain and the symbol of the antebellum nation's problem. If de Tocqueville is to be given any credit in this regard as a prognosticator, the proper conclusion proceeds from a straightforward reading of his words: it was the Negro's presence that threatened disaster, and those "future dangers" he foresaw came to a head not in some far off "racial confrontation," but only a quarter century later, with the Civil War and in the confrontation between slavery and freedom.

※※※

IT WOULD be altogether fitting if the Frenchman de Tocqueville were somehow to have been influenced in his opinion on the nature of the impending maelstrom in America by the writings of Thomas Jefferson. Jefferson has the dual virtue of being the most Francophile of American presidents and perhaps the nation's very first racial pundit, the founding father who was also the godfather of the Negro problem before it had that name.

Historians have been struck (and sometimes undone) by the many seeming contradictions in Jefferson's attitude toward slavery and African Americans.[50] He was sufficiently aghast at the deprivations "of a system he genuinely hated,"[51] and said so enough to be portrayed as "the patron saint of anti-slavery" at the time of the Civil War.[52] Elected to the House of Burgess in Virginia in 1769, among his first legislative actions was a proposal for emancipation. He wrote, "The whole commerce between master and slave is a perpetual exercise of the most boisterous passions, the most unrelenting despotism on the one part, and degrading submissions on the other."[53] But he himself always owned slaves, depended upon them nearly every day of his life, and in various ways manifested his loyalty to the plantation class whence he came.[54] He was a man of principle, articulating the best promise of America, but also a politician and an inconsistent one at that.[55] Jefferson was "alone among the spokesmen for the American Enlightenment" in moving in the direction of developing racism as a rationalized ideology by positing that black people "were probably inferior to whites in certain basic qualities." But this was done, Winthrop D. Jordan writes, with a "confused tentativeness."[56]

Jefferson, like Booker Washington later, was deemed a "man of action," but some of his contemporaries like Charles Carroll saw him as "a theoretical and fanciful man."[57] It is in that sense in which he assumes his greatest importance as a racial pundit. Contemplating the future of his nation, of the republic, and of the revolution that made democracy in America possible, Jefferson takes on the essential fact that the class of revolutionaries, of which he was a part, used slavery, as Edmund S. Morgan has insisted, like "a flying buttress to freedom."[58] This symbiosis, which Americans have ever been loathe to admit, and even historians who recognize it often have portrayed as an instance of tragedy or an irony of history, is the ground, at once fetid and fertile, from which the Negro problem eventually emerges. Jefferson's gambit was to set his mind to breaking that intimate connection: to sever by the word the foul roots of American democracy in slavery.

If one were of a mind to, one might engage in the exercise of imagining Jefferson at this project in his study at the manse of Monticello. Setting himself to the task, his mind, well trained in the leisure time provided by owning someone else's labor, instructs his skilled hand to dip quill in inkpot and write words on paper. All of these items having been purchased by slave labor; Jefferson and those slaves inhabit spaces within walls of a building on land that is his because of his family's ability to dominate their human property. With these instruments at hand Jefferson undertakes to make a new future, to conjure a nation free of slavery, to render an American pastoral free of the Negro, and thus to escape the conundrum and set liberty on a firmer footing for posterity. It is an extraordinary ambition, and Jefferson, about whom his friend and rival John Adams said he likes "better the dreams of the future than the history of the past," was just the man to do it.[59]

While Jefferson eventually settled upon the twinned policy of defamation and deportation of the Negro, his first, abortive, move in the direction of creating the Negro problem was to seek to erase slavery's staining of the American revolutionary enterprise by blaming slavery on the English crown. George III, he wrote in his original draft of the Declaration of Independence, "has waged cruel war against human nature itself, violating its most sacred rights of life and liberty in the persons of a distant people who never offended him, captivating and carrying them into slavery in another hemisphere, or to incur miserable death in their transportation thither. This piratical warfare, the opprobrium of *infidel* powers, is the warfare of the *Christian King* of Great Britain." Adding to the "assemblage of horrors" laid at King George's feet, Jefferson further scores him for promising freedom to those slaves who will rally to the King's banner and loyalism. The crown shows its evil purpose in "exciting those very people to rise in arms among us, and to purchase that liberty of which he has deprived them, by murdering the people upon whom he also obtruded them, thus paying off former crimes committed against the *liberties* of one people, with crimes which he urges them to commit against the *lives* of another."[60]

What a wonderful world it would be if it were so simple to manufacture an American freedom without American (as opposed to British) slavery.[61] What a miracle it would have been to make for America a truly new beginning through the dissolution not only of "the Political Bands" connecting the English and the Americans, but also of the tie between freedom and slavery. Unfortunately, history stood in Jefferson's way in the form of a living, growing peculiar institution that his fellow Americans sought to secure for equally exigent, if not so lofty purposes. Jefferson's clever circumvention of the tie between freedom and slavery would not fly with representatives to the Continental Congress from Georgia and South Carolina, and Jefferson's tour de force of constructing a new American past for the purposes of ensuring a different American future came a cropper.[62]

Words sometimes do fail, but to an idealist and dreamer like Jefferson, the failure of certain words only demands a return to the writing table to mobilize a new assortment of words for the same old purpose. If the fantasy history he made in the excised portion of the Declaration of Independence were trumped by the pragmatic principle expressed by others of the Founders, he would make his own antislavery pragmatism. The point was to make abolition and removal of the Negro seem both more exigent than staying the course, and a direct and inevitable consequence of the revolution. It had then to be a pragmatism built, as he wrote in *Notes on the State of Virginia*, of gradual emancipation and "colonization," undertaken "with the consent of their masters, rather than by their extirpation."[63]

The question arises for any person of humane and liberal principles of why must it be thus: why cannot Jefferson's antislavery principles be resolved simply in one form or another of emancipation, and let the post-emancipation chips fall where they may? Why does Jefferson insist upon the exigency of removing the Negro from the American continent? One answer is that for some Americans antislavery need not be resolved thus. However, the way in which Jefferson comes up with this seemingly sad, tragic, but inevitable conclusion, more than the resolution he advocated, is the key; therein, one finds his clever attempt to move matters from the problem of slavery—which only spells trouble in the nation's future—to the problem of the Negro in a free society—which can be whisked away if the nation only wishes it so. It is indicative of the true nature of things in this largest of slave societies that mere cleverness in the form of an idea was sufficient as a defense of what was reality—a strong and growing slave system, rewarding to any number of Americans in addition to slaveholders.

Jefferson, in the main, was no simple bigot; as such, and due to a general overattention in modern America to discrete racial attitudes (the degree of animus aimed at individual African Americans or at the group), it is possible to miss what is truly malignant in the radical gambit he undertakes in constructing the Negro problem and solving it. He articulates something of the perennial American lowest-common-denominator racism in writing of the Negro's peculiar smell and tendency to sweat overmuch: "They secrete less by the kidneys; and more by the glands of the skin, which gives them a very strong and disagreeable odor." These were malattributes of the Negro that Jefferson, unlike his French readers to whom the *Notes* was addressed, presumably was in a position to experience from a close-up perspective as he observed them working his fields. Another bit of Jeffersonian bigotry, derived from outside the area of his own witness, is his assertion that Negro men prefer to take white women as mates as an act of upward aspiration comparable to "the preference of the Oranootan for the black woman over those of his own species."[64]

Comments such as these suggest, however, a certainty about the true nature of the Negro that is belied elsewhere in Jefferson's writing. The chief question is not whether he was really, truly racist. He was a slaveholder after all.[65] Rather it concerns the use to which he puts such doggerel. Taken in context, Jefferson's utterances, which strike the modern reader as simply racist, have the aspect, not so much of ad hominem attack (who of any significance in the late eighteenth century needed to be convinced of black incapacity?), but of a trial balloon launched to seek a means of abstracting African Americans from the American reality. Are they beings of a different order from white people? Could they be up to the American snuff? Jefferson holds that the jury remains out on both these question. He does not favor the poesy of Phillis Wheatley, but that may be set down to a matter of taste; what he seeks is objectivity. With that in mind he corresponds with and about the astronomer and almanac publisher Benjamin Banneker as a test case for Negro intellectual capacity.[66] He terms an "experiment" the ongoing test of black ability for self-rule in Santo Domingo and Sierra

Leone.[67] About each case his view is not sanguine, but he remained agnostic on the question of the extent to which nature or nurture took precedence, a stance that places him closer to that of twentieth-century America than to most of his contemporaries. And it is here, removed from twaddle about smell and glands and taxonomy of supposed sexual preferences, that Jefferson engineers and embraces a truly vulgar and frightening barbarism.

Suppositions of the Negro's inferiority "must be hazarded with great diffidence" until such time as they may be treated as "subjects of natural history," Jefferson insisted, "submitted to the anatomical knife, to optical glass, to analysis by fire or by solvents."[68] While Jefferson, here, sounds quite mad (like one of those doctors produced by Nazi Germany tossing "patients" into vats of boiling water just to see what happens), there is no reason to suppose that what he proposes is anything more than a rhetorical gambit. His task is done once the Negro appears as a matter of intellectual curiosity, a subject of scientific inquiry, rather than children of the Enlightenment endowed by "their Creator with certain unalienable Rights." The Negro, in his person and collectively, then assumes the dimension of a problem, and the idea of the slaves being freed and remaining in America is an impossibility. Why not allow them to stay, Jefferson asks, and then answers his own question by providing a glimpse of the evil such folly would wreak: "Deep-rooted prejudices entertained by the whites; ten thousand recollections, by the blacks, of the injuries they have sustained; new provocations; the real distinctions which nature has made; and many other circumstances will divide us into parties, and produce convulsions, which will probably never end but in the extermination of the one or the other race."[69]

It will be race war, Jefferson predicted, an apocalypse of blood and death. Given his characterization of Negro incapacity, it may seem surprising that Jefferson is unsure of who would turn out on top in the Armageddon to come from "the insurrectionary spirit of the slaves": "from being local it will become general, and when ever it does, it will rise more formidable after every defeat, until we shall be forced, after dreadful scenes and suffering, to release them in their own way, which, without such sufferings we might now model after our own convenience."[70] With black people outmanned and outgunned, not to speak of outsmarted and outcharactered,[71] it is a wonder how Jefferson could end up in the 1820s sounding as if he were anticipating a more blusterous David Walker or a more talky Nat Turner.[72] Perhaps what Jefferson truly fears is the type of accounting white people will face if a just God enters the fray on the side of the Negro. Perhaps he is simply speaking out of the mind of a slaveholder made mad by the sin-ridden world he and his fellows have built up around themselves, hoping against hope that, in the liquidation of his class and their bête noire, a better way will be made for the non-slaveholding white.[73] Perhaps though, when he speaks of "the bloody scenes which our children, and possibly ourselves (south of the Potomac) [will] have to wade through,"[74] his anticipation of the Negro besting the white man hides a different, but more realistic Jeffersonian nightmare. Jefferson's rhetoric is itself a mask for a fear that the impending apocalypse will not turn out to be a race war at all, but a war between freedom and slavery, between free states and slave states. And he knows that when matters assume that complexion, his beloved South cannot win. If that is his real fear, however inchoate and even something he was loath to admit to himself, it would explain Jefferson's increasingly frantic mood in the last years of his life, a time, in many ways, in which slavery and the South seemed to be in the driver's seat when it came to national politics. But to Jefferson even as mild a compromise as that forged in Washington in 1820 over Missouri's entry into the Union seemed a sign of a bloody reckoning to come.[75]

The only solution to the Negro problem was emancipation and bidding good luck and good riddance to the Negro. Jefferson, at the end of his life, latched onto a plan, advocated as well by similarly motivated dreamers, whereby adult slaves would be shipped out of the country, while their children would remain to be raised (and rigorously exploited) under the care of their masters until they reached their maturity, at which time they too would be made to leave these shores. Stated with admirable humanity, it was a mad and evil plan, and even Jefferson had to take pains to finesse the horror, writing in a letter in 1824, "The separation of infants from their mothers would produce some scruples of humanity. But this would be straining at a gnat, and swallowing a camel."[76]

Jefferson should by no means be taken as a representative man of his times; he was too wealthy, too cultured and cosmopolitan, and, not incidentally, too much a slaveholding Southern gentleman to be dressed in the clothes of a typical American. Moreover, most of his musings on the Negro problem were, like "the generous and emancipatory thoughts for which his name is so justly praised," reserved for his private correspondence.[77] His awareness and imagination, the ambit of his intellect, set him apart even from the run of his revolutionary peers and mark his greatness.[78] His ruminations on the Negro problem assume their importance as much in his anticipation of what would be necessary to maintain an ideological modus vivendi between slavery and freedom, a basis for national consensus, as in his direct influence upon the compromisers of the antebellum period who manufactured that consensus. Thus he spins out of his head fantasies of incipient race war that can only be forestalled by deportation. This is equally fantastical due to its definite impossibility (as a practical matter) and unlikelihood (as a political and economic matter). As well, they might seem to be rendered moot by the ascension of King Cotton (the term used for market cotton's domination of Southern agriculture) and the dual revolution that followed in his train. Jefferson to his deathbed did not think it so. But beyond that, his formulation of the Negro problem has among its cardinal virtues the not quite ironic effect of evacuating the area at the center of Jefferson's plan of salvation so that advocacy of emancipation becomes the province of dangerous fools and reckless adventurers. Heeding the counsels of prudence, "the 'realist' could agree with the 'visionary,'" that the Revolution's principles demanded abolition, but "reality required that the Negroes' 'equal right to freedom' be consigned to that pantheon of ideals which evoked rhetorical respect but did not impinge on the immediate world of affairs."[79]

A corollary to this evacuation was the demonization of the anomalously free African American population in order to prove the rule.[80] The Free Negro was severely squeezed in the South, segregated in the North, barred from the territories, and, generally, much maligned, mobbed, and otherwise ill used as a matter of (de facto where it was not de jure) policy in the internal affairs of the states. Carrying forward Jefferson's dream of a final solution to the Negro problem, the American Colonization Society was founded in Washington in 1816; at its first meeting Henry Clay, exemplar par excellence of antebellum evasion, praised the society's resolve to "rid our country of a useless and pernicious, if not dangerous, portion of its population," the free Negro. This was required because they posed a threat to the completeness of the equation of blackness with servitude in the American imagination, the sign of antebellum America's pain.

In politics, evasion made a succession of tenuous and arbitrary antebellum compromises, enforced by gag rules and violence and "pragmatism," clear the way for political figures to say what Jefferson could not: "I am no friend of slavery," Clay proclaimed, but "their slavery forms an exception (resulting from a stern and inexorable necessity) to the general liberty in the United States."[81] The Negro problem provided license to say such things without having that "stern and inexorable necessity" be understood as the requirement of what James H. Hammond called a "mud-sill" class of permanently submerged, dispossessed workers.[82] It was a way out, a way of escaping the self-perception of a harsher political economy, a means to add color to the black-and-white picture of class hierarchy sealing the fates of Americans. Instead the South and the North—the United States—would have its cake and eat it too: experience the benefits of having a mud-sill that was not a mud-sill—because slavery was the only way to control the Negroes—while denying both its permanence and the organic nature of its relation to American society—because the Negroes will one day be vanished.

Once having achieved this shape the Negro problem, as such, solves itself, but formally surviving only to be invoked as a rear-guard action covering the flanks of the pragmatic consensus.[83] African Americans are fixed in their place. There, whether as victims of America or the nation's chief villain, their claims are abstractions, special pleadings isolated from the normal contest and conflict of American society. In this environment it is possible to be, like Jefferson, agnostic on the question of the primacy of nature or nurture without giving away the game: black people's peculiar debility may have its source in biology, the middle passage, slavery, or some combination of these; the salient fact is that they were wrecked. Assuming an idealist form, the political and intellectual problem posed by the treatment of African Americans being an exception to the rule in the American democracy is rendered as a matter not of contention between potentially clashing social forces, but as a matter of consensus among white people.[84]

Chief Justice Roger B. Taney's opinion in the Supreme Court's *Dred Scott v. Sandford* case is telling in this regard as an effort, only momentarily successful, to forge a national white consensus on the backs of African Americans and to rescue the nation's future by dubious but politically usable inferences made about the architects of the American republic. He wrote, "It is difficult at this day to realize the state of public opinion in relation to that unfortunate race, which prevailed in the civilized and enlightened portions of the world at the time of the Declaration of Independence, and when the Constitution of the United States was framed and adopted." "This opinion was at that time fixed and universal in the civilized portion of the white race. It was regarded as an axiom in morals as well as in politics, which no one thought of disputing, or supposed to be open to dispute." Those seeking sectional reconciliation picked up on this line of reasoning. Thus, the newspaper associated with President James Buchanan, the Washington *Union* of March 12, 1857, prayed that Taney's opinion in *Dred Scott* will "exert a mighty influence in diffusing sound opinions and restoring harmony and fraternal concord throughout the country." The court had demonstrated a "moral conservatism" that the Union found all to the good. But therein lies the problem: nowhere in the constitution is it said, with Taney, that African Americans did indeed have "no rights which the white man was bound to respect." It is precisely the Constitution's silence on this matter that indicates the "moral conservatism" of its framers among the American revolutionaries, and indicates as well the radical idealism of Buchanan, Taney, and their allies in seeking to bring on a revolution in the American system of government.[85]

Even the most sensible precautions sometimes cannot hold back a flood. Agreements dissolve and even white supremacy can erode under the weight of its own (nonbiological) contradictions. One might say that while the South was doomed by slavery, the North's tragic flaw was racism—that on the eve of the Civil War the regions were united in their contempt for black people. But racism and the accord that was the Negro problem once cast into the breach could not survive in their antebellum form. During the war African Americans, both free and slave, asserted themselves in great and small ways, overcoming the dissembling of politicians and, as it were, dictating terms that could not be evaded, but that slowly, grudgingly and then, in 1862 and 1863, with ever greater momentum demanding to be faced forthrightly. Moreover, faced forthrightly, as Frederick Douglass had always maintained, as a matter of crime and not of color. It was, in that time, a problem of a very different sort than the Negro problem of the past; it was a problem, moreover, not of discrete "racial" attitudes, nor merely of military strategy, but of what it meant to be an American, a citizen and, as well, a soldier. Abraham Lincoln spoke volumes by finally heeding the advice of Douglass, Martin R. Delaney, and others to utilize black troops in the Union Army. "We had reached the point where it seemed that we must avail ourselves of this element, or in all probability go under," the President said, and so "this element," previously of no account, could now take the field to be a part of the rescue of the Union. President Lincoln's new policy was action pointing in the direction of something like a revolution in social relations. But his formulation of the matter is also telling: "I was brought to the conclusion that there was no dodging this negro question any longer."[86]

In being true to the antebellum usage of the term, Lincoln's words are liable to be misconstrued as one of those types of fixes Jefferson, the colonizationists, and other fantasists conjured. However, in arming black men and otherwise, in responding to the ways in which African Americans struck for freedom, ennobling the aims of the Civil War and the American nation, he was not so much facing up to the Negro problem as evacuating it, setting the nation right on the matter of the exception posed by the treatment of black people to the rule of democratically organized American society.

That might have been that: the Negro problem dead at the feet of a new nation.[87] In 1865 there was born a new America, if not purged of every sin, then at least having paid, in being born anew, a wrathful penance, purging through the blood one of America's foulest ongoing sins, such a purging as only madmen the likes of Turner and John Brown had had the foresight to predict and welcome. The Negro problem, however, would after a fashion reassert itself. Even as the war drew to a close and his life neared its end, Lincoln, like so many of his predecessors before him, would continue to talk up colonization to Douglass and other visitors to the White House. But neither boorish behavior on the part of the president nor dire predictions of the freed Negro's imminent demise, nor racist violence and the traps set by a skewed economic system could spoil the fact that emancipation "had once and for all decreed that the struggle for freedom would no longer be a struggle against slavery." Heaven was yet to arrive on earth, and freedmen and freedwomen faced this new world with "at best only modest resources," Barbara Jeanne Fields has written. But meager and inadequate as these may have been, the freedpeople grasped tools "for facing those challenges that do not arise in slavery, but belong uniquely to the domain of freedom."[88] Perhaps the nation did not need any old Negro problem or the flurry of schemes for its solution.

%%%

ANOTHER DAY, another place, another funeral.

When Frederick Douglass died on February 20, 1895, at his home, Cedar Hill, in the Anacostia section of Washington, D.C., some good part of the nation took notice. He was "The Slave Who Ran Away," as one headline read, and articles charted his course up out of slavery and Maryland's Eastern Shore to freedom and the North.[89] Settling first in New York and soon thereafter in Massachusetts, he worked the wharves of New Bedford as a free individual. But personal salvation or redemption, accomplishment enough for most hearty souls, was not the end of his quest: others were still in chains. And so he offered up himself to the Massachusetts Anti-Slavery Society, as its agent traveling the circuit "telling his story" and organizing opposition to "Negro slavery." In that capacity, and later as autobiographer and editor of his own newspaper, *Frederick Douglass's Paper* (which later became *The North Star*), he played his part in "the long agitation in America against negro slavery."[90] While some of his abolitionist colleagues turned their faces from politics and counseled him to do the same, he would not demur and was on hand for, in their turn, the beginnings of the nascent Liberty, Free Soil, and Republican parties. And when the war came, he presented himself at the White House, persistently knocking on Lincoln's door, prodding the president to make the war about freedom, to make of Negro men soldiers, and, in so doing, to make himself into the Great Emancipator history and destiny demanded. That large task accomplished, Douglass went on to offer counsel to other presidents and to hold high appointive offices, being named Marshall of the District of Columbia in 1876, Recorder of Deeds for the district in 1881, and Minister of the United States to Haiti in 1889.

It was mostly on account of his civil service, perhaps, that some thought was given to honoring this "most illustrious citizen" by placing the body to lie in state in the rotunda of the Capitol. But that plan died aborning on the floor of the House of Representatives.[91] Nonetheless, many memorials were written to him and services held for him where his virtues were extolled and attempts were made to define the meaning of his life. *Harper's Weekly* pointed to an ineffable presence: a "something strikingly noble in Mr. Douglass's appearance," such that "whoever beheld him felt immediately sure that the man before him was one of note—a personage."[92] The Rev. Dr. Louis Banks, taking as his text the words "Know ye not that there is a prince and a great man fallen?" in a sermon at the Hanson Place Methodist Episcopal Church, Brooklyn, New York, spoke of Douglass as the greatest of the century's great self-made men: "the most picturesque historical figure in modern times." Though he was, among his people, a leader in championing the cause of Republicanism, even there he was "a broad-spirited, public man," and his rising above partisanship was demonstrated: " 'I am a Republican,' " Banks quoted Douglass as saying, " 'but I am not a Republican right or wrong.' " Illustrative of that same expansiveness of sympathy, note was made of the appropriateness of the morning of his final day finding him at Metzerott Hall in Washington for a meeting of the Women's National Council. Douglass had been there from the start, addressing the first women's rights convention in Seneca Falls, New York, in 1848, and so his unexpected attendance at this closed meeting was welcomed and a chair was found for him next to his old friend, Susan B. Anthony, an apt culmination of a nearly fifty-year period of active attention "to the equality of rights and privileges between man and woman."[93]

In some of the encomia to Douglass there is to a certain extent a suggestion that Douglass's life since the Civil War had been anticlimactic. The view that Douglass's last thirty years were not so great or dramatic as those years leading up to 1865 has merit, and even his most fervent supporters (or Douglass himself, likely) would not be too much troubled by it. If so, it is partly by virtue of the very success of Douglass's advocacy of abolitionism, political engagement (both before and after the war), and black people's enjoyment of the full complement of bourgeois rights. Expressed on the stump but also through the building up of institutions, this advocacy succeeded by the late 1860s in re-creating American citizenship to include African Americans and was instrumental in the rise of Radical Reconstruction and a class of African American political figures and elected officials—up to and including senators and congressmen and high positions in state government, but also and crucially sheriffs, justices of the peace, councilmen, clerks, and dogcatchers.

Perhaps mundane compared to the war years, this was the great accomplishment of Douglass and those in his generation who fought for freedom: not utopia or an end to racism and racist proscription but, rather, what might have been a permanent routinization and normalization, within the democratic context, of the problems and challenges faced by African Americans and a more or less efficacious check on the mischief of those inclined to agitate a problem with black people. In the 1860s and 1870s and even afterward when office holding became less frequently elective and more frequently of the appointive or patronage type, Douglass might be looked at as old sage or chief "pol," but never so singular or singularly heroic as in his youth. The times had changed; that war had been won.

However, interpretation of what Douglass's life meant to America in 1895 had also to be tied up inevitably with the burying of bloody shirts, endeavors to begin organization of Civil War veterans' reunions—wherein increasingly wizened "Johnny Reb" would grasp the hand of aging "Billy Yank" in an act of symbolic reconciliation transcending the years of animosity—and other contemporaneous efforts signaling sectional rapprochement. In this environment it was required that certain euphemisms be employed to describe Douglass's activities. He was "an orator upon subjects relating to slavery," which may be what the historian U. B. Phillips was training to be at that time, but hardly covered what Douglass did in the 1840s and 1850s. Even the somewhat more pointed descriptions—"lecturing against slavery" and "on behalf of the slave"—have a certain summer-idyll-at-the-Chautauqua flavor to them.[94]

The memorials to Douglass were themselves marked by the distance between emancipation and thirty years later, and by the conviction (which Booker Washington would soon come to articulate) that Douglass's heyday called for hostility and war, while now peace was in the offing, demanding "a policy, not of destruction, but of construction."[95] That fact makes for some mystification regarding the contemporary Negro problem. In the era of the advent of systematic segregation, for instance, what explains the *New York Times*' baffling statement praising Douglass for being "instrumental in advancing the work of banishing the color line"? Was not the color line being slathered all over the nation—onto signposts, buildings, and railcars? The explanation lies in the newspaper's implicit distinction between Douglass's aid in the destruction of slavery—the color line banished by the Thirteenth Amendment—and the advent of the freedmen, then, and the wholly other matter now of the lesser unpleasantries faced by free black people "owing," as the newspapers said of Douglass, "to the prejudice that was felt against his race."[96]

Withal there was nothing like an attempt to diminish Douglass or even the later Douglass as his resume and record of accomplishment spoke for themselves: "Though born and reared in slavery, he managed, through his own perseverance and energy, to win for himself a place that not only made him beloved by all members of his own race in America, but also won for himself the esteem and reverence of all fair-minded persons, both in this country and in Europe." In the end, he was, the sub-headline of the *Times* story announced, "the Most Representative African America Has Produced."[97]

The headline speaks volumes about Douglass's place in America and American memory in the 1890s. It was a time in which "war memories and ideals were rapidly passing," Du Bois wrote, "when the nation was a little ashamed of having bestowed so much sentiment on Negroes, and was concentrating on Dollars."[98] But the memorials suggest that perhaps there was some reservoir of sentiment remaining, or, perhaps, a new stream flowing in the ideological currents of the time heading in the direction of the Negro. Douglass was "most representative"—a singular, superlative version of the common late-nineteenth-century usage[99]—not just in the sense of being the best man Negroes could come up with, but, more: that his was a life in which Negroes and America could alike take pride. "His shade will be conspicuous in the ghostly company of William Lloyd Garrison, Wendell Phillips, John Brown, Henry Ward Beecher, Oliver Johnson, and Owen Lovejoy," but among them "the only man with negro blood in his veins, the only one who, in his person, had suffered the penalties and experienced the pains of slavery."[100] Simultaneously, then, Douglass was a Negro hero and, in striking a blow against slavery and thus confirming the heroic virtues upon which the nation was founded, an American hero; a shared symbol of mutual freedom from the peculiar American institution that was slavery; and a common point marking the nation's and its peoples' triumph—a triumph over not just slavery but also the past itself.[101]

"But whither the future?" some Americans asked. "There is great necessity that Frederick Douglass's mantle shall fall upon younger men," the Reverend Banks insisted four days after his passing.[102] Seven months later, Booker Washington, a man who had been a slave like Douglass, but was otherwise unlike Douglass in having few institutional associations, beyond his affiliation to the Alabama school for Negroes at Tuskegee, to the broader American public life, would mount a stage in Atlanta, Georgia, introduced to the assemblage there for the Cotton States Exposition as "a representative of Negro enterprise and Negro civilization."[103] He then commenced to speak, invoking his authority in his right to convey "the sentiment of the masses of my race."

The Negro, he said, has found himself lost in freedom, unable "to draw the line between the superficial and the substantial, the ornamental geegaws of life and the useful." He carried these oppositions back to the dawn of freedom: "Ignorant and inexperienced, it is not strange that in the first years of our new life we began at the top instead of the bottom; that a seat in Congress or the state legislature was more sought than real estate or industrial skill; that the political convention or stump speaking had more attractions than starting a dairy farm or truck garden." The Negro is so lost because he has been misled and blind the possibilities before him; that "when it comes to business, pure and simple, it is in the South that the Negro is given a man's chance in the commercial world," that "No race that has anything to contribute to the markets of the world is long in any degree ostracized," and that "No race can prosper till it learns that there is as much dignity in tilling a field as in writing a poem. It is at the bottom of life we must begin, and not at the top." He sought to drive this point home by way of an allegory: "A ship lost at sea for many days sighted a friendly vessel. From the mast of the unfortunate vessel was seen a signal, 'Water, water; we die of thirst!' The answer from the friendly vessel at once came back, 'Cast down your bucket where you are.'" A second, a third, and a fourth time, the signal was sent by the distressed vessel, and three more times the signal was answered, "Cast down your bucket where you are."

> The captain of the distressed vessel, at last heeding the injunction, cast down his bucket, and it came up full of fresh, sparkling water from the mouth of the Amazon River. To those of my race who depend on bettering their conditions in a foreign land or who underestimate the importance of cultivating friendly relations with the Southern white man, who is their next-door neighbor, I would say: "Cast down your bucket where you are"—cast it down in making friends in every manly way of the people of all races by whom we are surrounded.

To "those of the white race," Washington continued, "were I permitted I would repeat what I say to my own race, 'Cast down your bucket where you are." Cast it down among the eight millions of negroes whose habits you know, whose fidelity and love you have tested in days when to have proved treacherous meant the ruin of your firesides." Cast it down among those who need not "strikes and labour wars," but who are "the most patient, faithful, law-abiding and unresentful people that the world has seen."

> As we have proved our loyalty to you in the past, in nursing your children, watching by the sick-bed of your mothers and fathers, and often following them with tear-dimmed eyes to their graves, so in the future, we shall stand by you with a devotion that no foreigner can approach, ready to lay down our lives, if need be, in defence of yours, interlacing our industrial, commercial, civil, and religious life with yours in a way that shall make the interests of both races one. In all things that are purely social we can be as separate as the fingers, yet one as the hand in all things essential to mutual progress.

The alternative solutions to "the great and intricate problem which God has laid at the doors of the South" are clear: the Negro will be "a veritable body of death, stagnating, depressing, retarding every effort to advance the body politic" or the Negro and the white shall be tied together for mutual benefit, for "progress" (repeated seven times), and "a new heaven and a new earth."[104]

In less than a quarter of an hour his speech would be over, and he would have Douglass's mantle and more.

%%%

IN A perceptive review of *Up From Slavery*, the eminent turn-of-the-century man of letters William Dean Howells was moved to mull over related matters concerning Douglass and Washington, history and memory, slavery and freedom, the Anglo-Americans and the Afro-Americans, and, though he did not say as much directly, the collective Negro problem. "It is not well to forget slavery, and the memory of Frederick Douglass will always serve to remind us of it and the fight against it," he wrote, "But it is not well to forget that slavery is gone, and that the subjection of the negro race which has followed it does not imply its horrors." Unmindful of the change—of the real difference between that past and this present—and overly sensitive to the subjection, "the temper of the Afro-American mind" turns to "extremism" and "bitterness." Flailing away at the ghosts of "race ignominy and social outlawry," the Negro fails at self-consciousness. Lacking in perspective and ironic sensibility, black people evince an inability to enjoy or even admit the humor in black foibles or the muddle of human affairs that is endemic to freedom.

Washington, Howells believes, is different from those Negroes, set apart by "his constant common sense," his rising above bitterness, and "his unfailing sense of humor." His reasoned public utterances are "infused with the sweet, brave humor" that makes it possible for him to "enjoy the negro's ludicrous side as the white observer enjoys it." Humor and irony enable him "to place himself outside his race, when he wishes to see it, and to report its exterior effect from his interior knowledge." In this way Washington, in Howells's view, acts, where others merely strut and fret, applying "the mild might of his adroit, his subtle statesmanship" to the problem, "the only agency to which it can yield." "He seems to hold in his strong grasp the key to the situation," Howells concludes, "for if his notion of reconciling the Anglo-American to the Afro-American, by a civilization which shall not threaten the Anglo-American supremacy, is not the key, what is?"[105]

What is, indeed. Howells, in one way or another, touches upon the essential elements defining, with but a few amendments, what Washington represented to his age. It is useful then to show what Washingtonianism is and what it is not. It is not conservatism. Howells and others do use the word in describing Washington, but it is in the sense of a conservative turn of mind rather than a political, much less a philosophical, stance. Washington evinces no especial concern for the buttressing of the existing order (which he rather seeks to change) or reinvesting hallowed tradition (which only points backward to slavery, not even to speak of the Reconstruction, which Washington, with most of his supporters, views as a tragic era) or defending the treasures black people already possess.[106] Washington's watchword is ever "Progress"—indeed, it is his mantra, invoked fully seven times at Atlanta—predicated on the faith that loosing the fetters of the past will enable the nation to take a great leap forward into a new day of prosperity and peace. And neither do his supporters think Washington especially an accommodationist; taking him at his word, they see him as straightforwardly sincere in what he says and right in what he does for the Negro. Their failure to use such an unwieldy term may also be explained by its shedding little light on the matter under discussion: a situation that finds Washington and his "progressive" legions riding the wave of segregation's revolutionizing of the American scheme of government, while those like William Monroe Trotter and Ida B. Wells-Barnett, whom Washington tellingly called the "reactionary ones," seek democracy's preservation.[107]

"Accommodationism" is especially useless because every African American of any moment and not undertaking a revolution or immediate emigration is, in one way or another, accommodating the American scheme of things (just as most Americans, grudgingly or not, find themselves doing). Taking that reality into account, scholars discover Du Bois as "conservative," too, but not Marcus Garvey, a large admirer of Washington, who, had he not been unjustly imprisoned and then deported, might have remained in America for decades advocating his particular form of "back-to-Africa" nationalism.[108] The point here being that while, of course, there are elements of what Washington stood for—like the Negro getting out of politics—that can be deemed conservative, they are predicated on a foundation of radical idealism that holds that disfranchisement and segregation will result not only in Negro uplift, a dubious proposition in its own right, but also an increase in white good will, that will eventually lead, as Washington said at Atlanta, to "the enjoyment of all the privileges" and rights other Americans already enjoy.[109] Additionally, there is an objection to the general and promiscuous use of the terms "realist" or "pragmatist" as synonyms for those who, seeing no other choice, encourage black political quiescence and business activities. The notion of pragmatism implies a reasoned choice between different avenues. If one believes Washington and black people had no other choice (due to circumstances or whatever sort, political, social, economic, cultural, or racial), such does not make them pragmatists, but people on a forced march down a hard road. Calling that exigency "accommodationism" or pragmatism or realism hardly helps clarify the situation faced by those trying to positively change the odds and provide African Americans with more and better options. To say, then, that Washington is an "accommodationist" becomes either an excuse for his not accomplishing much—a certain thing as far as concerns politics and social freedom—or a reason for its latter-day exponents not to have to think carefully and deeply about the different exigencies of their own times.[110]

So much Washingtonianism is not. What it is is a set of attitudes, postures, and most of all an idea that rapidly amounts to a hegemonic solution to the Negro problem, a set of requirements for responsible Negro leadership, and a platform upon which Washington stands as the leader with the only feasible solution to the problem. Washingtonianism is "the common sense of the Negro problem," as he would have it,[111] meaning what white people—the best white people—are inclined to think; it is a confirmation of their prejudices (though not only in the pejorative sense of the word) toward the Negro and what they think the American nation reasonably ought and can do for this particular class of American people. Washingtonianism is an openness to white help and socially engineered and radical change. It is a style of Negro leadership predicated on the absence of bitterness, meaning a willingness to forgive the past's sins against the Negro people. "In his heart there is no bitterness," Howells wrote,[112] and Washington's reader or listener knows this to be so because he takes great pains to lay open his life and that of the Negro, lay them bare, and insists a fresh start can be made, a new history.

Washingtonianism is also a gentle and sometimes not so gentle ridicule of black people, homely homilies to the shiftless and picaresque that evoke a precise psychological mixture in which contempt and sympathy lose their precise definitions and become one.[113] Washington ingratiates himself with his supporters, entertaining them and saying what they might otherwise be loath to say. In so doing, he demonstrates his cardinal ability to be recognized as positioned both inside and outside the black mass. He is a black man, born of the peculiar circumstances of black life in America, in and of that world, and yet also in the white world in being of one mind with its inhabitants, and thus a kind of emissary straddling or rising above the color line that is figured between what Americans with Washington's aid led themselves to believe were two societies, one white and one black. He is a Negro leader endowed with special moral standing by his unique position and thus gifted with a special vision, encompassing past and present, and pointing toward a way out for all concerned into a better future.

Washingtonianism's most elusive element, although hidden in plain sight, forms the key to the mystery of Washington as both actor (through the expression of ideas) and pragmatic visionary. Howells properly calls it a notion—though subsequently it will assume the dimension of a fact of nature—"of reconciling the Anglo-American to the Afro-American."[114] "In all things purely social we can be as separate as the fingers, yet as one as the hand in all things essential to mutual progress," as Washington had declared at Atlanta. What obtains here is not so much Washington's framing "the *modus vivendi* of race relations," as C. Vann Woodward put it. That was taken care of by Jim Crow's henchmen, lynch mobs, and a complicitous federal government and judiciary. It was they who conspired to create an ugly reality. Washington's contemporary, the education reformer Robert C. Ogden, was closer to the mark when in lauding the Atlanta performance he spoke of its effect in giving "the race question a rapid impetus forward."[115] What Washington accomplished was the elucidation of a theory. This theory—not a theory *of* race relations, but race relations as theory—takes off from wide-ranging and difficult economic and political questions on the ground where black people live in order to render those issues harmless to the business of America and beyond the purview of any democratic creed.

In this theory, the Negro problem's cause and cure are one. The source of black people's misery and the general headache and worriment they present to America is bad race relations—that is, "ignorance," prejudice, hostility—and its putative solution is good race relations—the absence of strife of various kinds, racial harmony. And so justice departs, its place taken up by a naive distortion, "racial justice," that embodies the very double standard it presumes to oppose.

The Negro problem is not, Washington insists, an aspect of capitalism or of internal colonialism, and certainly not of "caste" (though that term for the Indian practice of vast antiquity will be applied inappropriately to the new and innovative American settlement of the 1890s); it is not a pogrom or a Prussian Road. The Negro problem does not find its source in any deep-rooted American antipathy toward the black, nor in any fixed laws of biological determinism; neither in anti-Americanism, nor in any antidemocratic tradition that has ever reaped the fruit of discrimination and exploitation. None of these, but bad race relations. That is to say, he offers an idea, a view, a formulation of what is happening in America, and extrapolates from that evidence attitudes and moods that can succumb to the properly chosen word.

With the Negro problem safely sequestered outside the democratic arena, the interests and aspirations of politicians and ministers (among Washington's first foils), workers and businessmen, parents and teachers would no longer need to be expressed by way of the normal, if potentially messy, institutional channels through which Americans settled their conflicts and competition. Instead they would be mediated through the good offices of "Negro leaders" ever mindful of where their mandate comes from and the requirement placed on them as a first principle "to cement the friendship of the two races." How? By going hat in hand to make what are inevitably special pleadings to white patrons.

Skipping lightly over or, rather, necessarily ignoring the neat manner in which the interests of older Southern forces that put black people in their place came together with those of New South and national interests to keep them there, the idealist conception of the Negro problem ("ignorance," "bad race relations") and its putative solution ("better race relations") was crucial to the "separate but equal" settlement being understood, as in *Plessy v. Ferguson*, as a rapprochement with "the Negro," an undifferentiated collectivity, rather than as an insult to citizens dispossessed of their rights. It was, then, "the Negro" America faced, rather than croppers and farmers,

workingmen and workingwomen, business owners and politicians, teachers and parents with various interests and deep claims on the American
nation; "the Negro," dependent and, following Washington's example, praying for consideration from behind an encircling wall of what white people
would bear.

Therein lies Washingtonianism's promise and appeal to idealism, its
buckets cast down, its hands upraised and fingers spread: the offer of a
means of escape (as Jefferson had hoped America could escape) from
seemingly intransigent problems that are by no means products of "race,"
but of the real difficulties, material as well as political and social conflicts
that Americans pour into the leaky vessel of race. The solution of the Negro
problem will not be found in an extension of democracy; neither is the
solution found in slavery or religion (for Washington, a mere instrumentality, a machine to make of Negroes better workers). No one of these, but
magical "Progress" to conjure good "race relations," a seemingly practical,
but in fact fundamentally idealist abstraction—how black and white people
feel about each other—as a solution.

Washington's own experience provides the basis of his theory; that is,
race relations' proofs. It is possible to see, in his moment at Atlanta, his
vision in operation:

> As I sat on the platform, with the flower and culture and beauty of the
> South on either side, and in front of me the black men who were slaves, and
> near them ex-Confederates, who only a little while ago were the masters of
> these black men, and as I saw these black men and these Southern men and
> beautiful and cultured Southern women wave their hats and handkerchiefs
> and clap their hands and shout in approval of what I said, I seemed to have
> been carried away in a vision, and it was hard for me to realize as I spoke
> that it was not all a beautiful dream, but an actual scene, right here in the
> heart of the South.[116]

The accounts of the speech and the reaction of many Americans to it bear
out the magic Washington describes. Widely distributed—it was claimed
that it appeared "in nearly every paper in the country." Clark Howell, the
editor of the *Atlanta Constitution*, called it "epoch-making," a "turning point
in the progress of the negro race," and "a platform on which the whites and
blacks can stand with full justice to each race."[117] It was, Howell concluded
a solution to "the great problem known as the negro question."[118] A Tennessee teacher proposed that "the new epoch" Washington's speech inaugurated could best be symbolized by a label button emblazoned with "an open

hand, fingers extended and diverging," that surely "would be bought and worn by thousands both white and colored."[119] Northerners were equally laudatory, one editorial praising the way Washington "bewitched" his audience and calling him "A Negro Moses."[120] A Massachusetts woman, an abolitionist and friend of Old John Brown (the wife of one of his "secret six" of supporters), called the speech "glorious!" and added that Washington had "struck the keynote of Twentieth century civilization in America!"[121] William Still, another old abolitionist, commended Washington for his articulation of "grand truths."[122] A New Yorker wrote as "a white man and old time abolitionist, an ex Union veteran" to say "we have entered upon the outer rim of the shining of the sun of the mellenial [sic] Dawn as it comes up over the Mountain tops."[123] And a Massachusetts-born scholar then teaching school at Wilberforce, Ohio, wrote to congratulate Washington for "a word fitly spoken."[124] Taken by the power of this reaction, Washington himself would write, "This is the year of jubilee of the negro. It is the beginning of an era," concluding that "there will soon be not only a new South but a new negro."[125]

The success of Washington's innovation in his own time lies not in its practical accomplishments. His appeal to the better class of white Southerner for protection and tutelage did not effect a real peace. It did not bring about a cessation of the racist violence or of the disfranchising efforts against African Americans, nor result in an improvement in black opportunities of various sorts in various venues, nor put any capital in black coffers that would otherwise not have been there. The Tuskegee Institute and Washington's "Tuskegee Machine," respectively the proving grounds and the vehicle for his self-help ideas, never functioned without a liberal application of philanthropic grease.[126] The Negro's share of the allocation of resources was meager indeed, insufficient, locking black people in a position where they were constantly losing ground to the whites.

The Progressive appeal of the race relations construction—and the source of Washington's ascendance—lies in its allowing democracy and racist proscription to exist hard by each other (indeed overlapping) seemingly without the latter affecting the former. It is here we find Washington's real wizardry and the real genius of race relations as an idea in providing a magic formula to create two worlds out of one world of difficult, perhaps even intractable, conflict, and, prospectively, offering up "the Negro" as tabula rasa: a clean slate upon which a better future could be charted, a worthy cause that Americans of good will surely might act responsibly toward, but for whose plight Americans and America were just as surely not responsible. This was the idealist rendering of the Negro problem.

Such idealism has been seen before—after the Civil War, not in the Reconstruction era, but in the contemporaneous Gilded Age, which might have extended throughout the nation but for the messy squabbling at the South. Then it was that a man on the make, a typical true believer without money for coal or wood, could fix a candle in his heat stove and reassure his freezing, blue-lipped visitor: "What you want is the *appearance* of heat, not the heat itself—that's the idea."[127]

Uttering the idea of race relations, the truth that won him the ovation at Atlanta, ensured Washington's success, but did not cause African Americans to be set free nor bring surcease in the warring against them. But, for the people who counted and heard from him what they wanted to hear, it was enough.

Washington himself came to see that it manifestly was not the good and pragmatic deal he had sold the nation, and he at last stopped saying that "the most harmful effect" of the raft of discriminatory practices and racist violence resided "in the permanent injury to morals of the white man" and tried to show that Jim Crow not only gave impetus to the twisted logic that seeks "to make wrong right or seem to be right," but that it was, as well, a crime and an injury to black people. Articulated first in his private correspondence in the last years of his life, and then in an article that only appeared after his death, he argued that "segregation is unjust," that it "invites other unjust measures," and that there is no symmetry to it, but rather, "The negro is segregated from his white neighbor, but white business men are not prevented from doing business in negro neighborhoods." (This last was an implicit rejoinder to what Washington himself had said at Atlanta in 1895 about the magic of the competitive market in lifting up even the most otherwise despised of races.) But it was too late.[128]

Explanation of how Washington came to discover the idea of race relations as a solution to the Negro problem, the personal and the political influences upon him, provides an opportunity to account for the creation of that dream, and, at the same time, how he and the nation came to meet at his vision. Those stories demonstrate how the Negro problem and race relations—ideas that transcend the distance between the two visionaries, Washington and King—came to constitute, along with what Du Bois called the strivings of black people, a central theme in African American history. Washington's persuasiveness, and the enduring appeal of his telling of his life story, also suggest that the source of the enduring twentieth century popularity of the race relations construction of the Negro problem, even after the dismantling of the Jim Crow system, lies in the transformation of Washington's common sense of the turn of the century into a hegemonic "common sense"—in Antonio Gramsci's meaning of the term, as "conception of the world" and "conforming norm of conduct"[129]—shaping the terrain upon which consideration of the fit and future of black people in American society took place. On this ground, race relations functions, as the Negro problem once did, as the central feature of a new social vocabulary with which Americans were able to shelter their democracy from what had been and would be done to Negroes, an explanation for the very contradiction that Jefferson and Lincoln conceived of as demanding colonization, that Myrdal conceived as a moral dilemma, and that King would combat with a combination of moral appeal and political mobilization. As such, its lineage constitutes a discrete chapter in the history of American racial ideology and the history of American reform, with the figure of Washington squarely at the center of their meeting.

He was an American, because attracted and repelled by the American scene. He was an American, because he was a native son; but he was also a Negro nationalist in a vague sense because he was not allowed to live as an American.

—RICHARD WRIGHT, "HOW BIGGER WAS BORN"

Chapter 2

"Negroes Whose Habits You Know"

The Slave Boy, "Booker," Progress, and "Racial Feeling"

N O SUCH person as Booker Taliaferro Washington was ever born. However, a slave named "Booker" did enter the world on an obscure farm near a not especially significant crossroads of Franklin County in south-central Virginia, and, as far as it can be known, did so sometime in the spring of 1856. The name of the mother of the child was Jane, and she was a black woman and a slave; about the father nothing beyond the hazards of guessing is known concretely except that, then and later, rumors swirled about the place, and the community of black people and the community of white people, that he was a white man of the neighborhood.

These facts have engendered three forms of slander against Washington, smoke from the flames of controversy surrounding him. The first of these defamations holds: that, of course, the man and leader Washington was not born, but rather had to be invented by the agencies of white supremacy.

Second: that the man who became the accommodating leader was born a slave and, as far as his personal psychology and social outlook were concerned, died one too. Third: that the possible paternity of a white person (true or not, and ultimately unprovable), serves either or both as a capstone explaining his compromised nature and illegitimacy as a black leader.

The Washington scholar might take note, here and there, of all these forms of attack from Washington's detractors and others with an axe to grind against him. In the former category there are those criticisms of Washington's cynical manipulations, his subjecting to ridicule various types of anachronistic "slavery days" Negroes, shiftless black dandies, pompous black politicians, and feckless Northern-based, big city black intellectuals coming upon the scene after the war, and, in general, his pandering to "prejudiced or race-proud white people."[1] He was nothing but a dexterous intriguer, an avatar of twisted logic, a salesman hawking platitudes and passivity, a "sell-out" deserving to be damned to a place of opprobrium with history's greatest traitors, the Buthelezis and Savimbis, the Quislings, Pétains, and those others making "obeisance before barbarian totems and absurd taboos."[2] Was he not a low-rent Vallandigham? A traitor behind the lines in a latter-day Civil War? A double agent in the new one on now between the Negroes and the whites, but unfortunately safe and untouchable because those African Americans who should have been in charge of dealing with black traitors were without the power or resolve to do with snakes what Lincoln did with his famous copperhead? Or perhaps he deserves less credit and a milder fate: shunted off into a corner where lesser men of putatively malign intent are warehoused, shut up in the rest home for toothless Uncle Toms.

If that line is not scathing enough, the second seems even stronger. Could there be a worse libel leveled at Washington than to wonder, as Washington's contemporary Kelly Miller did in 1903, if "but for Lincoln's proclamation," it would not have been probable for Washington to have "arisen to esteem and favor in the eyes of his master as a good and faithful servant"? Emma L. Thornbrough found hostile editorializing against Washington in the press that struck the same chord. She quotes a *Denver Weekly* reporter as claiming that if Washington had been born somewhat earlier "he would have had genteel, cleanly work about the house," a favorite of "old marster."[3] In his heart and mind, he "never fully lost the attitude of the favorite slave," another scholar claimed, never really embraced the challenges or hazarded the shoals of freedom; he never truly left the farm upon which he was born a slave.[4] His childhood personality, formed on the cusp of the distorted system of white mastery and black abjectness, fathered the weak man and false leader willing to settle for meager scraps fallen from white tables. Why else but a warped allegiance to the race of the father who denied him would he countenance egregious affronts to black humanity and savage attacks on black persons in the heyday of racist proscription and lynch law? What else but possession of a house slave mentality would explain his acceding to those forces behind segregation and disfranchisement seeking ever to throw African Americans "back again" into slavery? How else but through retention of the house servant's greedy calculus could he so selfishly promote a false racial peace, spinning out tales of racial harmony and personal success, while all around him his brothers and sisters are dying? All these make a prima facie case as to why he determined to cast his lot with the sure bet of latter-day "Massa" and paternalistic benevolence rather than with the long odds faced by his fellows in the fields of freedom.

But does such a case need to be made?

Taken together these notions, of Washington as invented leader opportunistically seizing the new times and Washington as never not thinking like a slave or house servant, appear on their face to be somewhat contradictory. However, both developed as species of the effort to topple Washington from the pedestal upon which he was placed after his performance at Atlanta in 1895. And they may have claimed, in Washington's own day, a certain rhetorical power for certain audiences. In that time, though, their efficacy was ultimately and decisively drowned out by the flood of acclaim and support Washington received from his white political and financial backers, and the general, if ambiguous black support he eventually gathered to himself as a result of that white help. It is instead at some greater remove from the age of Washington that the ideas of him as the creation of white power or creature of slavery have a stronger resonance. As perspective on the nadir that was his time, the inadequacies of his manipulated (and not simply manipulative) leadership, and as a retrospective attempt to theorize African American history, they share a common perspective that views his ascendance and Washingtonianism, both, as distorted developments of black politics, abominations and diversions from the righteous path of true or authentic black leadership in, as it were, struggle.

Some parts of this theory are correct, while other parts are woefully inaccurate. These views of him as an unauthentic black leader manufactured by the white powers-that-be and as a failed free man fall flat as estimations of Washington, his historic role and the whole program of Washingtonianism. William Monroe Trotter articulated both, scoring him for "ever and anon laud[ing] the benefits of slavery" and insisting that if he was "in any sense the leader of the Colored American people" it was so because he had been "chosen for that position by the white American race."[5] Trotter neverthe-less accurately recognized the turn-of-the-century dynamic that allowed white people to get away with precisely this type of fabrication, this Negro king-making, and, further, that in their doing so, their artifice assumed the form of concrete reality; they could not, in other words, be vanquished by the well-chosen calumny, but, coming on black people like a hurricane—a force of nature—necessitated his being confronted as such.

An important part of that strong force is the way Washington's support-ers thought of him and felt for him. "My life," he matter-of-factly reports to his readers, "had its beginning in the midst of the most miserable, desolate, and discouraging surroundings."[6] But they already know how the coming story, the upward march, will turn out—else why would *Up From Slavery* have been produced and distributed so that now Washington's life rests in their anxious hands? Therein lies a significant measure of the work's appeal in its own time.[7] It is an invitation to join him in his arduous and triumphant climb to making something of his freedom. They know, too, that while Washington's story at its beginning may be like that of other Negroes ("My case will illustrate that of hundreds of thousands of black people in every part of our country"),[8] unlike theirs, his life will not end up in tragedy or obscurity or invisibility or some other such troubling and pathetic dénouement.

But a black standard is not the only measure by which his supporters mark Washington's excellence. Washington, in their eyes, rather than being slavish or servile like the New South's misty reverie of faithful family retain-ers, was the best of free men, black or white. The sage of Tuskegee was the singular Negro, a rare one to know that freedom in no wise means license, that rights come accompanied—are indeed preceded—by duties. And that it was through this social and self-knowledge he would make of himself a truly free man. "It is not hyperbole to say that Booker T. Washington was a great American," Theodore Roosevelt would write, "one of the most useful, as well as one of the most distinguished, of American citizens of any race."[9] Striking the same, as they would have it, transracial or, better yet, univer-salist chords, O. K. Armstrong identified a vital element of Washington's appeal to his age in writing that his life and example "remind us to be con-scious primarily not of our race, but of our humanity." The lesson is not to be servile but to give service, and the challenge is not just for the Negro but for all: "In the long climb upward of that common humanity, few have done more to help so many on their way than that man of good will."[10]

There are ambiguities in this favorable, pro-Washington and, theoreti-cally at least, pro–African American view. Reasons, for example, to doubt the universalism of Theodore Roosevelt's touting of Washington for his mastery of the universal values upon which the republic was founded, when such praise is simultaneously wielded by the ex-president as a bludgeon against "the mass of ignorant, propertyless, semi-vicious Black voters," who he claimed were "wholly lacking in the character which alone fits a race for self-government." (And this particular effusion from the pen of the president was neither the first not the last example of such white stroking of Washington while swiping at the dignity of Negroes in general.) Reasons, as well, to doubt his champions' view of Washington as the one truly free Negro, predicated as it is, in part at least, by their ignorance of (not to speak of their bias against) African Americans in general, which, whether tacit or willed, allows them to think him apart simply because they do not (or would not) know any other similarly able black men and women. The former caveat—that Washington was the invented instrument of white power—needs to be placed within the dynamic of Washington's rise—a feature of his times he well understood and used to his benefit. The latter one—that Washington was ever a slave—is not so much a problem at all.

If it is true that Washington was born a slave and that he, unlike the great antebellum heroes—Douglass, Harriet Tubman—did not personally strike for his freedom, nothing but his youth need be offered in the way of an excuse for this lack. Further, as Washington himself would say, the Douglasses and the Tubmans were exceptional; the fact that he had no opportunity to emulate their example forms only a part of the rule, which in turn can be seen to make his rise seem all the more extraordinary. It is equally true that freedom came relatively quickly to him—by his tenth year. Freedom, first and more than anything else, shaped his ambition and character, and was abetted by the Reconstruction era enactments, the ensuing conflict over Negro rights, and, finally, the missionary education he received at Hampton Institute. This was a peculiar sort of education to be sure in terms of its content and curriculum, but in its duration and formality an education unthinkable in antebellum times for the vast majority of even free black people. The psychological geography of his life, then, is not restricted to the narrow horizons of the slave—isolated upon plantations and farms, the masses of them kept illiterate and "completely ignorant . . . so far as books or newspapers were concerned"[11]—but comprehends the wider world of freedom where an ambitious and intelligent boy becomes a striving young man. And the young man, in his turn, could gauge the best possibilities for making something of himself and, thereby, reach for and grasp "the main chance."[12]

%%%

ONE NEED not hold too closely to that furrow plowed by Washington's promoters—their values, reasoning, means and ends—to appreciate his abilities and attainments. Contrary to their Washington-centered myopia, however, he does not stand alone in having come up from slavery into a life of
accomplishment. His were but a part of the significant, mainly good, works
of the last generation of African Americans born into slavery, but coming
of age in the context of freedom. Born after 1848 or so, this generation was,
in a sense, privileged over their elders in their not having had to be slaves
for too very long and, particularly so, in being situated to take advantage
of the dramatically increased availability of education (beginning in Union
outposts within the boundaries of the Confederacy as early as the first year
of the war). Washington's generation also held advantages of a type over the
generation immediately following in having witnessed as youngish men and
women the drama and tumult of the Reconstruction era. In Washington's
case, he even played a part in it, although in some quarters he would not
want that career to become common knowledge.[13] These were Washington's
peer group in the South, men like the businessman John Merrick, born
in North Carolina in 1854, who founded the North Carolina Mutual Life
Insurance Company; the scholar and clergyman John Wesley E. Bowen,
born in New Orleans in 1855, who became the first Negro to hold a regular
professorship at Gammon Theological Seminary; John E. Bruce, born in
Maryland in 1856, who went on to become an influential journalist writing
under the pen name "Bruce Grit"; T. Thomas Fortune, also born in 1856 (in
Florida) and also later a journalist, though of even greater sway than Bruce;
the brothers Grimké, Archibald and Francis, born in 1849 and 1850, the
former a lawyer and the latter a minister, who went on to become leaders
of black communities in, respectively, Boston and Washington; William A.
Pledger, born around 1851, the son of a Georgia plantation owner who went
on to lead Georgia Republicans in the 1880s; and George H. White, born in
North Carolina in 1852, who entered Congress in 1896, the last black man
from the South to do so for the next six decades.

Washington's cohort also includes a man reputed to be able to "out-
Booker Booker,"[14] a cynic's cynic: the Alabama educator William H. Councill, born in 1849, with whom Washington refused to appear in public
because of, he claimed, Councill's "reputation for simply toadying to the
Southern white people," although it was also true that Councill was a main
rival for funding within the state of Alabama.[15] If Councill holds up the
soft extreme of the spectrum of making getting along with Southern white

people pay, Joseph C. Price, born in North Carolina in 1854 to a free mother and a slave father, and head of Livingstone College there, was, before his premature death in 1893, thought by some to occupy as a man of some firm principle and dignity the other end, a "Better Booker," perhaps, than the prevailing model. George Washington Carver's name might also be mentioned in this pantheon, as he was second only to Washington in the American public's estimation of the wonders of Negro progress—lauded as the black analogue of Thomas Edison just as Washington was compared to George Washington.[16] The list would also include persons who share Washington's Virginia background and slavery origins like George William Cook, born in 1855, who became an important member of the NAACP; another key NAACP member, Clement G. Morgan, born in 1859; and, stretching the criterion some to include a man born free, but only by a whisker in 1865, Adam Clayton Powell Sr., pastor of the influential Abyssinian Baptist Church in New York City, who shares with Washington the common background of having been born in Franklin County, migrating to West Virginia, and coming under the tutelage of G. M. P. King at the Wayland Seminary in Washington, D.C.

Serious strivers all, they will be men of the masses and men of the classes. A compilation such as this could also include ten or a dozen women, but the endeavor here is to suggest those who might have been available for hiring by powerful white people to occupy the symbolic position Washington did. It is for that reason in the nineteenth century that the relevant list consists only of men.[17] As good a way as any to convey the character, the élan, of this group of the best and brightest of their generation is to invoke the childish, but accurate words of one of their number. "Tell 'em we're rising," exclaimed a voice from the crowd at a Georgia freedmen's school when in 1868 the students were asked by General O. O. Howard for a message from the schoolchildren of the South to the schoolchildren of the North, "tell 'em we're rising." And "the black boy of Atlanta" of John Greenleaf Whittier's poem, Richard R. Wright (born a slave in 1855) did so, as a teacher, college president, political appointee, and association man.[18] Some of these former slaves will be "Bookerites," and others will be his opponents. Still others will be most unlike him in maintaining silence on the large-scale questions that would consume Washington and assure his rise to national prominence.[19] Among the Bookerite group many will seek to stake out positions of greater flexibility than his, standing, for instance, for economic advancement and for civil rights; among his opponents, there will be those who will be brought low by their apostasy and made to pay due homage to Washington and give obedience to his version of Negro leadership. At the very least, the variety in the different courses of their lives, their differing fields of endeavor and accomplishment, provide evidence debunking the notion that Washington and Washingtonianism were simply organic developments out of the slave experience, his Virginia slave background (Cook and Morgan), or of putatively having a white father (the Grimkés, Pledger).

That having been said, Washington remains the key both in the sense that his operation and program provided employment or opened opportunities for many of these notables; equally, his example set the crucial line of demarcation between permissible activities and productive advocacy from dissent beyond the pale. He was the center of the black world—because the white people who could say so and make it stick did so—overshadowing them all. The source of his triumph lies in his ability to construct an edifice for himself of the material of his (and their) past and present situation and sell it all done up in the gaudy trappings of progress as a vision of the nation's future. In that capacity, Washington is sui generis among the African Americans of his time; his rise cannot be explained in terms of a particularistic black science of politics, a black leader lifted up by black hands to sit upon black shoulders. Nor ought it to be understood simply in terms of his works and accomplishments and all he overcame—as compelling as all that may be to schoolchildren and others with lesser warrant for being overly credulous. Rather his career is more like that of the modern democratic politician, polling his constituency to find out the issues of importance to them, making himself electable through the construction of a platform and calculating the odds relative to his opponents and rivals. A comer, in short, and calculating, not a black version of Roosevelt or Woodrow Wilson, his close contemporary and fellow Virginian (born in 1856 in Staunton), but the thing itself—the man in the middle, the key figure—subject to many of the same requirements and dynamics. Except he never stood for any election.[20]

※※※

FRANKLIN COUNTY, Virginia, where Washington was born nearby Hale's Ford, sits hard by the Roanoke River. In the map of his life he was 120 miles and nine years away from Malden, West Virginia, to which he and his little family (his mother, a sister, and a brother) would remove themselves in 1865. From Malden he would set out in 1872 on the greatest journey of his young life, three hundred miles across parts of two states to Hampton, Virginia, from where it is a bit under five hundred miles to travel along the route crows could fly to Tuskegee, Alabama. In the historical geography of the Negro problem, Booker's birthplace in Franklin County is one hundred or so miles south-southwest of Thomas Jefferson's home outside Charlottesville, whence it is an approximately equal distance to the landmarks of Jamestown, where captive Africans are sometimes said to have first stepped foot in North America, to the southeast (on the way to Hampton), Southampton County to the south-southeast, and Harper's Ferry to the north. Harper's Ferry and Washington, D.C. (where the Supreme Court handed down its *Dred Scott* decision in the year after Booker's birth) are each about two hundred miles from Hale's Ford. Returning to Whiggish Franklin County from Democratic Monticello, one might split the difference by visiting Appomattox Court House, where the transformation of Jefferson's dream-turned-to-nightmare culminated in the death of the Confederacy and the destruction of the largest slave society anywhere in what we take pleasure in calling the free world.

Most of these places assumed their greatest importance to American history in antebellum times, and it is fair to say that none but the event at Appomattox in April 1865 made the slightest impression on the slave Booker's consciousness. Nevertheless, the matter of slavery is its own landmark in the life of the nation, a cairn built of the efforts to hasten or delay or a thousand times compromise away America's final reckoning with it. And slavery and its finish are central to the Negro problem in its post-Reconstruction incarnation and to the development of Washingtonianism, not least as benchmarks and evocations to reach out to various audiences: in the Yankee memories of a good but dire fight, but also in their resolve to effect a less costly peace in progress and prosperity for all (or, failing that, some plausible portion of all); in the hoary mythology of white Southerners of brave and chivalrous knights and fair ladies, and faithful "Uncles" and loyal "Aunties," "servants" and loved ones, but also in their fear and paranoia and the rending of the bonds between the children of the former and the children of the latter; and, most complicated of all, in Washington's relationship and appeal to African Americans, the sons and daughters of slaves and free people.

※※※

"I WAS born a slave on a plantation in Franklin County, Virginia. I am not quite sure of the exact place or exact date of my birth, but at any rate I suspect I must have been born somewhere and at some time."[21] With these disarming words Booker Washington begins the chronicle of his rise up from slavery to national glory. It is possible to find too much meaning in the fact that the boy who became the man was a slave; to find or invest in it all the rife associations that state and institution hold for the modern person; to permit it to serve as a trump or a veto, a gavel ruling out of order any and all objections to Washington's philosophy. Du Bois, late in life and at home in Ghana, remarked to a visitor how in his youth his aunts had sternly rebuked him for some slighting comment he had made about Washington. In the visitor's words, Du Bois was told "that it ill became one who had been born free to speak disrespectfully of a man whose back bore the marks of the lash."[22] But to what does that caution amount? It did not cause Du Bois to hold his tongue or stay his pen. Is the aunts' standard more than a contextual etiquette, a margin of grace like the respectful hearing that should be granted to people such as bilious veterans and boastful grandparents?[23]

Certainly it is relevant to a consideration of Washingtonianism just as Washington's slave origins certainly were significant to those in his own time who held the man in high esteem. But to them relevant as having been born to the Jews suffering under the oppression of the Egyptian pharaoh was relevant to Moses, and having been born in an America that would come to see itself, in its relation to the metropole, a captive of the tyranny of George III was relevant to George Washington. That is to say, enslavement was not the sum of the man. Nor could it ever be said to encompass him, but instead provided the measure of his character and greatness. As such it was an incident in the working out of his destiny, the sea he had inevitably to part, the Delaware he need must cross, in his passage to glorious victory. These were associations his friends must have had in mind when they called him "the Negro Moses" and asserted that he promised to do for his people what the General Washington did for the American nation. Two of Washington's greatest supporters, Andrew Carnegie and William H. Baldwin Jr., were among those who characterized Washington in this way. Carnegie figured Washington as "the combined Moses and Joshua of his people. Not only has he led them to the promised land, but still lives to teach them by example and precept how properly to enjoy it. He is one of these extraordinary men who rise at rare intervals and work miracles."[24]

On the other hand, rather than the link to the high-born, slaveholding patrician, a perhaps more appropriate analogy between Booker Washington and an American president—and one also brought out not infrequently during Washington's lifetime—might be to Abraham Lincoln, pregnant as such a comparison is with association to the Negro problem and high achievement from lowly birth. (Surely Washington would find much to concur with in Lincoln's objection to slavery as an interference with "the right to rise.")[25] "Except for the race ignominy and social outlawry to which he was born, the story of Booker T. Washington does not differ so widely from that of other prominent Americans. His origin was not much more obscure, his circumstances not much more squalid than Abraham Lincoln's, and his impulses and incentives to the making of himself were of much the same source and quality," so wrote William Dean Howells.[26] It is hard to imagine another African American (with the possible exceptions of Frederick Douglass in the nineteenth century and Martin King currently) being placed in such rarefied company. Such esteem illustrates the way in which Washington, by his supporters' lights, transcends in his life story particular "racial" circumstances, to offer lessons that are of universal application, and to enjoy broad popularity among, at least, the white people who count the most.

These ascribed characteristics make him wholly another sort of animal than the run-of-the-mill among leaders in Negro America before or since the age of segregation, a unique phenomenon of that time and situation. Indeed, one might wonder, given all this high regard, if Washington should not properly be considered as something more than merely a leader of a minority segment. He was a man who, as his friend, sometime opponent, and later lackey T. Thomas Fortune said, existed on beyond the parochialism of race that infected even the best of his black and white peers to inhabit a position as the sole Negro in the American pantheon of embracing leadership standing outside mere matters of local controversy.[27]

To set the scene, then: near the Roanoke River of Virginia, in Franklin County, there once was a crossroads known as "Hale's Ford." From there, it would have been possible to travel not especially well-beaten paths to places like Rocky Mount, the Franklin County seat, and auspicious-sounding locales like Big Lick (present-day Roanoke). Absent from modern maps of the state, it was hardly a place of any significance even in its day, offering (as was said about another, similar locale, Southampton Country, where a different sort of man made his mark) "nothing to distinguish it from any other rural, lethargic, slipshod Virginia neighborhood."[28] Booker Taliaferro Washington, or, rather, a child called "Booker," was born in those parts in the spring of 1856, and he grew up to become probably Franklin County's most famous son.[29]

%.%.%

"THE EARLY years of my life . . . were not very different from those of thousands of other slaves," Washington writes, "I was born in a typical log cabin," and it was there where he spent the better part of his first decade, which was the totality of his life as a slave.[30] By its outward appearance (preserved in photographs and, in a recreated form, standing today in Virginia) this one-room, dirt floor abode was surely a hovel, a slap-dash, 16' × 14' edifice of split oak logs cobbled together by aged and cracking mud. Without glass windows, the cabin "had only openings in the side which let in the light, and also the cold, chilly air of winter," Washington remembered; that, and the fact that there was "something that was called a door"—cracked and undersized—which "made the room a very uncomfortable one."[31] But not an especially mean hovel if judged by the standards of how some of the world's peasantries were caused to live in the nineteenth century (and afterward, for that matter). And, although Washington would later expound upon the especially malign effect of the one-room homes on the morality of the black family, his first home was probably not in affect or materially different from those in which President Lincoln and others of the nineteenth century's self-made men were born (and what striver worth his salt in the nineteenth century did not have a log cabin some whereabouts in the vicinity of his past whence to take wing?).[32] However, its inhabitants, Booker, his mother Jane, older brother John, and, by 1860, younger sister Amanda, were slaves. Their persons, their ragged clothes and meager furnishings, even the hole in the ground for storing sweet potatoes in winter that constituted the central feature of the cabin's single, dirt floor room, were part and parcel of the property of someone called James Burroughs.

Burroughs was a man of no especial significance beyond the narrow confines of Franklin County, a farmer—not a planter—of the middling sort for the antebellum South. Although in upcountry Franklin County he was wealthier than some of his neighbors (holding ownership, for instance, in a buggy), he was also worse off than others. In all, he was not any type of embodiment of Old South colonnaded splendor and gentlemanliness. His enterprise was based on the exploiting of the sweat of kith and kin, as well as slaves: "My master and his sons all worked together side by side with his slaves. In this way we all grew up together, very much like members of one big family. There was no overseer, and we got to know our master and he to know us."[33] The endeavoring of the massed hands sustained Burroughs's people and livestock; what was surplus went to market along with the Burroughs enterprise's cash crop of tobacco. Here, in Burroughs, was the stolid and independent backbone of the American republic; a yeoman of the Jeffersonian stripe, he possessed, according to the 1860 census, ten slaves and 207 acres (100 unimproved) of the Piedmont's red and yellow clay soil. The Burroughs's spread, like the surrounding region, included acreage that was somewhat undulating, but withal, fertile ground, its soil conducive to the cultivation of the kind of dark tobacco that, with careful tending, produced plug or twist chaw.[34] Burroughs owned no thresher, and so had to hire the services of one of the itinerant thresher operators who traveled from farm to farm, or else beg or rent one from one of his more prosperous neighbors thereabouts. The little more than half of the Burroughs acreage that was improved was—following the antebellum prejudice for open grazing—enclosed by a Virginia worm fence to keep the neighbors' livestock out (as opposed to the later convention, costly to the yeomanry, requiring the fencing in of all livestock).[35]

Washington, in his writing about his youth, called the Burroughs farm a "plantation" and their residence the "Big House," but his use of those terms can only be explained as products of a child's skewed sense of scale and dimension. The inaptly titled Big House was hardly much smarter than the four slave cabins—including Booker's, which doubled as the kitchen, mere feet away from the diminutive manse—spread around the place. It consisted of five rooms in "a small and very plain storey-and-a-half,"[36] a hewn log structure rather than the frame buildings favored by Franklin County's minor grandees.

As slaveholders, Washington said of Burroughs and his family that they were not "especially cruel . . . as compared with many others."[37] He did recall a certain willow tree from which was cut the switch with which he received his first thrashing.[38] More horrific was the image, so scorched onto his memory that it formed his "deepest impression" of slavery on the Burroughs place, of an adult relative, his uncle Monroe, laid bare and tied to a tree to receive an application of a cowhide whip from one of the Burroughs family. "As each blow touched his back the cry, 'Pray, master! Pray, master!' came from his lips, and made an impression upon my boyish heart that I shall carry with me to my grave."[39] Despite such scenes, the Burroughs were, in Washington's mature opinion, decent enough slaveholders. To provide a contrast, there was, in the neighborhood the likes of Josiah Ferguson from a nearby farm, whom brother John Washington remembered as "a cruel master and a bad man," the horrifying sort of abuser of slaves who freedmen and freedwomen would always point to as one of the more bestial aspects of slavery.[40] From the perspective of Washington's boyhood his own owner was a cut "above the average in the treatment of his slaves."[41]

"Although I was born a slave," Washington wrote in The Story of My Life and Work, "I was too young to experience much of its hardship." Washington articulates, not a survivor's statement in the modern therapeutic sense, but a self-conception of indomitability and pride: by an accident of birth I faced the raised whip hand and was not bowed or scarred by it. But

Washington also speaks to a more prosaic reality in his life: he had not had to endure, like so many thousands gone, the years and decades of grinding toil or the personal disorientation of being sold south, and the rending of family that accompanied that brutal practice.[42] Nor was Washington as a child called upon, he remembered, to labor very hard. As a result of his youth and the way labor was organized on the Burroughs farm, while a slave he learned none of the vaunted industrial skills he would later tout as virtues of "the school of American slavery."[43] Instead, young Booker worked at minor tasks around the farm: bearing water to field hands, cleaning the farmyard, and eventually becoming a houseboy working within the Burroughs residence operating something called a "fan mill," a $2.50 piece of machinery for the prevention of airborne pests disturbing the Burroughs family's mealtimes. Beyond that worthy occupation, he spent the greater part of his bonded time as a playmate and factotum for the young masters and mistresses.

At other times, there were occasions for fun, even moments of brief grace, as when his mother was able to attend to his needs, or when his brother "performed one of the most generous acts that I ever heard of one slave relative doing for another" by breaking in Booker's new flax shirt, Burroughs's sole provision against the weather for his young slaves, the wearing of which Washington compared to "the pulling of a tooth."[44] These elements of Washington's experience as a slave suggest a part of an explanation of why he would insist he harbored no bitterness about what he called, not "the time when I was a slave," but "the period that I spent in slavery."[45] Added together, there were these mitigating circumstances. First, there was the relative ease of his service. Second, that he was a part of a family of sorts in the persons of his mother and brother John and sister Amanda, and received the benefits afforded by the comfort of his connection to these loved ones. Third, that there was culture to be amid: pleasurable succor in the sounds of voices raised in song emanating from the quarters, the slaves' "wild and weird" music during corn-shucking time.[46] These were the "good times" for the company of slaves, abetted for Booker by the more uncommon fetes when his mother's companion, a lively and restive slave named Washington who was frequently rented out by the neighboring Fergusons to toil in the saltworks of western Virginia, would return to visit the Burroughs place and regale his fellows there with stories of the wider world beyond Franklin County.

Washington's retrospective observations about life on the "Old Burroughs place"[47] are not, however, a warrant to conclude that slavery was for him anything other than a cruel and brutalizing institution. There were these moments of kindness and decency, less frequently ones of grace and joy. But these were mere interludes for him between days and weeks down on the farm of loneliness, filled with want—the pain of sleeping atop "filthy rags"[48]—and most of all fear: fear of the whip, fear of the master's demand not being met, fear of strange neighbors and adults, generally, for their capriciousness, and, most especially, fear of slave catchers and patrollers.

These frightful features of life on the Burroughs place were only made worse by the advent of the Civil War in the spring of his sixth year when local patrollers were replaced by Confederate Army regulars. Washington also had a special fear of being snatched up and taken during the war years, when deserters haunted the forests of the neighborhood; they were alleged to cut off children's ears. And he had to deal with the fear engendered by hope: the threat that his mother's hope for freedom would never be realized. All this is to say that if he personally was not bitter about slavery, that resolve came about not in slavery itself but because of some subsequent adjustment, psychological or merely professed for other purposes, that caused him to make peace with an institution that cost him dearly, and sorely tested African Americans.

Later in life, when the occasion and the audience warranted it, Washington "strummed the same heart strings"[49] as the New South's nostalgists of the Old South. He gave no stint to the writers of the literary Southern or Dixie school who, beginning in the 1870s, made it big with the reading public by lavishing more praise upon the plantation legend than even some proslavery polemicists would have thought seemly.[50] Washington's theme, like theirs, was the contentment, generosity, and devotion shared between slaves and their masters, masters and their slaves. There was much in slavery, he said "besides its hardships and its cruelties, much that was tender, human, and beautiful."[51] He would rhapsodize at length on slavery days' yuletide celebrations and hard mutual labor to bring in the crops; and of the sure bonds of faith and love manifest (as Washington would say in Atlanta) in slaves "nursing your children, watching by the sick-bed of your mothers and fathers, and often following them with tear-dimmed eyes to their graves."[52] He would speak also of former slaves, made free by the war, but so loyal to those who were once their masters as to assist them in their infirmity and old age. As a symbolic reenactment of this sentiment at the end of a 1908 visit to the old Burroughs farm, Washington "plucked a rose from a bush in front of the house and laid it upon the grave of his old master."[53] The races, it would seem, had found a special kind of harmonious peace within the peculiar institution.

※※※

ONCE THE point had been established at the turn of the century that the ultimate measure of African American well-being and progress is the state of race relations, certain, but not necessarily all, other theoretical matters fall into line, becoming batteries passed which black people are not supposed to go. This is surely not strictly Washington's fault, but just as surely it is mainly his responsibility. And so, after engaging in a ritualistic memorial to those good race relations in slavery when he laid that rose on the grave of his former master, he then has to face up to the living, breathing Americans who inevitably wonder: if good race relations defines a good society and if there were good race relations in slavery then must not slavery be a good society? This was not always simply a moot point. Slavery's antebellum advocates would answer in the unqualified affirmative (any quibbles about the answer from segments of this quarter would involve the old worries about the black presence in America). But there are no slavery revivalists at the turn of the century. Instead, there are those looking for a more progressive means to impose slavery's effective controls over misbehaving or defective black people whose sin or ailment was manifest in their failure to be sufficiently malleable in response to the needs and desires of landholders and bankers, politicians and panderers, and everyday monopolists of public spaces. Added to that group are those other great scrutinizers of the racial character, the educators and reformers looking for an amelioration of the Negro's condition by means of concerted eyeballing. From among this mass there will be those who insist, with Washington, that there has been a decline both in Negro morality and race relations since the war, but, unlike Washington, predict that because the Negro as a race is "unprogressive" African Americans were headed toward extinction.[54] While slavery is itself a dead letter, Washington's answer to the challenge from this quarter would be a more qualified and complicated one about the specific character and consequences of the relationship between masters and slaves during slavery days because it involved a point that was not quite as dead as old man Burroughs.

There was, in fact, a more complicated story lying beneath Washington's treacle, a different portrait of slavery available to attentive Yankees and even Southerners (if they were of the stripe of a Thomas Dixon, the novelist behind the film *Birth of a Nation*, who never bought what he perceived as Washington's act and professions of friendship for the Southern white man).[55] On occasion Washington did not resort to subtext. As an indication of the way he shaped his message for differing audiences, there is his differing treatment of antebellum Christmas celebrations. In *Up From Slav-*

ery, the story is told as an example of the slaves' failings: "In their poverty and ignorance it was pathetic to see their attempts to get joy out of the season that in most parts of the country is so sacred and so dear to the heart." "The sacredness of the season seemed to have been almost wholly lost sight of." Upon another occasion six years later and, this time, addressing himself to Tuskegee students, Washington merely tells of his fond memories: "it seems to me that there was a certain charm about that Virginia Christmas, a peculiar fragrance in the atmosphere, a something which I cannot define, and which does not exist elsewhere in the same degree."[56]

An even more telling example of this text buried beneath the text is a story Washington related of a fallen-on-hard-times son of "old Mars' Tom" receiving graciously granted alms from the former slaves of the place:

> I know of a case on a large plantation in the South in which a young white man, the son of the former owner of the estate, has become so reduced in purse and self-control by reason of drink that he is a pitiable creature; and yet, notwithstanding the poverty of the coloured people themselves on this plantation, they have for years supplied this young white man with the necessities of life. One sends him a little coffee or sugar, another a little meat, and so on. Nothing that the coloured people possess is too good for the son of 'old Mars' Tom,' who will perhaps never be permitted to suffer while any remain on the place who knew directly or indirectly of 'old Mars' Tom.'

Left unsaid is how the debauched son got himself into such a fix in the first place. But what Washington does make clear is that scions like this one were not an atypical issue of a slaveholding class marked by decadence, lassitude, and what he would later call "non-progressiveness."[57]

There was, Washington believed, an underside to the seemingly perfect intimacy between master and slave: an intense connection and reliance on one another that spilt over into a morbid dependence, robbing both slave and slaveholder of what Washington would call their "manhood": those qualities in people—a taste for hard work, zealous initiative and activity, and inner direction—that make for greatness in individuals and nations. Slavery caused its people to look upon such qualities as bad, caused them, black and white together, to see "a curse in work."[58] Years later Washington would relate a story about what a bitter harvest this produced for one former slaveholder once without the slaves who were "the bulwark of the household." It was in the Reconstruction era, Washington reported, that the man began to realize "with a feeling almost indescribable, to what an extent he and his family had grown to be dependent on the activity and faithfulness of their slaves; then he began to appreciate to what an extent slavery had sapped the sinews of strength and independence, how the dependence upon slave labor had deprived him and his offspring of the benefit of technical and industrial training, and worst of all had unconsciously led them to see in labor drudgery and degradation instead of beauty."

It then begins to become clear how the South's reputation for borning the type of gone-to-seed sot Washington earlier referred to was earned. First, "there was halt in this man's life." Then, set aflame by "his weak and child-like condition," there was a turn toward bitter recrimination as "cursed the North and he cursed the Negro," as if they were at fault for his plight. Then, as if realizing the folly of such cavalier rejection of his own guilt, there was the self-imposed fall into "despair, almost utter hopelessness," there was the taking up of glass and bottle, and then the abyss:

> The temptation was to forget all in drink and to this temptation there was a gradual yielding. With the loss of physical vigor came the loss of mental grasp and pride in surroundings. There was the falling of a piece of plaster from the walls of the house which was not replaced, then another and still another. Gradually the window panes began to disappear, then the door knobs. Touches of paint and whitewash which once helped to give life were no more to be seen. The hinges disappeared from the gate, then a board from the fence, then others in quick succession. Weeds and unmown grass covered the once well kept lawn. Sometimes there were servants for domestic duties and sometimes there were none. In the absence of servants the unsatisfactory condition of the food told that it was being prepared by hands unschooled to such duties. As the years passed by, debts were accumulating in every direction. The education of the children was neglected. Lower and lower sank the industrial, financial and spiritual condition of the household.

To invoke an old saying favored by farmers and certain black nationalists, the chickens had indeed come home to roost on this sap. It was only a short while before "the whole mistake of slavery seemed to have concentrated itself upon this household." And from behind bloodshot eyes there dawned the realization of "the awful truth of scripture, 'Whatsoever a man soweth that shall he also reap.'"[59]

The extremity of this one man may not and need not be true of the whole of the class of slaveholders. Washington had other purposes in mind than simply portraying slavery's moral evil or creating a sociological account of the fortunes of the dispossessed master class. The sensitive reader, North and South, might be moved by the magnanimity of such a black man who could say that slavery had "wrought almost as much permanent injury upon the Southern white man as upon the Negro." To those types, Washington offers the balm of good race relations and greater education. To Northerners, to whom he spoke above the heads of his white, fellow Southerners, he offers the satisfactory image of the bedraggled Southern plantation, supplanting the colonnaded manse of fiction, to compare with the well-kept Yankee farm.[60]

The more acute reader finds something more.[61] Hidden beneath the fuzzy sentimentality for white Southern consumption, but available to those more interested in "cold, hard facts" than warm, soft pabulum, he derives lessons as to the source of just what was wrong with slavery as an institution—just what it cost all those involved in it: black people, slavers, slaveholders, and even non-slaveholding whites who wanted to own slaves, wanted to be slaveholders (or, equally bad, set themselves against slavery and its markets for subsistence farming that was by definition non-progressive). And for those readers aware of the convention of the Negro problem (friends and Negrophiles, alike) to picture African Americans as being solely defective, there is to be seen underlying Washington's sympathetic portrait an indictment, *sub rosa*, not just of slavery and its ways and means, but of the incapacity of the nominally better class of the white South, caused by slavery's sapping their strength and reflected in the degradation of "the proudest and bluest blood in your civilization."[62] And so how could they be expected to lead in the future after the Reconstruction has been bungled, the Redemption was not so great, and now mobs of white men are hanging Negroes from trees?

All these potential readings of Washington's view of slavery do more than reflect history. The contents of Washington's history are features of an advertisement for himself broadcast for the attention and donations of the nation. If he can be generous to white people, including former slaveholders, that stands him in good stead in his competition with rival Negro educators and other alms-seekers in the homes, offices, and churches of the North and South. For the do-gooders and "drys," there is the scourge of drink, and that, too, helps. The practical man appreciates his sober, but harsh indictment of sloth and lassitude, as likely, and with equal certainty, do the busy-working inheritors of family fortunes. And while all this may not make Northern white people at the turn of the century say Washington is the best man of the South and thus its natural leader, their inclining in that direction redounds to his benefit, too, because it means he will receive a decent hearing from them, and a hearing is a prerequisite to checkbooks being pulled out and purses opened.

There is theory here, too: a theory about the effects of slavery and a theory about the nature of racism as not simply being a legacy of the past, but as well a reaction to the past that finds its source in frustration and bitterness, blinding those caught up in it to the future, placing them in opposition to progress. And there is the theory that good race relations is not always such a good thing—not an end in itself.

But if Washington seems here to have rejected the race relations formula he himself did so much to promote, there is another side to the story. It is not a simple matter of black victimization. The Negro got something out of slavery that was progressive, lifting him up out of his heathen past and gifting him with Anglo-Saxon civilization. But slavery was also a system of exploitation: it involved using others for pecuniary gain. Who was responsible for the establishment of such a system? "Three parties were responsible for the slavery of the Negro in the United States," Washington wrote. He indicts the usual suspects: the Southern white man (although he insisted it was wrong "to assume that the Southerner was ever solidly in favor of slavery"), and Northerners and Englishmen. But, startlingly, "First of all, there was the Negro himself,"—not warring peoples in Africa, but "the Negro"—"who carried on the slave raids by which his fellow-African was captured and brought down to the coast for sale."[63] Here, back again and revived, is the moral universe of race relations, where all fault is divided, where errors exist on "both" sides, and moral parity reigns. Where it is possible to manufacture a race where no race existed, cause them to engage in self-destructive acts when by its very nature the participation in the slave trade by differing African groups involved the "other" not the "us," and, by inference, the people who got the short end from all those others are just as accountable for their lot as anyone.

It is as if no one's hands are clean from America's original sin; no one comes out of slavery innocent and untouched. Or, perhaps, one does come clean: the little child who will become the man to lead them all.

%%%

IN DESCRIBING his youth, Washington attributes to himself precocious powers of seriousness and observation that would be completely implausible if they were not in one way or another attested to by others who knew him in this period. Thus he writes that "there was no period of my life that was devoted to play," and the positive meaning of the line is carried by its completion—"though I think I would now be a more useful man if I had had time for sports"[64]—suggesting this was not so much an aspect of his oppression, but an inborn feature of his character. Is it a lacking, imposed or otherwise, or more like the brag of the Wall Street raider who purports to get by on four hours sleep a day, the type-A personality who boasts of her single-mindedness? Booker was different even as a child, "a unique character" separate from his peers, and watchful of them. One is most impressed by his stillness and quietude, self-reported and confirmed by others, amid the hurly-burly activity of the Burroughs place of his antebellum years and in other places just after the war. Soon after the turn of the century, a visitor to Malden, West Virginia (where, in addition to Booker's family, large numbers of former Franklin County slaves had settled after the war) found evidence of this alienation or exceptionality in discussions with a number of older persons who knew him as a slave. The visitor, Byrd Prillerman, reported, "I one day met an old woman who lived at the place of his birth where he was born. How delighted she was to tell of his early life. She said that 'Booker' was not like other children of the slave plantation; that he would not play with the other children, but would stand around and watch their play." This quality of young Booker's, "His frequent standing in one place and looking 'North,'" was, as Prillerman understood it, "a curious omen to many of the old slaves." Dixon was also moved to make mention of this strange habit, retelling it, however, within his own métier: "a little ragged, barefooted pickaninny who lifted his eyes from a cabin in the hills of Virginia, saw a vision and followed it."[65]

What type of omen? What type of vision? What was he looking at? What did he see? It may be that these accounts of young Booker as a golden child of the Burroughs farm (at least to some black people) are products of the imaginations of people impressed by what he became rather than recountings of who he actually was when a slave. But if what they and he say is true then, first, he was not like most other slaves, escaping the malign effects of slavery on the rest of the cast. And, second, his account of those effects and his escape is like an actor speaking in asides to an audience, describing and directing attention toward particular features of the action on stage. He is, in the telling, the main actor, the star of his life, and observer and somehow, as well, critic of the production taking place around him: taking the measure of the other players; and, in regard especially to the slave community, diagnosing the problem of black people and preparing, if prematurely, to take their lead. An omen, then, indeed it was: a second sight of his rising to the leadership of his people.

Washington's view of what slavery cost African Americans, told in the form of anecdotes from his personal experience, and through miscellaneous statements, speeches and stray aphorisms, is not particularly consistent on some points. For instance, on the matter of black people's attitude toward work, he might in one venue claim a sound, proud African heritage of honesty and industry: "The Negro in his original native state was an honest race; it was slavery that unmanned him in this respect."[66] In another venue, he might praise the way slavery inculcated the Negro with decent work habits as well as craft and artisanal skills (which, he would insist, also without consistency, petered away during Reconstruction). And in still another venue, he might make a statement of quite a different character altogether, piled high with causational hyperbole: not just Africa, not just slavery, the Negro problem is a problem of "dealing with a race that has little love for labor in their native land and consequently brought little love for labor with them to America. Added to this was the fact that they had been forced for two hundred and fifty years to labor without compensation under circumstances that were calculated to do anything but teach them the dignity, beauty, and civilizing power of intelligent labor."[67]

However, it is possible to locate certain themes in his account of slavery, especially in regard to the moral degradation of the African American manifest in the slave's lack of inner direction and their attachment to their master's lives and needs. "In slavery days," he wrote, "the traditions of the people who lived in the cabins centered almost entirely about the lives and fortunes of the people who lived in the 'Big House.' The favorite stories around the cabin fireside related to what this or that one had seen on some distant journey with 'old master,' or perhaps to the adventures they had when master and they were boys together."[68] The Burroughs family's smallish Big House was "the centre of the only world" the Burroughs slaves knew, and it was in and around the place that young Booker and the other slaves heard conversations from which they learned about "the great white race in America" and how it had traveled across the seas to America. Denied them was realization of the "desire to know something about their [African] ancestors." This was a desire Washington perceived to be true of all young people, boys as well as girls: "no matter how obscure their origin," he wrote, "each will feel a special interest in the people whose fortunes he or she has shared, and a special sympathy with all that people have lived, suffered and achieved." Such desire was a needful thing, the fulfillment of which was necessary for true pride of place and identify. Instead of such nourishment, slaves like Washington's peers received paltry helpings of denigration, opprobrium served up in the form of invidious comparisons and assiduously insulting asides off the cuff of their superiors. He recalled "many and sinister references" to "the long and terrible journey by which my ancestors came from their native home in Africa to take up their life again beside the white man and Indian in the New World."[69]

Many, and perhaps, Washington felt, most—"the masses" of Negroes— suffered from this lacking. "There were always some among them, like Frederick Douglass, who were different and distinct from the masses. They became the fugitive slaves."[70] However, the ruling, psychologically unhealthy, situation Washington perceived about the slave quarter on the Burroughs place, their identification with "their" white folks (reflected in the "airs" put on by Virginia slaves as against their deep South counter- parts), meant, Washington insisted, "the life of the Negro was so intimately interwoven with that of the white man that it is almost true to say that he had no separate history."[71] It created within them a stultifying dependence on their masters that had consequences for black people just as malign as slavery-bred dependency had for the pitiful, helpless former slaveholder.[72]

Pursuing this thesis, Washington argued that the Negro was cursed by a sentimental, otherworldly religious feeling "which banks everything in the future and nothing in the present."[73] The slave's Christianity was the oppo- site of an effective system of moral stricture, and consequently of no help— either in slavery or afterward—in the building up of honesty, reliability and other virtues. Instead, the slave community was infected with immorality and fecklessness, a view that he would later convey to his audiences with one of his store of homilies: "During slavery the people reasoned some- thing like this, 'My body belongs to my master, and taking master's chicken to feed master's body is not stealing.' One old colored man whom his master caught stealing his chickens said to the master, 'Well, now, massa, you's got a few less chickens, but you's got a good deal more nigger.'" The difference between white people and black people, Washington would later assert, "is a difference produced by the unequal opportunities. To argue otherwise is to discredit the effects of slavery."[74]

Washington was different in that bondage did not seem to have this degrading influence on him. In contrast to his fellows, the slaves, the desire to know from whence the Negro came, and the consciousness of their intel- lectual and spiritual deficits stayed with him, shaped his consciousness: "All this helped to increase . . . my desire to know what was back of me, where I came from, and what, if anything, there was in the life of my people in African and American to which I might point with pride and think about with satisfaction."[75]

How did he do it? How did he escape the trap set by slavery and the slavers? In Washington's telling, it might seem a miracle. He had a family of sorts, a lucky circumstance as far as the life of a slave child was concerned, but perforce insufficient to change the basic reality that the beginning, middle, and end of family was a wholly owned subsidiary of the Burroughs enterprise. Examination of the parameters of Booker's familial relations serves to probe the point.

Washington's mother, Jane (later Mrs. Washington Ferguson), was to her son a good woman who was a victim, and as she was a slave that is hardly surprising. Her family background, which Washington later tried to investigate, was a dead letter, lost. "No doubt, my ancestors on my mother's side, suffered in the middle passage of the slave ship while being conveyed from Africa to America," but beyond that lay a mystery. He was able to determine little more about his mother's own story: "Her addition to the slave family attracted about as much attention as the purchase of a new horse or cow," he wrote.[76]

Mother Jane, however, was more than those things, and when the war came he remembered her "fervently praying that Lincoln and his armies might be successful, and one day she and her children might be free."[77] This was perhaps Washington's first lesson that slavery was not necessarily to be his final fate, that some other destiny might possibly lay before him. In that way, his mother was one source of his ambition. She gave him his first book, and when he had begun to make something of himself at Hampton Institute, her kindness and example drove him to achieve "a position in which I could make my mother comfortable and happy."[78]

She was "my sainted mother," and, in the recalling, he could warm all but the coldest hearts with tales of her virtue and self-abnegation.[79] All that having been said, however, his mother was a slave, and slaves were property, legally bought and sold, swapped or squandered as a gambler's stake, and eternally subject (even if not perfectly so) to their owner's will. The truth of that statement, though, hardly conveys the reality of what it meant to a young child coming to the realization that one's parent's first duty was to another. This meant that by the very nature of her condition she was a negligent mother. The training and nurturing of her children was a task peripheral to her main responsibilities, a matter of Jane "snatching a few moments for our care in the early morning before her work began, and at night after the day's work was done." She loved her children, but even that was mediated by loose morality induced by her servitude: for example, when she awoke her children in the dead of night for the purpose of feeding them a chicken she had most likely purloined from the Burroughs coop or larder: "Some people may call this theft. If such a thing were to happen now, I should condemn it as theft myself. But taking place at the time it did, and for the reason it did, no one could ever make me believe that my mother was guilty of thieving." Instead, he concluded later, she was "simply a victim of the system of slavery."[80]

One might excuse Washington's mother's pilfering as simply taking back a part of what was being stolen from her on a daily basis, simultaneously providing a late supper for her children and just desserts for those living off the backs of exploited slave labor. One might explain his remembrance of her "crime" as being refracted through the lens of a Victorian sensibility; even the entertainment of the question of her guilt demonstrated a failure to consider fairly an oppressed class's perspective on matters of right and wrong. Such reactions, however, miss the point Washington is driving at, which is that slavery brought his mother low, and, in so doing, made her a failure as a mother. In turn, this means that from the perspective of, especially, his moral development—not all the children of slavery, but the man he became—he was, in his telling, made an orphan by slavery.

Indeed, the notion of young Booker as being orphaned by slavery is hardly an overstatement, but fits with his account of the general state of affairs as he apprehended them and later recalled: "I cannot remember a single instance during my childhood or early boyhood when our entire family sat down to the table together, and God's blessing was asked, and the family ate a meal in a civilized manner." In the slave quarters at the Burroughs place "meals were gotten by the children very much as dumb animals get theirs": "It was a piece of bread here and a scrap of meat there. It was a cup of milk at one time and some potatoes at another. Sometimes a portion of our family would eat out of the skillet or pot, while some one else would eat from a tin plate held on the knees, and often using nothing but the hands with which to hold the food."[81]

If the woman who gave birth to him could not by reason of her condition properly raise him, the man who was his father simply never entered the picture: "whoever he was, I never heard of his taking the least interest in me or providing in any way for my rearing . . . He was simply another unfortunate victim [of slavery]."[82] Despite the real moral difference—rather papered over by Washington's making each a 'victim'—between what his mother might have hoped to do for him and his father's willed neglect, the sum of her circumscribed actions hardly amounts to more than his total inaction from the perspective of young Booker's development. Neither Washington's mother nor his father (whoever he was) could or would rescue him from the jealous desire that came upon him when he witnessed white children enjoying treats that he would never have. Nor was any person available to make amends for the crushing experience of accompanying one of his young mistresses to the schoolhouse door, carrying her books, but not being able to cross that mysterious but golden threshold. No one intervened to rescue him or engineer his salvation, and in this and other ways, great and small, Washington's slave experience was very much like that of millions of other hereditary bondsmen at the South. They all, Washington would write, wanted freedom, but in the fix they were in before 1861 that was no more than a vain hope, a wisp of an aspiration held in abeyance by slavery. Each was victimized and all were trapped, "entangled," he would write in a particularly Jeffersonian formulation, "in the net of slavery," with no way out.[83] But, somehow, the boy Booker did make it out.[84]

%%%

WHAT WASHINGTON offers in his remembrance of his youth is nothing less than a portrait of an elaborated wreckage of what today would be called "black culture" left by slavery, a disaster his experience embodied but overcame. His answer to the question of what two and a half centuries of bondage cost African Americans (but seemingly not him), then, is nearly everything of importance to a nation of people: all but the most minor, window-dressing remnants of the African past; all but an impotent pantomime of familial ties and bonds. Lost, too, he believes, was the opportunity for black people to take part in the founding and building up of the American republic, and so to be able to claim the patriotic inheritance that was a prerequisite of effective and productive citizenship. Or, alternately, the resolve of a strong and independent people endowed with the collective will to strike for real freedom, to make of what they did possess—a collective experience of oppression, and with it something of fellow feeling and esprit de corps—their own nation.

Are his standards too high? Or, are the standards here imputed to him ones that he did not in reality hold?

Some might see in Washington's treatment of the slaves a too-harsh judgment of black people swamped by slavery. First in this connection is the seeming conundrum of how to explain the good results of his life given that he lived through the same circumstances as other black people. How to explain his succeeding swimmingly while they drowned or merely trod water? Answers to this question came more easily in the environment of a segregated America where vast numbers of African Americans could appreciate and even be buoyed up by the accomplishments of this "first" or that "pioneer." It was an age when "contributionism"—in contemporary affairs and historical studies—ruled the day, although not to the exclusion of sterner types of publicity from bigots and race experts. Only latterly has the nature of black achievement and its trumpeting come to be posed in the form of a conundrum, tied up as it now seems to be with controversies over social policies, with underinflated role models made to strain inadequately to lift up the earthbound, and with exceptional men and women being forced into the category of narrow rules that all can achieve if they set their minds to it. Opposition to these free-floating panaceas, abetted by those egalitarians who unthinkingly believe equality as a political goal demands perfect equality in individual ability, makes a problem out of what really needs no explanation.

Washington was set apart from the rest, a distinction remarked upon by those who knew him. His lifetime accomplishments were out of the realm of the possible for the average person of that time. If there is a conundrum there, arising from his achievement as compared to other black people, like him, living in a racist society, at least a part of the knot can be loosened by recognition of the simple fact of the abilities of fortitude and intelligence he possessed in greater measure than they (exceptional qualities he of course shared with those like Ida B. Wells-Barnett and other prominent African Americans of the time). He was different from the run of slavery's mill. This difference was reflected by a singleness of purpose, an ability to concentrate, that made him, as he saw it, a kind of a rock in the center of the storm while those all around him were flitting and flying about, caught up in the wind of blithe irresponsibility.

If Washington's treatment of slavery runs afoul of one early-twentieth-first-century convention that holds that all African Americans are equally endowed by nature, he also violates the convention that one must not admit any debilities on the part of the Negro even if they are induced by oppression. This proscription proceeds from the understandable fear that if black failings are admitted such an admission will provide ammunition to black people's enemies: that given the uncertain moral and intellectual compass with which Americans locate the right side on matters racial, if one finds evidence of the wrong of slavery (or segregation or racism or late capitalism) in the persons of African Americans, this will divert umbrage or criticism from the offending institution itself; that it opens the door for a kind of halfway admission that black people deserved the treatment they received; that it is another species of "blaming the victim."

Others would claim as well that the standards Washington uses to judge the slaves are the wrong ones: that he is guilty of judging the black masses in slavery by the standard of a class-biased, Victorian or other equally anachronistic perspective. Certainly there is more than a passing resemblance between Washington's portrait of the slave as abject, other-directed and feckless with the contemporaneous view of Southern nostalgists and latter-day advocates of the positive-good argument for slavery, who, viewing the Negro from a perspective both relativistic and racist, emphasized slavery's (unfinished) project of civilizing the primitive and heathen African.[85]

That having been said, Washington, unlike some of his contemporaries, makes no quibble about "the cruelty and moral wrong of slavery," writing in his autobiography, "I condemn it as an institution as we well know in America it was established for selfish and financial reasons."[86] Rather than the superficial similarity between Washington and the pro-slavery writers, a more intimate connection lies between Washington's version of slavery and that portrayed by both later liberal proponents of the "damage" school of slavery historians like Stanley Elkins, and with the general view of the black past championed by certain advocates of black nationalism.[87] Both these schools of thought, like Washington, emphasize black people's "white-orientation," their cultural amnesia, and political impotence. And, for all their differences (the first claiming objectivity, the second making explicitly political readings of the past) these are not strange bedfellows: both groups despise slavery, both emphasize the middle passage as a fall— whether from psychological adjustment or simply from grace—and both make casual causal linkages between the supposed legacy of slavery and contemporary black "pathology." And both groups' readings of the black past make inexplicable the mustering of black energies that created the civil rights movement and ultimately broke the back of segregation.

Washington's historical and autobiographical writings on slavery and its consequences contain within them fodder for either of these intellectual tendencies. It is possible to see at the root of those writings a crucial perspective on the harm of slavery, a perspective, indeed, that lay the basis for his possible future assumption of leadership. What type of leadership he would provide would have to be worked out, but, nonetheless, a leadership based on his first-hand insight into the lives of slaves and the consequences of the stultifying dependence and other bad effects of slavery he as a leader would wish to make right.

As presumptive leader of black people—as Moses and George Washington in one—Washington has necessarily to be concerned about the black masses and their attitude toward work, family, crime, and general morality. And if he believes slavery-induced sloth and thieving are of little help in African America's plight, the argument rests not with what he says about slavery—what he saw in slavery and believed about its effects—but about slavery's post-emancipation legacy and the postbellum Negro problem, matters about which he is engaged. If what he is talking about is not hold-

ing slaves but free black people to a high standard, the people he is proposing to organize, that casts in a rather different light some of his more
roseate statements on slavery that seem only to be appeals to turn-of-the-
century nostalgists. For example, Washington, seeking to dispel the notion
"that there was bitter feeling toward the white people on the part of my
race" on account of their prosecution of the Civil War, insisted that "In the
case of the slaves on our place this was not true, and it was not true for any
large portion of the slave population in the South where the Negro was
treated with anything like decency."[88] Secure in the knowledge of the type
of leader Washington became, one might quite properly view this statement as an appeal to sentiment and sympathy, as Washington seeking to
drum up charity for the abject Negro.

On the other hand, it might pay to question whether Washington's views
on slavery fit so perfectly into what Washingtonianism turned out to be.
Marcus Garvey, ensconced in Jamaica on the eve of departing for the land
of his greatest opportunity, and with, it must be admitted, a less than perfect
understanding of the United States, the plight of the America Negro, and
the contours of the domestic Negro problem, saw in Washington's interpretation a springboard for a very different and black nationalist politics, a
foundation for work on black people's real needs, preparatory to the formation not of a liberal-pity party to bring alms to the Negro, but a nationalist
war party to deliver the Negro out from under the cyclical movement of, on
the one hand, scorn and neglect, and, on the other, an insincere American
pietism that offers alms but denies responsibility for the Negro's plight.

In setting off for his pilgrimage to Tuskegee in 1915, Garvey may have
missed the boat on just what type of leader Washington had become by
the 1910s, but his reading of the content of Washington's writing on what
the Negro needs as laying the groundwork for a strong black nationalism
is not inapt. It explains why many intelligent nationalists initially lauded
the Atlanta speech in 1895 because of Washington's attention to the way
in which African America in freedom remained divided against itself:
in America but robbed of the benefits of American citizenship; a nation
within a nation, but without the self-consciousness to act upon that special status to determine a different course from that laid out for it by white
supremacy's purposes for the Negro. The absence of bitterness among the
slaves and former slaves, read in this light, is not a positive attribute, but
one of the Negro's failings; the absence of self-conscious resolve, a sign of
what they needed. *Up From Slavery* is liable to just such a nationalist reading, one, for instance, that would highlight the inherent absurdity (though
not necessarily the complete truthfulness) of Washington's observation that

"to defend and protect the women and children who were left on the plantations when the white men went to war, the slaves would have laid down their lives."[89] Indeed, can there be any greater indictment of the lack of political consciousness of "a slow-to-anger people"?[90] Garvey, the black nationalists, and other interested parties like Du Bois saw something of this in Washington and were gladdened. But their initial view was based on a quick, superficial, and, as it turned out erroneous, reading of his words and intentions; they heard him and, based on the situation faced by black people, believed, for a time, in what Washington might have been rather than what he in fact became.[91]

Washington was but a slave, and so any insights gleaned during his travail in slavery are notable merely for their latent potential to be acted upon, a matter that demands a suspension of judgment and a holding in abeyance of the political and philosophical meaning of his analysis. And yet Washington's most obvious break with the damage school, and a further connection with the nationalists (and others) rests in his observations on the slaveholders, and his assertion that dysfunction was not merely an element of bastardry, biology (Washington's and his parents') or the Negro condition, but covered the Burroughs place like the dust of a stinking mold.

Here the political function of his declaration of not being bitter becomes realized. If on one hand Washington violates one kind of twentieth-century code by proclaiming the infirmities of black people, he engages in a seemingly more serious—even deadly dangerous—violation in criticizing white people, and doing so without being seen as overturning his public's acceptance of his self-proclaimed status as not bitter.

Washington did not invent the judgment by which black leaders are evaluated as either bitter or not bitter; rather, the criterion predated him, but his influence on it was telling nonetheless. As prim a figure as Harriet Beecher Stowe, the author of *Uncle Tom's Cabin*, recognized the difference between productive political opposition and destructive personal bitterness. Upon meeting Frederick Douglass, she was pleased to find "no deep stratum of bitterness" in his demeanor or his abolitionism. Stowe's judgment on the difference between the two—not an especially great accomplishment given her schooling amid the antislavery fight—is a distinction largely lost in the late twentieth century's evaluation of African American figures such that "bitterness" becomes the ultimate criterion for categorization. This has much to do with Washington's influence, because Mrs. Stowe's distinction is a distinction Washington seeks to obliterate.[92] For example, in asserting that "the members of my race entertain no feelings of bitterness against the whites," that in contrast there are myriad examples of former slaves "tenderly caring" for their former owners, he deliberately confuses the personal and the political. Feelings for a broadly construed "family" in slavery—"a strange and peculiar attachment to 'old Marster' and 'old Missus,' and their children"[93] did not translate to white people in general, as Washington surely knew—else why would he have to offer up his politics of reconciliation? For Washingtonianism, "bitterness" is a catch-all for, among other things, all types of political activity that directly address the conflict between black people's interests and white people's interests; thus, he ascribes bitterness to Douglass and the abolitionists in their fight against slavery, bitterness to the Reconstruction era politics, and calls "hard and bitter" the statements by racists intended to put black people in their place.[94]

In contrast to these bitter fruits, Washington will eventually offer good race relations, such that are made possible only to the extent that black people and white put aside hard feelings and hate. In discussing slavery in the context of this purpose, Washington's aim is not so much truth as reassurance to both those who believe in the fable of contentment down on slavery's farms and plantation and those who do not. His Yankee supporters insist on a validation of the sacrifice they and their ancestors made, but slavery cannot be made to be so bad—so evil, so productive of bitterness—as to leave a legacy, the bloody shirt, the scarred back, as evidence, upsetting sectional and racial reconciliation. To accomplish this task Washington seeks to write an alternative history of slavery in line with the politics of the turn of the century: "notwithstanding the cruel wrongs inflicted upon us, the black man got nearly as much out of slavery as the white man did." Washington can claim this because he does not discuss what in fact slaveholders and white America got out of slavery, certainly not that it formed the basis for a particular type of high civilization, now rendered a moot point by the war. The questions he has inevitably to leave unanswered are: How did slavery exist? And for what purpose? Instead he offers up the good news:

> Then, when we rid ourselves of prejudice, or racial feeling, and look facts in the face, we must acknowledge that, notwithstanding the cruelty and moral wrong of slavery, the ten million Negroes inhabiting this country, who themselves or whose ancestors went through the school of American slavery, are in a stronger and more hopeful condition, materially, intellectually, morally, and religiously, than is true of an equal number of black people in any other portion of the globe.[95]

Here is the coming to fruition of the race relations idea in historical interpretation of slavery. It is the meaning beyond the moral parity sleight-of-hand—

in service to Washington's contemporary project—that retrospectively divides up responsibility for slavery between the white race—in Northern, Southern, and international groupings—and the Negro race. Manufacturing a "black" racial responsibility back in Africa (where, of course, neither race nor a black race existed before the age of discovery by Europeans, themselves not previously equipped by race either), and making white people who have no business to do with slavery a part of white racial responsibility for slavery is more racial ideology; more "race" with which Washington gives a clean, smooth, black finish to the pile of bodies of thousands upon thousands, millions upon millions, who might have been something more—in Africa, in America—were they not caused to be slaves (for, of course, it is not just the deaths caused by the slave trade but also the stunting of the potential of those who lived in slavery that mark it a crime). Washington varnishes the heap with race, and his brush is relativism. He gifts the nation with an essentially moralistic accounting—black Africans versus Negro Americans—that obscures the only relevant comparisons for judging the costs and benefits of the peculiar institution, which is between those who were slaves in America and what they were left with, those who used slaves and the slave trade in America and what they have, and those other Americans who derived the benefits of freedom without the aid of owning someone else's bodies for their own purposes. If slavery were wine-making: someone drank the wine, someone got paid to make the casks and barrels, likewise to ship the wine-filled casks and barrels to other drinkers, and someone did the picking and squishing. Washington's comparison is between those not even in the vineyard, but thousands of miles away, and those laboring to make someone else's wine. In his accounting the opportunity of the latter to drink the dregs is the most salient feature of the enterprise, a tasteful bottom line for those looking for a cheap forgetting of who really got drunk.

Washington's waving a wand of race—Swish! There it is, the black, the white—over the ledger of slavery's assets and deficits is evidence on the point that his race relations theory is most assuredly not about the observing and affecting of relations between black people and white people in various capacities in a specific time and place. If this were simply so he would not be called upon to theorize the meaning of slavery at this high level of abstraction—so high, indeed, that it almost offends the sensibilities. Rather, race relations serves as a means of making himself available to America as a moral beacon, promulgating the meaning for decent people of the indecencies committed upon African Americans. The radical nature of this innovation, with Washington placed on a throne that Douglass, tied to the quarrelsome and tragic past, never could have occupied (even had he wanted to), lies in his faith that white people will allow him this license: to speak with a universalistic voice of authority, rather than a particularistic voice from the Negroes. He derives his standing and moral authority from giving forgiveness to all those "entangled in the net of slavery." It is a slavery without a single victim, but one in which all are victimized, white folks equally with black folks.

Old man Burroughs may have been a hardworking, rough-hewn man and more decent than most owners, but his very success in the enterprise of utilizing—depending upon—slave labor doomed his sons and daughters to their fate. Slavery robbed them of "the spirit of self-reliance and self-help," that might have enabled them to make something of themselves, to get them aboard that engine of progress improving the land and bettering the lives of people outside slavery's grip. None of the Burroughs boys "mastered a single trade or special line of productive industry." Neither were the Burroughs sisters "taught to cook, sew, or to take care of the house." All the white people of the place "unconsciously imbibed the feeling that manual labour was not the proper thing for them" with the result that tasks were not done "in the most improved and thorough manner." Washington recalled further that "fences were out of repair, gates were hanging half off the hinges, doors creaked, window-panes were out, plastering had fallen but was not replaced, weeds grew in the yard." Within doors, the Burroughs family's decor was hardly less slovenly, and their taste in cuisine for their own consumption hardly more elevated than what they provided for their slaves: "As a rule, there was food for whites and blacks, but inside the house, and on the dining-room table, there was wanting that delicacy and refinement of touch and finish which can make a home the most convenient, comfortable, and attractive place in the world."[96]

These were insights Washington derived from his youthful but prescient perspective on the occupants of the Big House, whose ways he was singularly situated to judge from the vantage point off to the side of their dinner table, where he would operate a fly-fanning contraption for the masters' comfort.[97] His portrait of them as not striving enough, as unprogressive and not endeavoring with all their resources to make it big in the antebellum world is scathing, and pitched directly to Northern ears. He places the Burroughs such that they may be judged from the cultural and economic standards of another world far removed from rural, western Virginia, and in that light finds them wanting, a sharp contrast to Northern progressiveness, energy, and industrialism.

If there is a contrast between the Burroughs family's slovenly ways and the neat farms and factories of the North, Washington also asks his readers to compare their evaluation of him with how the Burroughs (and slavery) assessed the boy, Booker. Washington became a houseboy for the Burroughs around 1862, when he was about seven years of age. He was said to be a great favorite of his young mistress, Miss Laura Burroughs,[98] but given the opportunity to claim a part in his success, she denied teaching him to read, and, in so doing, revealed much about her own lack of refinement: "My folks say that I learned him his letters, but I do not recollect much about it." Literate and enlightened, she summed up the limits of their relationship by saying, "But not on your life do we believe in social equality."[99] This was the type of person slavery allowed into the schoolhouse, while barring the door to young Booker.

Why was Washington made a house servant? Is it possible that some one of the Burroughs saw a potential in him as did his slave peers? The evidence on these matters is mixed. It may have redounded to his benefit that he was perceived to be a "mulatto." The importance of that ascription, much more than whether or not the rumors about his parentage are true, may be evidence a member of the household saw him as more intelligent than the other slaves—"white blood" being the singular explanation racists could fix upon to explain a black person with singular intellectual gifts. Contrary evidence, however, exists to suggest rather the opposite conclusion as to why he was taken up out of the quarters to work beside the Burroughs table. One Burroughs informant reports that Booker was somewhat dim; "rather slow," he said, speaking it seems for the family, and that it was his older brother, John Henry, who was the "cleverer" of Jane's sons.[100] And John Henry was an able boy, but of the "jack-of-all-trades-master-of-none" variety that made him useful around the farm, and later of great service to his younger brother in the building up of the Tuskegee Institute. Washington, in those later years, was quite critical of the way in which slavery tended to manufacture these handymen, who he believed were increasingly anachronistic in the industrial world of technical sophistication. John Henry's early roles at Tuskegee were eventually taken over by a number of other men, each possessed of a specialized expertise that was a product of greater training.[101] Washington's perceptions of how the white people looked at both his brother and him may have been a part of what helped him form perspective on slavery's values. What may have taken place was that the more, perhaps, mechanically adept John Henry was seen as more intelligent—"bright as a dollar"[102]—simply because he possessed a wider range of skills useful in the running of the place; Booker, of less use, perforce was a dullard. Adding to that may have been the white people's observations of the very same qualities of stillness and quietude in Booker that caused black people to see the potential for great things in him, but that to myopic slaveholders signaled only a fitness for fanning flies.

Washington eventually discovered just what he meant to the Burroughs, quite literally the final analysis of the worth of "1 negro boy (Bowker)" as assessed by slave society in the 1860 census: $400.[103] He knew he was worth more, that slavery sorely underestimated him. Kept from learning, he at least prized the idea of what might be found within the pages of books: "The idea that books contained something which was forbidden aroused my curiosity and excited in me a desire to find out for myself what it was in these books that made them forbidden fruit to me and my race."[104] Here, Washington follows in the footsteps of slaves like Douglass.[105] He had learned something about the limits and provincialism of the slaveholders—the erstwhile better class of Southern white people—used them up as far as concerned what he could gain from them. But if he did not want to be a slave, then what?

%%%

WASHINGTON'S TREATMENT of his life in slavery operates on several levels to accomplish the seemingly impossible task of simultaneously distinguishing himself from the other slaves and making himself a man of the masses. He does this by portraying slaves in general as hollow shells, bereft of ancestry, desiring a lot different than the one set out for them by slavery, but without the means or will to achieve freedom. He is one with them, but of sterner stuff, empty—without ancestry—and yet filled up with potential for greatness. Thus there is sympathy for him, a mixture of pity and contempt for them. Here and throughout his writings and speeches he elaborates a quintessentially American merit principle: "The crucial test for a race, as for an individual, is its ability to stand upon its own feet."[106] Who accomplished this, they or him? The personal is political insofar as it allows him to be grounded in a time and place, all the more to make greater drama of his rise.

In the heyday of his ascendance, Booker Washington would call on certain devices from his speechmaking arsenal secure in the knowledge that this bit of rhetorical irony or that nugget of homespun lore would elicit a predictably favorable response from his audience, whether in the North or the South. Such confidence was won atop hundreds, even thousands of speaker's platforms before probably more than a half million listeners altogether; the persuasiveness of his oratory, or short of that, the basic ability to connect with those listeners, forged in the fire of his audiences' reaction to his words. Experience and psychological insight make the responses predictable: you tell them the one about the lazy man toiling under the hot sun who all of the sudden falls to the ground and announces " 'O, Lawd, de cotton am so grassy, de work am so hard, and the sun am so hot dat I b'lieve dis darkey am called to preach!' "[107] and a part of the audience will smile, another part will chortle, and not a few of the gathered of a more emancipated temperament will erupt in gales of laughter.[108] Washington comes to know his audience, and wins them through his gift of evoking this common past to which they respond knowingly, as if they arrived at the point, the idea, or the rationalization even sooner then he did; as if they and he were in on the telling of the story together. In gratitude for this, they return Washington's favor with the gift of support and money or, at least, acclaim.

In this collaborative process (rather a lost art in today's age), Washington's telling jokes on the Negro is not the least part of the source of his popular success—aiming low, after all, is still aiming—but a part of his means of ascendance rather neglected by the defenders of his "pragmatism." But do his constant iterations of this darkey story or that fallen-on-hard-times Negro politician allegory not poison the moral well, thus making it more difficult for African Americans to get to the place Washington and his contemporary and latter-day proponents ostensibly all wish them to go? Is the substance of what they sense themselves sharing not made up of his listeners' gentle or not so gentle racism? This was a matter about which he was occasionally criticized even by his supporters as they began to get a glimmer of the corrosive effects of too frequent repetition of his "dis darkey" humor.[109]

Whatever the usefulness of the homely homily in his effort to effect a meeting of minds between himself and his constituents with a taste for tales of black foibles, these were not his sole oratorical props, but were accompanied by certain creedal statements of Washingtonianism: good race relations above all else; "progress"—invoked fully seven times at Atlanta—a faithful watchword for the future; and the absence of "bitterness" on the matter of slavery.

There are reasons to reject Washington's claim that he was not bitter about what he suffered through as a slave, just as it is important to recognize what such a declaration about himself and black people symbolized to his supporters, and to understand just what Americans mean when they ask of the Negro whether he is bitter.

Slavery in retrospect can be many things to an individual, once a slave, now a person: idyll or exile; tragedy or comedy; or, oddly enough, merely a childhood. To develop a portrait of the institution of slavery, historians may take in aggregate all of the remembrances of individuals who, unlike Washington, are in history, but not seeking to make it, with all the faint or false focus and forgetfulness of vast distances—time, place, circumstances—that mark the difference between history and certain memory. Washington has no such luxury as have average freedmen and women, like the Works Progress Administrations interviewees who formed the long-lived rump of his generation down to the 1930s, to tell a good tale or prosaic lies or just what strikes their mood. Even though he promises only to tell "a simple, straightforward story, with no attempt at embellishment,"[110] he, a larger man with greater ambitions, has a task different from simply telling the truth. He is not arguing for or against slavery—an academic exercise—and in that sense he is not a philosopher: he has bigger game to bag than long-dead slaveholders. His endeavor is to construct a usable past for his program. To make himself one with the people, and so to fit humbly among them, and yet not one, but better, an actor not a object, a visionary and no mere survivor, and thus fit to be their leader, the nation's avatar. The notion of he and they not being bitter is crucial to this distinguishing. It is Washington speaking not to exalted Clio but to the here and now of the turn of the century; speaking directly to the hope of good race relations and harmony in settlement, not in a renaissance of the dead letter of slavery days (for who but the reactionary or the fool would want back into that feeble, weak, pathological dystopia), but in the progressive now of the 1890s, a world rid of the nasty, regnant elements of the past and solving its strifes peacefully with less building of battlements and more scientific engineering.

The natural reaction of many in Washington's world to his portrayal of the slaves is: "I'd be bitter" or "I'd never let such a thing happen to me and mine in the first place" or "I'd fight to the death, slay the slavers." And some souls draw an obscuring line between their white nature and the putative nature of Negroes without sense—or courage or manhood—enough to embrace the full and appropriate purchase of hatred for oppression. The drawing of that line is margin enough to open the door to a special solution to the problem of the Negro that is segregation and disfranchisement. And other, better souls draw a different line, finding goodness in the souls of black folk: what a peculiarly humble flock of God's children to forgive the sins against them and not be bitter toward slavers or white people or me? Such a flock needs not conflict in politics but a good shepherd to lead them, and that is Washington and his sermon of good race relations.

Slavery in the past for Washington means not looking back, and because of the Civil War and the fight to define freedom it engendered, not needing to look back in anger—bitterness is not necessary because the nation fought, in the bloodletting, the question of what to do with the Negro and the forces of freedom prosecuted their negative on slavery. He cannot look back with complete honesty because slavery in prospect is death for one such as him. The question of whether he would have been a good slave is a false one because it misses his measure completely. Could he have settled for slavery, earned the Burroughs family's respect, added to their estates as a faithful vassal; his advancement, his knowledge, his acuity, his greatness only the compounded interest on the $400 (U.S. or C.S.A.?) America judged him to be worth in 1860 while slavery still reigned?

The appropriate question from the perspective of Washington's psychology is not whether he was bitter. Rather: believing as he did about slavery's limitations as a civilizing agent, about the way his slaveholders—white people—undervalued and misjudged him and his abilities, about the way America fumbled the freedom and misled black people, about the absurdity of political squabbling—about all the things that demanded he take the reins of black America and lead them, the question becomes: how did he channel the muddle of anger, insight, and will to power to make his value to the nation and its purposes for the Negro be of inestimably greater value?

Did it have to turn out this way? The problem is only partly his holding himself up as a paragon as against the rule of black people. There is some warrant for that because he is different, better, stronger and so on. But looking out over the next years of his life, circumstances set before him offered up the chance of taking the lead. The road he ultimately travels takes him to a destination where he is *the* Negro leader and is proclaimed thus in significant measure because he is also entertaining white people at the expense of black people. Did he have to? What would have made him take on this role as part sociologist and part scold, part missionary and part minstrel?

There was latent in Washington at least some potential possibility to go the way he did, but equally qualities within him that would have made him a quite different type of leader. These potentials bespeak a dilemma posed to an energetic and capable person rising up from black America and on the lip of a career. As for the slave boy he was, what he makes of the meaning of these incompletely formed insights, even the chance to develop them and choose a course, was predicated on a revolutionary change making any move possible.

There remains that image, accounted by his fellow slaves of young Booker gazing fixedly out over the fields, looking north. For whom or for what was he looking? Was he looking for his father to come to claim him? Was he looking toward freedom, or, seeking out and anticipating the time to come when it would be the right moment to escape? With the advent of the war's nearing Hale's Ford, might he have been looking with an expectancy of approaching cannonade, fearing or welcoming the let-loose dogs of war? Perhaps he was looking away from Dixie toward where he might imagine the only place in America where a future for one such as him could lie? Or, may he simply have been looking, not just for freedom, but for an angel of salvation, a chariot to swing low, to take him to a new world of possibility?

%%%

THE WAR came, and with it came the doom of slavery. The Burroughs slaves, with an army of liberation near at hand and freedom's ring in the air all about them, remained true to their own conception of duty and honor, guarding their people's silver and other valuables from the coming of marauding Yankees or, at least, from the rumors of those marauding Yankees, and that was enough. The Burroughs sons rode off or walked off or were carried off the place to protect what their people had built up, or to defend Virginia's honor, or to valorize the glories of the Southern way of life. One was killed, two others were injured, but it was not enough.[111]

The South had grown civilized and prosperous riding the backs of slaves, but the North had grown powerful and rich. That a portion of this Northern abundance was, by the reckoning of a later moral economy, itself traceable back to the North's taking of its own pound of flesh from the backs of slaves was a better left unrecovered memory; the section had invested that bounty wisely, compounded its profits, added to its numbers with aliens from other nations who quickly became Americans, while free Negroes and slaves were made to stand down. The South, its prevailing sector conservative and reveling in having its way with slaves, was nothing like so welcoming of strangers and industry, and what poor newcomer would even entertain the idea of making a start where all that was good was taken up already by slaveholders?

The vast dimension of the North's wealth and population, in proportions unimaginable at the founding of these united sections, would prove all the difference needed once the centrality of slaves and slavery came to the crucial fore. Then, Washington would write, against "doubt and distrust," and while "the cause of Union seemed to quiver in the balance . . . the Negro was asked to come to the rescue in arms."[112] They did so, and the world, in a moment, had changed: black men were soldiers, enlisting at the behest of Douglass and the abolitionists, but in the fulfillment of their own different sense of duty and honor. Then there was the vision, the best of impossible dreams, of black men fixing bayonets and shouldering rifles, their weapons aimed accurately at the present defenders of slavery; dedicating themselves to this good fight; consecrating the ground where their blood was spilt, and making a tribute to the many thousand gone where they caused their enemies to fall in great pools of American gore. One of them wrote a letter to the slaveholding woman who held his daughter in bondage: We come *en masse*, he said, arrayed with "a powrer and autherity to bring away and to exacute vengeneens on them that holds my Child." "This whole Government gives chear to me and you cannot help your self."[113] And they marched on: from the raw recruits thrown under the gun at the siege at Island Mound, Missouri, through the bloodletting at Port Hudson in Louisiana, to the "heroic souls" of the Massachusetts 54th,[114] wrapped up in glory at Fort Wagner, South Carolina. And in the end, Washington noted, "It was a Negro soldier who hauled down the Confederate flag" when Weitzel's crack black troops took the capital at Richmond on April 3, 1865.[115]

It would be understandable, given what Washington came to stand for, that such a scene would appear to him—as to the nation—as a nightmare best forgotten. And yet the enormity of this phenomenon, momentous if fleeting, demands his attention. Perhaps most of his readers missed the hidden irony—a remarkable irony—that beyond the significance of the black soldier, it was the forbearance of the stay-at-home slave who did not flee to the Union Army that enabled the Confederacy to pursue its fight for independence, to stay in the fight secure in the knowledge that their loved ones at home were safe, thus perpetuating the bloodletting, the sapping of the white South's strength, and, ultimately the demise of the slave South. Washington claimed, up until the last years of his life, that the Negro could always endure the abuse whites heaped upon them, but that the real harm in racial oppression was to the whites themselves. While this is dubious as a general principle, the Civil War does shed a different light on Washington's claim.

And so a portion of those who benefited from slavery, and some who did not, lived or died, but slavery was destroyed. One thing, though, was clear: lions did not lie down with lambs, as the Rev. Hollis Reed and so many others like him would have wished when proposing that emancipation be followed closely by colonization back to Africa; the American nation did not cleanse itself by the extirpation of its Negro numbers.[116] Freedom was at hand, but the freedpeople were not carried down to the sea; those storied ships did not come in; the people were not borne across the ocean back home to a place they had never been before. And so, the dreams some had dreamed for the perfecting of a white American Zion and the manufacturing of a black African Zion were held in abeyance, and it was left up simply to Americans to resolve the matter of what was to be done.

After he became famous, Washington received correspondence from persons sharing warm memories of having known Booker in those earlier days of slavery and freedom—that is to say, "I knew you when"—or, more commonly, writers responding to his words' kindling in them warm imaginings of what it would be like to know him in those antebellum times. Paying no heed to the prophesied torrent of blood that gave meaning to the war, setting aside the meaning of that fall into conflagration—for it to be a true and biblical fall and not just the nation's tripping headlong into disaster—for an easier, less challenging measure of moral or moralistic concern, these remembrances, real or artificial, one part nostalgia, another part celebrity worship, look to Washington for affirmations: for some, that white blood tells; for many, the salving of consciences because slavery could not have been so harmful if one such as him made it through; for all credulous readers of all times, that slavery could never have been so sinful if one such as him rose from it. In a way, it was as if he were America's favorite former bondsman—every man's ace boon Negro—their friend.

If there is a corollary in literature for the white regard for Washington, it is more from the work of Twain than of Stowe. Some Americans might sometimes have seen Washington as Stowe's character "Uncle Tom," long suffering but remaining dutiful to the end, his living and dying having no other purpose than to reveal the immorality of slavery, a good soldier become cannon fodder in the war for white sympathy for slaves. It seems more likely that he was to them like Twain's "Jim," coming into sharp focus away from the big or not so big house of bondage, distanced if not completely removed from slavery, and always ready on the raft for a deep adventure on ancient, muddy rivers with his white public playing the role of permanently innocent "Hucks."[117] Like Twain's character, these white persons were perhaps naive in the ways of the world, and maybe approached him too forthrightly, or even with a little bit of condescension. But with more or less ardor seeking out the encounter with the black man who was something like the muse of their imaginings about their fate and that of the Negro; they with eyes wide, and, there on the river—America's other great and metaphorical river—hands cleansed of the dirty business of doing evil to black people. Like that "Jim," Washington would always be their patient preceptor, willing to forgive their trespass upon his time; ever ready to take them, not as they maybe are, but in the light of their best possibilities. The analogy makes sense for it is necessary both for the white people who approach Washington and for his own gracious inviting of them in to his life, that time be suspended on the river where it possible not to see black peonage and white profit, or to witness the execution of pogroms, or to catch whiff of black bodies crackling upon lit faggots piled high or rotting like strange fruit hung too long from trees under hot Southern skies. It is only floating down those rivers of the mind, down the meandering streams of best of intentions, that in the age of segregation that is the age of Washington, the white (but a cleansed whiteness) and the black (but Washington alone because superior to jealous thoughts of "racial feeling") can find afloat an ideal basis to begin the quest for common ground.

This good race relationship composes a part of "the Washington legend," or what one of his teachers recognized as the "romance" of his account of "the transition life from slavery to freedom," a potent symbol for the nation's setting things right, for American progress, and the here realized potentiality of black and white meeting where their souls reside.[118] Adding to that legend was the type of "little speech" Washington gave that was similar in tone to ones he often gave during the fullness of his glory days. This time, though, it was given on the occasion of a visit back to the Burroughs place and before an audience of white people and black—before "the old aristocracy of the region" and their former slaves some of whom were "grim fellows, showing in every line and lineament of face and figure, the efforts of continuous and severe labor." Washington was reported to have had no regrets: "that he had never been sorry that he was born there, and born as he had been, a slave." Washington said "he had learned a great many things about life, coming up as he had, from that lowly condition in life which he could not have learned if he had been born in any other or higher station." The most important of these lessons was of "the opportunity that there was in this country for every man, whether he was white or black, if he had the heart and courage to work." Washington then plucked a rose and told a story the point of which was that "there was something precious, and something real in the kindly, and often tender relations which bound master and slave together, in the days before the war. The new generation that has grown up since that time, as a rule, did not understand, and did not value those old relations of kindness, and good-will which had bound the two races together, in the old days." Concluding his remarks, he reminded his former neighbors "that it was not too late for them to begin, if they had not already done so, to save a little money to get a little home, and to make something of themselves."[119] Washington had been there: slavery was not an end or an excuse. Even in the discouraging circumstances in which free people sometimes found themselves, there was always hope. There were people glad to help if asked.

I am black and I have seen black hands, millions and
millions of them—
Out of millions of bundles of wool and flannel tiny black
fingers have reached restlessly and hungrily for life.
Reached out for the black nipples at the black breasts of
black mothers . . .
And they've held balls and bats and gloves and marbles
and jack-knives and sling-shots and spinning tops in
the thrill of sport and play . . .
They've held pens and rulers and maps and tablets and
books in palms spotted and smeared with ink,
And they've held dice and cards and half-pint flasks and
cue sticks and cigars and cigarettes in the pride of
new maturity . . .

—RICHARD WRIGHT, "I HAVE SEEN BLACK HANDS"

Chapter 3

"They Will Pull Against You the Load Downward"

The Freedpeople's Failure and Booker Washington's Rescue

THE GREAT war ended and freedom came to the South and to the Burroughs place. After Virginia had seen Fredericksburg, and Chancellorsville, and Virginia masters and Virginia slaves had received word of the happenings eastward from Hale's Ford at Appomattox Courthouse, after night had fallen on the Confederacy, then there was a jubilee. Booker, "clinging wonderingly to my mother's skirts," heard "her shout hallelujah because we were free."[1] It was, Washington recalled, "a momentous and eventful day to all upon our plantation." In the days preceding, the people there had taken up the chorus of what had heretofore been slave songs—songs of work and songs of sorrow sung in the lonely voices of people seeking solace now and deliverance in "the next world." Now those songs, no longer merely a balm in Gilead, were reprised by the entire company in full voice "to let it be known that the 'freedom' in their songs meant freedom of the body in this world." Now the people threw off the mask and there was "great rejoicing, and thanksgiving, and wild scenes of ecstasy."[2]

But the joyous mood soon was quieted, and the singing of songs of freedom was to be followed by more somber moments. First, there were the feelings of "pity among the slaves for our former owners," victims themselves, Washington would say, for whom recent times had been especially hard and would only get harder. Washington insisted that the war and the shortages it had spawned had had a harder effect on the Burroughs family than on their slaves: "As the war was prolonged the white people, in many cases, often found it more difficult to secure food for themselves. I think the slaves felt the deprivation less than the whites." This point is not merely an expression of unctuous sympathy but another of Washington's clever means of drawing a distinction between hardy slaves and soft slaveholders, as is suggested by his explanation of why it was the case that the whites suffered more. This was, he writes,

> because the usual diet for slaves was corn bread and pork, and these could be raised on the plantation; but coffee, tea, sugar, and other articles which the whites had been accustomed to use could not be raised on the plantation, and the conditions brought about by the war frequently made it impossible to secure these things. The whites were often in great straits. Parched corn was used for coffee, and a kind of black molasses was used instead of sugar. Many times nothing was used to sweeten the so called tea and coffee.[3]

Then there came upon the newly free people the creeping realization of the magnitude of the task laid upon their laps, a realization that, if Washington's account is correct, came as more of a surprise to his fellows than freedom itself: "The great responsibility of being free, of having charge of themselves, of having to think and plan for themselves and their children, seemed to take possession of them." A "deep gloom" replaced elation in the quarters, uncertainty crowded out carelessness as to the future, and there was the sense, young Booker saw, that "freedom was a more serious thing than they have expected to find it." The jubilee and the joyous noise of the freedom songs were silenced for the sake of quiet councils on the matter of what should be done next.[4]

In the days and weeks after the emancipation, "there were two points upon which practically all the people on our place were agreed," and, Washington wrote, "I find that this was generally true throughout the South." First, there was the resolve to dip toes, cautiously or willy-nilly, into the waters of freedom. This the newly free did by scurrying off their place of previous captivity. Most of the freedpeople undertook such a sojourn "at least for a few days or weeks in order that they might really feel sure that they were free." Accomplishing this, testing themselves through small adventures with differing results, there followed the return, in triumph or crestfallen, home.[5]

The second matter, seeming to the people to be a pressing one, was acting upon their desire to take for themselves a last name. "When they were slaves," Washington explained, "a coloured person was simply called 'John' or 'Susan.' There was seldom occasion for more than the use of the one name. If 'John' or 'Susan' belonged to a white man by the name of 'Hatcher,' sometimes he was called 'John Hatcher,' or as often 'Hatcher's John.'" For people without surnames this would seem a part of the serious business of freedom, a requirement of free persons and certainly, among other things, a prerequisite for or useful aid in the establishment of legally recognized personal and familial identities, in the acquisition of property, and the entering into of contracts—the bits of paper that are the accouterments of soon-to-be citizenship. Washington, however, details the matter of names as rather comical, making the freedpeople's manner of choosing seem frivolous. He saw developed "a feeling" among the freedmen "that it was far from proper for them to bear the surnames of their former owners." Thus as "one of the first signs of freedom": "'John Hatcher' was changed to 'John S. Lincoln' or 'John S. Sherman,' the initial 'S' standing for no name, it being simply a part of what the coloured man proudly called his 'entitles.'"[6] This was a minor bit of the folly of "a new race," as Washington would have it; or, alternately, the fixing on baubles and shiny ornaments that is to be expected of a child race.[7]

On the dawn of freedom, Washington writes, "In a few hours the great question with which the Anglo-Saxon race had been grappling for centuries had been thrown upon these people to be solved. These were the questions of a home, a living, the rearing of children, education, citizenship, and the establishment and support of churches." It was, he felt, "very much like suddenly turning a youth of ten or twelve years out into the world to provide for himself." It is, he later explained to an audience of Northerners, "with an ignorant race as it is with the child; it craves at first the superficial, the ornamental, the signs of progress rather than the reality. The ignorant race is tempted to jump at one bound to the position that it has required years of hard struggle for others to reach."[8]

At this point "Booker was only nine years old . . . still clacking about on his wooden shoes, wearing his single shirt."[9] Where does a child, even a precocious one, a gifted and unusual one, born of a child race go for guidance?

%%%

IT IS not known if in August of 1865 Washington's mother took for herself a last name, but whether or not so suitably clad in the clothes of free adulthood she, nine-year-old Booker, his brother and sister pulled up shallow material stakes but deeper emotional ones and headed westward for a new life in freedom to West Virginia. They had been called there by Washington Ferguson, formerly a slave on a neighboring farm who before the war had entered into what apparently was a type of unofficial marriage with Booker's mother, and who surely was the father of Washington's younger sister. When freedom came, Washington Ferguson sent for the little family to join with him in the Kanawha Valley of West Virginia. Following his bidding, Mother Jane would be among the first of the Burroughs family's property to take permanent leave of the place.[10] Their few clothes and household goods were piled into a horse-drawn cart provided by Ferguson, and they set off on a journey of tedium and discomfort that lasted for weeks, bouncing along on the cart or, more frequently, walking, and sleeping in the open air. Camping one night in rare shelter, the family was menaced by "a large black snake." This, perhaps, was an omen of things to come, a symbol of the jeopardy in which they would soon find themselves. The party nevertheless endured, journeying on to reach the little town of Malden, below Charleston, in the new state of West Virginia. There Ferguson had "secured a little cabin for us to live in" near where, now as a freedman, he had resumed one of his slavery days occupations, working in a salt furnace.[11]

The house provided for the family by Ferguson was "no better than the one we had left on the old plantation in Virginia." In fact, it was a good deal worse than the slave quarters at the Burroughs, where at least its bound occupants had the benefit of freely breathing the fresh air. The new place, on the other hand, "was in the midst of a cluster of cabins crowded closely together, and as there were no sanitary regulations, the filth about the cabins was often intolerable." Adding to the ordure—indeed, seeping in the waste about the new place—the neighbors were a "motley mixture" including other African Americans (presumably freedpeople like the Ferguson family), and "the poorest and most ignorant and degraded white people."[12] (According to the 1870 census, their closest neighbors were white persons and families).[13] Young Washington, used to the open spaces and placidity of the farm, suffered his full measure of shock at the world freedom (and, it would come to seem to him, Washington Ferguson as well) had wrought. There was chaos beneath the stench, he saw, and an atmosphere filled up with all manner of dangers including the "drinking, gambling, quarrels, fights, and shockingly immoral practices" that were nightly occurrences in the district where black and white people lived.[14] It was amid this sordid interracial comity that Washington grew to young manhood, where he began to form habits of mind that would last him throughout his life, and where the unfolding of his life increased old hurts and created new wounds.

"I was made a free child," Washington wrote,[15] and it requires no great stretch of the imagination to apprehend the content of young Booker's idealized version of freedom, the shape of his youthful dreams: it would be for him the straight path ahead once the walls of slavery were down, the sturdy ladder to climb for one possessed of "intrinsic, individual merit." He would get him a book, conquer it and learn to read; secure an education, be smart and not merely achieve the cleverness encouraged in slaves; work with his mind and not just with his hands; work to be useful and not just for someone else's selfish uses. He would serve his family, work for his and their prosperity and safety. And lead: his quest for an education was spurred on by his desire to follow Douglass's example, to study his "wonderful life and achievements," and so to emulate the great man.[16] Only the sky would set a limit on what he could do, rising up on the hot air "of the great human law, which is universal and eternal, that merit, no matter under what skin found, is, in the long run, recognized and rewarded."[17]

Because that straight-line course to the good life had, like names, like literacy, been among the things denied to slaves by their condition as property, it is reasonable to assume that young Booker was not alone in feeling this way about the promise before them; a general feeling, or a similar optimism, grouping many mixed motives about what freedom meant as the river swelled, bursting over its banks. But what, indeed, is the good life, and what are the responsibilities and duties of citizens in a democracy in pursuing that bounty? Freedom alone is sometimes not all it is cracked up to be, and rivers sometimes really ought to obey their banks. It was, in Washington's telling, the freedmen's headlong rush into freedom, disregarding those traps and snares that made a muddle of the whole process. Perhaps it was the case that the young Booker, childishly partaking of the illusory view of freedom his elders maybe had entertained at the dawning, believed that freedom meant improved conditions and the absence of want; if so, he was quickly disabused of that meaning of freedom. And he had other disillusions take its place: that the freedom in the offing meant to be free of the more or less effective protections slavery afforded to slaves by their masters' paternal and fiduciary interests. And thus, if no other able protectors come to the fore to bar the door to dangerous wolves, free to be shadowed by dangers and privation; free to starve; free to be overcome by circumstances; and free to be used by those who take advantage of the opportunities afforded by freedom to embrace their freedom to exploit. In the rough environment of postwar Malden, a hard-living, hard-bitten town on the Kanawha River, there were no shortages of all these type of threats and dangers, and they came in black and white, as friend as well as foe. Sometimes, Washington soon learned, the most dangerous of the wolves were those residing on this side of the door.

%.%.%.

WASHINGTON FREQUENTLY averred that he detested the living in towns like Malden and larger cities, both personally and for black people in general. He advised his Tuskegee students to steer well clear of cities if at all possible, telling them in no uncertain terms that "we serve ourselves best, we serve our race best, when we keep away from the large cities, unless we have good cause to go to the city to do work that no one else is doing, unless we are sure we can do better work, unless we are sure that more lasting and effective work can be done than it is possible to for us to do in some country district."[18] Washington was insistent on the point based on his observations of what happened to black people going to town. Despite his stated lifelong aversion, or perhaps adding vehemence to it, he seems also to have recognized Sodom's allure; he, too would one day be caught up, if only for a brief and controversial time, in the teeth of big city violence and vice.[19]

Country folk went to town attracted by "all its excitements and temptations," the hubbub and agitations not found in rural areas. Filled up, as Washington once would seem to have been, with hayseed wonderment at the dash and dazzle of it all, they were ill prepared to stay out of the traps and snares threatening all who entered with the degradation of body and soul. And many did indeed become so trapped, caught in the allure like an overawed deer, frozen in place by the headlights of its oncoming doom, unable to effect its own salvation as nature meets modernity in the middle of busy highways.

Washington believed there to be "a large idle class," forming "too large a proportion" of the black city dwelling population. Such could be found in New York and Philadelphia in the North, Montgomery and Atlanta in the South, and in many smaller cities and towns as well, laying up "in shanties, flats and sheds." These idlers live "in constant want." Where that unenviable station did not obtain, it was only because they live outside the law, dishonestly "get[ting] their living by women working and feeding them." For their own good and for the good of the race, Washington advised those women caused by their men to slave over washtub, cooking stove, and ironing table to rid themselves of these "worthless creatures, who would be better dead than alive." If there is a deficit of morality in the Negro, he said in 1900, "I feel very sure that the weakness of our race is in the large cities and towns" among these people: "Idleness leads to immorality, it leads to sin, and following in the wake of idleness in the large cities is physical weakness."[20] The result of this, along with "bad whiskey, poor food and poor houses," was a higher incidence of mortality among African American adults compared to white persons. Adding to the problem was, as he knew from personal experience, the poor ventilation in the ramshackle places that black people called home.[21] Some of those same factors were also surely involved, he believed, in a "lack of care and attention" that resulted in the deaths of large numbers of black city children. All this amounted to the scourge of black families and a drag upon human progress.

Washington saw the change from slavery to freedom and country to town in much the same light: both tended "naturally, to unsettle, to intoxicate and to lead the negro to wrong ideas of life."[22] But while the shock of transition represented by movement to the city affected white persons, too, the black world he found in Malden, West Virginia, amounted to the addition or multiplication of the two transitions: a double shot of intoxicating experience in the rollicking river town. The freedman left plantations where he had been "surrounded by restraints," for "the freedom and temptations of the city [that] was too much for him. The transition was too sudden."[23]

While Washington is not especially graphic about the details of what it was like living hunkered down "right in the midst of the salt furnaces" in hardscrabble Malden, his revulsion at the type of roughhouse conviviality between the black and white denizens, the camaraderie of cock-fight and razor, of throwing bones and bare knuckles in the close quarters of juke joints and back alleys found there is readily available to the imagination. Malden, its decline since the 1850s only temporarily spelled by activities spawned by the war, was not a large city—even its rising neighbor Charleston was then but a biggish town. Relative to what he had seen previously and with its own substantial industries of vice, his virgin eyes told him he had been delivered unto Babylon.

Presumably there was much to be averse about. What he witnessed of the concentration of corruption in which both black people and whites participated, but centered on the places where black people lived, was the wave of the future. From the passage in many states after the war of "black codes" to set things on their proper, racial course, to the age of Washington at the turn of the century, segregation never prevailed in these nominally black precincts. Even when segregation reached its absurd heyday in such state-sponsored attention to the minutiae of where people ought and ought not to be in the Jim Crowing of telephone booths and escalators, and throughout succeeding decades it never reached into the world of the demimonde. Instead, vice and other forms of lawful or unlawful organized disorder were often located in black districts or slopped over and ever encroached upon them. (Squalor and corruption seeming to have a certain tolerable flavor to authorities when it was so situated in inaccurately named "black" communities.)[24]

There were some bright spots, areas of possibility as wide and compelling as the deep green darkness of the mountains and valleys, the abundance of natural beauty, painted on vistas so wide as to astound the eye, that Washington would ever after remember in keeping his West Virginia beginnings close to heart. In the state, for example, there was no passage of "black codes," because unlike their Confederate cousins across the freshly painted state line in Virginia and elsewhere in the South, authorities in Unionist West Virginia saw little reason for such regulation, which was counterindicated, anyway, by their hopes of achieving rapid statehood.[25] Washington recalled his excitement at seeing "a young colored man reading a newspaper to a group of colored people who surrounded him with gaping mouths and wondering eyes. He was almost a god to them," a lesson not lost on the ambitious boy.[26] Nor, as a general matter, lost on the other freedpeople, already manifesting an "intense desire . . . for an education," he noted, "it was a whole race trying to go to school."[27] Nevertheless, the picture, as Washington saw it, was ugly in those first days of freedom. Even the seemingly unalloyed good of educational opportunity was distorted somehow: "The Negro boy," Washington recalled, "immediately after the Civil War was confronted by—or at least it seemed to him—two propositions which in many cases were liable to exert a serious influence upon his life. One of these was that freedom from slavery brought freedom from hard work; the other was that education of the head would bring freedom from hand-work." The freedmen, Washington added, were "not directly responsible for either of these ideas, but the fact remains that in a large degree they prevailed."[28]

Equally unpromising in Malden was the grim reality of the salt furnaces and coalmines. The former was the town's main industry—Malden was originally called "Kanawha Salines"—and the work available there, loading salt into barrels, was difficult and unremunerative for the workers (for the owners of the enterprise the story might be a different one). But the mines were worse. An adjunct to the salt industry, the mines were created to provide fuel for the furnaces that were central to the extraction of the salt from the brine,[29] the mines also produced restive workers set on edge by the poor pay and the dangers of their job, a fact that likely produced the off-hours violence and squalor that at first blush so impressed Washington. Horrible death and class warfare were fixtures about the mines. Washington may have known about the 1868 mine fire in neighboring Pennsylvania that killed 175 men; in Malden and elsewhere in the region were minor and major strikes like the general strike that came up out of the mines in Martinsburg, West Virginia, in 1877.

Returning home to Malden from school in the early 1870s Washington found the salt furnaces cold, and the coal mines inactive. This was "on account of the miners being out on 'strike,'" he wrote, "this was something which, it seemed, usually occurred whenever the men got two or three months ahead in their savings. During the strike, of course, they spent all that they had saved, and would often return to work in debt at the same wages, or would move to another mine at considerable expense." Washington's observations of this morass, aside from turning him evermore against "the professional labour agitators," proved to him the futility of mild or militant labor action: business was not getting done, the economy was harmed, and "the miners were worse off at the end of the strike" than they had been at its outset.[30]

In the late 1860s, though, "Every one worked in the mines," a Malden acquaintance from those days wrote Washington years later.[31] In such an environment, the best one could generally hope for was merely to live to toil another day. Even those who survived, Washington believed, often wound up "physically and mentally dwarfed."[32]

Most times and being politic, Washington would describe settings such as this as one more site for the beneficial workings of the market, the aboveboard and progressive way in which relations are worked out (in the absence of unions) in "the commercial world."[33] He had to know this was but a quaint euphemism for the often violent relationship between labor and capital in Malden in those days. Likewise, while he would one day recall with nostalgia the sight of the mines, he also recalled their misery: their entrance appearing not so much as a hole but more like a mouth, a maw where spirited boys see their ambitions consumed. The nostalgic view harks back, perhaps, to young Booker's first days in Malden, when the mines would appear to him, beginning his education and fully flush with the excitement of every possibility, simply as someone else's destiny.

But this was another of the illusions of freedom for young Booker, a boy no more than nine or ten, was to find himself taken out of school and cast into the world of work, first in the furnaces, and soon thereafter, down into the coal mines. His stepfather, Washington Ferguson, "discovered that I had a financial value" and thus could not be spared from work to join the newly opened school for Negro children in the Kanawha Valley.[34]

Ever after he would remember the nightmare of this dread-filled experience when "although quite a child," he was thrown into the dangers of the mines.[35] There was, first, "the fright which going a long distance under the mountain into a dark and damp coal mine gave me."[36] This entailed going downward a mile "in the blackest darkness" to the face of the coal. Washington would later comment, "I do not believe that one ever experiences anywhere else such darkness as he does in a coal-mine." Imagine the horror felt by the boy, his candle gone out, finding himself lost in the different "rooms" of the mines, the panic of "wander[ing] about in the darkness until by chance I found some one to give me a light." The work was dirty—"it was a very hard job to get one's skin clean after the day's work was over"—and "not only hard, but . . . dangerous. There was always the danger of being blown to pieces by a premature explosion of powder, or of being crushed by falling slate."[37] Not for nothing does Washington call the time he spent in the mines "dark and discouraging." And the fact that it was Washington Ferguson who caused him to suffer this fate must have only added to the pain of it. He had been set free from the bondage he was born into by a mere accident of birth only to suffer a different sort of bondage to a man who was, like the slaveholders, using him without regard to his future interests and personal progress. The combination of being taken from school, forced down into the mines, robbed of his earnings was, he would recall, "one of the keenest disappointments that I ever experienced."[38] It would, however, not be his final fate.

%%%

ONE OF the reasons why Washington escapes the opprobrium of being a theorist is his ability to leave things like causes and motives unsaid if being explicit serves no purpose or would actually hinder understanding of his point. Why, one might ask, had he been cast down into the mines? But providing good explanations is beside his point. Better to let those matters lie and rely upon the alienation engendered by distance, time, class outlook, and racism to direct attention not toward the nature of an iniquitous system, the intractable situation faced by a poor man with mouths to feed, but to mystification as to Ferguson's motives, leaving his audience, sympathetic to the Negro but sensitive, as well, to black pathology, to come to their own conclusion.[39] It may be that it was the worse for him because unlike the plain Negroes he admonishes to take the work available to them—put dignity into common labor—he was fitted for better things. As well, his being cast down into the mines appears not as a necessary thing but as an act of perfidy and greed on the part of his stepfather. The problem is not the system, but the personnel, not political or economic but personal. Harlan writes that young Booker responded to this discouragement and challenges in this stage in his life "in Horatio Alger fashion,"[40] but there is more to that than meets the eye: the transformation of history into fairy tale.

Horatio Alger published his first story the month before Booker was born; in April 1856, he published his second story, "Cousin Jim." More than the coincidence in the timing of these events provokes comment. The boy hero in Alger's stories and young Booker, the hero of Washington's story, which may have been taken as the Negro's story, are each recalled as quintessential "rags to riches" characters in "the Work and Win, Upward and Onward" narrative of American rugged individualism, avatars of capitalist triumphalism and the patriotism of laissez-faire. And what was once said about Alger could be said with equal validity about Washington: that he "put into simple words and a standard plot the hopes and beliefs of a nation."[41] At least in the case of the fiction writer, however, this was not by virtue of what Alger had actually written. Alger, his biographers write, was no capitalist ideologue, nor does he deserve his "reputation as a success mythmaker." He was, to be sure, a follower, from the war to the end of his life in 1899, of the Republican line in politics, but opposed usury and crass acquisitiveness even after those values were nailed securely into the Republican Party's Gilded Age platform. He also was an advocate of cooperatives, and, far from simply worshipping at the altar of the free market, could muster a dissent from its values, warning his young readers in "Paul the Peddler" (1877) of the malign effects of competition when it meant employers could depress wages.[42] And the irony of all this, of the transformation of the meaning Alger's work, and the Alger hero's concordance with the image of Booker T. Washington, is that the actual stories bear an even closer relation to Washington's life than the parodic modern advertisement or alleged capitalist boosterism.

In the typical Alger story—*all* his stories are typical—a boy, seemingly bereft but possessed of moral character, rises to middle-class respectability and that is all; he does not become a millionaire through hard work. And it is not because of the existing system that he has this moderate success, but despite it, as anyone with more than a passing acquaintanceship with Alger's writings and his large sympathy and affection for all the boys in his stories, regardless of whether or not, like his heroes, they are fated to make it. His boys are down on their luck or literally down in the dumps of American cities, sons of dead or absent fathers or orphaned altogether, but possessed of a piety inexplicable in the circumstances in which they live. Alger's boys are good, and goodness means waiting for fate to intervene, waiting for a fairy godmother, waiting for a *deus* to come from the *machina*. He is not really waiting, but more precisely settled into his immediate fortunes, soldiering onward with an innocent determination and endurance. Despite all circumstances, one acts good, one obeys the golden rule. That is the reason why good fortune in the end smiles upon the virtuous urchin, the plucky newsboy, and all the other diamonds-in-the-rough populating Alger's tales. Thus Alger's first stories—as old as Washington—set the pattern. The young doctor, forced to choose between marrying for love and marrying for money, opts for the first and gains the second not because he wanted it but because he did not. The fatherless son, a mere boy of twelve seeks the advice—not the money—of his rich uncle, is spurned by the grubbing squire and his arriviste wife, but triumphs in the end when an even wealthier relative, having viewed events incognito, takes the boy under his wing, becomes a father to him, and rescues him from his "season of adversity."

Alger's description is of a fantasy of escape from forbidding and stringent circumstances—moral melodrama—rather than an elaboration of normal means of ascent within the political economy. And he must have seen it as rather an unpromising social framework that would demand miraculous and unlikely interventions.[43] Indeed, the true Alger pattern reminds one of nothing so much as the tradition as old as the oldest fairy tale and as recent as the latest pulp science fiction in which the peasant boy, offered the throne, disavows his ability for such high office and finds that his denial is the ultimate sign of his qualification (told or written in a time when there was a large certainty that peasant boys were not qualified for high office and an even larger certainty that they would not be asked). Thus, it is an idealism sprung from a realistic appraisal of just how difficult it is to rise, and the attraction is that, in nineteenth-century America, heroes such as Alger and Washington described did really seem to exist and in spades. Just as it takes but one well-publicized million-dollar jackpot winner to sustain the amateur gambler in his belief against all odds in the likelihood of hitting the right number, the example of an Andrew Carnegie, coming to America next to penniless from Scotland and through combinations of gumption and good fortune becoming a tycoon, is sufficient to gild a whole century of dreams.

So, too, it is with Washington.

The cynic may view Washington's autobiography as nothing more than an adornment of platitudes, a thin tissue of lies or misrepresentations, strung upon a fatuous tale of the rags of slavery to the riches of prosperity and influence, but its power to carry Americans along with it even one hundred years after its first telling suggests the potency of its blend of romance and ideology, fact and fantasy, in a life lived by one who avers that all is possible in America, and can prove it with his own example.[44] But freedom in mind is not the same as freedom in person. No story ever effected the emancipation of real world slaves, nor the collective deliverance of worthy boys held back by circumstances. Even the fabled meeting where Abraham Lincoln is supposed to have said upon being introduced to Mrs. Stowe—"So this is the little woman who wrote the book that made this big war"—recognizes this principle.[45]

Commenting on the matter of his being born with no fortune behind him—indeed, a certain thing—and without a name, he describes his aspiration in a way that provides a direct contrast to Ferguson's misconduct and failure: "I have sometimes had the feeling that if I had inherited these, and had been a member of a more popular race, I should have been inclined to yield to the temptation of depending upon my ancestry and my colour to do that for me which I should do for myself. Years ago I resolved that because I had no ancestry myself I would leave a record of which my children would be proud, and which might encourage them to still higher effort."[46]

In Washington's telling the Reconstruction is the story of a river at war with its surroundings, and he, but a boy huddled with his mother in the ramshackle cabin provided them by her husband, could tell that its mindless pursuit of that course could only lead to disaster. He wanted to learn, to win an education and so to make himself useful to the world, to begin the long haul up from slavery at the bottom of life, and do for his family what Ferguson had been unable or unwilling to do. There, even on the most flood-prone terrain, is where foundations are built, seeds sown and tended, is the place where rich and productive lives are begun. But that was not the orthodoxy of black Reconstruction; nor, it appears, was it the stepfather's course.

If the man who was in the place of his father failed in providing adequately for him and his mother; if Washington Ferguson left him unprotected from the more malign vicissitudes of the world, and instead preyed upon him, was a parasite using him in the same way slaveholders had used their slaves without a thought to their charges' futures (but a worse form of using because his earlier condition was merely an accident of birth), he would strike out and escape Ferguson's depredations, would fight to get free of what freedom had wrought and the whole tragic situation freedpeople were in during Reconstruction.

Washington describes other chapters from his experience of similar import: instances of black misbehavior and the messy and bitter race relations that ensued. He may not have fully understood just what was wrong—the sources of black obstreperousness and pretensions to grandeur—only that he knew no good would come of driving a wedge between the races. But the outlines of his critique of emancipation and, if Washington is to be taken at his word, his receptivity to his mature theoretical system, began as a child seeking a means of ascent. In turning this page in his life, his mother was his first teacher.

※※※

WRITING ABOUT what he gained from his experience at the Hampton Institute, Washington said, "back of all else, the lesson which General Armstrong was trying to teach us was the same that my mother had taught me." At Hampton it was gained "through the medium of books and tools and through contact with my teachers," but nonetheless his mother had imparted the same eternal verities: "namely, to distinguish between the real and the sham, to choose the substance rather than the shadow, to seek the permanent good rather than the passing pleasant." That there are no free lunches: that hard work and genuine effort, self-discipline and thriftiness, patience and propriety are their own rewards. "The lesson which I learned in this simple fashion at home was of great value to me, " he said, "in trying to lead my race in the direction of things that are permanent and lasting rather than merely showy and temporary."[47] The stories from his boyhood that he tells on himself and other black people are not so much metaphors about those lessons, as they are the ostensible substance of his social theory. This is one theory central to Washingtonianism: that what ought to guide an individual's living is equally applicable—he extrapolates—to the problem of the Negro's general condition and the basis for black people's reformation. He offers his own Reconstruction era example of the way it is possible for African Americans to escape the trap of their own pathology and redeem their claims to American citizenship.

Young Booker was himself not immune to the blandishments of extravagance and the thin but colorful material culture of consumerism, the valuing of some of "the ornamental gewgaws of life" over that which is merely useful, as he phrased it in Atlanta.[48] He tells a story, illustrative of his just folks, man-of-the-black people humility, of his own scrapes with stupefying superficiality the moral of which serves also to demonstrate how he grew to be different from the common folk, how he stood up and thus stood out from the mass of Negroes. Having "long cherished a desire to own a suit of 'store' clothes," the young Washington saved to scrape together ten or twelve whole dollars, and with this horde proceeded apace to the local haberdashery. There, the tailor, sizing him up as a sucker and a yokel, gushed that he had just the thing for his young patron, an imported suit—"a Dolly Varden suit"—brought just for his young customer, and all the while taking the measure of the bulge in Washington's pocket where he kept his money. Filled up with a rube's excitement and seeing his heart's desire in this "flashy, showy" suit of many colors, Washington was at the moment oblivious to the fact that the coat was short of sleeve and worth at wholesale, he later supposed, about half what he paid for it. He paid his savings to the pleased tailor, and the next Sunday "wore it with great pride" to church. On his way home from the church, however, a downpour came "that drenched both me and the suit." The next morning he hung the suit out to dry. "Presently," he recalled, "I noticed that the colors had begun to flow. In fact, they had gotten all mixed up with one another and the whole suit seemed to be in the process of disintegration." When his prized garment fell apart like a cheap suit, a chastened Washington was told by his mother "that it would be wiser to spend my money in buying some 'homespun' cloth which she promised [she] would make into a good, sensible, and serviceable suit." He did, and she did, and while the resulting clothes were not showy, they lasted for several good years.[49]

The principle here is that what is good for the individual can be applied with equal force to the race. Years later, at Tuskegee, Washington would expound on this lesson to his eager charges during the Sunday evening talks that were an important part of the Tuskegee curriculum. From the head of the room he would declaim on the "great power" found in simple dress: "the best dressed person is the person whose dress does not attract attention. Whenever a student is so dressed that his dress attracts attention, then he is not well dressed. He is over dressed. The same is true of a woman. Whenever she is so dressed that her hat or her ribbons or anything about her apparel attracts special attention, she is not well dressed." And concluding with words that might well suit another, more recent undertaker of cultural revolution, Washington said, "Modesty and simplicity give strength."[50]

Another story from the annals of the black propensity for paying more for gaudiness but getting less of usefulness was a lesson in humility that likely happened before the Dolly Varden suit incident. But once again he was his mother's avid pupil. The boys and young men about Malden had taken to "a rather new institution" in freedom: the wearing of the "store hat." Submitting to the group pressure, Washington began to feel "quite uncomfortable" going about hatless while "all of the other children wore hats or caps on their heads." He had never possessed such a thing; indeed, he writes, in slavery no one "even thought anything about the need for covering for my head." But now his peers pressed in upon him, taunting his uncovered head and the fact that he had no money to go to the store. His mother, though, found a way out of his difficulty by sewing him a "home-spun" or denim cap. "Since that time," Washington writes, "I have owned many kinds of caps and hats, but never one of which I have felt so proud as the cap made of two pieces of cloth sewed together by my mother."

To finish the story, Washington related how "several of the boys who began their careers with 'store hats' and who were my schoolmates and used to join in the sport that was made of me . . . have ended their careers in the penitentiary, while others are not able now to buy any kind of hat." This was something he subsequently learned and noted, "without satisfaction, I need not add" (as he disseminated their sorry fates to the reading publics of America, Europe, Africa, and elsewhere). Those well-topped boys become men in the penitentiary. Why? Washington portrays the difference between himself and them as a matter of "strength of character," the example provided by his mother of not relying on credit, and, generally, not being "led into the temptation of seeming to be that which she was not."[51]

Accepting the notion that giving themselves over to such temptation paved the road to imprisonment for those others, Washington's position is rather a different one from more traditional ideas that sinners are always among us, and that the sinner will be made to pay, or the merely rhetorical flourishes of black conservatives (although even for them their drawing of distinctions between the pathological and the productive turn on the question of amelioration and its limits rather than on an embrace of hierarchy). Washington instead intimates a different sort of tragedy in their dooming themselves through their acts. They could be helped, they could be reformed, if someone who knows the right behavior—who knows the ropes of freedom—were to be put in charge of them, hold their parole. The people can pursue simplicity and substance or showiness and superficiality; can take the first path and wind up successful; can take the second course and wind up in penitentiary like the young conspicuous consumers who taunted him and, due to their own hubris, were made to pay in the end.

The dire consequences for the black purchasers of the "store hat," are suggestive of the tendency toward hyperbole Washington developed on the stump. (Were none of these boys working to pay for their new hats? In making one point of this kind Washington, unwittingly strikes at another, laying bare African Americans, calling into question all elements of their entree in society, erasing alike their just and unjust deserts.) However, the point is not that the African Americans cannot learn to behave—to save and delay gratification, to persevere in the face of long odds and discouragements—Washington is proof of that—but that at their first freedom they had never learned those lessons, or denied them like children out of school who forget their lessons and turn away from books. Or they ignored them in their rush for mere things. "Individually, the Negro is strong," Washington would say, but "organically he is weak,"[52] meaning without collective organization, unity, and purpose. If individuals can be changed and re-formed in a new culture, then it should also be possible to make over "the Negro People," the aggregate of all the mutable but strong individuals through the use of some device or technique, with the proper home life, in the country rather than the city, and with the right guidance.

But how does one rise from a dysfunctional family amid a superficial people in a dog-eat-dog world? The obvious answer is that one must escape to a more secure and helpful environment, but first one must be cured of the debilities marking the freedmen, and so to prove one's self worthy of assistance. His answer of that question and his surmounting that challenge create the platform on which he lays claim to leadership: he had the cure and had himself been cured.

One gray day when he was free—free of slavery, but not free of being used for the purposes of others—Washington came up from his daily sojourn in the mines where Washington Ferguson had cast him feeling sick and worn down, put out by his labors and discouraged by his present prospects. A neighbor, seeing his mood, offered him candy "to cheer me up and make me feel better." The proffered candy was pleasing to the boy's eye, and so he eagerly hied home to enjoy the pleasures he knew it would offer. Once home, however, his mother had another diagnosis. Knowing better his true needs, she insisted, "it was not candy I needed, but a good big dose of vermifuge." This was a brand-name product supposed to eliminate worms; it was marketed then like a patent medicine as a cure-all, Washington recalled, "for almost every real and imaginary ailment." It was also "about the worst tasting and smelling medicine, I firmly believe, that was ever concocted." Washington, taking what he knew to be the worst part and spurning his mother's prescription," took the candy and put the vermifuge aside." That decision was to his regret: the next day he felt no better and the day after he was worse. By then he knew what he would have to do. Finally heeding Mother Jane, he would take his medicine: "So I threw back my head and held my nose while my mother forced the nasty stuff down with a large spoon." The next day he felt better.[53]

Whether the patent medicine actually worked, or was merely a placebo (or, perhaps, more likely, had as its main ingredient alcohol) is not important. Neither is it important whether Washington actually had worms or something else the dose treated; nor whether he was able simply to exercise will power over the ailment, control his symptoms with his mind. No one of these questions about the tangible matter of cause and cure makes the slightest bit of difference. It is, Washington suggests, the turn of mind that allows one to make evident proof of one's willingness to be cured, to submit to the taking of one's medicine, that makes all the difference. He felt better, and indeed, he was better not because he was now rid of the mines and the whole sorry situation his stepfather created for him, but rather in the same way Horatio Alger's characters are better than their surroundings, and thus able to live decently in indecent circumstances.

But this was the limit of Jane Ferguson's good ministrations: she could assist him in the attainment of a proper sense of his responsibilities but not save him from those circumstances. Booker bided his time, or rather made useful his time in the mines by seeking to cipher the nature of numbers and words from "the letters and figures" marked on the sides of barrels into which salt was packed; at times, he paid luckier children able to attend school to tutor him, and poured over a Webster's "blue-back spelling book" his mother had somehow procured for him.[54] Like Alger's heroes, he was made ready for salvation, but young Booker still needed an angel.

%%%

AT THE low point in his life, when Frederick Douglass felt himself "made to drink the bitterest dregs of slavery," he took advantage of rare moments of leisure to stand on a spot overlooking the Chesapeake Bay, "whose broad bosom was ever white with sails." He stood there to "pour out my soul's complaint": "O God, save me! God, deliver me! Let me be free!" And, as if in response to his lament, "the moving multitude of ships" appeared before him as freedom's "swift-winged angels."[55]

In Washington's account, his being cast into the salt and coal, not slavery, was the low point in his life, made worse than slavery because slavery and the uncertainty and want it produced were only temporary. Now that real freedom (through education and effort) was obtainable, and with it the opportunity to make fast work of the impediments before him, he found only that this freedom was less a clear field than a thicket, with not just white hands, but black hands, like branches and briers, slowing his pace. Into this miserable scene comes salvation, taking the form, not of the incognito blood relation of the Alger story, but a variant on that theme: the friendly savior coming on in the second to last act like a fairy godmother. Here, in Washington's story, she arrives in the person of a white woman, Viola Ruffner, who Washington "soon learned to look upon her as one of my best friends."[56]

Viola Ruffner was the wife of General Lewis Ruffner, and in contrast to her greater relative importance in Washington's rise, it was mainly on account of the general, rather than any special contribution of her own, that the couple composed one of the two or three leading families in Malden. They became, according to Harlan, "the proto-types of those Southerners 'of the better class' with whom Booker Washington later sought alliance."[57] The husband, in his sixties when Washington encountered him, had married before, fathering a large family of children before his wife died in the 1840s. He had long been in charge of the extensive salt and coal mining operation the family owned. Before the war he was the owner of a considerable number of slaves (twenty-six by the 1860 count) but, too, a larger number of white workers, then and later, added to his coffers. He was a member of the American Colonization Society, and like other ambivalent, betwixt-and-between Virginians before him, simultaneously holding onto to the slaves who made him wealthy and, seemingly with equal resolution, holding onto the principle that the nation would be better rid of Negroes. He opposed secession, and when hostilities broke out in 1861 he did his part in the forming of West Virginia, joined the Republicans, and served as a major general in the state militia. After the war, he remained a significant figure in Republican politics and in business.

In her early fifties when Washington met her, Viola Knapp Ruffner, for her part, was no Southerner, unionist or otherwise. She was born poor in Vermont, and worked hard to win an education only to find that Vermonter parsimony extends to teacher salaries as with all other matters fiscal. She taught in schools in North Carolina and New Jersey; it was from there that she secured for herself a situation as governess to Ruffner's motherless children. Some time thereafter she married her employer and with him had two children.

The Ruffners lived in a large house on a hill built to accommodate his large first family, but by 1867 occupied only by General and Mrs. Ruffner while their son and daughter were away at school. While in the mines, Washington heard of an opening in the household, and so he sought and won the job of

Mrs. Ruffner's houseboy. The change in his life was as if from night to day, or how a Malden miner might feel climbing out of General Ruffner's mine (the opening was called "Ruffner's Gate") for the last time before moving on to brighter pastures. His four or five years with the Ruffners inaugurated just such a new day for Washington, her strictures and the eventual trust she invested in him washing away the squalor and degradation to which he had been exposed like dust beneath a summer's rain. It was, he writes, "the most valuable part of my education."[58] But of just what did this change consist?

Some opportunistic aspects to the change are incontrovertible: he was allowed to attend school part of the time, and, boarding with a retired teacher with a willingness, as she said, to "help and direct" his course of study, who "encouraged and sympathized with me in all my efforts to get an education," allowed him to make rapid progress daily or more often, nightly, when fellow students paid off by Washington tutored him on missed lessons.[59]

Another candidate is business. Mrs. Ruffner had a substantial garden, and Washington, after a time, began peddling produce up and back the road from Malden to Charleston. It was work of which he became "very fond."[60] But despite his fondness then and his later emphasis on economic enterprise, Washington never participated in wholesale or retail marketing again (discounting his secret control of a number of newspapers and his widely successful efforts at marketing himself as an entrepreneur of racial good will, neither of which were, in the main, profit seeking ventures).[61]

The proper conclusion is that there is something intangible that comes from the relationship, a magic quality to their intercourse that, he writes, "I confess to you, in a large measure enable me to do the work for which I am given credit,"[62] an ineffable thing that set him on his course, gave logic and trajectory to his rise, a purposefulness to his passage upward with the assistance of a succession of white people like Mrs. Ruffner and her husband, the first in a succession of white fathers, who awakened in him a new sense of "pride and hope."[63] Closer examination, however, suggests a more narrow and personal meaning to the relationship when he actually experienced it, and that the idea of race relations holds rather more significance in solving the ideological dilemmas of the Negro problem than the practical problems of Negroes.

%%%

IN SEEKING to make sense of Washington's later project for segregated America, once race relations becomes the means to ameliorate conditions for African Americans and to solve the Negro problem, one response is to wonder if only there were indeed enough white women to go around to satisfy all the worthy black young men who could benefit from their experience and culture. That such a response came from the ruder sort of pro-segregation controversialist should not take away from its inevitability. Thus Dixon and others of his ilk would insist that Washington's covert scheme was to effect race amalgamation—mulattoization and subsequently quadroonification, and onward to an octoroonized America (as one imagines the benighted users of those inherently racist nouns might spin them off into the ether of their nightmares). They cast the same stones at the NAACP throughout the age of segregation, Dixon's labeling it "Villard's interracial marriage service" being a notable early example.[64] This mocking, humorous gambit, of indeterminate effectiveness (and a precursor to the harsher fighting words of "would you want one to marry your daughter") was not solely a weapon in the arsenal of the army against social equality. Washington, too, used it against the liberal rivals, covertly fostering negative publicity against a 1911 "black and white dinner" of the Cosmopolitan Club in New York City planned and attended by a number of individuals actively involved in the NAACP. (Washington's desired effect was presumably achieved when the ensuing coverage took the tone of "Fashionable White Women at Board with Negroes, Japs and Chinamen to Promote Their 'Cause'—Yellow and Black Representatives Show Most Enthusiasm" and "Intermarriage of Kinky-Haired Peoples with Caucasians Keynote of Blow-Out at Cafe Boulevard—Africans Have Time of Their Lives, But the Waiters Are Sorely Puzzled.")[65] There may be something ironic about Washington, having inaugurated the idea that social reform may be effected by racial reconciliation, attacking efforts to embody the solution to the Negro problem he did more than anyone else to create (while also demonstrating the lengths to which he was quite willing to go once rivals sought, unwittingly or otherwise, to steal his race relations thunder).

Nonetheless, the rearing of the social equality bugaboo in the form of a tableau of unseemly intimacy or merely absurdity is an inevitable consequence of the looseness of Washington's formulation of just what he gained through his intercourse with Mrs. Ruffner and the direction to which it aimed.[66] However, just as fairy tales cannot work if every child has a fairy godmother—a point about which Alger was certainly cognizant—the romantic edifice of his salvation should rather be seen as the elaboration of his personal exceptionalness in contrast to the general Negro rule, not about social equality but a critique of black worthiness.

Here, again, Douglass's story provides the illuminating antecedent.

%%%

IN "THE history of American slavery epitomized in a single human experience,"[67] a bright black boy is transferred from one division of an extended family enterprise to another where he is a houseboy brought into happy contact with a transplanted Yankee woman who, recognizing his gifts, begins to teach him to read. In the subsequent history of a freed boy that becomes an autobiographical solving of the Negro problem, a bright black boy gains a transfer from one division of a family enterprise to another where he is a houseboy brought into happy contact with a transplanted Yankee woman who, recognizing his gifts, assists him in his rise to true freedom. In the former case, the Northern woman, "a kind and tender-hearted" Yankee woman, a weaver who had made her own way in the world practicing her trade before her marriage ended that career, first encountered the slave boy with her heart and head free from "the blighting and dehumanizing effects of slavery." Teaching him to read followed from her supposition of how "one human being ought to treat another." Their tutorial together was barely begun when it was aborted by her husband. Thomas Auld, more experienced in the exigencies and requirements of administering human property, intervened because of his belief that teaching Frederick to read would spell his ruination as a slave, making him " 'unmanageable' " for his master's part, and " 'discontented and unhappy' " for his own, that slaves must be made to remain "in mental darkness." Although redemption comes to this sad situation in the message Douglass gleaned from his owner's prohibition, for Sophia Auld the result was strictly malign once she "commenced to practise her husband's precepts." Douglass recalled that "the fatal poison of irresponsible power was already in her hands, and soon commenced its infernal work. That cheerful face, under the influence of slavery soon became red with rage; that voice, made all of sweet accord, changed to one of harsh and horrid discord; that angelic face gave place to that of a demon." Sophia Auld was transformed into a wretch by slavery, but Douglass discovered one key to his freedom in the uncoupling of his fate from the vicissitudes of white mastery.[68] It may be that had Sophia Auld continued her instruction of young Frederick, he, with the same sort of personality and intelligence, would have been the slave who stayed to home; that, however, would be a different sort of slavery from what was practiced in the American South, a slavery of a more ancient vintage unimaginable, as men such as Auld surmised, with the nearby siren song of liberty calling him to escape, the white-winged angels spied from the banks of the Chesapeake pointing north toward freedom.

In contrast to the sad dissolution of the nascent friendship between Auld and Douglass, Ruffner and Washington began a friendship important to both parties that lasted until her death in 1904, and that Washington would use it as a perfect illustration of the differences between slavery and freedom and the possibilities for good and mutually productive race relations once, crucially, the chains of servitude, psychological as much as physical, were broken. Here he is, a free boy, once again under the control of whites, but this regime of race relations, unlike slavery with the Burroughs, pointed upward toward personal growth and self-realization.

Other boys had found their way into Mrs. Ruffner's employ, but none was able to stick beyond a few weeks. Washington explains this as their being undone by the high, New England standards of "order and cleanliness and truth" she demanded. He, too, was for more than a little while cowed by her, even quaking in her presence. "He left me," she recalled, "half a dozen times," but always returned.[69] Washington's phrasing is the more telling. "I ran away," he writes, like a slave taking flight rather than a free man taking leave from a job; ran away, indeed, to the Ohio River (like so many slaves before him), and hired on with a steamboat captain plying the route between Malden and Cincinnati. But soon he returned to her and "acknowledged my sins."[70] He may have realized the absurdity of his flight and the fact that back at the Ruffners lay not iniquitous bondage but good opportunity. Ultimately, he came to see Mrs. Ruffner's standards as a godsend, writing that even years later that "I never see bits of paper scattered around a house or in the street that I do not want to pick them up at once. I never see a filthy yard that I do not want to clean it, a paling off of a fence that I do not want to put it on, an unpainted or unwhitewashed house that I do not want to paint or whitewash it, or a button off one's clothes, or a grease-spot on them or on a floor, that I do not want to call attention to it."[71]

As a consequence of Washington's studious cultivation of this image of himself, it has been concluded that the main value of the relationship was his imbibing of Mrs. Ruffner's own hatred of dirt and his inculcation of "the New England message of cleanliness and good order."[72] (Another conclusion is that it was more a reaction to his long night in the general's dusty dungeon, with coal dust clogging his pores, mouth and nose, that caused his antipathy to dirt, but that too might best be seen by him laid at his stepfather's feet.)

Washington later constantly stressed the importance of his teaching the Negroes the value of keeping proper toilet and personal hygiene—his version of industrial education included "that each pupil should come to school clean, should have his or her hands and face washed and hair combed and should keep the buttons on his or her clothing,"[73] and he willingly and lengthily expounded on the significance of "the use of the tooth-brush" in the Tuskegee system, and its effect "in bringing about a higher degree of civilization among the students."[74] This was of such importance to him that he even proposed "a chair in some strong university for the science of scrubbing." (He elaborated: "Yes, the common art of scrubbing. Seldom do we see clean floors; the art seems to have passed away.")[75] Cleanliness was next to self-reliance, untidiness a close kin of sloth and indolence, and the education too many Negroes received tended only to make matters worse, ill fitting them for the tasks of freedom. "One of the saddest sights," he ever witnessed, "was a colored girl, recently returned from college, sitting in a rented one-room log-cabin attempting day by day to extract some music from a second-hand piano, when all about her indicated want of thrift and cleanliness."[76] Then there was the black college man, a French scholar, encountered when Washington was a child: "I noted the poverty, the untidiness, the want of system and thrift, that existed about the cabin, notwithstanding his knowledge of French and other academic studies."[77]

At the height of his power Washington will receive correspondence from critics, usually of the friendly sort, pressing him on the matter of his publicizing of negative portrayals of African Americans—his scoring of them for their lack of hygiene or resistance to work. One such writer, a civilian in the wars over Washington's leadership, wondered if his constant telling of "chicken stealing" jokes did not have a detrimental effect on the white regard for black people and on black people's own self-conception. "It may be foolish of me to think of such things," she continued, "and I want you to tell me what you think about it." Washington's reply was that a race that can laugh at itself is a race that has gone a long way toward recognizing its problems and then solving them: "My experience teaches me . . . that white people have a good deal more respect for us when we tell them on ourselves than they do when we try to make ourselves believe there are no such jokes going around."[78] Scrutiny is a welcome thing, a judgment no honest, right-living person need fear. There are two ways of helping the Negro, Washington would tell the First National Conference on Race Betterment in 1914. This is done, first, "by praising him just a little more" when he does right, and, second and all the rest of the time, "by being frank with him, telling him about his faults."[79]

This is what had gone wrong after emancipation. Black people in the great leap from slavery to freedom, in their hubris and haste to taste the fruits of freedom, had turned their backs on white people and the best standards by which the best white people judged themselves.[80] "It is with the ignorant race as with a child: it craves at first the superficial, the ornamental signs of progress rather than the reality. The ignorant race is tempted to jump, at one bound, to the position that it has required years of hard struggle for others to reach."[81]

Changing the analogy makes the problem as Washington saw it become clearer. The lesson of civilization, as Washington would later put it, is that "freedom comes through seeming restriction."[82] The reality as it applies to black people after 1865 is that they leave out of prison without anyone holding their parole. The freedmen are not responsible to anyone: not to the Southern whites, not to Northern whites, and not even to themselves, owing to their underdeveloped consciences. The post-emancipation Negro, this "new race" and new to freedom, too, was not willing or able to assimilate these values and character traits; chafed, contrariwise, at the notion that taking the bridle was a good and necessary thing for them to do; could not comprehend that that was just what the white civilization had demanded of white people. Internal constraints that Anglo-Saxons had assimilated over long centuries had not been developed in them—never in Africa, not in slavery—and the external influences that might have helped were neither in the offing. The ties binding them to their traditional minders, the Southern whites, had been severed by the war and by the meddlings of carpetbaggers. All of this caused them to exist in an individually indulgent, corporately irresponsible and disorganized fashion, surviving on credit, for example, or living parasitically off others or the government till.

Picture dandies and fops cakewalking on a high wire with fancy little parasols good for show if not for balance; these Negroes were bound to fall and without a net to save them. It is an image of the freedpeople largely in keeping with the type of Thomas Nast caricature appearing in popular magazines in the late 1860s and afterward; a black world of bounders and jackanapes and coxcombs. They put on their flamboyant outfits, their fancy ribbons and bows, they skulk around back alleys shooting craps and gambling, quick with a blade or a blackjack, a scheme or a confidence game, and promenade down busy streets, crowding out decent folks. Adding to this image is Washington's disparagement of the "educated Negro" who takes up geography with not a clue as to where he really is, who learns Latin and Greek but refuses to communicate politely to his neighbors. The younger generation of freedpeople and those born after slavery scoff at the labors and the endurance of their formerly enslaved parents (who, "ignorant as they were," if nothing else, "taught us patience"),[83] but develop no means of support in the trades or service or agriculture for their own livelihoods.

Washington typically tells the stories of such archetypes in the vein of one of his humorous anecdotal homilies intended, as Howells recognized, to soften the sting of the offense taken by white persons at black misbehavior. As well, they present an opportunity for Washington to suggest that the inevitable comparison of grand white achievement and black people's more modest deeds is an invidious one, that, in the white regard, the Negro should not be judged "too quickly or too harshly" given from whence he came.[84] On the other hand, any party seeking the resuscitation of Washingtonianism, or wishing to claim he said one thing, meant another, and secretly accomplished three or four good things to help the Negro has to contend with the strong concordance between his portrayal of the bungling of freedom and Reconstruction and the dominant views of his time disparaging "black" Reconstruction. A part of those holding such views constituted the intellectual wing of the national movement to cast African Americans out of civil society. And while this bit of entertainment may somewhere or other have its desired effect (and at least lead to funds being placed at Washington's disposal), one has to wonder whether, in propagating an image of black people as leeches and fools, its effect is rather less than amusing.

Washington insists that the source of black people's predicament lies in internal and intangible elements; that it is the Negro's own folly, creature of the deficit within him in the intangible elements of higher civilization, that in turn create the predicament of bad race relations: pretentiousness, high living, the rush for the outlandish and showy but shoddy, and other ways of acting such that inevitably it would "alienate his Southern white neighbours from him."[85] W. E. B. Du Bois's statement of this matter is too subtle. It is not Washington's picturing of "a lone black boy poring over a French grammar amid the weeds and dirt of a neglected home," Du Bois would write, that is "the acme of absurdities." The caricature is, in fact, broader than that. The aggregate of his portrayals of black misbehavior might better be imagined in the figure of a black bounder in an alley with that French grammar under his arm, waiting for the other idlers, scroungers and parasites and similarly feckless girls who have rejected their mother's industry, to make their way (as Washington suggested at Atlanta) to the opera house. And while Du Bois "wonders what Socrates and St. Francis of Assisi would say to this," there is a firm historical record of what white Americans said and what they did.[86]

The kinds of activities Washington describes—these black deeds, products, he would say, of racial proclivities and inclinations as well as of society—are those that are bound to get under white persons' skin; those ill behaviors that will create the category of "uppity" that will become the long-lived catchall for certain kinds of Negroes, and the equally long-lived justification for violence, entrapments, and other double-standard ways of punishing black people for the improprieties white people, high and low, usually get away with.

If his opposition to black misbehavior sounds like the white South's position, it is different in relevant ways. Washington has a more complicated opposition to black extravagance of dress, their saunter and strut. He would not do it, to be sure. It offends one's neighbors and others with the potential to offer one something along business lines, or education, or other useful intercourse. It is not good for the general demeanor of black America. It is not dignified, as well as not realistic, and harms black people's self-respect because it perpetuates the false knowledge that black people are something they are not. The substance of this thinking as far as Washington's directions to black people is one matter. But what of Washington's effects on white thinking, North and South?

Commenting on Washington's propensity to make sport of black people before white audiences, Ida B. Wells-Barnett felt certain that he was well aware "that the Negro is the butt of ridicule with the average white American, and that the aforesaid American enjoys nothing so much as a joke which portrays the Negro as illiterate and improvident; a petty thief or a happy-go-lucky inferior." This knowledge was, indeed, the secret of his success with the whites who "hail with acclaim the man who has made popular the unspoken thought of that part of the North which believes in the inherent inferiority of the Negro, and the always outspoken Southern view to the same effect."[87]

His publicizing the Negro's weaknesses was a part of an attempt to create for the Negro behavioral benchmarks that were once operational slavery, to lay the Negro open to the healing powers of harsh judgment, "whether honest and candour for the time being pleases or displeases him."[88] Or, as he said on another occasion: "We can benefit a race only as we can an individual, and that is by dealing honestly, truthfully with it—by giving it that truth which shall make it free indeed."[89]

Upon his first encounter with Mrs. Ruffner, Washington himself had turned away, and time and again sought refuge from her strict scrutiny. This was his sin, self-confessed and amends made; that, as when he was sick and rejected the vermifuge, he initially rebelled at Mrs. Ruffner's good prescription, but he returned to her, took his medicine, and learned from her those things essential to learning to stand on one's own feet. His embrace of the scrutiny of white people is a part of his conception of how he rose— his separating himself from other African Americans—and likewise it is a solution for black people's problems. "If only they too could pass the test," one might hear sympathetic persons say, with a blithe disregard for the contradiction at the heart of the challenge.

※※※

WASHINGTON LIVED with the Ruffners, off and on, for the next four or five years, and describes his contact with them as the key to his understanding of freedom and central to the later project of Washingtonianism. His experience there in this good race relation and its effects on him cause problems only to those who choose to read Washington critically. Here is the problem. His constant advice to black people is to embrace the work before them, challenging them to be "perfectly conscientious" whether working in a field, a factory or some other pursuit.[90] But faced with the work in the mines, he scrambles out to find work in a white woman's house, and callously dishonors his stepfather in one smooth move. Following his own advice, he would have stayed in the mines. Added to the hypocrisy is bad faith; what warrant does he have to conclude that black people's problem is an absence of hygienic mores rather than the availability of the wherewithal, such as toothbrushes and clean running water, that are the means of such good habits? And piled atop the bad faith is an absurdity: since as a slave Washington was a houseboy and in freedom he ended up following the same line of work—what type of progress does that represent? How hard could his work for Mrs. Ruffner be—when he was eleven or twelve is one thing, but did it pose the same difficulties at sixteen?

It is hard not to conclude that the whole banquet of platitudes Washington serves up is but his effort at pandering to white prejudices. May this simply be, as Harlan suggests, the inaugural of Washington showing two faces to the world, one for white consumption, the other facing into the black?[91] The advantage of the idea of there being two Washingtons is that it clarifies a seeming contradiction in his story. That contradiction might be phrased in this way: one can conceive of Washington's submission to Mrs. Ruffner's strictures as leading to him turning into a very good houseboy for her or some other equally lowly pursuit, but in no wise does her scrutiny make realistic sense as the source of his later prominence as, his supporters would say, a very good leader of black people. He would have stayed to home—in her home in Malden—but he would not have ended up running a college in Alabama; he would have wound up cleaning rooms, rather than raising money and running the Tuskegee machine out of hotel rooms all over the country. To say he is two-faced is to call into question the genuineness of his expressed experience. This may contribute to consideration of the riddle of Washington's personality, or "multiple personalities," as Harlan would have it,[92] but this way of reconciling questions about his youthful psyche and questions about his later politics rather disserves both. As an alternative, one might give more serious attention to what might be made of his relationship to Mrs. Ruffner, from whom he received his first lessons in the ideology of the Negro problem.

%.%.%.

IN SHARP contrast to Frederick Douglass's momentary mentor, Auld, before her fall from grace, Viola Ruffner seems to have been quite miserable before Washington met her. In the accounts collected by his biographer, a portrait of her emerges as a sad and lonely, seemingly friendless woman, often anxious and forlorn, occasionally hysterical. She was the second wife, alienated (as sometimes happens) from her husband's grown children, who had once been in her charge. But added to that troubled dynamic was her cultural difference, a kind of foreignness to those parts. A Northerner in the rural South, she appears in Washington's description and that of others as a lonely and solemn avatar, there in her transplanted redoubt upon a West Virginia hill, of shut-in Yankee virtues, besieged by the surrounding coarseness of what to her were slipshod Southern folkways. And given her origins in egalitarian, unchanging Vermont, perhaps equally beset by the tracked-in dirt stirred up by an overabundance of too-rapid social change and too great a distance dividing the different elements of the local populace. "She is a perfectly unique person," said one of the general's kin just before Washington came into her life, "the most sensitive person I ever saw," but due to that she was most of the time "the very embodiment of wretchedness."[93]

It cannot be said for certain that her hiring of Washington made a significant change in her mental health, but probably it did. What is clear is that however she felt about herself she was quite willing to take the measure of those around her, and in the case of the African Americans she spied from her perch, to judge them especially harshly. One imagines her fussing about in her rooms, almost a prisoner there, contemplating the quiet dust settling momentarily upon floors and furniture, and the loud Negroes making spectacles of themselves out of doors, in alleyways, and unsettled streets. The former is the muse of poets, the latter of pundits of the Negro problem. And she was indeed a racial pundit of the advanced amateur sort, combining the wisdom of her two fields of expertise into words of wisdom for the boy and later the man. Down to the end of her life, half-blind and infirm, she was divesting herself of her opinion (in an 1899 letter to "Dear Booker") on just what was wrong with black people to the effect that "they are still too much influenced by the past & make little effort to be independent by their own efforts. Those about the place are still under the influence of slavery."[94] Washington, on the other hand, was different, she told an interviewer: "He never needed correction or the word 'Hurry!' or 'Come!' for he was always ready for his book. There was nothing peculiar in his habits except that he was always in his place and never known to do anything out of the way," which, she concluded, "has been his course all thru life."[95] Washington attributes those good qualities to her tutelage, but the success it brought him, and not those other boys who failed to shape up, had more to do with him than simply good fortune or luck, a notion he told Tuskegee student was "nonsense."[96]

Instead, he earned his way into Mrs. Ruffner's good graces, subjecting himself to her scrutiny, embracing her challenges to him, and passing her tests. This sets a pattern for him of rising to the occasion when hurdles come his way, turning his taking of those short hurdles into great leaps forward in his apprehension of life's reality.

‰‰‰

THESE ARE the origins of Washingtonianism, the onset of the notion of him as a man of action, the start of his discovery of the race relations idea as a solution to the Negro problem. Mrs. Ruffner is the first to grant him that laurel. She herself recognized that the work she asked of him was not especially difficult. On the question of whether she had any inkling that his sights were set on occupations higher than being a career houseboy, no evidence survives. "He seemed peculiarly determined to emerge from his obscurity," she recalled, "ever restless, uneasy, as if knowing that contentment would mean inaction."[97] Such a comment, consistent with the way many black people noticed him, is proof of her sensitivity, and the bond they shared. But it is evidence of her own hubris that she registered no surprise at his high stature, a testament in her mind, perhaps, to the way the inculcation of personal fastidiousness translates into a general occupational competence, portable into any field of endeavor including race leadership. This is so because in the successful intercourse between them, the transfer of values she presented him, the specific skills gained are not what is important, but the mentality attained; not in the work, any work, but in the manifesting of the willingness to work; not in a job well done, but in the unctuous commotion with which he shows himself getting the job done. It was not obsessiveness that caused Washington to clean the room at Hampton three or four or five times. This seems absurd, when efficiency and common sense would indicate doing it once and right. But the scrutiny of women like Viola Ruffner and his Hampton teacher (another white woman who became "one of my strongest and most helpful friends")[98] is not especially about efficiency; their aim as taskmasters is not a kind of thumbnail Taylorism. Their demand is for art more than science, the flourishes of culture more than bottom-line outputs of economies, a pantomime of toil sufficient to satisfy Mrs. Ruffner's own jackleg version of the Negro problem. The show is the action, polishing the apple, or more precisely, scrapping away the incrusted barnacles off a boat left in the river too long. And how it moves the white scrutinizers to feel is action, too, as they witness him transmute their ideal Negro, which is also their idea of what is wrong with the Negro, into reality, thus freeing him of his predicament and, in the case of Mrs. Ruffner, elevating her morose contemplation of her predicament. Their agreement, the meeting of minds, the black and the white, is action as well, a movement of theoretical possibility: they did it together, joined in good race relations, and so why not others? Put another way: if one Negro can escape then why not all? If only one Negro does win this white embrace then he is the exception that proves the rule that probably most Negroes are not really worthy of that sympathetic support. If Washington says they are both worthless and worthy, broken but fixable, and that he will fix them then his worthiness is all the greater.

Therein, Washington would say, lies a real test of "my worthiness."[99] And, equally, therein lies both his claim and his platform for leadership, a dream of good race relations spread out like a balm over the whole of the nation wherever black people are needful and resent it, and wherever white people are disappointed and resent them; there Washington would be, the key man holding the whole of the regime together.

%%%

ONE DAY while out peddling Mrs. Ruffner's produce, Washington was approached by an older man of his acquaintance, who snatched one of his employer's peaches, and then, with the half-joshing, half-threatening tone of bullies everywhere, asked Washington to make him a gift of it. Though younger and smaller than his accoster, Washington stood his ground, got back the Ruffnerian peach, and sent the bully on his way, if not fully chastened, then at least with his paper-thin bravado slightly tattered.[100]

The experience of encounters like this one, along with the assistance of white helpers like Mrs. Ruffner, are some of the substance from which

Washingtonianism is formed, aphorisms and platitudes that are derived from his experience, bright pearls of wisdom that are but products of the minor irritations of dark oysters.

He tells of the misadventures of a whole cast of faulty, humorous black individuals; they are this way, to be sure, not because of their race, but because of past wrongs bearing bitter fruit. Among these are the damnable effects of slavery in its "constant tendency . . . to destroy the family life," a damage which would require years to overcome.[101] These malign consequences were readily understandable; for example, the way in which a people denied any type of standing would allow racial feeling to cloud their judgment once freedom came, listening to bad advice from selfish men, and becoming overly concerned with matters of status and form. "Ignorant and inexperienced," he said at Atlanta, "it is not strange that in the first years of our new life we began at the top instead of the bottom; that a seat in Congress or the state legislature was more sought than real estate or industrial skill; that the political convention or stump speaking had more attractions that starting a dairy farm or truck garden."[102] Pretensions to grandeur, the desire to be that which the freedpeople were not, set them on the road to ruin.[103] This was the wrong way for them, and it had more negative consequences in driving their white neighbors into colliding with them.

Matters need not have had to come to this turn, or so it might have seemed to Washington safe within the Ruffner home, as the black and the white during the first freedom and Reconstruction threw themselves at each other, flailing away in contests of greater and lesser moment. But politics was the most highly charged of these contests, black and white in violent conflict being the apotheosis of Reconstruction's disordering of race relations.

This was the time of the Ku Klux Klan, who like the slave patrols, "operated almost wholly at night," but with even greater cruelty, seeking "to crush out the political aspirations of the Negroes," but not confining themselves to those deeds, and instead putting the torch to churches and schoolhouses, and attacking not just politicians but "many innocent persons," as well. "The 'Ku Klux' period was," Washington writes, "the darkest part of the Reconstruction days."[104]

In December 1869 tensions came to a head around Malden when, as Washington tells it, a dispute between two men caused the races to array themselves against each other in angry mobs. After an initial exchange of gunfire, the black group retreated where they were met by General Ruffner, coming on at a trot and followed by his houseboy, Booker. "He tried to defend the coloured people," Washington recalled, and, in so doing, found himself interposed between the two groups. One might imagine the feelings that came over General Ruffner as he came upon the scene of free blacks and whites at each other's throats, enacting the hellish scene about which Jefferson had warned. This was the American Colonization Society nightmare now come to pass in his own backyard. And then a brickbat was flung from amid the white mob, striking General Ruffner on the head. He was knocked unconscious, "and so seriously wounded that he never completely recovered." If that was not sad enough, the general's departure from the field led to a return to the fray: "It seemed to me as I watched this struggle between members of the two races, that there was no hope for our people in this country."[105] He escaped, however, because he held himself above the fray, did not participate in the foolish charade; he kept his mind at some remove from the whole, sorry mess, aloof from the animus on each side that threatened, as race-relations believers always fret, to tear the nation apart in a bloody race war.

Here putting aside "racial feeling" stands as an Olympian objectivity: a righteous neutrality in a pointless conflict, to be sure, but more than that, a sociological and political perspective gained by distance when emotion might call one to join in on the fray. (The "friends of humanity," he advises, ought to follow his lead: "raise yourselves above yourselves, above race, above party, above everything.")[106] On the other hand, some might see in this an erroneous and self-serving, even cowardly neutrality, standing aside in a righteous conflict. But even those critics will have to admit that if Washington is sinning, his sin mainly consists in failing to validate the Reconstruction partisanship as a matter of historical interpretation: his failing to contest a battle already lost in the gainsaying of that politics.

Conflict is not inevitable, Washington believes, and here he may have been in disagreement with the brave general. His experience in the Ruffner home, however, may be seen as the basis for his later ideas about "mutuality" and the "identity of interest" between the races. There, in the Ruffner preserve, it was from all according to their abilities in separate capacities—as businessman, housewife-entrepreneur, and houseboy-marketeer—and to all according to their need—the Ruffners' need for a clean and tidy house and young Booker's to not be in the mines, with the added benefit of the reward the stern, former teacher received in helping in his instruction and the benefit the boy received from that instruction. They all contributed in their separate ways and capacities for the greater good. "The wisest among my race understand that the agitation of questions of social equality is the extremest folly," and that because it is unnecessary. His own history constituting the truth of the aphorism he announced famously in Atlanta in 1895:

"In all things purely social we can be as separate as the fingers, yet one as the hand in all things essential to mutual progress."[107]

Freedom, to Washington, does not mean immersion in the river of black struggle, going with the flow of black Reconstruction, but breaking with it, departing the waters, crossing over to the other side. In freedom it was incumbent upon this free boy to cross over the river, just as slaves fleeing the South had to cross over the Ohio River. His crossing however, was not so much marked by spatial dimensions as by psychological ones: an escape freeing himself from his family, and from the false or perishable freedom that was the product of a mishandled emancipation, freeing himself through the embrace of white hands in order to face better the tests that would gain him a true and enduring freedom. This was the freedom that most other Reconstruction-era Negroes hoped or wished or demanded was theirs in a grasping misapprehension of what freedom means and a premature declaration of the river's arrival at its final destination. Washington arrived there, free and clear, an arduous portage rather than mere floating, a product of his striving and good race relations rather than conflict and bitter politics.

"It was unfortunate," Washington would later tell a group of Unitarians in New York, "that the burden of the government in the South was so largely thrown upon our shoulders."[108] It was also unfortunate that "no strong force was brought to bear preparing the Negro to become an intelligent, reliable citizen and voter." White Southerners of the better sort should have fulfilled this role of leading Negroes by keeping "in close touch and sympathy in politics," but they were otherwise preoccupied.[109] But Washington, even as a child, saw inevitability in the disaster, saw that "mistakes were being made" in Reconstruction, that policy was being made based on "a false foundation, was artificial and forced," and that "things could not remain in the condition that they were in very long." The freedpeople looked to the federal government "for everything, very much as a child looks to its mother."[110]

There were, Washington averred, two types of advisors to the Negroes. First, there were those who stand face to face with the Negro, and, with no selfish purposes at heart, speaking words black people, often, would prefer not to hear, but words of wisdom that are right and true. On the other hand, there are other advisors of selfish purpose and conniving calculation who sidle up to black ears whispering softer words filled up with pabulum and panaceas, reminding black people of old grievances and what they are owed and what they owe the Southern white man. They offer, in short, the sweet mother's milk of black dependence on the federal government, and the bitter formula of politics as a means of payback and vengeance for slavery. Black ignorance and inexperience made the freedpeople most receptive to the latter, which in turn opened the door to the unscrupulous "Carpetbagger" and treacherous "scalawag," who were, with few exceptions, users of Negroes just as mean and greedy as slavers and slaveholders had once been, "yield[ing] to the temptation to use them as a means to lift themselves into political power and eminence."[111]

Similarly, Republican politicians sought "to punish the Southern white men by forcing the Negro into positions over the heads of the Southern whites." This resulted—because of the venality behind it, because of its violation of the merit principle—in a distortion in politics, which Washington believed, in its natural functioning, should work to enable the able to rise to the top, and the less able to stay in their lesser, but safe place. The distortion led to a black political class in Reconstruction that Washington characterized (again holding out some exceptions) not as able men sensibly concerned with making friends with their white neighbors and harmonizing the interests of the two races, but as clever careerists and trimmers, as well as far too many fools and buffoons weighing in on questions well beyond their competence and weighing down the interests of the race almost to the point of drowning the whole of it. Washington wrote: "I saw coloured men who were members of state legislatures, and county officers, who, in some cases, could not read or write, and whose morals were as weak as their educations." "Not long ago," he related, "when passing through the streets of a certain city in the South, I heard some brick-masons calling out, from the top of a two-storey brick building on which they were working, for the 'Governor' to 'hurry up and bring up some more bricks'. . . . My curiosity was aroused to such an extent that I made inquiry as to who the 'Governor' was, and soon found that he was a coloured man who at one time had held the position of Lieutenant-Governor of his state." While this anecdote has the happy result of the 'Governor' ultimately falling to his appropriate station in life, Washington's point was that "the general political agitation drew the attention of our people away from the more fundamental matters of perfecting themselves in the industries at their doors," securing property, and making friends of their neighbors, the whites.[112] Instead, Reconstruction politics, the tenor of which, Washington held, was rooted in bitterness over slavery and the war, became itself the source of even greater bitterness on the part of Southern whites.

In the education field, as with politics, the Reconstruction period saw the distortion of black life and the problem of bad leadership. Indeed, Washington claimed there were "two ideas constantly agitating the minds of the coloured people, or at least, the minds of a large part of the race. One of these was the craze for Greek and Latin learning, and the other was a desire to hold office." During the era in every part of the South, schools, "both day and night, were filled to overflowing with people of all ages and conditions, some being as far along in age as sixty and seventy years." The freedpeople's desire—"the ambition to secure an education" as a way out of poverty and ignorance—would have been all to the good, "most praiseworthy and encouraging," were it not in part the product of the former slaves' flight from the responsibilities of labor; that "in some unexplainable way" once educated one "would be free from most of the hardships of the world, and . . . could live without manual labour." Those who became teachers, as well as those who ministered to the black faithful, embodied this notion that "a little education" provided a means to "an easy way to make a living." They were as ignorant as their charges, and less principled. On the scene, of course, was that Washington perennial, the source of more humor than any other component of his public utterances, the "dis Darkey am called to preach" faker. And there were teachers too, "of this type," like the prospective educator who wandered into Malden one day scrounging for employment. When the question arose "as to the shape of the earth and how he would teach the children concerning this subject," the man explained, "he was prepared to teach that the earth was either flat or round, according to the preference of a majority of his patrons."[113]

What all this amounted to in terms of the future interests of the African American people, Washington believed, was a disaster of inestimable proportions. "The crucial test for a race," he would tell the centennial convention of the A.M.E. Church, "as for an individual, is its ability to stand upon its own feet."[114] This is as civilized people do of necessity, but equally because it is their way, a product of their very breeding: "The very fact that the white boy is conscious that, if he fails in life, he will disgrace the whole family record, extending back through many generations, is of tremendous value in helping him to resist temptations. The fact that the individual has behind and surrounding him proud family history and connection serves as a stimulus to help him to overcome obstacles when striving for success."[115]

And so the boy was at odds with his environment and the orthodoxy embraced by too many black people in the age of Reconstruction. Washington recalled one of the first of his encounters with this orthodoxy in his initial enrollment in the local school for free children. His teacher, he writes, claimed "that the chief object of education was to enable one to speak and write the English language correctly." Precociously, Washington sensed that this was not true. "While at that time I could not formulate my ideas well enough to express disagreement with my teacher . . . this definition grated rather harshly upon my ears, and did not seem satisfactory to my reason." He thought of his mother, "at the very moment . . . living in the most abject poverty and want," and wondered how correctly articulated words could help him "make life a little more bearable—and, if possible, even attractive—for her." It seemed to him that there was more to education and the struggle of life than that: "I wondered if my ability to speak and write correctly was going to fit me to help very much in relieving the condition of our family."[116]

As it turned out, Washington's "ability to speak and write correctly," was precisely what he decided on as the best means of his achieving a successful career. Grammatical matters, as he suggests, were not the key to his success, but rather the political and ideological correctness recognizable in his story of how he learned to stand on his own feet. One might say this is not a true story about how he came to be, that there are other ways of rising that Washington buried in his past. That would be truer story than the one Washington tells. On the other hand, simply disproving Washington's autobiographical account explains neither why he dissembled nor, more important, how he came to see the need for leaving those other Washingtons behind him. Inquiry into the shape of some of his earliest dreaming provides a way of answering both those questions.

※※※

ONE WONDERS at the fine mess Americans fixed themselves with in the era of Reconstruction. And wonders, too—even in spite of the way the literature of the period has been so well reformed since the civil rights era of the late 1950s and 1960s—at what a paradox the period represents. It does not fit comfortably within the neatly ordered pattern in American history of black people set in their subordination. This was a condition so normal in other times that Americans able to count on little else remaining the same amid the whirlwind expansion of the United States could count on the Negro's being in place: down in the dirt and mud of the farm or attentively waiting next to sideboards or in kitchens, held still for beck and call. There are, of course, exceptions to the rule, scattered around in antebellum times and post-Reconstruction—these make up the river of black struggle. But the striking feature of the history of the Negro problem in antebellum times and in the age of Washington and afterward is just how little actual big trouble African Americans caused.

Reconstruction cannot be made to fit comfortably within the general narrative. In the Reconstruction era, those efforts at black empowerment were the rule rather than the exception. It was the river's realization, with black people's hopes and aspirations no longer locked down by institutional authority or legal dictate, the margin becoming the mainstream of their own lives, their course coming together with an American promise previously denied them. (A very fine illustration of this point is an 1872 drawing of Lincoln County, Georgia, voters fording a stream with guns held aloft on their way to the polls.)[117] But the river was dammed or diverted or strangled down to a trickle, and because this was so it is possible to deny Reconstruction's reality. Or diminish it with false analogies, such as calling the civil rights movement of the 1950s and 1960s a "second Reconstruction" and thus missing the fact that what was lost in the earlier era could hardly have been regained in the more narrow enterprise of the more recent time. This was the promise of freedom, and then the defeat, counted in the dashed hopes of the freedpeople for land and independence and a republican self-sovereignty, and lesser aspirations for political power as an armor and a weapon against the forces arrayed against them. The nation sped forward through seventy or eighty years of Jim Crow down to the time of the civil rights movement and the commencement of legal changes and the gaining of greater opportunities, and it would seem the height of ingratitude to say that a quarter-century of special attention does not outweigh the loss of three-quarters of a century of normal access to the levers and means of rising in American life, of movement within institutions, the accumulation of experience and acquaintanceships, of democratic participation and wheeling and dealing in the acquisition and distribution of resources, the calculations of conflict and compromise.

To master the time—to make it more in keeping with the rest of American history—Americans, if they have occasion to think about it at all, might make it a mere precursor to the civil rights era; and, if so, Reconstruction is not important for its own sake. Or they might hold that nothing of lasting importance was accomplished then; and if that were true, then the efforts of African Americans were in vain and of no account—another generation of helpless victims of American white supremacy. They may see it thus because of the civil rights movement's triumph and the diminishing of the degree to which they and their compatriots are willing to participate in certain of the rituals of race relations. While some aspects of our social and intellectual life have surely changed, others just as surely have not; this is especially so with regard to the conventions of historical memory. Americans today, as a general matter, do not see the era of Reconstruction all that differently from how they did in the age of Washington (despite the good efforts of some historians). So it is and so it was. A quarter-century removed from Reconstruction and "the troublous character of the times,"[118] and with three or four decades of Gilded Age rising and fortunes being made and work being done behind them, Americans under Washington's spell looked backward to say that Reconstruction was an especially bad period in race relations that now, with luck, will get better.

But there is the rub. Reconstruction was a time of disorder and tumult and the seeming chaos of real competition and conflict in town and country over the land, over politics, as well as wages and hours and conditions of labor, and the schooling of the nation's children at the South. It was a time of men and women composing themselves in their various parts—as individuals, in families and in private and public associations—seeking to find the best place for themselves in the world, restless wanderers and careful planners going about the business of being free. And it was the time's very disorder, reflected in the tumult engendered by the revolution of civil war, and constitutional amendments and the commitment of efforts by and on behalf of the freedpeople as a result of their being armored by those rights, aid, and allies that should prevent its being given the structure and calm of any sort of race relations. The period in which Washington came of age is characterized not by "race relations," but by their absence. It is a time out of the mind of the Negro problem.

※ ※ ※

RETURNING TO Malden in the autumn of 1901, nearly three decades after taking leave of the place to seek his fortune and just weeks before his dining at the White House with President Theodore Roosevelt gave evidence of his striving having brought him to the highest pinnacle of success, Washington looked out upon the small world of his first freedom and reflected. He remembered the location of his first school, the old church where he attended Sunday school, the Ruffner house where he worked as a houseboy, and the location of the first schoolhouse where he taught immediately after his graduation from the Hampton Institute. The salt furnace was gone now, the tanks and the vats and the old pump house long since removed or scavenged; only the stone chimney remained, a remnant of an industry gone to seed, a strange anachronism crumbling in a cornfield. And he remembered the mouth of the mine down into which it was his unhappy lot to travel in his first weeks of freedom in Malden; he had not forgotten, could not forget that place, his fear, and the man he felt responsible for casting him down into that purgatory. But only a purgatory and, because that was so, he could recall something else about being a boy in the place on the Kanawha River which had been his home and the hills that formed his horizons. "When I was a boy," he said, "I used to look up at these hills here, and wonder what was behind them. I used to wish that I could climb up to the top of the highest one, so that I could see what was in the great world on the other side."[119]

When he did leave Malden in 1872 after his years with the Ruffners, venturing out to test himself in the wider world, he did so with a clear sense of purpose in mind, determined, he recalled in 1899, "to attempt to do something to improve the conditions of the millions of my race in the far South." This is an odd, meaningful statement by Washington. Odd because of its intimation, not just of the importance of what he learned in Malden in setting his fate, but also in his experiences there giving explicit direction—southward to the Deep South—to that fate. He was but a young man in 1872, bound for Hampton, where he would spend more than two and a half vital, formative years, then back again to Malden to engage in political campaigns as well as to teach, where he stayed for four years (less a brief, ill-fated sojourn at a seminary in Washington, D.C.) before being called back to Hampton. Indeed, it was not until the summer of 1881 that Washington embarked on his life's work at Tuskegee, more than eight years before he set foot in the Deep South and began his work with the benighted masses of the black belt and began his proselytizing of them—but "not alone to benefit my own race"[120]—and so, too, their white neighbors on the virtues of good race relations.

His aim was set once he received his education in the intangibles of civilization: to head off for the Deep South, to sally forth as a missionary preaching the gospel of mutuality between the races. His statement of this may well spring from a desire to give logic and trajectory to his rise as a service to his later interest: to find a purposefulness to his passage upward through the assistance of white persons like Mrs. Ruffner and her husband—the first in a succession of adopted white fathers—and the Hampton principal, Samuel Chapman Armstrong, the greatest hero in his life, that selling himself in that way had to be a help in his efforts to divest white philanthropy of funds in support of Tuskegee and his other enterprises. But there may also be still more reason to believe that Washington only later invested that rise and those relationships with a higher meaning and a greater importance in his life than they did actually bear. In his endeavor to cast his dream athwart the present and future of turn of the century America, he cast backward the turn of the century's solution to the Negro problem, imposing the balm of race relations on the difficulties of his own young life.

Here are things he learned in his decade-and-a-half-long experience of freedom before he went south to Tuskegee. They can be adumbrated with some specificity: housekeeping skills and the value of white help from the Ruffners; the farce and folly of black politics; the Hampton Institute's teacher-training curriculum. The rest are intangible things: about how white persons relate to black people, how they want to see and feel about them, as well as about how Washington related to African Americans, what he wanted and could expect from them. It is from this category of intangibles that difficult but fundamental questions can be posed: how he saw himself, what composed his identity; how he came to understand his special gifts and purpose in the world, why he decided to pursue his destiny in the far South. These matters were resolved in the crucible of Reconstruction, its end, but also its heyday of strenuous and enthusiastic black political activity, amid the triumphs and travails of the people in what were also the crucial years of Washington's adolescence and early adulthood.

I am black and I have seen black hands, millions and
millions of them—
They were tired and awkward and calloused and grimy
and covered with hangnails,
And they were caught in the fast-moving belts of
machines and snagged and smashed and crushed . . .
And they grew nervous and sweaty, and opened and
shut in anguish and doubt and hesitation and
irresolution . . .

—RICHARD WRIGHT, "I HAVE SEEN BLACK HANDS"

Chapter 4

"Gathered from Miscellaneous Sources"

Democratic Possibilities and Other Kinds of "Racial Feelings"

THERE IS a certain irresistibility in the idea that great men, when they are young and before they are great, somehow were alive to the possibility of what they would become. They must be dreamers of great dreams that account for their destinies, small bits and pieces of conscious and unconscious invention, mere wisps of notions coming together, dissipating and reforming until they become something more substantial, clouds of glory falling to earth as a plan or course of action. In unpromising circumstances, those dreams serve to buoy or protect a young man's purposes, to succor a kept quiet identity faced with naysayers and doubters and their counsels of despair; they are armor for a self-conception that insists, "I will be someone" or "I shall show them all." These dreams are means for a young man to set things right on the planet, even if that fixing occurs only in one's head, refashioning the world to make it comport with one's own sense of its proper shape. Sometimes those large thoughts become warped by the frustrations of a world that will not change or refuses to acknowledge the dreamer's existence, demanding adjustments from heroes without honor, diamonds in the rough who turn out to be mere chunks of coal, lost in their own anonymity, bursting their dreams or turning them into nightmares filled with mad rancor and violence.

But sometimes the dreamed-of greatness comes true, as in Washington's case. And so to the chaos of what was and to the long dream of a solution to the Negro problem, he offers the promise of what could be. It is as if the lessons of his experience cause him to announce calmly what Richard Wright will later cry out: "This is the culture from which I sprang. This is the horror from which I fled."[1] But not, as in Wright's explanation, as a culture encompassing folkways and circumstances—the black and the white in hierarchical arrangement. Rather, Washington's flight is from the tawdriness of the freedmen's endeavors: the negative example of Reconstruction policies and politics, and the negative example of the freedmen's inability, personified by Washington Ferguson, to juggle the multiple responsibilities of making livings and families and friends with their neighbors. Thus he takes refuge with the Ruffners and lays the groundwork for what he will offer up as Washingtonianism. It is his great dream of good race relations, with himself as the key man to hold the whole of the regime together saying to the nation: follow me to a place of peace and prosperity and mutual progress. No conservative, he seeks to change his present and the nation's future, offering his life in evidence of the benefits and rewards of being open to white help and equally evidence of his exceptionalness, his striving before their intervention being proof of his worthiness (just as black self-help at Tuskegee will be fueled by white charity). His infinitely compelling and usable past, a tale complete with evil black stepfather and white fairy godmothers, functions as proof of his theory and a rejoinder to all those who dissent from his leadership and the race relations idea; a rebuttal to all the lynch mobs and eggheads, white haters and race baiters, the white supremacists and those agitators standing firm on the quicksand of "Negro rights." Some look at the age of Washington and see all around him the ruins of African America in poverty and the spoilage of other people's dreams withered on the vine. Opponents can shout words to the effect of "He's an Uncle Tom!" But wrapped up in his dream, his commonsense prescription that solves the Negro problem, his supporters look and see him dining at the White House. Wrapped up in the race relations idea, questioning the truth of his telling of how he arrived at his conclusion is tantamount to reading the story of Cinderella and being concerned with how the stepmother's traumatic experience of having lost her two husbands might mitigate negative evaluations of her parenting.

A question arises about whether Washington's telling of his life story delivers an accurate portrait of how he came to be and a truthful one about the early forming of his ideas about black progress and white help in America; whether the political truth of his dream in adulthood might not mask some of the dimension and content of his dreams in the past or otherwise conceal some variations in his dreaming. For example, he offers scant evidence of black hands helping his rise—a little help here, good wishes there—for to do so would contradict his story of continually swimming against the tide of the main currents of black life. It is not because of humility alone that he gives no hint that his African American neighbors saw him as a rising star in Malden, that they, as much as if not more than the Ruffners, cherished his promise, afforded him opportunities to grow, challenged him, but with tests of a different sort.

There is a seeming irony in black West Virginia recognizing his potential—recognizing in him the seeds of future greatness—in the gathering of precious nickels and scarce dimes to help him along his way to the Hampton Institute. These were Negroes whom Washington, in the main, portrayed as bereft, embittered, ridiculous, a feckless child race of people. Perhaps they, like the slaves of Hale's Ford viewing his gazing as a portentous thing, were simply overawed by him or superstitious, and thus their noticing of him means next to nothing; even dim bulbs shed some light. A surer conclusion is that this evidence means something important about Reconstruction, a democratic promise that offers Washington another path to greatness, and one well traveled by him at least down to 1879. This was not the treading of an imagined road, but real footsteps leaving tracks in evidence in the memories of black people.

In his autobiographical writings, Washington rather tends to ignore or neglect that acting, political work, to stint his immersion in the social and cultural swirl of Malden and its black outskirts, a place called Tinkersville, to make it into the road not taken for reasons that may have to do with his reckoning that it was a dead end, and that the practical man as autobiographer need not tarry too long in an account of his journeying there and journeying back to the fork in the road where he finds and begins to trod his one true path. In general, Washington's story rather tends to render what must have been to him as a boy and young man complicated and vexatious matters relating to his identity and emotional and political commitments as simple as quaffing some vermifuge. At the same time of retrospection, he leaves a number of important matters relating to the influences on his life of black people, generally, and Washington Ferguson, in particular, to appear in but a dim light—a light, perhaps, that Washington either consciously or unconsciously wanted turned down low in order to hide other kinds of actions like rights and democracy once available to African Americans, but no more in the age of Washington. He chooses to conceal as well the reasons for a black family's difficult choices made in seeking to be a family rather than separate economic units presenting themselves at muster. Perspective on the whole of his early life leading up to Tuskegee suggests that it was a more difficult progression that culminated with Washingtonianism. Contrary to his telling, the race relations idea, rather than being his only idea, is one of several dreams he entertained; that rather than one dream, his rise up from slavery gave rise to a series of dreams; and, indeed, that race relations was the least of young man Washington's likely dreams, his last dream but not his first at a time when he had before him a number of other possibilities. Foremost among these was to be a part of a family, to be no longer the fatherless son he had been as a slave. Booker's first dream was to gain a last name, and then to make that name outstanding.

%%%

ON THE general matter of the black family in freedom, Washington took some pains to distinguish the problems faced by the families of freedpeople as distinct from those of other poor and embattled white persons, "Anglo-Saxon" families, in the back of whom, ensuring their success and endurance, are "thousands of years of harmony in home life." He drew a portrait of dysfunction and incipient pathology within black families, the source of which was found in slavery. In 1900 he believed that still the Negro "has not had time enough to collect the broken and scattered members of his family." In support of his argument he cited his own example—"a personal reference." "I do not know who my own father was; I have no idea who my grandmother was; I have or had uncles, aunts and cousins, but I have no knowledge as to where most of them now are."[2] It was as if the consequences of the past were returning to doom the black family even before it really had the chance to begin. The tragedy, in his telling, is an obvious one: that he, who apparently knew so well the strength and support shared by members of white families, wanted to be a part of a family, a unit and an enterprise for the betterment of its members, especially the young, wanted to be in on the building up of the solid base of family, with caring mothers and providing, protecting fathers, and children governed by loving parents, who would bar the door to the odd dangers abounding outside home and hearth, the wild wolves anxious to get at the souls within. In so doing, families would make better lives for succeeding generations while providing a haven in a frequently hostile, heartless world—one type of progress unneedful of philosophical explication. This had been denied him as a slave, but now free of the chains, he would be a son, protected and cherished, safe within the bounds of family, defended against the predations of strangers, and at the behest of nothing but his own best interests. But then he was cast into the mines.

Because Washington makes no effort to supply Ferguson with anything other than a selfish motive for this action--a reasonable explanation of it--one might take from his other comments on post-emancipation families either or both of two conclusions. One is that Ferguson was simply a parasitic exploiter of children, a Negro exploiting other Negroes once he discovered that Booker "had a financial value."[3] The other explanation emphasizes incompetence rather than malfeasance. The black families encountered by Washington in Tuskegee who were without sense enough to send their children to school, but rather the whole of the family flocking into the cotton—"planted up to the very door of the cabin" and so leaving no room for garden plots—where every child "large enough to carry a hoe was put to work, and the baby—for usually there was at least one baby—would be laid down at the end of the cotton row."[4] The Fergusons were like that. Or like that ship lost at the mouth of the Amazon River about which he famously spoke at Atlanta, the crew dying of thirst because the captain of the vessel had lost his bearings. The first mate, Washington's mother, was good and true, and sought to hold the line, but it was not her hand holding the tiller. The consequence of Ferguson's squandering, as the man at the helm, the opportunities offered by freedom, or simply not keeping up to the demands of freedom was the family's floundering, lost and dying of thirst in the midst of fresh water. Washington's portrait is clever: what are in fact the impersonal forces faced by the Ferguson family—by the landless freedpeople, in general—are made to appear as personal: a liability suffered as a result of Ferguson's failings; and by inference his readers may understand Negro poverty and collective suffering as at least in part the result of the bad judgment or selfishness of thousand upon thousands of black fathers like Ferguson. Thus does the odd conservative Washington wage war on family and the generation before his own, which came into adulthood under slavery. But what is Washington's warrant for thus convicting Ferguson? And by what measure can it be said that the Fergusons were not successful in shouldering the duties of freedom?

Note should be taken of the fact that, whatever other cause there was of Ferguson sending for Jane, John, Booker, and Amanda, he owed them no legal obligation; and further, that with the tumult surrounding the end of the war, there is no reason not to think that if he so desired he could be free of this fifty-year-old woman (by all accounts an old fifty as a result of her good services in benefit of the Burroughs family) and their daughter, not even to speak of her two sons. Is there reason to believe his assumption of these burdens represents anything other than an expression of pure sentiment? Of love and assumed responsibility causing him willingly to give up a part of the full freedom that was legally, if not morally, now his? Indeed, what kind of man was he?

There is the fact that he set Booker and John to work, alongside him, in the salt industry, but even there one wonders if, based purely on selfish reasoning (a rationality placing the quality of one's individual standard of living over all other consideration of emotional attachment and feeling), he would not have been better off going it alone, without this ready-made family. To this family of five was some time soon after added a sixth, a boy named James (later James B. Washington), an orphan. (Was he abandoned by some other, less responsible father, perhaps?) Washington would have this adoption be the work of his mother alone: "notwithstanding our poverty," he writes, "my mother adopted [him] into our family."[5] But this is pure spite. It is as if, on the one hand, Ferguson tyrannically dictated to the family, imposed his desires on them, and, on the other, was sleeping at the wheel when the mother's benevolence brought aboard another mouth to feed.

If Reconstruction was so much a barren place, and Washington Ferguson so much a bad father figure, how did Booker, and not just him, but the other children—John and Amanda and the adopted boy, James—end up fairly well off relative to large numbers of black people in the half century after freedom? If Ferguson expropriated all his earnings from the Ruffners, from where did the boy Booker get the money to pay for the tutors he employed to supplement his studies? As well, from where did his brother and mother get the money that helped him pay for his schooling at Hampton? A close observer can see an answer to those questions in a rather different assessment of Ferguson's stewardship of the family with Jane Ferguson. One can see too that even those aspects of Ferguson's role in Booker's life that Washington resented can fairly fit with his hale willingness to carry a burden not mainly his own, and thence to move the story up and out from the flat surfaces of melodrama and an Alger-type sob story to achieve more real and human dimensions.

In contrast to Washington's portrait, Ferguson might better be seen as one type of hero, even though a minor one, in the reconstructing of the nation and the establishing of American freedom. Someone who, as a freedman, manifested those good qualities that historians, further revising the understanding of emancipation and Reconstruction that came to predominate in the age of Washington, identify with many hundreds of thousands of freedpeople seeking—and with some success—to define freedom to their own best advantage. What kind of alternate accounting can be made on Ferguson's stewardship of his family?

First, Ferguson's resistance to Washington going to school rather than working alongside him in the mines is no difficult matter. It may have been a hard decision, and it was one he eventually relented on, but it is not unreasonable to see it as the simple, conservative common sense of a former slave, unlettered well past middle age, valuing more the solid foundation of work that is before one over the uncertain benefits of reading, writing, and arithmetic. That is to say, he may have made something like the same calculation his stepson would insist that common sense demands when he was foisting industrial education upon black people. But in Ferguson's case, this was because he was conservative and perhaps because he could conceive of no other course, as opposed to the case of the younger man who will later laud necessity, nostalgically invoking how the Negro "brought forth treasures from the bowels of the earth," at Atlanta as if it was not a perfectly miserable business.[6] Was he indeed guilty of exploiting the children? One may offer the reasonable explanation that this subjecting of children to the world of work was required of people in the nineteenth century, and not just African Americans. The problem is manifestly not some carryover from slavery, the detritus of that toxic condition; if the Fergusons are floundering or merely struggling to survive, that struggle is in fact a product of the present and not, in any strict sense, of the past. But does the case need making? Only when the alienation produced by the distances of time and place, and of the racism of one hundred years ago intervenes to obscure reality is explication necessary of the hard decision made by Ferguson, and likely Mrs. Ferguson as well.

Indeed, it is not even clear that Washington and his brother's expropriated wages "barely paid for their support." Following Washington's lead, a biographer concludes that Ferguson "pocketed their pay." The image of Ferguson, at leisure, lining his own pockets with money taken from the two boys, which it would seem was the image Washington himself sought to convey, is rather at odds with Louis Harlan's elaboration of the mitigating circumstances possibly explaining the situation: "Perhaps he was too poor

to do otherwise; the exploitation of children was widespread in the nineteenth century in agriculture, textile mills, mining, and all low-wage industries." Harlan may be right, but Washington offers no hint of the exigencies
of survival for the family, supporting the contention that his intention was
to transform a decision of necessity into an allegory of the depredations of
some meaner Negroes upon other weaker Negroes.[7] What if their wages
were less than what it cost the parents to feed and clothe them? The fact is
that it is just as impossible for us to know for certain the answer as it must
have been for Booker himself.

On the other hand, the one authority in a position to know was General
Ruffner, and he is silent on the matter, and the only evidence available
is the fact that the Ruffners were sufficiently provided for to send their
children away to school, to maintain a large house and have the need and
wherewithal to employ a houseboy. That is to say, that after Booker's escape
from the mines, those like Ferguson left behind at the bottom of the salt
game paid for Booker's upkeep and that of the Ruffners. It is the relation of
these two exploitations that is the key; to avoid them is to avoid the central
dynamic of the freedom so graciously granted to the emancipated slave.
The demand came down from on high—from landowners, from banks,
from civil and martial authority, and from many of the Northern missionaries—that man and woman and their children present themselves singly
before the market. The Ferguson family, a product of sentiment rather than
law, was buffeted about by these forces; their journey is a new story, native
to freedom, not to slavery.

The evidence on this matter is fairly clear: a marriage that lasted until
Washington's mother died in 1874. Before then, Mr. and Mrs. Ferguson,
like many another couple when freedom came, strove mightily to make a
family. But new forces of exploitation demanding all black people muster
out into lines to present themselves individually for hiring was not popular
among the freedpeople who recognized the promise that demand held to
tear their little families apart. Washington, on the other hand, embraces
that individualistic notion gladly. "More than once I have tried to picture
myself in the position of a boy or man with an honoured and distinguished
ancestry which I could trace back through a period of hundreds of years,"
he wrote, imagining being a boy "who had not only inherited a name, but
fortune and a proud family homestead; and yet I have sometimes had the
feeling that if I had inherited these, and had been a member of a more popular race, I should have been inclined to yield to the temptation of depending upon my ancestry and my colour to do that for me which I should do
for myself." Concluding with what might be seen as a direct slap at the man

he came to see as a failed father, Washington "resolved that because I had no ancestry myself I would leave a record of which my children would be proud, and which might encourage them to still higher effort."[8] He felt himself used, misled, and thus was required to escape through the means of his employment at the Ruffners', and thence to Hampton and thence to the far South.[9]

What is left after the rejecting and scorning of the paltry patrimony a poor black man can afford a child, whether his or someone else's? It is as if the sole significance of Washington Ferguson's life was to provide history and his stepson with a name to defame.

But what is in a name?

%%%

ATTENDING HIS first day of school in Malden, after his fellows doffed their "store hats," and the teacher began asking the names of his pupils, Booker found himself in "deep perplexity." All the other children, he discovered, had two names—"some of them even indulged in . . . the extravagance of having three"—while he had but one. "Before going to school," he related, "it had never occurred to me that it was needful or appropriate to have an additional name." When it was his turn, and the teacher asked him what his full name was, he answered smartly "'Booker Washington,' as if I had been called by that name all my life; and by that name I have since been known."[10]

It is a precious story in his telling, and so slight in detail as to make his selection fodder for romantic elaboration by his later partisans. One type of romanticism would point toward the name "Booker Burroughs" as an obvious one for "just plain 'Booker'" to adopt. But despite his later willingness to participate, for the purposes of Washingtonianism and New South nostalgism, in publicity opportunities back at the old homeplace,[11] that relationship had run its course. He would not claim them; the not-so-big house occupied by the Burroughs, whether it ever had any real emotional allure for one such as him, was now no longer the center of his world. Those race relations had run their course.

Placing the selection into another type of romantic narrative, a Washington hagiographer offers a quaint and quite positively apocryphal rendering of the occasion: "Booker, aiming as high as he could, said it was Washington. And indeed he became the father of his people."[12] While this story, one of a number emanating from Washington acolytes, is of extremely dubious provenance, the association with the nation's first Washington is irresistible both for the reasons of their common name and their shared Virginia roots in the state at one time in American history called the cradle of the presidency. However, the idea, as Washington's Hampton teacher, Mary F. Mackie, would say, that he was "wisely *guided*" in his choice, is insensible on its own terms as evidence of Washington's predestined greatness. If it were indicative of the latter, what is to be made of all the other black Washingtons (not to speak of black Lincolns and black Johnsons, all of the Jacksons and the Jeffersons) in African America, some of whom have been men and women of note, but the majority of whom have as their outstanding feature of their lives simply their averageness?

There is equal illogic in the idea, a product of segregation and equally its appeal, that the two Washingtons have similar functions in the building up of distinct nations. It is said, in this fantasy, that the earlier Washington, by a revolution, fathers a people within a discrete geographic dimension and border, within which Negroes await the latter Washington to found, without revolution and warfare, their nation without borders, and, then, to lead this imagined community of a fictive nation without recourse to democratic rights in the actual nation within which it is engulfed. Mackie, the Lady Principal at Hampton Institute, would articulate the more sensible version of this view, writing to Washington that in his sharing a name with "the 'Father of his country' you too by your earnest, wise, unselfish life are adding fresh laurels to the same name which future generations shall blend together as belonging to a name which all Americans both white and colored, shall honor as leaders of the two races which make our commonwealth. I feel quite sure 'George' would be proud to grip hands with our Booker in recognition of the honored place he has made for himself in this country." James Merville Pyne, who described himself as a white person, took perfectly seriously the idea of the second Washington fathering a country, writing, "George founded a great Nation for White men. I am wondering if Booker will not found a great Nation for Black men. The time is ripe." (He proposed this nation consist of the southeastern states and the West Indies, with its capital at Tuskegee.)[13]

Washington, himself, all humble (and endowed with the humility of someone who has others to do his bragging for him) makes no such grandiose claim, saying in *The Story of My Life and Work* simply that he choose "the best name there was in the list,"[14] suggesting no fatefulness in the decision—no destiny—but leaving the legend intact: "I think there are not many men in our country who have had the privilege of naming themselves in the way that I have," he wrote upon one occasion.[15] And on another, "Yes; I think I realized whose name I was taking."[16]

Despite the mythmaking and obscurantism of the legend that makes mysterious how Washington got his name or confuses the matter as "an exceedingly picquant bit of boyish conceit,"[17] the riddle is easily unraveled. Washington, indeed, provides two kinds of hints as to the real story. First are his derisive comments on how the freedpeople frivolously claimed names as a part of their "entitles." The second is that the next paragraph following the previously quoted statement from *The Story of My Life and Work* is on the subject of Washington Ferguson. A Washington biographer has a part of the story right by ignoring the romantic notions of some of Washington's biographers. But, following Washington's account, he concludes that Ferguson was an important figure in Washington's life only in a negative way. Thus, on the matter of his taking his stepfather's name for his own, Harlan sees as possible only ironic inadvertency—"a confusion about the nature of first and last names by a small boy recently out of slavery"—or self-conscious rebellion—"a deliberate decision to give himself another name than that of his rather unsatisfactory stepfather."[18] A more likely truth is that, regardless of biology, he was his father's son; that, in that time, he was "Wash's Booker" become "Booker Washington." This is speculation, of course, but there is no special warrant in favor of concluding that Washington's attitude had reached a point of terminal alienation from Ferguson at this time; neither that he was mistaken in taking Ferguson's name (although obviously he was mistaken about which name to adopt), nor that Ferguson had indeed proved his inadequacy as a father, surrogate or otherwise.

In retrospect, Washington gives thanks to a long list of white persons—high and low, and almost too many to be named—all of whom helped and guided him in various ways, starting with a white woman who took him into her house and taught him to cherish work. This assistance will be available to Washington, as a child and a man, because of his openness to it, which in turn, is a product of his rejection of bitterness toward the white man. But added to that is another part of his outlook: the notion of his having no ancestry. If freedom and the franchise are a part of the river of African American struggle, Washington distances himself from that part of the river, from the disaster of black Reconstruction—in his account, a product made up of equal measures of hubris and foolishness, receptivity to bad influences and to bitterness. He crosses over to a different sort of promised land on the other side, then disavows the river and affiliation with those in it. Singularly among those is Ferguson, who he will call "my mother's husband," or grudgingly, stepfather, and who is the only person in his autobiography for whom Washington expresses bitterness. Washington will come to rely on what Harlan terms "a succession of fatherly white men."[19] These later will be the material from which the house of Washingtonianism will be built. Before that edifice gets thrown up—before it can stand—underneath the lumber from which it will be erected lies buried the first man to claim the role of Booker's father. Ferguson's fathering of him will become in Washington's life as he enters adolescence a free boy, the crucible in which his identity is formed, the negative example against which Washington bases his own life course.

In an inquiry into Booker Washington's relationship with Washington Ferguson and his eventual denial of any familial relation with him—that any honor is owed the older man for his role in Washington's success—the point is not so much about Ferguson, but about the changes in Washington: about how he resolves the conflicts in his life and how he portrays his overcoming them. That is the tension: between the subjective, purposeful portrayal which leaves out any hint of psychological ambivalence (just as his portrayal of these years in politics admits no explanation of black behavior beyond bitterness and bacchanalia in explaining why the Reconstruction era was a negative example of how to elevate the Negro); two negative examples of how to uplift the Negro race: the close at home one of Ferguson and the general failing of Negroes. This leads to Washington's aiming south to follow another course, while at the same time it is a part of his larger course in separating himself from any taint of the past that might hold him back: self-realization through the embrace of white foster parents, white teachers, white fathers. This provides a satisfactory explanation for why he is not bitter, but less so for why he aimed south.

%%%

THE CONTENT of someone's dreaming presents a particularly difficult problem, theme and variation in the interpretation of dreams not being the usual fodder for historical analysis. Best to stay with feet planted firmly upon the safer ground of what can be proved or disproved. Frederick Douglass looks out upon the Chesapeake and the sails of boats become white winged angels, and his vision is paid off by freedom. Who would wonder if Douglass, standing on the banks of that river, might not have wished that those gentle angels of liberty would turn into avenging angels of retribution? In the primal division in African American history, there are those like King said to be dreamers, and yet it is the practical accomplishments of the civil rights movement that, most would conclude, defines the substance of his dreaming. Present political matters—like linking one's position on the state's being color-blind to one or another of King's rhetorical flourishes and phrase-making—similarly earthbound King's dreaming, grinding it down such that keeping faith with his hoped for "beloved community"—an untrodden place perhaps so foreign to our own that it escapes precise definition—becomes a matter of merely professing the resolve to cause black people and white people or white people and people of color to get along better in the coming year.

That race relations idea was actually a dream Washington elaborated years before, but evidence to that effect has been neglected in categorizing of Washington as a realist. Insofar as he is credited with having an interior life at all he is thought merely to have been a cipher for powerful white men, or, otherwise, his covert actions along the same lines as those sought by his black opponents like Du Bois is mustered in evidence of a mysteriously divided soul, that in turn leads to questions of about which of the Washingtons was genuine. Here again, a man's commerce in human affairs precedes understanding of his personality, determining how the inquiry into his psychology proceeds: the problematic is simply the supposed difficulty of accounting for two different policy positions in the operation of the mind behind his "sphinx-like" visage, his "complex, Faustian character" and "Delphic public utterances."[20]

Consideration of how Washington came to be that way centers on his relationship with various "fathers," but a more fruitful inquiry would turn the matter around: to view it as a question of personal identity as opposed to ideology; rather than looking backward from the turn of the century, a different perspective on his relationship with Washington Ferguson is gained by looking forward from slavery. For whom had Washington been looking when as a slave he gazed off toward the horizon? It is a reasonable surmise that the first focus of his longing then was Ferguson. Washington recalled him in the period just previous to the end of slavery as "a man of about fifty years of age," and, reflecting his later attitude, takes pains to disparage him as "employed merely as a common labourer," which one supposes is Washington's way of distinguishing Ferguson from those slaves "employed" or making careers in more lofty fields of endeavor.[21]

Other evidence suggests a different kind of figure represented to the slave boy. Ferguson was the property of a tyrannical, abusive owner, but he was restive, and, if the account of John Washington is any indication, would not stand for his master's mistreatment, and so was hired out to work outside the neighborhood. By Washington's own account, Ferguson was missed by the company he left behind. Jane and her children suffered "his long absence from home."[22] He "seldom came to our plantation," Booker Washington remembered, making his entrance as infrequently as once a year at Christmastime.[23] But when he did return home, those were the big times for Booker, filled with his telling tales of his adventures out in the wider world. "I recall that I would sit for hours in rapture hearing him tell of the experiences he had had in a distant part of Virginia, where he and a large number of other coloured people were employed in building a railway, he wrote, and "in my boyish ignorance at that time, I used to wonder what interest he could have in a railway of that kind; whether or not he owned any part in it; and how it was he was so much interested in the building of a railroad that he could remain away from home for five or six months and sometimes longer."[24] This is as close as Washington comes to admitting the true feelings the present account is suggesting he once had for Ferguson.

Once the war commenced, according to Washington, Ferguson was either "carried off by a party of 'Yankee' raiders" or had in some other way "wandered into West Virginia," seeming to suggest no more animation or willfulness on his part than what could be evinced by the silverware the Burroughs worried over.[25] Brother John provides a different account of what happened once the war came. Rather than being toted away like a parcel by the Yankees, he suggests, Ferguson absconded to the Union Army, like thousands of other, self-liberated "contraband," joining up with General David Hunter and going back to West Virginia, "where he was free," and from where he sent for the family.[26]

Here was a man unmastered by slavery, and thus it is possible to understand him as cutting quite a figure in the eyes of a young boy seen and seeing himself as different from other slaves, proudly if privately holding himself in reserve, still, and thinking himself not subject to their big house orientation. The combination of what he thought of himself and what he looked for in Ferguson makes for a potent mix. The scene at the school is readily imaginable. His teacher's first question—"What is your name?"—confounds him, just as Washington reports, his perplexity stemming from the fact that he may indeed never have thought about it before. Then the teacher, perhaps with some experience and understanding of from where such confusion comes, asks the clarifying follow-up: "Well, who is your daddy?" or "What is your daddy's name?" and this is a question Washington can answer, a name gladly taken, an identity willingly assumed.

It is needless to deny the influence the Ruffners had over Washington's life, but his portrait of their positive effect and Ferguson's negative one cannot stand alone. When, at the turn of the century, inquiries were made as to how Washington "is regarded among the neighbors of his childhood and youth," he was not disremembered, as one might expect if the main part of his time was spent cooped up, duster in hand, with Mrs. Ruffner. Rather he was recalled as a full-fledged participant in the social swirl that was black Reconstruction in its local West Virginia version. His neighbors, those "who knew him best in childhood and youth," recalled him as "thoughtful" and "diligent," but active as well. He was "an industrious Sunday school teacher, a careful church clerk, a successful school teacher, a ready debater and a Christian young man." He was, they all agreed, "great in Malden and great in West Virginia."[27]

Father Lewis Rice, pastor of the Colored Baptist Church in Malden, tells of his baptizing Washington on the shores of the Kanawha River: "He was about fourteen years old, but he was old for his years. He was so reliable, and was able to read and write so much better than most of our people, that not long after that he was made the clerk of the church."[28] A student of Washington's during his tenure back in Malden in a letter to Washington recalled for him the annual church picnics they attended, and Washington's addressing the gathered flock.[29] Even earlier than that, and before Washington left Malden for the first time to attend Hampton, his prowess as an orator was acknowledged by black Malden. As "a mere boy," a local minister told a visiting journalist, Washington was entered into the lists for the Malden Debating Club against a powerful, adult debating society from neighboring Charleston: "The Charleston Club was composed of grown men, but they conceded that 'Booker T.' was the force which gained the victory for the Malden Club."[30]

This was another kind of training than that which he received from Mrs. Ruffner with her each-one, teach-one approach to slapdash social engineering on the cheap. The temperamental differences between the two cannot be overstated. She was a shut-in, from her perch atop the hill, scorning and perhaps also fearing her narrow and bigoted white neighbors, the resentments of her husband's thralls and minions and their mates, the violations of etiquette committed by pushy arrivistes tracking mud onto her pristine space.

Young Washington, unlike his white mentor, was a joiner, immersing himself in the out-of-doors, and within the institutional life created by the freedpeople. He was a star there in a theater built by black people, who, for their part, noticed the qualities of strength and intelligence he displayed as a young man. Her practical demands on him (as opposed to the psychic ones having to do with her scrutiny of Washington and the dust mites) were not so great, leaving him with plenty of time for other activities, including latterly disreputable political acts, the outlines of which rather call into question his stress on what he learned from Mrs. Ruffner, and provide some clues as to his sense of self, and his conception of his role in the affairs of men based not on what he became, but on his future looking forward from youth.

There was every reason to believe he was well along on the road to being some kind of leader, one among many, taking in the whole of this rising generation, and rising up to lead it by the choice of democratically constituted polity. This was his life, as a teenager, his life in a normal world not rid of racism or deprivation. But, before Reconstruction was ended and before the Negro problem was reasserted into the vacuum created when democracy was abandoned and defeated, it was a world of significant opportunity for education, debate, politics—activities all springing from government intervention and the desires of the people to be active citizens, to improve and protect themselves, to have their say and influence too.

Washington embraces the opportunities, created for those of his generation by black hands, early on: part of the impetus for his wanting to learn to read was in order to read the life of Douglass, and so to emulate this other hero of his youth.[31] And many others of his generation followed such leads in 1870 and 1871 and 1872, a ripe time for a young person to rise. especially so because, as Father Rice recognized, those former slaves who were coming to maturity, who like Washington were entering early adulthood when Reconstruction was in full flower, gained the benefits of education at an early age, but, additionally had neither spent whole lives in slavery, nor assumed the full burden of adult responsibilities.

The confluence of these two factors explains why it was that it was Washington who acted as secretary for the local cadre of the Republican Party when it convened in the summer of 1872 (a meeting chaired by another sixteen-year-old). Washington's report on their proceedings, the first surviving piece of his writing, is telling about the times and his emersion in them. Tinkersville Republicans pledged to "stand by and support the principles enunciated by the Republican party," and not to "support any candidate who comes out in opposition to the regular nominees of the Republican National, State, and County Convention"—standard procedures of American party politics any time. But Republicans at Tinkersville also had particular concerns, and so, over Washington's signature is their avowal to "not countenance or support any man who is in any way hostile to the colored people."[32] This resolution suggests nothing so much as that Negroes around Malden knew what they were about and what was about them: that they sought to be both partisan and democratic, to embrace the particular and the universal.

Later, these matters will be presented by Washington as an either-or proposition fumbled by the freedmen. In the first years of freedom, we were presumptuous, forcing ourselves upon our neighbors rather than making them our friends, and meddling in politics rather than building businesses, and, generally, talking when we might have been doing. We were wrong; we were as spoiled children, wanting to start out on top of it all, rather than working our way up from slavery.[33] Unlike the later Washington, all theoretical solutions to the Negro problem and embracing nearly any white man willing to stop short of calling for the colonization of Negroes elsewhere, the Reconstruction-era Washington and his comrades stood on principle and did not seek a solution to ideological conundrums about the fate of the race. They did not wave wands and effect the perfecting of race relations; did not embrace the false logic of the Negro problem, but offered, rather than solutions, the redoubt of political struggle and alliance-making.[34] As a participant in a movement within American politics—and again unlike his later stance—Washington and his fellows placed themselves before the public where they and their candidates could judge and be judged, lose or win; that is to say, to submit to tests and contests, be subject to higher standards because unlike, for instance, the tidying of a room, the results of group politics within a democracy are objective, concrete, and readily verifiable.

With all his talk of being bereft of ancestry and the "tremendous mistakes" made by the freedmen in Reconstruction, this reality, this other path Washington walked down, is largely obscured, even erased. That erasure has much to do with the turn in the nation after Reconstruction. From the perspective of what things become, one might fail even to consider the possibility of politics fueling Washington's dreams. In lieu of a straightforward statement of those aspirations, Washington writes,

> In those days, and later as a young man, I used to try to picture in my imagination the feelings and ambitions of a white boy with absolutely no limit placed upon his aspirations and activities. I used to envy the white boy who had no obstacles placed in the way of his becoming a Congressman, Governor, Bishop, or President by reason of the accident of his birth or race. I used to picture the way that I would act under such circumstances; how I would begin at the bottom and keep rising until I reached the highest round of success.[35]

Mindful both of racist proscription and the focusing lens of race relations, Washington's followers might bemoan—in the abstract—the reality that one so worthy as he could not freely dare to dream so high; some may even say this is one of the ways Washington articulates just what is wrong with racist America. But these intertwined views miss the point of what is extraordinary and unique about the Reconstruction era and the new free-dom of that time. The outstanding feature of his comment is that it may be the best evidence of precisely just what Washington aspired to as a young man of sixteen or seventeen: to go before the people in order to become an elected leader at some high level of authority. And this was no will-o'-the-wisp, either, for free people in Reconstruction, which, Eric Foner writes, "transformed their lives and aspirations in ways unmeasurable by statistics and in realms far beyond the reach of the law."[36] Then it was certainly not completely unreasonable given democratic opportunities—given the wide vistas seeming to open before the freedmen and given his own sense of his specialness and ability and faith in "intrinsic, individual merit." This was a new (and, as it turned out, perishable) faith, unimaginable for the young of antebellum times. Later generations of African American boys and girls, of course, had little reason to allow their minds to wander toward such pos-sibilities, and even those in the post–civil rights generation, with good rea-sons for being cynical about their relation to the American polity, may not yet so blithely engage in such reverie. But, in Reconstruction, Washington could indeed "picture" himself occupying a seat of power—even the most important one at the White House.[37]

Consideration of rising to such an august station, or, in the short term, assisting others in rising to less lofty, but crucial positions of authority, entails also a reckoning on one's opposition. During Reconstruction, Afri-can American cadres within the Republican Party like the one in which Washington involved himself encountered opponents who considered them not just opponents but also enemies to be vanquished, killed, or, at least, ridden out of the American body politic—where they had never belonged from the beginning, a band of "ignorant, stupid, demi-savage paupers," as one of their political rivals said.[38]

In his various autobiographical writings, Washington is inconsistent about when he discovered what we would now term "racism." In *Up From Slavery*, he states that it was not until his 1872 venture to Hampton Institute (when he found himself denied accommodations "at a com-mon, unpainted house called a hotel") that he discovered discrimina-tion: "The difference that the colour of one's skin would make I had not thought anything about," he claims, "This was my first experience in finding out what the colour of my skin meant."[39] While his assertion stretches credulity, it may indeed be true that this was an occasion, his first time away from home to really contemplate the meaning of racism in America; to pull together and seek a synthesis of his experiences and knowledge of the wider world, as well as to come to terms with fugitive thoughts on the possibility of his taking much sterner action than any acting indicated by Washingtonianism.

%%%

A STRANGE phenomenon of the Negro problem has emerged, since the 1960s, of our guides in matters racial revealing their soul's dark nights: those public speakers parading their former "street" credentials before credulous white audiences, and white professors of "race relations" studies averring as to how they, like all white persons, are racist. As a precursor to these showy displays of politics and moral authority manifest in performances of exhibitionism, at least a couple of times in his career Washington, for reasons of his own, implicated himself in racism, inaugurating a heretofore unhonored tradition in the history of the Negro problem. "I used to be a hater of the white race," he told an audience gathered for the first National Conference on Race Betterment in 1914, "but I soon learned that hating the white man did not do him any harm, and it certainly was narrowing up my soul and making me a good bit less of a human being." As with the vermifuge, he resolved to stop: "and so I said, 'I will quit hating the white man.'" Malcolm X, in the last months of his life, came to the same conclusion, say those who would cast him in a supporting role in what they see as the melodrama of 1960s race relations, a louder, more secular King. But Malcolm X would never come around to Washington's discount universalism—his four-square, post-partisanism: "I am interested in the Negro race," Washington told the conference, but "I am equally interested in the white race in this country."[40]

Perspective on Washington's vantage point in the political environment of the 1870s, however, suggests he did not yet see firm, stalwart advocacy of particular black interests either as an expression of bitterness or chauvinism; rather, that he observes the clash of black and white and other incidents of mob action and Klan or other affiliated aggressions against the freedpeople with quite different commitments than he lets on later. His stated opinion that all was for naught, that there was "no hope" for the nation, is belied by his continuing commitment, down to at least 1879, at which time he was still working as a political campaigner and still aspired to be a lawyer or minister—the professions providing the main springboards for black men to enter public life and seek office.[41] His notion that the situation was hopeless, then, might not best be understood as the race relations liberal's decrying of any sort of racial disharmony or conflict. Instead, it is better understood as a perspective coming from position of partisanship in those conflicts, his taking the measure of black people's opponents, allies, and the Negro's own abilities to organize and mobilize, and, concluding, with much chagrin, that the odds are not on the side of the angels.

But who did Washington, at the time, see as with the angels and who did he see as the minions of the devil? Washington the historian, describing his and General Ruffner's encounter with the two opposing mobs of black and white, casts the general as the sole hero of the dramatic scene, illustrating the depths to which race relations descended in Reconstruction. With training to forage for and pick out racial factors, those who follow Washington cast a blanket explanation—bad race relations—over the encounter. And if it is simply race relations being worked out here, little consideration needs to be paid to the diversity of motivations—political, personal, even to the irresistibility of joining in mobs—that might engender such violent action. Thus, Harlan writes that two lessons were taught Washington, the first being about the "danger incurred by a black man who transgressed the racial codes of the whites," and secondly, "a class one, that the white paternalist was the black man's only friend, albeit never a perfect one and in this case an ineffectual one."[42]

Washington, however, is not simply a historian or dramatist, but working in the tradition of the Negro problem and in his capacity as a racial pundit. The hegemony of the race relations ideas causes one not to see Ruffner as the big man about Malden, the mine owner, but as a valiant knight representing white Southerners of the better sort entering the lists to protect Negroes and peace, nor to look at the riot as an occasion for one of his disgruntled white workers to mete out a bit of class politics at the boss man's head. But what of the general? What fears preyed upon other parts of his mind? Did it strike him that among both the mobs were his workers? Might he have had a shock of recognition, once the brickbat had struck home and just before his consciousness slipped away, that it might have pitched at him for reasons other than his acting as a racial peacemaker— that one of the white mob might well have taken up the opportunity to seek a pound of the bossman's flesh, to exploit the tumult, not for reasons having anything to do with race relations and racial peacemaking, but much to do with the workaday world of specific and personal resentments against filthy exploitation? Washington and the race relations idea give little cause to wonder about Ruffner's reaction to his braining (and anyway, there is little evidence one way or the other). But one does wonder if, during the general's recovery, he did not experience a terrifying epiphany: once this was why we needed colonization; now this is why we need segregation.[43]

Staged as race relations, Washington casts himself as a nonpartisan observer, a critic rather than a player, a moral beacon, who would advise his listeners to follow his example and "raise yourselves above yourselves, above race, above party, above everything."[44] Upon other occasions Washington offers a different history of his encounter with racism. In *The Story of the Negro*, which appeared in 1909, he makes the fullest statement of all, dating it back to his schooling when the image of the African—or what some of his teachers might have called "the Negroid"—was presented in "an unnecessarily cruel contrast with the pictures of the civilized and highly cultured Europeans and Americans." It seemed to him that "the best among the white people was contrasted with the worst among the black"—all invidious comparison of George Washington, embodying "the best among white people," with "a naked African, having a ring in his nose and a dagger in his hand," made to stand in for "the worst among the black." This made "a deep and painful impression upon me."

> It is hard for one who is a member of another race and who has not had a like experience to appreciate the impression that has often been made upon me, and upon other members of my race as they have listened, as inexperienced boys and girls, to public speeches in which the whole Negro race was denounced in a reckless and wholesale manner, or as they have read newspapers and books in which the Negro race has been described as the lowest and most hopeless of God's creation.[45]

Washington here articulates what may be seen as his general experience or what he learned elsewhere, but one wonders if he might also be speaking more specifically, if guardedly, about his experience with his white mentors: Mrs. Ruffner and General Ruffner, she the sad harridan, the sharp-tongued shut-in, and he the prolix anachronism, the errant knight. And, later, his experience with General Armstrong, the Hampton principal under whose sway Washington would fall, who, for his part, outdoes them both in his resort to racial punditry.

Such a surmise is suggested by his statement that as "a young man, I was driven almost to despair by the hard and bitter, and frequently, as it seemed to me, unjust statements about my race. It was difficult for me to reconcile the ruthless denunciations which men, with whom I was acquainted, would make in their public speeches, with the uniform courtesy and kindness which they had shown me and others of my race in all their private relations":

Even now it is difficult for me to understand why so many Southern white men will allow themselves, for the purpose of enforcing an argument or in the heat of a political discussion, to go so far in the denunciation of the Negro as to do injustice to their own better natures and to their actual feelings toward coloured people whom they meet, perhaps, in business, or toward the servants employed in their own household, the woman who cooks their food, looks after their house and cares for their children. I mention these facts because they serve to illustrate the singular relations of interdependence and opposition in which the white and black people of the South stand to each other to-day, all of which has had and is having a very definite influence upon the development of my people in the South.[46]

There is no irony in these friends of Washington gifting him with fundamental lessons in the racist ways of white persons, for while it demands a different perspective on his relationship with them, his being formed in the belly of a perverse, idealist paternalism—filled up with solutions for all that ails the Negro and churned by a desire to make go away an aching conscience—actually goes far in demonstrating that Washington's alliance-making is not with Southern conservatives, but with racial liberals and progressives whose prejudices and foibles he knows well.

But this was a plan and program he would arrive at in the future. In the early and mid-1870s he had not the discipline to make peace freely with their variant of racism, much less more virulent varieties in thought and action. His ears bombarded by "hard and discouraging statements" about the incapacity of the Negro, and with black people in the Reconstructed South, generally, assaulted from various sides, Washington felt himself compelled to some type of action. His first reaction is "to seek rest" and escape, "to go away to some distant part of the earth and bury myself where I might be a stranger to all my people, or at least where the thing we call race prejudice did not exist in the way it does in the Southern states." Ultimately, he tells his readers, he arrived where he arrived, endowed with, he writes, "a determination to spend my life in helping and strengthening the people of my race, in order to prove to the world that whatever had been its feelings for them in the past it should learn to respect them in the future, both for what they were and what they should be able to do." "I made up my mind," he continued, "that in the end the world must come to respect the Negro for just those virtues for which some people say he is despised, namely because of his patience, his kindness, and his lack of resentment toward those who do him wrong and injustice." In this, he remained all the time consoled by the hope that others would "recognise what seemed to me the wrongs of my race."[47]

That curious phrase—"the wrongs of my race"—stands out, like the term "the Negro problem," for its ambiguity. It suggests a Washington with one foot in the obscurantist future of race relations advocacy, ever bending to the will of his white supporters, one foot in the Reconstruction time, all straight marching into battles, political, pitched, or otherwise, that neither he nor anyone else of any seriousness could be certain African Americans and their allies would inevitably lose. One might see that the notion of fleeing the field of conflict in Reconstruction has little attraction to one who aspires to lead, and who, despite not a few statements to the contrary, maintained a belief in the benefits and necessity of "race pride and race consciousness."[48]

It is an indication of the uncertainty Washington felt in this period that he also considered for himself the resort to violence. He says he pondered doing "something desperate" that would make the world know that evil was being done.[49] This turn of mind links Washington with the Walkers, Turners, and Browns of antebellum times, "desperadoes" and bad men like Robert Charles (a close contemporary of Washington who famously shot up turn-of-the-century New Orleans) in Washington's own time, as well as the often but not always full-of-hot-air black revolutionaries of the 1960s. More than that it also is an affective connection tying Washington to many, many other black people (the young more than the old, certainly; young men most probably more than young women): those who in anger and frustration at the state of things find their thoughts turning to a consideration of a gesture of some sort as a sign of their will to put a mark upon the world. A "revolutionary suicide," Huey Newton called it; but it goes by many names, this idea of what the Negro ought do if he must die at the hands of the whites, and takes many forms. Chester Himes conceived it as the enduring, eternal "Plan B," fallen back upon after one's efforts to vindicate the rights of black people have proved unavailing. For Suffren Griggs, it is a black conspiracy emerging from an "*Imperium in Imperio*," slouching toward Gomorrah. It is a bitter dream, to be sure, arrived at authentically though when all other hopes seem to be gone, and the mind is caused to conjure dreams of revenge and revolution; the paying back of blood with blood; terror bashed backward at terrorist; not legalisms like justice and equality, but "a Mao-Mao," Eldridge Cleaver said, to vanquish black enemies; to take the fight to the proud, bragging "nigger-hazer and nigger-killer,"[50] whether garbed in hood or uniform, Red shirt or white collar, the cracker and the *Bourbon*, North and South.[51] It is self-realization through acting, a perfection of rightness through attack on what is wrong in the world.

Washington's admitting to his entertainment of such thoughts in Reconstruction is not quite the violation of his later ethic and the politically correct line he held to in the age of segregation it may seem. Rather, it is quite
likely to figure his supporters taking this as more evidence of his superior-
ity: he was once like those others whose sole notion was to stand up in
opposition to reality, fighting against the whites by voting or organizing
politically, or otherwise caviling and carping, but he had the good sense
to rid himself of such retrograde notions and embrace good race relations,
Washington's advocacy of which, here, means a therapeutic deliverance
from black animus.

On the other hand, Washington's statement that he once had occasion to
visit the depths of this "racial feeling," once could conceive another role for
himself other than acting as race relations mediator, is especially significant
as a uniquely unqualified statement of partisan allegiance—a black warrior
rather than good shepherd. So much did Reconstruction do to him. But
Reconstruction would ultimately be ended, necessitating the damping of
certain fires so that one day Washington would be thought the very last
Negro "to do anything dynamitic to the structure of society."[52] Nevertheless, in the time, one suspects that freeing himself of them, adopting a more
progressive view of whites and resolving the confusion marking "my own
feelings in regard to my race," required a stronger remedy than his mother's
dose of vermifuge.[53]

%%%

WASHINGTON'S LOOKING outward from Malden so as to ponder on the
nature of the wider world beyond the surrounding mountains and his
eventual resolve to seek his fortune in the deep South may be just as telling
about his mood as his consideration of desperate acts or revenge: both are
but versions of a desire to escape more or less unpromising circumstances,
a turn of mind from hunger, a second sighting when the available courses
are washed out or not adequate enough to satisfy one's sense of destiny.
As such, they point Washington in the direction of a critique of the insufficiency of black politics in West Virginia during Reconstruction, the black
aspect of that unfolding being the proximate one, that which is both most
closely connected to the fate of his own fortunes of the time, and, abetted
already by his experience of white scrutiny, most definitely available for
scoring.

One looks at his looking first and sees that his turning to the horizon is
a reflection on Malden. The black population of West Virginia was small.

Leaders emerged from, especially, churches and schools, as well as civic organizations. But outside the eastern panhandle, where the forming of Union Leagues helped organize a larger relative black population, this did not lead to an effective machine for the launching of black candidates for statewide and federal office. Generally speaking, then, black West Virginians were cultivated, with varying degrees of success, by white politicians in both parties looking to them as a swing vote to turn the tide in closely contested elections. This meant they "possessed some bargaining power and therefore some significance in matters of education, civil rights, social reform and economic development," and, particularly, led them to prize the vote and politics as the cardinal badge of their freedom. (This faith led to a consensus among politically active freedpeople that the principled stance was to oppose disfranchising even treasonous Confederate rebels lately waging war on the United States). They followed the political course with humility—a white journal, the *Spirit of Jefferson*, commended them for being "respectful in their intercourse," manifesting "no disposition to be turbulent or offensive"—but much of their effort came a cropper due to their lack of numbers. Despite all this, African American men, according to historian Carter G. Woodson, could become political players, but "only with white acquiescence or support."[54]

There is a twofold problem in this situation as Washington might have apprehended it. First, there is the futility of voting without much consequence—of being free without the means of making that freedom the broadest vista, and, second, there is the dependency of black politicians on white patronage, which later bothered him not at all. At the time, however, a young man with the aspiration of rising to high office would feel disappointment at the way the numbers and the politics boded ill for that aspiration. Looking outward to the horizon and the wider world beyond, he might also have looked longingly at the far South, where black majorities and near majorities were indeed sending black men to significant state offices and to Congress. Looking at his looking in this second way suggests a rather different dimension to his thinking about a career: that his aspirations pointed him south, bearing not the gospel of race relations but carpetbag, with the aim of cultivating a real constituency to catapult him to the highest rung of success.

Some aspects of this story may be inferred, while others require speculation. The record on these matters is quite unclear. Later there will be the certainty that great mistakes were made by the freedmen; that in the "great leap from slavery to freedom"[55] black people fell flat on their faces. That the suddenness of the change in their lives leads "to excesses and mistakes" contributing, Washington says, to "moral and physical degeneration," to the inevitable negative reaction on the part of white people, and thence to bad race relations.[56] Nonetheless, it would seem that before 1879 (when he returned to Hampton Institute as a postgraduate teacher) he continued on his course in politics positioning himself as a nascent leader among the black polity: their man, a creature of their politics as well as their advocate. The corollary to this is that he had not fully fallen into the embrace of white help, of what whites could do for him—how they could, in the absence of the turmoil of black political participation, lift him up and place him atop a depoliticized, demobilized black mass. This was a matter that he had to work out at Hampton and afterward; he could not solve it in Reconstruction. Further, it seems clear that he was not yet prepared to devote the problems of the freedmen to either plain black incapacity or a special racial debility engendered by slavery—for how would he go before a black electorate with jeremiads of black haplessness?

This is to say that the Washington of Reconstruction times was not the Washington of more modern times; that he had not yet established the proper, sufficient distance between black people and himself he later achieved, or rather, proper distance on their insufficiency to throw his lot in with race relations. Still the kernel of the critique of African Americans was likely in place: not from Mrs. Ruffner alone had he learned to scrutinize harshly the freedpeople's strengths and weaknesses. From his precocious experience in politics he may well have begun to wonder, can they stand up to the odds against them as an enduring force worthy of my leadership, a constituency, not simply worthy of, but capable of carrying me on their shoulders to high station?

Washington claims that early on the sneaking suspicion arose that all would turn out for naught: "Though I was but little more than a youth during the period of Reconstruction, I had the feeling that mistakes were being made, and that things could not remain in the condition that they were in very long." Nevertheless, his more nuanced comments suggested a more ambiguous situation likely was beginning to form in his mind. There are, he insists, "several kinds of freedom": "There is a freedom that is apparent, and one that is real; a superficial freedom, and one that is substantial; a freedom that is temporary and deceptive, and one that is abiding and permanent; one that ministers to the lower appetites and passions, and another that encourages growth in the higher and sweeter things of life—a freedom that is forced, and one that is the result of struggle, forbearance, and self-sacrifice."[57] While Washington attributed the freedpeople's "tremendous mistakes"[58] to, among other things, bad faith and vindictiveness, the Negro's taking the wrong path during Reconstruction was more the product of a noxious combination of hubris and childlike ignorance (although apparently not such a child as himself) that drove black people to acts of folly and into relationships with exploiters, charlatans, and other types of false leaders. It was "unfortunate," he would write, that "some strong force" was not brought to bear on the situation.[59]

Therein lies a harsh assessment of the leadership provided by and afforded to the people in Reconstruction for it is the absence of strong and effective leadership that feeds Washington's dreams of revenge. They come when one senses the imminence of inevitable, reoccurring defeat to which one says—with a will even if only to one's self—"I must act, defend, attack" because others have failed to make a proper defense.[60] They are the conjuring of castles by bullied boys after lines in the sand have been drawn and redrawn, crossed and then obliterated by succeeding incursions and changes in the tides of history. And the dreamers, the bullied, find themselves backed up so far that no beach remains; and, lying there, flat on battered backs in grassy dunes, dream of unassailable fortresses.

Such a perspective on the freedom and Reconstruction is echoed in Washington's impatience with otherworldly religion, with nominal leaders acting the fool and leaving the Negro anesthetized, asleep, too concerned with superficialities and appearances to understand and really comprehend all that was being robbed of them. But Washington's position in these affairs, as opposed to his perspective on them, is more complicated because he was yet to have worked out his relationship with the black polity. Divided, and ambivalent, wanting to lead and wanting to be someone, he cannot simply reject the people. But he can begin to wonder whether one rises most surely up from among the people or as strictly an independent agent: whether in stringent circumstances it is not better to flee than to fight—to be a free bird in flight from the rest of the flock. The sign of this ambivalence, and a part of the process of its eventual resolution is embodied in his relationship with Washington Ferguson, who becomes for him not a hero of the freedom, but a scoundrel and a parasite; the receptacle for all his bitterness.

One might view the jokes Washington told on black people as simple entertainment: a means to win over white audiences to his more serious message and purpose. On the other hand, with a view in mind of his political ambitions, they might be understood in a different vein, as reflective of his genuine perspective on the inadequacy of black people—bitter humor because black people are unable to realize their role in his dreamed of greatness, thus forcing him to rely, unfortunately and unhappily, on the whites to lift him up. Seen in the first light, the sport he makes of the people's choosing of names—where slaveholder Hatcher's slave John becomes John Hatcher or John S. Lincoln or something similarly highfalutin'—becomes a way for him to draw a distinction between himself and other former slaves. Only a few pages removed in his autobiography from his caustic character-ization of the freedpeople—all pretentiousness and hubris and filled by a sense of broad entitlement—he claims, nonsensically, "the rare privilege" of naming himself. This is a statement tantamount to a boast: he, unlike them, earned his name; he made himself.[61]

But Washington neither made himself nor named himself, or at least not in the way and to the extent that his promoters wished when they portrayed him as the second coming of the original Washington—the singular Negro to properly take advantage of the freedom, and thus destined to lead. He was one among many of a rising generation—"tell 'em we're rising"—and the dynamics that produced the man he eventually became produced as well different and divergent personalities. That need not lessen the importance of Washington to what would become his age, after all. The existence of one such as Ida B. Wells-Barnett, up from slavery with a story to tell wholly as dramatic as Washington's, but cutting quite a different figure in the age of Washington, does not make her an alternative to him (as it sometimes seems suggested), but instead illuminates his connection to his peers. Rec-ognition of those facts suggests a different, hidden meaning to his joke on naming, and, perhaps, equally to the scores of others he tells on Negroes.

The trick of Washington's treatment of his naming is that the joke here is one only he knows he is telling on himself: that in exposing the folly of just freed slaves he was retrospectively scoring his younger self for his own folly in placing himself within the Washington Ferguson line; for being naive and for personally investing too much faith in this black man; and, in turn, for politically investing to great a hope in the ability of black people in gen-eral to make a go of freedom through their independent action.

This further suggests a way of understanding the deeper meaning of his employment of what two of his biographers call "the much-abused funny story" in his speeches and writings—his utilization of the Negro as chicken stealer homily that brought down the house at Atlanta, the "dis darkey am called to preach" parable that invariably had them rolling in the aisles out in the sticks, and the rest of his arsenal of racial funniness. His defenders insist that Washington does this only for the end purpose of more "effec-tively driv[ing] home whatever point he happened to be making," or, with Howells, that the jokes are means of setting his white audience at ease, bringing speaker and audience together. His constant telling of stories on feckless uncles and precious aunties, and the aphorisms and cryptic wisdom gleaned from their fractured diction, may have had that effect. If this were indeed the case, however, one still has to wonder if at some point Washington did not grasp the limitations of this oratorical strategy when the jokes spread as far or even farther than did his supposedly more serious message. As Emma L. Thornbrough notes, "many people who knew nothing else about Washington knew these stories for they were often published by themselves in newspapers all over the country even when his lectures were not reported."[62]

On the other hand, figuring the jokes he told on the Negro as Washington's own private and bitter humor, as reflecting Washington's real, true feelings about black people, rather tends to draw a distinction between the guffaws of a white house he brings down and what Washington reflects about himself. That is to say, one might identify each as contemptuous of African American ability, but Washington's is a scorn born of disappointment rather than the too-ready denigration that proceeds from never having had any expectation that the Negro could amount to something other than a laughable mess—a hapless race of Sambos—or destined for permanent thralldom. Both insist that black people are worthy of such scorn, but Washington's says would that they were not this way, and further: if only some sense could be knocked into their heads.

※※※

IT IS well nigh impossible to determine precisely when Washington began to see as ironic his naming himself after Ferguson; what is clear is only that he did not and then he did so see it. What is clearer still is that early on—even as a child in slavery—he was introspective, and that that quality in him must have been intensified by the tumult of the 1870s so as to force upon him questions at once personal and political. These were questions of an ambitious young man's identity: Who am I? How am I different from my peers and family and others? How am I to succeed in a sometimes inhospitable world? What can I make of my ability to navigate among the whites? Equally: why do I see folly where other black people see promise, but, perhaps more, promise where white people see only folly? Why am I the man who can do something about all this?

Washington takes the anger and bitter opposition to the whites standing in his way and in the way of African Americans actually achieving something enduring in this country, and for the purposes of his own rise and psychological well-being projects it onto his stepfather, makes him his foil. How is this fair? Ferguson was a good, conservative man, a man whose wife stayed at home (to work) in preference to answering the muster of the outside economy—not, then, any sort of parasite at all (and, as Washington well knew, the annals of man's inhumanity to woman provide numerous instances of even sickly women like his mother being turned out by their husbands). He was marked present at meeting of church and party. But Ferguson was not a leader in either place, and, further, was poor and limited in his ability to provide protection for his family; he was merely a mediocrity. like most people in their traverse through life.

Washington, in his evaluation of Ferguson's role in his life, does not have to be fair. It should not be expected that Washington especially as an adolescent or even as a young man would have any objectivity on the dilemmas faced by his family. If a part of him perceived himself as being all but done in by Ferguson, those feelings, for all their subjectivity, are his own, although other feelings are also in evidence. Take, for example, his claim that his mother adopted the orphaned boy who takes the name James Washington. It may have been the stepson's perception that Ferguson's failure resides in the fact that he did not put his foot down by vetoing his wife's decision when, as Washington complains elsewhere, the five members of the family were living in want. And perhaps there were other sins of which Ferguson was guilty, but unmentioned by Washington, although this seems less than likely given his willingness to make a show of parading the most intimate of dirty laundry. Instead, the Oedipus dimension may be no more complex than what is present on the page, consisting of what transpired within the Ferguson family, and in the strange thoughts and chronic angers come alive in mixed (step-) families and even in unmixed ones (indeed, even in the Anglo-Saxon families Washington was so hot set on black people emulating).

Is it possible for the black story to fit easily into those deep veins of family and psychology that lock fathers and sons into soul-crushing conflict until one or the other gives up or dies? That it is simply a variant on the universal story of manhood achieved through the son's striking out for a distinct course from his father's? Or is it an endeavor to slip the yoke of the Negro problem in order to say, this is a story just about the characters in it—something that happened in my family, but is not meant as fodder for the Negro pathology mill. But Washington's story, his disclaiming of any ancestry, fits so readily into that political enterprise, in the variant that sometimes seems like a *putsch* against black manhood and fatherdom, as to make one wonder if that is not his purpose. True or not, the notion of Ferguson as nothing but a failed father is an impression taken from his treatment. If his audience heeds his message and says he did indeed make himself—could see while all around him others were blind—they may as well say here was a "rather unsatisfactory stepfather," as one Washington biographer has written. Another biographer follows Washington's lead even farther. Why did he send for Jane and the children? "The outstanding motive," was "that he might use their labor for increasing his own sparse earnings. He was a thriftless man, with no strength of character or skill of hand that would fit him to support a home or guide the children." The "Negro stepfather . . . was shiftless, selfish, and short-sighted, and in so far as Booker was concerned, he made all the wrong decisions."[63] Or even more recklessly say, here was no father figure at all, and therein lies the root of the problem—the absent foundation, the cause of broken or defective families, the robbing of heirs, sons and daughters, of the legacy that should be passed on to them, why they are dependent in turn, handicapped. The failure of protection, the strong line all fathers aspire to draw around their people that says, past this line you may not come, to give up their lives if need be in defense of that line. The failure of a man set in the place of authority makes him no father at all, and neither is he a man.

This is not to discount the possibility that Washington's treatment of Ferguson reflects a simpler instrumentality: the revenge motive in memoir has a tradition, if not an honored place. Upholding that part of Washingtonianism that insists at once that the Negro must assimilate the American virtues of family and hard work, while kowtowing to the whites, he simultaneously violates other rules of decorum: pride in patrimony, for example, and if that value is impossible to uphold, if the wounds of childhood are too deep, that silence is a more noble response than slurs. But it is not simply a personal matter or private either in the long history of the Negro problem that is witness to a multitude of plain fathers gone without honoring, done in by racism and oppression. If they are especially unlucky they will be hung up like so much laundry from the walls of Southern shacks and Northern slums by literate Southern refugees and eternally naive manchildren fumbling their way down mean streets in the promised land; there on permanent display with no moment to speak in justification of the things they did; but rather lain on the altar of the Negro problem, offerings for the purpose of their sons and daughters to receive greater sympathy for having escaped their clutches—vindication via vindictiveness.

If this is indeed true about Washington, it is but a more personal than usual variant of the oft-repeated declaration by succeeding generations of black thinkers and publicists that theirs is a generation of New Negroes not willing to settle for the lot of their parents, or otherwise better equipped to handle those challenges that surpassed their parents. For Washington, as for other New Negroes, then and later, it is a way to signal certain ability:

a promise to make a splash, to not be held back, to make a great leap forward into progress, to break free from the conventions restricting African American life; a pledge of honor that this generation will not fall into the traps ensnaring previous leaders.[64]

There is a certain reasonability to the desire of some black people of Washington's generation in the age of Washington—that era of blithe progress and segregation's elaboration, of Darwin and Freud and the Dunning school, of scientific racism and lynch mobs —would in unself-conscious frustration, but also self-servingly, look askance at the generation of their parents. Laud the mothers for at least being there and passing or excelling the more limited test, as he sees it, presented to them. (But even that lauding is mitigated by Washington's simultaneous celebration of the role of women like his mother in their capacity as servants to whites; his nostalgic invocation at Atlanta of black women "nursing your children" may be seen as a backhanded compliment when one recognizes that this means they were not available to nurse their own children.) But slay, by the word, the fathers for their inadequacy in the too-large tasks presented them. And then, for the orphaned New Negro abandoned by the old variety, break free and through to make one's self anew or at the least a free agent unencumbered by ancestry or family ties and thus more available for adoption by prospective patrons.

The boy Booker, as a boy becoming a young man, comes to find the adult Washington Ferguson lacking: less than a man, a failed father figure. Washington then is made available to adoption by the Ruffners because of his stepfather's failings, and it is as if he says: pity me and love me, for I have been denied love. And the boy, when he grows up, insists he will be a man and promises to gift his children with a paternal legacy, vows further that he will not be consigned to the older man's fate—an average man in Malden, or maybe slightly above average, but still a man of no moment in the wider world. Washington's evaluation of Ferguson is a personal matter without necessarily being also politically pointed (although, as with the sport he makes of other aspects of black life, Washington's attributing his success to white help serves well the cause of his ascendance), but personal in such a way that to understand what he went through in his early years—how some of his dreams died and others were born, and how he came out a different person—requires some suspension of inquiry into the politics of his life and life story, and focus on, not the politics of the freedom, but the problem of Washington's forming psyche at a crucial stage of its development.

Washington has family in Malden and opportunities to grow. He takes advantage of these and shines, forming an identity between himself and the rising expectations of the freedpeople in Malden and thereabouts during Reconstruction. But there are limits there as well as good possibilities. Those limits involve readily identifiable forces, like racism, opposing Washington's advancement and that of other African Americans. They also include demographic facts that are politically indifferent in origin, but, nevertheless, place a cap on the heights to which even the most able—most intrinsically meritorious—black boy can reasonably aspire. Finally, and implicit in Washington's retrospective evaluation of the "mistakes" of the era and of black people, there is the inability of the freedpeople to lay a strong foundation for their future freedom; the insufficiency of their efforts at mobilizing a strong force and a sustainable posture relative to those forces arrayed against them. And so he turns to other means of ascent including the relationship with the Ruffners and his disembarking for the Hampton Institute in fall of 1872, seeking out more white help and more training. Neither of these moves on his part, however, indicates his rejecting of a political career or, otherwise, his seeking to be leader emerging up from African America (as evidenced by his continuing participation in the politics of Reconstruction even after his graduation from Hampton). Rather, they show Washington's turning to other steps than the more narrow and brittle homemade ones before him while still in his stepfather's house. The evidence of that turn, and in connection with other elements of Washington's thinking about the abilities of black people, about racial capacity and his forming of the idea of race relations, and about his relationship with Washington Ferguson, suggest as well his attention turning to a different self-conception than one too tightly tied to the fortunes of black Reconstruction; an endeavor to gain purchase on a liberated fate for himself—a possibly more progressive or more efficacious over the long haul, self-identity. But where to look?

In freedom as in slavery, Washington's fellows took notice of his propensity for gazing off to the horizon. Looking once again at his looking—the standing stock still and fixing eyes off toward the North that the other slaves remembered, it is possible to conceive of just what he was doing—to see both seer and the object of his gaze. Here it has been suggested that Ferguson was the person for whom he was looking, expectantly awaiting his return from his sojourns to western Virginia laden down with stories and news of the wider world; a world in which he was an actor in both senses of the word—as storyteller, and, more heroically still, as a slave acting despite his station with the élan of a free man. But what happens to the seer when Ferguson does not return to him, as had inevitably to happen because Ferguson was a slave and not some weekend parent regularly arriving on schedule bearing gifts. What happens to the boy's first sight then? And what happens, after freedom, when the man appears upon the second glance of the now older boy, a young man, as with feet of clay? Casting his eyes outward toward a world he means to conquer, what other visions appear before his eyes?

%%%

ONE OF Abraham Lincoln's most recent biographers has found evidence that his subject early on went through something like the same kind of searching attributed here to the young Booker Washington. Like Washington, young man Lincoln was endowed early on with a prophetic sense of his own greatness, David Herbert Donald has found. Also like the younger man, Lincoln came from unpromising and tumultuous circumstances. His rearing during the 1810s and 1820s may be seen as almost taking place on the back of a wagon heading west; indeed, his family's movement from his birthplace in Kentucky on to Indiana and then to Illinois virtually embodied, as Lincoln himself liked to say (quoting Gray's "Elegy"), "the short and simple annals of the poor,"[65] the story of the poor whites' sorry fate; of a failing yeomanry denied access to good fortune and dislocated from the good lands, or, alternately, of the unwanted—of trash—obtruding themselves on more virtuous and able persons in a series of backwater locales and burgeoning frontier towns.

It is the American convention to see no trouble in that; that those who do indeed turn out to be great men simply soldier on, noses to grindstone, bootstraps lifted—like, as it were Horatio Alger's boys: nothing can hold back a striver. In real life, however, and given the lack of promise in the circumstances of his life, believing in himself in that way brought Lincoln face to face with a contradiction with the result that he could not believe one such as him could be born into so seamy an apparent lineage as that provided by his parents. About Nancy Hanks and Thomas Lincoln, the son stated in 1859 that they "were both born in Virginia of undistinguished families—second families, perhaps I should say." To help explain his feeling of being "different from the people with whom he grew up," he fixed on the fact that his mother was born illegitimate, which was an opening for him to claim a Virginian of more outstanding stock, a nobleman, perhaps, as a forebear.[66]

Americans, and especially great heroes of American democracy, are not supposed to think this way, but instead are to embrace the principle of individualism that holds that fairness dictates the making of one's fortune or the failing at that—rising or falling—based solely on one's own merit. Lincoln, though, did not see it that way, at least in regard to what he felt was needed for him to rise or to explain how it was that he rose. Instead he adopted this imagined ancestor as plausible sire to his own sense of special endowments: "ambition, mental alertness, and the power of analysis" (in Donald's words). This was the psychological hook enabling Lincoln to expect a different fate for himself than that of his "ordinary and limited parents," but particularly so in regard to his hapless father. The alienation the son felt from the father apparently was intensified by the mother's incapacity due to illness and ultimately her premature death at the dawning of his passage into young manhood. Lincoln "began to distance himself from his father," about whom can be found "not one favorable word" in Lincoln's collected works and the stories and recollections in the vast troves of Lincolniana.[67]

The passing resemblance between the troubled relationship between Abraham and Thomas Lincoln and the equally alienated one between Booker Washington and Washington Ferguson may only be an interesting connection: a brief note on the irony of filial pietism buried at the back of a neglected file cabinet in the annals of great men. But a small irony and a superficial one of limited and uncertain meaning because the example upon which it is based takes up, in the former instance, the wedge driven by a son between himself and his real father, while in the latter one assumes an already existing and perhaps inevitable gulf between a stepson and the man he grudgingly referred to as his stepfather; that is to say, that where no paternal connection ever exists, notice can hardly be paid to the riving of that bond.[68]

Here, however, it has been suggested that the relationship between Washington and Ferguson was, at least for a time, more intimate and inspiring to the younger man than he was later willing to admit; that, Ferguson, indeed, was his father in all but one of the usual senses of term—as husband to Washington's mother, protector in providing shelter for the boy, and the man who gave him a name. And thus that Washington's disparagement of him and denial of their connection represents a more needful action on his part: a bitter blaming of Ferguson onto whom Washington projects his feelings of hurt and disappointment at some of the circumstances of his and the freedpeople's lives, and for what he considers to be the unpromising prospects for the fulfillment of his ambition. It is those circumstances, rather than Ferguson's failure as a father, that cause him to deny the only man who acted in the role of father to him and refuse to acknowledge that it was Ferguson who gave him his name; that color the young man's view of who he is, to whom he belongs and with, and how he means to make his way in the world.

Therein lies a deeper connection between Washington and Lincoln. The circumstances that drove Lincoln's family westward to Illinois also apparently may have caused Lincoln to doubt that Thomas Lincoln really was his father, paying heed to gossip back in Kentucky that said that he had been rendered impotent by the mumps.[69] In Washington's case, circumstances that placed him in West Virginia cause him to pay heed to gossip back in Virginia and circulated about the Burroughs place that his father, as he writes, "was a white man who lived on one of the near-by plantations."[70]

Perhaps this notion had meant something to Washington previously. Perhaps in those slavery days he had considered this a possibility, when standing watch waiting for Ferguson he had grown angry with a child's imperfect, impatient sense of time and desire, and with that feeling, began to imagine another father than Ferguson, but more powerful—freer—swooping in upon the Burroughs place, proclaiming "My son, at last!" and then to deliver Booker and Jane from their plight. And perhaps that thought had been driven down into the recesses of his mind, when that father, bathed in white, had never come, and war and Washington Ferguson had been his deliverer, only to be dredged back up again when Washington came to see that Ferguson and black people could not deliver on all that he expected was his due in freedom.

Discarding for now any question of whether the rumors are true (because whether they can, by objective means, be absolutely proven or not, has little relevance to the seriousness with which they were considered by these young men), it is possible to imagine Lincoln and Washington both in contemplation of the meaning of it all: of two forgotten fathers of sons destined for greatness; and of two fatherless sons—changelings almost—delivered down into the wrong lives, but not willing to leave it lie there. One finds, in the connection between the two young men's self-conception, not an irony of surfaces, but a deeper psychological irony beneath the surface of biological truth, in the suggestion that both these self-made men felt the need to lean on the crutch of superior heredity even if they themselves have to be the designer of their own improved genes.

Lincoln's conclusion was that he had an intelligence and a fortitude about him that could surmount any obstacle. To Washington, it likely means the same thing: however black his past and present were, his future is likely to be brighter. But the way he comes to that conclusion requires some greater examination of his thoughts on "the Negro of mixed and unmixed blood."[71] How he came to have those thoughts demands attention on Washington the beholder, but, as well, on him beheld, and what it means to Americans encountering him when they reckoned they had seen a mulatto.

%%%

BOOKER WASHINGTON is "a very competent capable mulatto," Samuel Chapman Armstrong said.[72] The former characterization is, of course, a value judgment; it is either true or untrue. But what of the latter? One might exhume the body in order to chip off a bit of proof for scientific analysis, or, short of that, seek to find out about his actual appearance—what were his physical characteristics—and survey all the accounts of his career, all of the descriptions of his person from friend and foe, alike. Doing so would hardly lead one any closer to a meaningful truth about him or his heritage.

Washington was, of course, a "mulatto," or, at least, so said plenty of his contemporaries. Howells called him "this marvellous yellow man."[73] H. G. Wells thought he had "a face rather of the Irish type," and added that Washington "is certainly as white in appearance as our Admiral Fisher, who is, as a matter of fact, quite white." Some of his contemporaries, however, thought Washington's appearance proved something quite different, denying him his reputation as a mulatto and, instead, insisting he was strictly a standard-issue Negro. An example of this sort comes from an Englishman visiting the United States, William Archer, who related that Washington "is a negro in every lineament, and not, one would say, of the most refined type." "His skin is neither black nor copper-coloured, but rather of a sort of cloudy yellow, to which the other shades are, perhaps, aesthetically preferable. His hair, ears, his nose, his jaw, all place his race beyond dispute." (Evincing the high level of acumen that typifies the entrance of glib foreigners into the Negro problem, Archer's comments must be understood in the context of his shameless embrace of what he calls "the irrepressible instinct of race-superiority.")[74]

The term "mulatto" however, has or had at least two meanings in the United States: one being simply a person holding heritage from both Africa and Europe and the second, more restrictive one, being the progeny of one African American parent and one of European descent. Because of this semantic difficulty, the man of letters, Howells, chooses his words carefully in describing Washington and Douglass as "of one blood with their fathers or forefathers."[75] Louis R. Harlan is careful, too, in his attribution: Washington's "medium-brown skin, reddish hair, and gray eyes suggest that he was the son of a white man." But Harlan, who labels Washington "colored," "black," or "mulatto" with no apparent special meaning attached to any of the usages, explores only the possible paternity of several white men about the Burroughs place. Whether his failure to explore other candidates is due to a lack of awareness of the more than one way a person might end up looking like Washington did or because these white men seem most plausible to him is not clear. In fact, the only warrant for concluding that Washington's father was white is the lead provided by Washington, who, in his turn, pays heed the gossip he heard as a child and small boy. Harlan reaches the conclusion he does by taking at face value those rumors and then seeing a white father in Washington's appearance, thus giving materiality to subjectivity. Census-takers in the nineteenth century did the same thing by spending a few moments in a home, making a best guess at the genetic inheritance of the inhabitants, but also perhaps reading in their faces something of their destinies. It is not clear that they held this to be a foolproof and historical determination of identity and paternity.[76]

The diversity in opinion that comes from these and a wide variety of other sources on the matter of what a mulatto is and who Washington was is telling. Telling about the origins of the word's malign application to humans, and the corollary that figures such "mixed bloods" as something queer and sterile or queer and metaphorical. It is also a telling adjunct to this diversity that black nationalists will write commending Washington and expressly excoriating "the negro (?) of mixed blood" as traitors to the cause and pawns of the white man, as, for example, John E. Bruce did in a letter to Washington written over his pen name, "Bruce-Grit."[77] This is because the meaning of race and race mixture borne through the blood is the most subjective of subjects for race men and racists and reforming friends of the Negro; the truth then, and contrary to the certainty of those who fixed Washington in this way or that, lies all in the eyes of the beholder.

And the beheld?

‰‰‰

FOR WASHINGTON, the ultimate meaning and specific implications of all these circumstances and conjectures was for the future to determine. Washington might overstate the matter somewhat when he claims in his autobiography that it was not until he embarked on his sojourn to continue his education with Armstrong at the Hampton Institute in the fall of 1872 that he had occasion to discover that "the colour of one's skin" could be used to harm one.[78] This was, he says, his very first encounter with segregation and discrimination. Nevertheless, the personal usefulness of his embrace of a white father is clear, offering him assistance in achieving some type of clarity from the clouded feelings associated with his identity and place in the world; what had happened to him and what he could expect from the future. He had left his black stepfather's house.

Leaving Malden, Washington, at sixteen, must have thought himself nicely on the go, a free wheel rolling on to his large destiny. The distance he placed between himself and black people's past in slavery, and between himself and Washington Ferguson's bad example, would now allow him to go on to greater heights at Hampton and afterward. He would complete the making of himself, and leave for his children a legacy that neither of his two fathers had seen fit or been fit to grant him. He was now Booker T. Washington. He may or may not have been looking for a new and different father to give the lie to the notion that all the work of making himself was complete, but at Hampton that was indeed was in the offing.

By the fall of 1872, he was, he would say, a young man with no ancestry and no alibis, and each of these qualities about him was to his advantage. For all his looking out upon the horizon, though, there was much—at this, the height of African American participation in the politics of Reconstruction—he could not see. The question of whether he would accomplish things of significance and win renown is not the right one. But given his sense of the vulnerability and tenuousness of black Reconstruction, another question might have occurred to him, if only in a distant and cloudy way: to be outstanding as among the tallest and sturdiest trees in a forest or to stand out, a transplant onto a bare plain where a forest once stood. Black West Virginia had equipped him for its own purposes and groomed him to assume his role in the former capacity—to teach, to protect, to defend, and to lead. This grooming had also been done for others like him, including many young men and women who would join him at Hampton. But those were the purposes of a group of citizens in a democracy when a leader among black people—in that post for black purposes, by the decision of black people, and thus thrown up like something organic from soil, seed, sun, and rain—was a rather different person than "the Negro George Washington" he was created as in 1895.

The question was: to stand out on a barren plain or to be outstanding? Circumstances would change and that organic development up from the fertile ground of Reconstruction would be given over to the axe of white supremacy, creating a barren plain where most all the remaining trees, old growth and new, were caused to whither and die, or, otherwise, to be potted in too small vessels and thus to become stunted and distorted. Only then would he say, back in West Virginia where he started out his journey to freedom, of his black leadership: "In all this work I have sought not alone to benefit my own race, but by lifting up the black man at the same time to assist the white man in removing the burdens that have come to him as a result of American slavery. . . . The two races are to live in this country together, and he is an enemy to both who tries to array one race against the other."[79]

This generous quality of spirit in Washington was something his soon to be mentor, a new and (as he would see it) more able figure in his life, came to recognize during Washington's years at the Hampton Institute. Booker Washington is an able "mulatto," Samuel Chapman Armstrong said, in recommending Washington to his eventual employers at Tuskegee, and, upon another occasion: "He is no common 'darkey.' "[80] Both his characterizations, but also Armstrong's punctuation of the last one, are suggestive.

Chapter 5

"Prepared for the Exercise of These Privileges"

A New Negro and the End of Democracy

YOU CAN look out upon a river and know with a positive certainty
that it has ever been and ever will be thus: elements of earth and
water, rock and wood, combining to form a definite and concrete
thing, a tableau captured in a painting or reproduced in a photograph.
Such frozen certainty, however, wholly depends upon placement and perspective: on where you are in relation to the river; on how far your field of
vision extends, even on the temporal intersection of your observing with
a moment in the life of the river. Back there, the river finds its modest
origins, betraying nothing of its glory downstream in waterfalls and white-
water. Here, the river rolls along in rapids, with no intimation of other
aspects of its meandering course through space and time; in another season
it might become but a shadow of itself, strangled down into a trickle bleeding through a dry and dusty bed. Up close, an eddy might be taken to be the

sum of the river, roiling, but in an arrested whirl, going nowhere in every direction. At a distance, the same section appears, no matter how fast it turns inward upon itself, as no movement at all, but a placid pool fixed to the riverside where waters are stranded or merely resting.

And to the skewing perspectives of time and place must be added the slant of the pragmatics of the looking. A captain of the river, on ferryboat or barge, sees in his mind one specific image of the safe or safest passage through hidden dangers and obstacles in but one slice of the river's longer course on which he traffics. What occurs upstream matters only insofar as it affects navigation upon his river. Circumstances downstream matter not at all, and so the lower river exists for him merely as a receptacle for the effluvium of his enterprise. A cartographer in the fulfillment of his purposes describes the river as an unchanging part of the surroundings, a fixed feature of the landscape. His map says nothing of the dynamic interplay of water and terrain, living, inseparable entities tied together and animated by the unfolding of nature; nor, in describing the river's course, does his map speak of the true ecological consequences of the interfering work and hindrances imposed on the river by human beings. When surveyors and engineers are brought down to the river, they commence the building of levees and canals and dams that alter the course of the river, harnessing its power, providing a basis for life and commerce in the flourishing of some fields, while simultaneously damming existent and potential life of other fields, depriving it of the requirements of growth, drowning it in a manufactured swamping, or leaving it to wither and die in the sun.

In the fullness of time and in the seasons of some years, the river breaks free from artificial disciplines. Shrugging off the routines of its past, jumping its banks, it seizes a new course and marks the land, taking it in a natural flood. But that is not an end. Even the evidences left by the wild forces of nature can, with a will and the wherewithal to do so, be erased by human genius from a marred terrain. Then, with restraints reimposed, the river once again appears to the eye of the observer in all its natural beauty, a creature of providence.

All the consequences of the meeting of man and river may be accessible to those trained and committed to the uncovering of the river's natural history, and the seemingly supernatural history that is humanity's troubling of the waters. The river may speak to them eloquently of its passage through time and space. But the river's own story is buried in its passing and by its passing, and the river itself is voiceless, made mute, and thus dependent upon others to sing its song. Geologists and ecologists may make encomiums to the beauty found in the long, slow confluence of earth and water, offer erudite statements on the deep eloquence of common nature, or provide linkages between the shaping of this river's contours and those of other rivers. But ultimately, their refrain is muted, too, drowned out by the presence of figures from on high, great men and heroes for whom bridges and waterways are named. Drowned out by those captains and surveyors and engineers employed to fix or perfect it for man's uses with their plans and machines. And drowned out by those closest to the river, witnesses to its surging, some of them beneficiaries of its bounty as well as survivors of its floods.

Washington is just such a man when he completes his speech in Atlanta, sealing his deal—for if it is a racial compact, it is one solely between himself and those who see justice in the race relations idea. He is their hero because he was down by the riverside, had gotten wet (even wetter than they knew), but had not been taken in the flood. For him to be a special American hero, he has to be a Negro saying what he says as proof positive of the potential salvation of all those others who lost and will lose their bearings in the turbid waters. As a Negro, he compels the most rapt attention because he survived when others drowned, bore the brunt of the river's raging, its ebb and flow, the twists and turns of the river's passage, and endured. It is for this reason that he merits posting as captain of the ship bearing forward the Negro's destiny. It is why he is placed at the helm to navigate, between banks, the river's course, battling the river, and casting his and the nation's dreaming fore and aft of the present.

%%%

WHAT IS it that might be said about a man famously involved in a compromise resulting in the ceding of the rights of black people for the sake of racial peace and the harmonizing of relations between the sections? Who, without even the most minimal consultation with African Americans— elected officials or leaders of institutions and private associations—entered into a compact with representatives from the white South, hoping earnestly that black people's bodies and rights would be respected or at least left alone? Who proposed to sit by while some of those bodies and the usable portion of those rights were destroyed? Who then, once the sealing of this rotten deal ensured his ascension to the highest success, situated himself above the political squabbling about Negro rights, and, instead, devoted himself to the Negro's industrial education? Were the man Booker Washington, common sense would know exactly what to say: his participation in affairs in and after 1895 made him the black leader of all time. Somehow words of praise like "interracial healer," much less "sensible black leader," do not attach themselves to the person of Rutherford B. Hayes. But two decades before Washington, he was voicing the outlines of what in the age of segregation would be deemed a visionary and sensible solution to the Negro problem. Washington was considered by many to represent the best of America, a perfectly first-rate man; on the other hand, Hayes was thought, by Henry Adams at least, to be a "third-rate nonentity."[1]

Perhaps it was Hayes's misfortune to be a visionary before the value and beauty of that vision was recognized, making him a prophet without honor in the home of the Negro problem, one of America's profoundest racial pundits, but unrecognized as such. Possibly it was, too, that Hayes simply did not have the same type of standing, even as president of the United States at the final end of Reconstruction, when democracy was not yet in abeyance and segregation had not assumed its full force, that could be mustered for an obscure black man at the dawning of the age to which he would give his name.

Nonetheless, Hayes arrived first at the vision the Age of Washington embraced as the solution to the Negro problem. It was he who first told an audience of white people and an audience of black people:

> We would not undertake to violate the laws of nature, we do not wish to change the purpose of God in making these differences of nature. We are willing to have these elements of our population separate as the fingers are, but we require to see them united for every good work, for national defense, one, as the hand.[2]

Hayes made this speech May 20, 1880, at Virginia Hall on the campus of the Hampton Institute, where Washington was then employed as a teacher. As such, it is abundant evidence that Hayes made a significant contribution to the education of Booker Washington, as well as playing an important role in the lineage leading to the inaugural of Washington as a certain type of Negro leader a little more than fifteen years later.

%%%

WASHINGTON ENTERED the Hampton Institute in October 1872, fresh from conducting his duties as secretary of the Republican rally back in Malden. His first catching sight of the place "seemed to give me new life. I felt that a new kind of existence had now begun—that life would now have a new meaning. I felt that I had reached the promised land, and I resolved to let no obstacle prevent me from putting forth the highest effort to fit myself to accomplish the most good in the world."[3] It was the heyday of Reconstruction, a time when Louisiana's next governor, P. B. S. Pinchback, could discourse on how a man might be dutiful "to his nation, his party and his race." This was Reconstruction's promise in Louisiana and elsewhere in the South, the key link between what appeared later to be "the Chinese Puzzle" of top-level partisanship and the urges drifting up from "the great forces below."[4]

Washington, as he later noted, was not alone in coming to Hampton filled with aspirations for greatness. Speaking for his classmates in his capacity as president of the Hampton Alumni Association, he would recall how they all "came . . . with no capital but stout hearts and brawny muscles and untutored brains," and Hampton "gave us a chance."[5] Those without much money, like Washington, probably did as he did when asked to give evidence of their enthusiasm for a Hampton education: cleaning rooms under the strict scrutiny of Mary Mackie, the lady principal of Hampton, or some other faculty member. In Washington's case, this meant sweeping the room three times, dusting it four times, moving around the furniture, and cleaning in the corners of the closet until the room was rid of every "particle of dust." "The sweeping of the room was my college examination, and never did any youth pass an examination for entrance into Harvard or Yale that gave him more genuine satisfaction," he recalled, "I have passed several examinations since then, but I have always felt that this was the best one I ever passed."[6]

The difference, however, between Hampton's entrance exam and whatever it took to gain admission to those other schools resided in the fact that one could never rest easy in the knowledge that one had truly made it at the Negro school; the tests continued. The new students of Washington's class may not have known it, but they had not entered a school so much as been wheeled into what Hampton's founder and trustees saw as a "race laboratory."[7] Their responsibility was not to excel academically but to outperform their fellows and thus win the role of most well-adjusted Negro.

Washington's emphasis on neatness and hygiene is inescapable: the seeming overzealousness and concentrated fastidiousness that led him to continue to show himself fussing and neatening long after he ceased being responsible for such tasks, after he was able to employ Tuskegee students or hired help to tend to such matters. There is an irresistibility to the urge to satirize this, to make Washington out to be a dimwitted Uncle Tom, or to take it overly seriously such that he appears to be a neurotic. Doing so, and thus making a problem of his personality, might seem a way of explaining his constant harping about the need for Negroes to keep clean. But what explains it if we discount the idea that African Americans were any more unclean and odorous than millions of other Americans similarly situated? Taking as a starting point Washington's reputation as an obsessive sweeper and duster, Wesley Brown, in his play *Boogie-Woogie and Booker T.*, has Washington compulsively cleaning the room he occupied before the important 1904 Carnegie Hall conference in New York; cleaning it as if his life and future depended upon the tidiness of his room rather than his impending joust with black rivals before an audience of white philanthropists. Brown's conceptualization of Washington dramatizes the way in which Washington was, in a sense, never off stage: always prepared to perform his star turn as the Negro who best assimilated proper values.[8]

A playwright may have a special advantage in recognizing a player when he sees one, especially one so inclined as Washington to chew up broad sections of the scenery when it suited his purposes. Thus, it is not obsessiveness that caused Washington to clean the room at Hampton three or four or five times. This seems absurd, when efficiency and common sense would indicate doing it once and right. But the scrutiny of women like Mrs. Ruffner and his Hampton teacher (another white woman who became "one of my strongest and most helpful friends")[9] is not especially about efficiency; their aim as taskmasters is not what they pretend it to be. Their demand is for art more than it is for science, for the flourishes of culture more than bottom-line outputs of economies, a pantomime of toil sufficient to satisfy their own jackleg version of the Negro problem. The performance is the thing, the staged show is the action, polishing the apple, or more precisely, scraping away the encrusted barnacles off a boat left in the river too long. And how it moves the white scrutinizers to feel is action, too, as they witness him transmute their ideal Negro (which is also their idea of what is wrong with the Negro) into reality, thus freeing him of his predicament. In the case of Mrs. Ruffner, this action means relief, elevating her morose contemplation of her predicament. For the Hampton faculty, there is the confirmation of their prejudices, but also a logic for the rationing of scarce resources. Their agreement with a student like Washington, the meeting of minds, the black and the white, is action as well, a movement of theoretical possibility: they did it together, joined in good race relations, and so why not others? Put another way: if one Negro can escape, then why cannot all? If only a small number of Negroes do win this white embrace, then they are the exception that proves the rule that probably most Negroes are not really worthy of that sympathetic support. If Washington and his classmates say, by their willingness to submit to each and every demand placed before them, that black people have been worthless but still are worthy of a chance, broken but fixable, then they have earned their way and explained away the general lack of opportunity available to African Americans for secondary and more advanced education.

If, in the Hampton laboratory, the students were the mice made to run through mazes, General Samuel Chapman Armstrong, the Hampton principal and professor of "moral science," was the laboratory's chief scientist and lead experimenter in conducting research on social engineering. He was, Washington was later sure, almost "superhuman," a great man and "the noblest, rarest human being that it has ever been my privilege to meet," and of a type with "that Christlike body of men and women who went into the Negro schools at the close of the war by the hundreds to assist in lifting up my race."[10]

%%%

ACTUALLY, WHO Armstrong was and what he represented to his students is somewhat more complicated than that. Some who went into the South after the war believed that the freedmen and women needed tangible skills and material goods. If they seemed to be abject, it was because of a deprivation in these areas. Asked what would help them, Sarah F. Smiley, a postwar missionary to the South who reported on her experience at the 1890 Lake Mohonk Conference on the Negro Question, replied that the women needed to learn how to sew; they knew how to wash and clean, but needed soap, "tubs and brooms," and these were given them. At Hampton, this attitude was reflected in one part of the Hampton philosophy: offerings of practical courses for teachers, more advanced work for better-prepared students, and opportunities for students to do some sort of work or another to answer the practical problem that most of them did not have sufficient capital to fund their schooling. On the other hand, and very much more in evidence in Armstrong's publicity for the school, there was "industrial education" predicated on the notion, as Armstrong said in the same venue at Mohonk, that the white man can give to the Negro—feed him and clothe him and build him a home—and even "give him knowledge." But, "that does not necessarily build up character. That has got to be worked out." Armstrong was quite precise about what Hampton's industrial education curriculum offered his students: "An able-bodied student represents a capital of perhaps a thousand dollars. We propose to treble that."[11]

Washington would later laud the "atmosphere of business" at Hampton, and how his experience there awakened in him the feeling of "what it means to be a man instead of a piece of property," but how he reconciled himself to the bottom-line ethic Armstrong used to judge him is another matter.[12] That is not the only regard in which there are differences between the mentor and the protégé, differences that might best be understood as those between the true believer and the initiate.

It is not clear how Armstrong came to judge his students and to look at the matter with such a concrete accounting as he had absolutely no experience in running or even participating in a strictly business enterprise. He was born to missionary parents on Maui, Hawaii, in 1839, and educated there and at Williams College under the tutelage of its president Mark Hopkins. After two years at Williams, he was graduated into the Union Army in 1862, serving with distinction and, in 1865, brevetted out from the ranks as a brigadier general. He then worked with the Freedmen's Bureau until 1867, at which time he succeeded in convincing the American Missionary Association to fund a school at Hampton.

Spending the full entirety of his adult life in the employ of the federal government and a charitable and educational concern for the remaining twenty-five years down to his death in 1893 was, however, no impediment to Armstrong's theorizing of the Negro problem. Indeed, he may be taken as a second-generation racial pundit. Armstrong's father and mother, Richard and Clarissa Armstrong, had undertaken their mission to the islands of the Pacific in 1831, that year of blood being spilled in service to a higher call, filled up with the desire to walk Christ's path at whatever cost. Armstrong's father had written at the time of their disembarking that "he who does not love Christ more than houses or lands . . . cannot be his disciple." Pursuant to this noble goal, they settled on the island of Nukuhiva. But this was an inhospitable place, and so they moved on to Maui. There, the Armstrongs, along with their missionary colleagues, set about establishing "a Protestant theocracy," according to one historian. This entailed chasing out their French Catholic rivals like jackals or hyenas might chase away lesser sorts of predators from a cornered and near dead prey. The native Hawaiians, indeed, were dying in frightening numbers, with their total population declining from 300,000 when the British first came to the place in 1778 to 100,000 or so when the Armstrongs settled there in the 1830s to fewer than 75,000 by 1853. To change this morbid arithmetic, Richard Armstrong offered conversion to "the heathen" Hawaiians, but he was not especially good at this. He then became a first-generation advocate of industrial education and deeply involved himself in island politics, reckoning that the problem was not simply heathenism but a deficit of civilization. This led to criticism of his secular strivings by his missionary colleagues as his personal mission came to seem less the devout Protestantism of an awakened New

England and more the bullish pretension of an incipient American imperialism. His vow of poverty went next as he departed the spartan quarters of the mission's compound to live in one of the King of Hawaii's more palatial digs.[13] Thus does doing good become living well, even as the example of the Lamb of God recedes like so much flotsam and jetsam in the wake of a fast-moving Pacific steamer.

Raised in this environment, the younger Armstrong would perhaps inevitably reject the ministry, enthusing to his mother that "I should rather *minister* than be a minister." Inevitable and in spite of the myriad differences between the now free children of slavery who placed themselves in his charge and Hawaiians who had been free to live in their own nation in perfect contentment, before the missionaries came, with most of the provisions of paradise, Armstrong saw strong parallels between the two groupings of backwardness. Both races were ignorant, but it was "not mere ignorance, but deficiency of character" that was the challenge, "the true objective point in education" being "to build up character." Pursuant to this Armstrong created a "Spartan regimen" at Hampton that was like "an army camp, whose distinguishing feature is not battle readiness but close order drill," in Louis R. Harlan's useful phrasing. Industrial education was, for Armstrong, Harlan writes, not just a means to equip able Negroes with useful skills, but "a quasi-religious principle, for the temporal salvation of the Negro race."[14]

Within the church of industrial education, the challenge for the student was to make abundantly clear their obedience to that principle. As the father sought to make over previously well-fed Hawaiian heathens living in a Polynesian paradise now dissipated by alcohol and undeclared germ warfare into spare Protestants dutifully worshiping at the altar of work, clothes, and civilization, so, too, the son sought to fix the broken Negro. This was not mainly an academic venture—what Washington would ever afterward disparage as "mere book education." Instead, it was lessons in culture, character, and civilization. Washington writes:

> I learned what education was expected to do for an individual. Before going there I had a good deal of the then rather prevalent idea among our people that to secure an education meant to have a good, easy time, free from all necessity for manual labour. At Hampton I not only learned that it was not a disgrace to labour, but learned to love labour, not alone for its financial value, but for labour's own sake and for the independence and self-reliance which the ability to do something which the world wants done brings.[15]

These were Hampton and Armstrong's standards, which is to say there were no standards except giving evidence of willing subservience to the notion that one embodied the deficit in all Negroes, but was trying hard to, as Armstrong said, "live down prejudice."[16] Thus, there was a built-in explanation for the low graduation rate at Armstrong's "race laboratory" where only one in five made it through to graduation.[17] In itself the fact that the vast majority of students left early was precise proof that Armstrong's zealous diagnosis was the right one; their failure, not Hampton's, was the best evidence that Hampton's civilizing measures were, like the vermifuge the boy Booker took at his mother's insistence, just the right cure.

Washington depicts himself "learning" these lessons so often in writing and speeches that it is possible to arrive at the mistaken conclusion that he was a dullard (as certainly some of his contemporaries did). But these stories are always a means of expressing his thankfulness to his mother, Mrs. Ruffner, Armstrong, the Hampton faculty, and other white persons, low and high, who gifted him with insight. He was not thickheaded, did not need the same lessons pounded into his head. Rather, those lessons were neither so much what is suggested by his platitudinous descriptions of them—platitudes his audience wanted to hear because they suggest a rationale for why Negroes are in a fix—nor lessons even Washington necessarily believed Negroes needed above all else to learn. Instead, their repetition in his writings and speeches offer continuing occasions for him to prove himself worthy: his telling about taking the vermifuge, in smaller and larger doses, when it was proffered him not because he was or is ill (or messy or slothful), but because white persons like Mrs. Ruffner, the Hampton faculty, and other friends of the Negro want reassurance of his exceptional and continuing willingness to submit to what they are quite sure is one of the main problem ailing black people.

In that sense, personal history and later politics become one and may be why so many of his supporters consider Washington to be singularly the one Negro to make exemplary use of his freedom. How he becomes that exemplar and what he stands for as a leader are but versions of the constant test inherent in the Negro problem as it shapes up just before the turn of the century. In fact, the high dropout rate is more likely explained as a result of students getting what they could out of the "mere book education" (perhaps in combination with financial concerns, having enough with the make-work they were forced to do, or both), and departing to take up teaching positions elsewhere. If Hampton and later Tuskegee can be accounted as doing good work for African Americans it is because of the teaching of those who passed through the schools, graduates and dropouts both. It is the former students' good efforts that are the really concrete accomplishments of the schools, regardless of Armstrong's claiming that the main work was inculcating Negroes to the value of manual labor.

Nevertheless, as a setup for a pitch to potential donors, clearly this was a lesson not lost on the founder of Tuskegee, who likewise would uphold Armstrong's advocacy of alliance with *"the progressive men of the South"* and do what he could to cover up the fact that industrial education did not come near to paying for itself.[18] The graduation ceremony coming at the end of Washington's third year at Hampton—three years of Armstrong's evangelism—points to what he learned. Washington, newspaper accounts recorded, "gave a most terse and vigorous argument" against Cuban annexation, expounding on the belief that the United States had quite enough former slaves already; "that annexation would flood the country with ignorance and crime, and above all, would increase the power of the Roman Catholic Church."[19] He, however, was not the star of the day, according to a reporter who witnessed the event. The valedictory, given by another graduate, was notable for its denunciation of the carpetbagger and sound "comprehension of the ignorance and superstition of the black race."[20] This was music to the ears of many of the white persons in attendance, and while it may have been an acquired taste for some students like Washington who retained political aspirations, it was a tune always called for by Armstrong, who welcomed Reconstruction's end, thought it was a tragedy, and, figuring himself *"in loco parentis* to [his] students and to black people generally," was well convinced by 1875 that the Fifteenth Amendment had been a mistake.[21]

Washington was a success at Hampton, of that there can be no doubt, but not an overwhelming one. His good showing at the conclusion of his tenure in Armstrong's laboratory might be taken as a premonitory event—one like Martin Luther King's second-place finish in an oratorical contest at Morehouse College years later—that is to say, rife with ambiguous possibilities, but a turn not yet fateful in a great man's life.[22] The date was June 10, 1875, Hampton's seventh annual commencement, on a day African Americans had been celebrating for a slightly longer time. Harlan quotes a friend recalling that day to Washington: "I remember," he wrote, "the very expression on your countenance, as you stood on the porch of the Virginia Hall for a few moments on the day you graduated. I thought then, as I looked at you that you looked like a conquer[or] who had won a great victory. Who could have thought then that such great deeds would be achieved in years to come by the youth, Booker."[23]

His term at Hampton, however, would not be his last tenure there, nor did it bring an end to Armstrong's influence on him. And Rutherford B.

Hayes had already begun his own processional to the presidency and, thence, his slouching toward a rendezvous with Washington and the Negro problem at Hampton's Virginia Hall in May of 1880.

%%%

AND SO Washington, despite his avowal to conduct himself to the far South, headed back home to Malden and thereabouts, determining "to face the situation just as it was."[24] What it was, he found, was ugly. Various depressions in the late 1860s and into the 1870s caused the salt industry to stop hiring, and dissatisfaction and frictions of one kind or another spread widely down in the Kanawha Valley and elsewhere: the Molly Maguires in neighboring Pennsylvania, the Whiskey Ring scandal, a confrontation at Little Big Horn, a heated debate over the Civil Rights Act of 1875 in Washington and in newspapers throughout the country. This was the larger environment in which Washington began his adult career. As a teacher, he encountered students of differing abilities, some of whom "were over fifty years of age, whose desire to learn was in some cases very pathetic."[25] They warmed to him, however, and "seemed to have the greatest confidence in me and respect for me and did everything in their power to make the work pleasant and agreeable."[26] A former student recalled that Washington "would stop teaching arithmetic and grammar to lecture his pupils on the care of their nails, hair, teeth and clothing, and on the importance of the formation of right habits."[27] His fastidious and stern former boss, Mrs. Ruffner, as well as the two generals, Ruffner and Armstrong, could not have been less than pleased with this proselytizing. Washington had learned his lesson well and gave "special attention" to "the tooth-brush and the bath." "I am convinced," he writes, "that there are few single agencies of civilization that are more far reaching [than] the proper use of the tooth-brush and the bath."[28]

Washington's comporting himself in this way consistent with Armstrong's philosophy is not evidence that he had swallowed whole the Hampton ideal. Indeed, he continues in his interrupted political work down through the 1870s, acting as a spokesman for the campaign to establish Charleston as the West Virginia state capital and traveling about the state giving speeches to mixed black and white audiences. The popularity he was winning as a teacher is not inconsistent with this political project, but rather may be seen as his effort to build a constituent base (a goal that, of course, would contradict Armstrong's strictures on proper Negro conduct). And mindful of the political dynamic engendered by the African American minority in the state, he strikes themes he likely considered to be of the greatest utility to his rise, offering up, as one newspaper noticed, "much sound and sensible advice in regard to their general course in voting, calling their attention to the identity of interests between the races, *etc, etc.*"[29]

By 1877, however, the course indicated by the aspirations of his larger dreaming—to be a real player in politics—might have seemed to him to be closing; that river running dry. He spent an uncertain amount of time at the Wayland Seminary in Washington, D.C., but that alternative seems not to have taken. He tried to pursue the law, but eventually was dissuaded from doing so by Armstrong (a happy result, Washington thought, in direct contrast to what Malcolm Little would feel when told by his teacher to heed the counsels of prudence that being a lawyer was "no realistic goal for a nigger").[30] But what and where were the better alternatives? Could he transplant himself and thrive upon a quite different terrain? And would those who caused the drought upon the once fertile soil of Reconstruction, who killed the leaders and shut off the tap of democratic promise, see in him a way out, another way for Negroes to grow?

%%%

IT IS commonly averred that Washington could not provide leadership to white people—be a black leader of white people, or, merely a leader—because of racism. But this is merely a pretense, a cop-out or an excuse for not addressing Washington's real role. Washington quite obviously was not able to stop racist paramilitaries or lynch mobs; he did not endeavor to do so and would have failed (at much cost to himself and his school) if he had tried. And further, he made no move to meet such groups with a force of his own to repel them; he would not train such a force, much less mobilize it for the defense of black people's homes and persons. And he would not call upon federal authorities to intervene. The type of black leader he was contraindicated his occupying any of those roles; rather, African Americans were called on to modify their behavior, and in so doing, to disarm themselves as a combustible element in the lives of white Southerners, who would in turn disarm themselves under the good regime of good race relations.

But Washington's criticism of black misbehavior may have the effect of disarming someone else as well as the two main components of the Southern problem. Once the point has been established that the ultimate measure of the well-being and progress of African Americans is the state of race relations, certain but not necessarily all other theoretical matters fall into line, and those that do not are, in their ambiguity, tilted to the detriment of black people. The problem, as the devotee of the race relations idea sees it, is the contest: black people are playing a slow game of checkers against the white, and white people are playing an angry, martial game of chess against the black, when the whole of the South, the whole of the nation should be looking at life as a game of solitaire, of all together for the one good end.

And so, after paying tribute to the good, personal relationships he experienced with the Ruffners, Armstrong, and the rest of the Hampton faculty—available to all Negroes if only they would be open to them—as well engaging in ritualistic memorials to bygone good race relations in slavery, as in his laying of a rose on his dead master's grave, he has then to face up to the living, breathing Americans who inevitably must wonder, if progress means taking the conflict out of the game, whether "Negro rights" are not just a luxury, but expendable and superfluous.

Washington's response, that the Negro will eventually earn the respect of their white neighbors and the nation and thereby gain the enjoyment of all the rights previously denied them, however, rather than deciding the matter, only deepens the lock race relations has on the question of African America's fate, tightening the stranglehold of race and racism around their necks. This is so because while Washington asks America to look at the matter without "prejudice, or racial feeling" in effect just the opposite occurs.[31] Because he has accomplished this objectivity "beyond racial feeling," he asks to be allowed to be above the normal Negro's chauvinism and mere racial partisanship and thus to set for all the terms of the consideration—to lead white people to the proper, progressive conclusion (which is to say, to be their leader). But the terms that allow him both to claim that African Americans are better off than the world's other Negroes and to insist that good race relations will make them even better are tenable only through the omission of the one relationship that is relevant to consideration: that is, African Americans with their fellow Americans. That relationship, in which it is not necessary in the ages of slavery or segregation to depend as a first principle on relative cultural differences and attainments, instead focuses attention on the proper terms of gain and loss and on the relativity of white power and black subordination to that power. Washington's leadership in evading consideration of that, as it were, interracial bottom line, and the putting in its place of a fictive intraracial relativity, makes for what is an essentially racial accounting, both for the purposes of establishing good race relations in the present, and, in its turn, enshrining and purifying a benevolent whiteness, which he presumes will then be free to make friendships with an incapacitated (but not unprogressive) Negro.

Washington's rendering of the story of the nation's passage from slavery to Reconstruction illustrates how the race relations idea obscures the questions that that transition raised and seemed, for a time, to have answered about nation and citizenship, and puts race in democracy's place as an answer. His emphasis on black misbehavior and incapacity, especially, has the consequence of uniting incensed and offended Southerners with disappointed and offended Yankees, who might otherwise feel a call, as Americans, to stand against the lynch mobs; to endeavor a quick response to evil as citizens (but surely not as white people for that capacity is explicitly filled by the mobs and their apologists). Indeed, Washington rather seeks to tie the knot between white Southerners and white Northerners.

Hindsight on the civil rights era suggests that this was just the opposite of what was called for. The reconciliation of the white North and the white South together, created the perspective and the resolve that ended Reconstruction. A score of years later the burying of the hatchet of sectional animus engineers or capitulates to, abides or embraces, the systematizing of segregation and disfranchisement. In other words, if Washington's notion of freedom is that it means restriction—socially imposed where it is not assimilated, which is to say, where Negroes are free—America took this advice and mandated racist proscription.

Washington's complicity in this is self-evident. Promulgating a philosophy of either-or-ism—Latin or labor, opera house or opportunity, Congress or crops, rights or respect—that he, his supporters, segregationists who supported him, and those who did not, apply to black people's business and no one else's, is there any mystery about the effects of this prism on those who might otherwise be moved to act against segregation and disfranchisement? This Hobson's choice is a feature of segregation and nothing else, a proscriptive prescription scrawled out by doctors like Washington and other reformers with the very best intentions?

Washington wishes a different fate. He sees black life in Reconstruction to be all surfaces and superficiality and the facade of being whole, freedpeople acting as if they were completed and up to the task before them. But their activities resound with the hollow echo of empty shells, the bluster of false pride, the crackle of partisanship and the crumble of paper citizenship, not the quietude and strength of independent mindedness; that the sound and fury of the Reconstruction era, signifying nothing more than that the task laid at their laps surpassed them, and all they could do was beat breast and howl about the depredations of Southerners, or how unfair it all was, or demand, loudly but with a shrill and hollow ring, "the Negro's rights."

An example of this difficulty is Washington's dissertation on "an ambitious, high strung young fellow," who had been to college and learned "to speak Latin." He "had studied books, but he had not studied men. He had learned a great deal about the ancient world, but he knew very little of the world right about him. He had studied about things, through the medium of books, but had not studied things themselves. In a word, he had been infected with the college bacillus and displayed the usual symptoms." The young man, because he had been to college and because he was high strung, became, according to Washington, "exceedingly sensitive concerning the 'rights' of his race, and propounded to me the very popular theory that the only reason the Negro did not have all the rights coming to him was that he did not protest whenever these rights were infringed upon. He determined to put this theory into practice and so wrote a very learned lecture that he delivered on every possible occasion. The subject of his lecture was 'Manhood Rights.'" This dissertation was "quite popular" for a season, and its author "was invariably present at every indignation meeting" convened to carp on "some wrong meted out to members of the race." But what was "totally overlooked" by the nervous man and his cohort of indignant Negroes was "the really thrilling fact that never in the history of the world before were there ten million black men who possessed so many rights and enjoyed so many opportunities as the ten millions of Negroes in the United States to-day."[32]

Here, there is something sensible in what Washington says, a nugget of truth in a pile of theoretical abstractions passing for the "common sense" of the Negro problem. It is the principle that Martin King and those in the civil rights movement surely learned: that rights, including "Negro rights," are not a line in the sand one's enemies dare not cross, but rather a line it is incumbent upon the would-be citizen to cross if she would be free. Rights do not protect. The rule of rights does not a democracy make; rather, the exercise of those rights protects the citizen. This is what a democracy is. This is the hard-line logic most Americans currently need not ever face: the higher law and the deeper truth of societies this side of heaven, that even in a democracy governed by the rule of law if one will not or cannot fight for one's rights, if the citizen is not vigilant in their defense every day, those rights will lose the dimension of rights and be merely dusty bits of paper filed in important looking buildings, the doors of which are barred to you.

But, recognizing this truth, Washington makes no proposal of how to achieve the vindication of those rights except for dependence on the good graces of white persons. He will not be the standard-bearer or general in that fight, out in front of a black army on the march; when he rises to prominence, it will not be because he leads black men and women, but because he presents an idea and an image of himself taking their lead.

It is in retrospect that he claims Reconstruction was an impossible situation for all the elements of the Negro problem—the Southern white man, the Northern white man and the national government, and the Negro him-self. Each element, however, in its own way, made the situation worse.

The criticism of the conduct of emancipation and Reconstruction, offi-cial policy and de facto practices and dynamics they spawned, that Wash-ington, misleadingly, says he inaugurated as a boy and developed over the course of his lifetime was predicated on certain rules for "the progress of the race," by which he meant a distinctive grouping of people and the devel-opment of their "civilization" and "character"—their culture as the term has come to mean today. These rules were, he believed, eternal and universal. "No race," he would say at Atlanta, "can prosper till it learns that there is as much dignity in tilling a field as in writing a poem. It is at the bottom of life we must begin"—because presumably all nations of people do so—"and not at the top." As another example from Atlanta: "No race that has anything to contribute to the markets of the world is long in any degree ostracized."[33] Being of universal application, the promulgation of those principles under his stewardship of black America was not intended to set a limit on black aspirations. Defending Washingtonianism, he would insist, "I have not sought to confine the ambitions, nor to set limits on the progress of the race. I have never felt that the Negro was bound to behave in any manner different from that of any other race in the same stage of development. I have merely insisted that we should do the first things first; that we should lay the foundation before we sought to erect the superstruc-ture."[34] But how this can be done in an already civilized country is the ques-tion of the moment.

If Washington is to be taken at his word, it would seem his receptivity to this theoretical system began as a child: "back of all else, the lesson which General Armstrong was trying to teach us was the same that my mother had taught me." At Hampton, this was passed on "through the medium of books and tools and through contact with my teachers," but nonetheless his mother had imparted the same eternal verities: "namely, to distinguish between the real and the sham, to choose the substance rather than the shadow, to seek the permanent good rather than the passing pleasant." "The lesson which I learned in this simple fashion at home was of great value to me," he said, "in trying to lead my race in the direction of things that are permanent and lasting rather than merely showy and temporary."[35] The stories he tells on himself and other black people are not so much meta-phors about those lessons as they are the ostensible substance of his social theory. And it is this theory in Washingtonianism that, what ought to guide an individual's living, is equally applicable—he extrapolates—to the prob-lem of the Negro's general condition and the basis for black people's reformation. He offers his own Reconstruction-era example as evidence that it is possible for African Americans to escape the trap of their own pathology and redeem the claims to American citizenship.

The problem with black people was that they were not so prepared; they would not hold their noses and submit to taking a backseat in line with their attainments as Africans, slaves, and newly minted freedmen. There is the implication in Washingtonianism that a kind of intermediary stage of freedom—a second class of Americans could be manufactured for the Negro (as opposed to the condition produced by the erasure of African Americans' rights as citizens in the age of Washington that is sometimes erroneously and unthinkingly called "second class citizenship"). This, at least, is implied when he makes statements to the effect that Reconstruction policy erred in that "too much stress was placed upon the mere matter of voting and holding political office rather than upon the preparation for the highest citizenship."[36] Washington's Tuskegee, ostensibly, exists like the Hampton Institute and like the Ruffner home, as an institutional mechanism for the Negro's imbibing of those values, but absent, in the main, the presence of white persons. Tuskegee, as Washington describes it, teaches "civilization, self-help, and self-reliance," and, in so doing, "lay[ing] the foundation for the pleasant relations" between the Negro and the local whites. But with a crucial difference from Hampton's laboratory:

> I knew that, in a large degree, we were trying an experiment—that of testing whether or not it was possible for Negroes to build up and control the affairs of a large educational institution. I knew that if we failed it would injure the whole race. I knew that the presumption was against us. I knew that in the case of white people beginning such an enterprise it would be taken for granted that they were going to succeed, but in our case I felt that people would be surprised if we succeeded. All this made a burden which pressed down on us, sometimes, it seemed, at the rate of a thousand pounds to the square inch.[37]

One sort of pressure comes from the fact that Washington's program ups the ante so that it is not just the individual Negro who is scrutinized because he is a Negro, but that the whole weight of white scrutiny falls on Tuskegee as the singular means of black salvation. But, as with Hampton and its good problem of numerous students dropping out before completing their course of study, continuing or multiplying evidences of black poverty, infirmity, and simply causing trouble redounds to Washington and Tuskegee's benefit.

In terms of the notion of a transitional stage of subcitizenship, Washington does not develop a program or specific policies to hang along this line, likely because both it cannot lead anywhere and the extreme nature of its precepts would expose the radicalism that beats under his common sense philosophy. But Washingtonianism, with its emphasis on black deficits in civilization, the good in denouncing political participation, and advocacy of making over African Americans for the purposes of gaining the higher regard of "white people," surely points in that direction. Contrast this with the Edisto petitioners, insisting on the absolute right, not to speak of necessity, of their retaining possession of the land upon which they long labored, or with a hundred and more similar examples of African Americans, unwitting as to the Negro problem, asserting with simplicity and with democratic faith their understanding of the basic requirements needed for them to make a start—to have a chance in freedom.

In problematizing the African American as a citizen, or African America as an element of the democratic citizenry, Washington, for the post-emancipation era of freedom and legal equality, acts in the tradition of Thomas Jefferson for antebellum America, following the older man in transforming what is, from a democratic perspective, a simple matter of a widely embracing polity into a matter that has as its first principle an invidious scrutiny of black capacity.

Who is the conservative and who is the radical? Washington or, to give but one contrasting example, the Pennsylvania State Equal Rights League on the eve of the blossoming of black politics in Reconstruction in which the promise of "the vote of one black man," not the right, nor the idea, but rather, the League insisted,

> the vote now—to-day—right here in his native land is worth to the nation, to liberty, to the securing of our right as American civilization, and the establishing of the Republic on the eternal foundation of truth and justice, more than is involved in the theory of civilization of all other parts of the world. It is America that you have to civilize, to Christianize, and compel to accept and practically apply to all men, without distinction of color or race, the glorious principles and precepts laid down in her immortal Declaration of Independence.[38]

This, like Pinchback's notion of a black person doing duty to, at once, nation, party, and people, is a profound idea, at once conservative and traditional in its expression of ideas about citizenship in a democracy, and radical in that the times and their application to the Negro form them into a militant shape.

Of course, they provoked a radical response from the various forces on the ground in the South, in Washington and in the North, where citizens in places like Michigan and upstate New York had of necessity to come to terms with the fact that it cost a good deal more to create governments of the people in the South than it did to do the same thing in the North, and that an African American's vote or that of a Scalawag or Carpetbagger entailed a much greater investment of resolve and fortitude than did a Northerner's casual processional into polling places. But that was the cost of democratic Reconstruction, and its genius and promise was that affairs did not so quickly sort themselves out in the way they would when the forces of white supremacy carried the day. It was possible before then to conceive of the matter in democratic terms (and in terms of Republicans and Democrats) and in keeping with the American promise of liberty and equality for all Americans.

Washington's ultimate position, on the other hand, is that what is true and right for Americans is not true for Negroes in the state they are in after 1865. There are the norms of democracy, but the Negro is not prepared for them, and that ill preparation has sown the seeds of animus and bad race relations. Under those circumstances, democratic rights are a positive harm to the Negro; it was a time of crisis and of opportunity, and he would ask something better of them just as the crisis times did. But their failure, their unthinking and tacit resolve to spurn the better part, indicates their sickness, and thus the necessity of taking other measures.

Describing those other measures in a sketchy and preliminary way, Washington will speak in terms of the remedial work to be done, not to aid African Americans in their citizenship and political activity, but rather to prepare them to be citizens—a "provisional submission," William Dean Howells called it.[39] This will be done, of course, based on the principle of nominally universal fairness, but addressed to the specificity of the Negro problem: literacy tests and property qualifications for voters, for example, "applied fairly and squarely to both races."[40] That is not the position his mentor, Armstrong, advocated. But what is Washington's warrant to think this equitable result would occur? What would the means be to do such a thing? Is it certain for success? Would the Constitution have to be redrawn to allow for it? How especially would this be done when the drafters of disfranchising legislation had to tread lightly and sometimes illegally in opening the can of worms they did lest the insurgent yeomanry turn them into bait? This is an abstraction, personal memory turned to rhetorical excess obscuring reality. It is as if to say the clock can be turned back, the genie placed back in the bottle, Pandora's box refilled and sealed. But Washington is the one who insists that "progress" is an inevitable and one-way street. He is simply not serious about this or merely rationalizing for the sake of his supporters what already is an established fact in the age of Washington in terms of the Negro's place. But in the mid-1870s he also knew, if nothing else, that slavery's string had run out.

But it is not sufficient to say of Washington that he is merely addressing political reality when he claims the removal of the black voter from voting booth and candidate list is a boon to their long-term interests, weaning them away from the breast of federal intervention. While it may be conservative to oppose overreliance on the federal government, Washington's position here is not clear-cut. He actually wished there had been a greater federal commitment to education during the Reconstruction period and subsequently.[41]

But more than that, it is not conservative to propose a rewriting of the Constitution—not just the Fifteenth Amendment—but the whole of the notion of government by the people in order to get one class of the people who have already participated in that democratic compact out from under the putatively overwhelming burden, and then to place African Americans in an intermediary or preparatory stage before they can take their place as citizens. They would be a sort of minor-league American. The notion that this ultimately would benefit black people—that they could earn their way back up to the "Bigs"—is indicative of Washington's radical idealism. He takes American professions of commitment to democracy as sincere, which is why the civically defective Negro's presence in politics is problematic, and he holds that the disfranchisers and their Northern sympathizers are seeking only the preserving and protecting of the Constitution, which is why there is vote fraud and electoral warfare. Taking all these professions of honest purpose far too seriously or leaving them unchallenged, he places himself in a position where he cannot possibly do anything to stanch the flow carrying black people out of the body politic.

Or he simply does not care, thinks democracy is irrelevant. One might think this a conservative opinion. But what is implicit in the logic of Washington's position that show it in a different light: that African Americans can advance their interests without availing themselves of the means by which Americans seek to get the good; can do so though mainly bereft of tools and implements or the money to purchase either; can do so without stores of capital, without geographic unity, concentrated in a depressed agricultural industry in a financially prostrated region; and can do so while barred from the vehicle of guilds and apprenticeships that were a poor man's means of acquiring a living. If the point is that African Americans had to do this despite the odds, that is one matter. But making a virtue of a forbidding necessity—and more than a virtue, a promise and a guarantee—is as radical as it is foolhardy, a flight of fancy that is anything but conservatism.

A part of the unreasonableness of Washington's commonsense plan lies in its leap from the individual's case to that of the group. In *Up From Slavery* and elsewhere, he insists that the merit principle does win out in the end, and that the Negro must put maximum effort into even the most mundane and unremunerative situations for the soul's own purpose, if nothing else. That may be common sense and true of individuals (good advice, anyway, even if it is not all the time true), to try hard, strive to succeed, to get along with the neighbors and do good in all things. But, as a "racial" matter, it is a theory as it applies to large numbers, a theory perhaps mainly useful to explain bad results for the mass of black people, and a proposal for some large-scale social engineering of a new kind of Negro.[42] It is high level meddling of the type easily pondered and promoted (at least when it comes to black people) but less easily put into practice (one thinks, in this connection of "back to Africa," busing, and the perennial hectoring of black people as an inducement to having better families). Indeed, the proposal is just as distant from the realm of the possible as the most grandiose scheme of colonization.

On the other hand, it is not as if the post-emancipation Negro had not already been subject to the kind of jolting makeover or cataclysmic reformation Washington would eventually propose. Had their not-so-distant ancestors not been snatched and grabbed and jerked around and crowded in and made to don different clothes, bear different names, shuffle along different country lanes and city streets? Had their forced passage from Africa, to the Caribbean and then to America, not been a great feat of social engineering—easily the greatest such feat ever known—and an extraordinary paean to progress? Even the slaves' long march west and southward, perhaps the greatest forced migration in the history of the world up to that time, that changed the demography of American slavery and the relations of masters and slave while mastering for America the then-frontier, can be offered up in evidence that all types of undertakings are possible when it comes to this problematic but certainly mobile and malleable people. "Considering the qualities which the Negro slave developed under trying conditions," Washington once noted, "it does not seem to me that there is any real reason why one who wishes him well should despair of the future of the Negro either in this country or elsewhere."[43]

In their daft fantasy of escorting black people "back" to Africa, the colonizationists said something like this, too, but Washington hopes for a future here in this country where the adjusted Negro can be made to realize his true potential, even if that making is as painful or more so than a child's taking a bitter dose of "vermifuge." Whether the cure fits the cause of the ailment, it is the adherence to just what the doctor orders that is the ultimate proof of this sick race's readiness to be healed. So did the "negative example" of Reconstruction teach this once-upon-a-time slave, now a child of freedom who would become doctor, minister, and judge at a special place, the Tuskegee Institute, where Negroes could go to take the cure. For Washington, the differences between Armstrong's straightforward denunciation of the Negro's playing a role in politics, and Washington's own more subtle evasions of the question or his inconsistency on the matter are of no great moment as long as black people are, en masse, political participants, as they were while he was in school and in the Reconstruction West Virginia he returned to after his graduation. As abstract formulations, they are no more than thought exercises of the type students and mentors often toss around. But when terrorism, corruption, and a diminishing federal and Republican Party role in the South begins to steal the life out of black Reconstruction, there is a shift that throws the argument decisively in Armstrong's direction. The support for his thesis, which had been reality, and Armstrong's antithesis, merely his plain punditry as to the character of backward peoples, now is thrown up in the air. The seeds of that revolution were already being laid in the mid-1870s. The problem, for Washington, but not for Armstrong, is that, just as the peculiar institution's endtime had come, American democracy's string could run out, too.

‰‰‰

WHILE WASHINGTON was out beating the hustings to win the capitol of West Virginia for his Charleston, President U. S. Grant, hero of the war and savior of the nation, in seeking to find a backdoor out of the commitments of his oath of office and Party, was saying of the Fifteenth Amendment, "It had done the Negro no good, and had been a hindrance to the South, and by no means a political advantage to the North."[44] His calculations may have been inexact or misleading, but he expresses a kind of realpolitik.

Grant's presumptive heir, Rutherford B. Hayes, was thinking some of the same thoughts. In January 1875 he answered a challenge from his close friend and college mate, a Texan called Guy M. Bryan, to accept the white Southerner's prejudice that the Negro could not be fit into the democratic system. Resisting the bait, Hayes replied that more education would lift up the Negro. Bryan, joined by Carl Schurz and some others, became in the coming months Hayes's preceptor in an effort to adjust his conscience into alignment with the emerging reality Grant had articulated. Bryan, whom one historian figures in this role as "a kind of Southern Rasputin," asked Hayes to consider the justice of restoring home rule to the South so as to let white persons have their way with the Negro. By July, Hayes was inclining in that direction, replying to Bryan that "'the let alone' policy seems now to be the true course. . . . The future depends largely on the moderation and good sense of Southern men. . . . I think we are one people at last for all time."[45]

This was the opening of the wedge: the honoring in principle of an abstract color-blind universalism. His advisors made the point more explicitly than Hayes ever would, but they set a standard for a kind of disingenuousness Hayes carried the potential to grow into. Earlier, Schurz advised Hayes that the trick was to come out for "the equality of rights without distinction of color according to the Constitutional Amendments." This principle must be absolutely and in all cases upheld. The rights of the citizenry "must be sacredly maintained by all lawful power of government," Schurz continued, except in those cases when the exercise of those rights proves unpopular with a significant element of the local population, in which case the "Constitutional rights of self-government must be respected." As a presidential candidate, Hayes ought to simply declare that we have "a nation of equal citizens," and then let the chips fall where they may.[46]

Schurz was quite sure this was a reasonable course for a Republican presidency to take, but Hayes was less than convinced, replying to Schurz that the phrase "'local self-government' . . . seems to me to smack of the bowie knife and revolver. Local self-government has nullified the Fifteenth Amendment in several states, and is in a fair way to nullify the Fourteenth and Thirteenth." But the breech had been opened as Hayes added: "But I do favor a policy of reconciliation . . . and, therefore, suppose you and I are substantially agreed on the topic."[47]

When Hayes received the Republican nomination, his letter of acceptance amplified on his growing solicitude to the Bryan-Schurz paradigm. "What the South needs most," he said, is peace, and peace depends upon the supremacy of law." If elected, a Hayes administration "will regard and cherish [the South's] truest interests—the interests of the white race and of the colored race both, and equally." Such sentiments might have given some succor to Republican regimes hanging on by the skin of their teeth in the South, but cold comfort for leaders like Governor Adelbert Ames, lately chased from the state of Mississippi by redeemers (to those deceased Republicans already fallen under the good offices of "let-alone," of course, it meant nothing at all).[48]

Even after the closely contested election, Hayes's preceptors still sweated him. Schurz was joined by the governor of Ohio, who wrote him late in January 1877, suggesting that it was necessary to "moderate the kindled ambition of the colored people to fill places which neither their experience, nor their knowledge of business or of the laws fit them, for." Hayes, the gaslight finally alit above his head, found his way through the emphasis on Negro incapacity.[49] A week later Hayes wrote to his diary on the matter of the remaining federal troops in the South: "There is to be an end of all that." And after a mid-February meeting with Frederick Douglass, Hayes noted that African Americans approved of his approach. "My course," he wrote, "is a firm assertion and maintenance of the rights of the colored people of the South . . . coupled with a readiness to recognize all Southern people, without regard to past political conduct, who will now go with me heartily and in good faith in support of these principles." By the time Hayes was ready to give his inaugural address, he was saying all that Bryan, Schurz and the rest had advised him, but he had been worked hard to arrive at his new principle by men more comfortable with combining expedience, bad faith, and knee-jerk acceptance of the notion of black incapacity. They went on about their business. The remnants of Hayes's older conscience told him something more needed to be said about "the two distinct races whose peculiar relations to each other have brought upon us the deplorable complications and perplexities which exist in some states."[50]

Historians have been impressed by Hayes's good intentions in regard to the Negro. They take him at his word and believe him to be sincere, and stress his work after the White House as first president of the Slater Fund seeking to support Negro education, which from the start Hayes had believed was the answer to the problems of the South.[51]

This reading of Hayes seems likely to be the case, but with a crucial amendment: kindness may allow for the conclusion that he was sincere, but good judgment insists that his later commitments reflect some guilty feelings about what he had done or allowed to happen when circumstances called him to stand on higher principle.

%%%

IN 1890, Hayes was in the chair when the inaugural Lake Mohonk Conference on the Negro Question was convened in western New York. The intervening years had been a time of flux, but now events in the South were picking up with an illegally constituted body meeting in Mississippi to foment a plan for ridding state politics of the corrupting Negro element. That body had as one of its number a single black person. The Lake Mohonk Conference, on the other hand, had not a single African American, the consideration of its organizers being that "rash words" and too great emotion would upset the proceedings.[52] This was an affair to put the house of Northern liberalism in order; to find a way of reconciling earlier, neo-abolitionist commitment to the changing reality in the offing in places like Mississippi and similar stirrings elsewhere in the South. Armstrong was there, expounding on how "the Jew store" and the deficits in the Negro's character kept black people down.[53] The Rev. Lyman Abbott was there, too, on the path from being antislavery (but not abolitionist) that would eventually lead him to use "every art of his remarkable gift of casuistry" in the adaptation of the parable of the Good Samaritan into an argument for segregation.[54]

Dissent was represented at Mohonk in the person of Albion Tourgee, Reconstruction politician and lawyer. For all the Conference's talk of the Negro problem, and of the Negro as a drag on the nation, Tourgee thought they might make a resolution thanking black people for 250 years of "unrecompensed labor," and for having "planted by their voice and votes in the fundamental laws of [the Southern] States the free public school system, never known there before, and then opposed by three-fourths of the white voters of those States, whose blessing and beneficence twice as many white as colored children enjoy to-day."[55] Those wise comments were, however, only a sidelight to Tourgee's real threat to the equanimity of the proceedings. Dissenting, Tourgee announced that those gathered "have sought testimony about the Negro from his avowed friends and confessed enemies, and think we shall obtain the truth by 'splitting the difference between them.' The testimony of the Negro in regard to his past and present conditions and aspirations for the future is worth more than that of all the white observers that can be packed upon the planet."[56]

One man had an answer to Tourgee's challenging of the undemocratic, segregated proceedings. One man had a name that would show that their contemplation of the Negro problem was on the right course, an implicit trump negating the sentiments expressed by Tourgee. "Mr. Booker T. Washington," Armstrong said, "is ahead of us all in this matter."[57] This was a time for a manufactured Negro leadership to embody an answer to the challenge posed by Tourgee's principle, and it was as if to say, "Here, is our diversity, our partner! Here is a basis for accord manifest in black and white!"

Washington was in a position to provide leadership to teetering white reformers because Armstrong in 1881 recommended him for the position at a new school being founded in Tuskegee, Alabama. In doing so, Armstrong was breaking with a convention that held that such positions ought to be reserved for white men.

%%%

BY 1881, Washington had been back at Hampton for a little more than a year, invited in the first place to deliver a "Post-Graduate Essay" at Armstrong's behest. "The idea," Armstrong wrote him, "is to bring out the facts of actual experience, to show what clear heads and common sense colored graduates of this school have attained." Washington answered the call and in May 1879 delivered an address, "The Force That Wins," that at least one observer believed was up to the standards of Harvard and Yale.[58]

By the fall of the next year, Washington had been made dormitory supervisor of "The Wigwam," placed in charge of the Indian students who were assigned to Hampton as prisoners of the federal government, and taken over the writing of the series "Incidents of Indian Life at Hampton," for the school paper, the *Southern Workman*. Throwing himself into this work that also provided abundant opportunity for self-promotion, he described teaching his charges to put down the bow and arrow and pick up the toothbrush, and, generally, imparting to them, as he wrote in one account, "the white man's civilization."[59] His Indian students, among them a grandson of Tecumseh, were "slow to learn that when they adopt the white man's dress, they must also adopt his health laws and that when the weather was fair "it was their great desire to sleep in the open air with no covering but their bare skin." To forestall this dangerous practice, Washington undertook midnight inspections "to see how far they observed the laws of health and neatness in their sleep." Directing a discussion of "the very delicate subject" of lying ("about which so many untruths are often told," he was impressed by their responses and gladdened while lecturing on the subject of "the four conditions of man" to overhear "many subdued whispers" repeating "We savages, we savages."[60]

Some of Washington's commentary on his students struck the same themes that he would make famous with his nostrums and homilies about African Americans, as is the case in his explanation of why Hampton offered "an Indian class in Natural Philosophy": "Yes, like other ignorant people, they need to be taught to understand and appreciate nature, which is near to them, instead of something far off." Or his report on one young man seeking to shirk his duties who prayed thusly: "verily, verily I say unto you, that shalt not work to-day because too much rain."[61]

Washington's main thesis, however, revolved around the intertwined themes of the opportunity given the Indians to transform themselves and the "generous spirit" of the Negro in helping them in this transformation. That this was fundamentally an advertisement for himself—his "generous spirit," his passing "the true test of civilization" in helping a "more unfortunate" race—need not be dwelt upon except to point out how readily Washington in this phase of his life and near the end of his education adapts to the language and rhetoric of problematic races.[62] Illustration of this new turn of mind, or, perhaps, new ideological sophistication comes from his last "Incidents," in which he describes Bear's Heart's transformation. James Bear's Heart was a member of the Cheyenne nation captured in the Indian Territory and held as a prisoner of war for three years in Florida before coming to Hampton in 1878. At the time of his imprisonment he was "clad in a blanket and moccasins, with his long hair flowing down his back, his ears jingling with ear rings, and his tomahawk and bow and arrows swinging from his side." Now, "instead of the weak, dirty, ignorant piece of humanity that he was, with no correct ideas of this life or the next—his only ambition being to fight the white man—he goes back a strong, decent, Christian *man*." "Who knows," Washington concludes, "but that the capturing of Bear's Heart and his associates marked the beginnings of the solution to the Indian question." James Bear's Heart then returned to his former home where he, like a large number of other Hampton Indian students, died a short time later.[63]

By this time, perhaps, Washington was reconciled to the fact he would never be a senator or congressman; or, perhaps not, and believed that his work at Hampton would be decent launching pad for his political career. And it did not seem any contradiction to him that he was acting as the fount for this acculturation—not of American ways—but "the white man's." Giving up on the other ambitions of his past, "ris[ing] above mere race prejudices" in service to other men, Washington had passed Armstrong's test. He was, as Armstrong would say in recommending him to the Alabamians, "a very competent capable mulatto, clear headed, modest, sensible, polite and a thorough teacher and superior man. The best man we ever had here."[64]

By this time, surely, Washington knew what he was about, knew his role in the affairs of the world and the contribution he could make to the resolution of the Negro problem. A part of this consciousness was political: the influence of Armstrong on him; his sense that some "strong force" other than politics needed to be brought to bear on the Negro; the certainty that he would not be marching into the black belt as a candidate toting a carpetbag with him. But another part was personal and psychological as well. This has as well to do with Armstrong's influence on him, or, more accurately, the bond between them, and what Washington might have understood about Armstrong's description of him.

%%%

THE RARE instance of Washington's humor actually providing amusement to someone in our more enlightened and delicate times comes when the joke is not on the Negro but on the absurdity of the Negro problem and America's peculiar obsession with race. Apropos of this, he tells in *Up From Slavery* "a rather amusing instance which showed how difficult it sometimes is to know where the black begins and the white ends." It is the story of the dilemma of a train conductor duty-bound to enforce segregation. One day the conductor was "perplexed" to encounter a man entering the Jim Crow coach, who, unbeknownst to the conductor, was "well known in his community as a Negro," but who looked "so white that even an expert would have hard work to classify him as a black man." Thus the dilemma: if the man were indeed a Negro, directing him into the white coach would be a violation of custom and law, but if the man were a white man, the conductor's asking him if was a Negro would be a grievous insult. Observing this, Washington saw the conductor closely examine the putative Negro but potential white man's hair, eyes, nose, and hands, to no avail—he could not tell the man's real race. "Finally, to solve the difficulty," Washington reported, the conductor "stooped over and peeped at the man's feet. When I saw the conductor examining the feet of the man in question, I said to myself, 'That will settle it'; and so it did, for the trainman promptly decided that the passenger was a Negro, and let him remain where he was. I congratulated myself that my race was fortunate in not losing one of its members."

While this joke is just as artificial a confection as Washington's more typical array of amusing appeals to white persons' prejudices, it has the attraction of the large likelihood that is humor was lost on the vast majority of his audience (although surely most Americans today can see what is funny about it) because it is about the absurdity both of race proscription and the notion that a person who gives every appearance of being one thing is actually precisely the opposite.[65]

The single question Washington was asked the most was "What is the relative ability of the Negro of mixed and unmixed blood?" His consistent reply was that he felt sure that "where the environment has been equally favourable, there is no difference in ability."[66] Washington, generally speaking, was ever so much the patient preceptor as to entertain even the most foolish or insulting queries, but on this question he did not give his correspondents the answer they wanted, which was that "white blood" tells.

Two examples of this species of argument illustrate its quality. Albert Stone, a Mississippi gentleman-scholar and author of *Studies of the Race*

Problem was reported in the press to say that the intelligence found among Negroes is due the fact that "the white strain does tell, and that practically all of the men of so-called negro blood who have done anything in the world are of the mulatto type." Stone's argument was to the effect that Washington and Du Bois covered up this fact, denied the telling of white blood, because it would reflect badly on their benighted, pure black fellows. Stone was quoted thus in the *Washington Post* but immediately objected to Washington that he said nothing of the kind. The words attributed to him are, however, consistent with the argument in his book. In the same vein, the unnamed author of a sociobiological essay entitled "Changing the Angle of the Forehead: That Is the Problem That Confronts the Negro," rejected the idea that the accomplishments of Douglass and Washington prove the potential of the Negro. On the contrary, "anyone who reads the life of Frederick Douglass or Booker Washington gets no idea whatever as to what negroes can do. The lives of Douglass and Washington tells [*sic*] us what a half-breed white man can do, but they give us no information at all in regard to the negro. The skulls of Washington and Douglass are not negro skulls, and their brains are not negro brains of the pure type."[67]

Washington would have none of it. This is supported by the example of Washington's reply to an Alabama Congressman, George Washington Taylor, who wrote him in 1904 seeking data "on the percentage of mixed and pure blood negroes in the United States." Taylor had concluded from Tuskegee staff photo that there was "but one full-blood" Negro on staff. Washington replied that he could not agree with the congressman's point "that persons with mixed blood have been those who have exhibited the most strength of mind," citing a myriad of examples. Washington held to this ground even though this and other of his correspondents sought his confirmation of their prejudice. There was no difference, he insisted. But, he adds:

> When it comes to the matter of executive or organizing ability and tenacity of purpose, I agree with you that those with mixed blood have shown superiority, in a word, in those matters where the feeling or imagination plays a large part I do not believe that there is any difference; in the application, however, of education or mind development I think I have the feeling that there is a difference.[68]

The suggestion here is not that what might be termed mulatto consciousness was at the center of his self-conception, much less an encompassing statement of who he was. But rather that it was a part of his self-conception following from his turning away from Washington Ferguson and heeding the rumor his was a white father. This means some things, but not others. For one thing, Washington speaks of "mixed" and "full blood Negroes," but does not speak of "mixed blood whites." And, he speaks of "the race to which I am proud to belong," without any confusion on the matter at all.[69]

The further suggestion is that this is a personal matter for Washington. His reticence about it, and his general refusal to jump to the bait offered by his white interlocutors, are evidence that whatever might be gained by agreeing with them is of less importance to him than consistency and personal principle. A principle because he does indeed not see a fundamental difference between Negroes of various sorts, and personal because embracing that part of his identity and heritage clarifies his conception of his role in the world as the man in the middle, straddling the color line and holding together the race relations regime and, of course, while others beholding Washington might think it fitting that he is, supposedly, a child of one white and one black parent, not all who see him in that way do so. As well, conceiving of the Negro problem as race relations is not the exclusive province of what are now called "transracial" peoples.

This conception may also be seen as of use to Washington in explaining his sense of difference (although, again, Taylor's belief aside, this need not lead to the conclusion that Washington sought out other people of similar self-conception as friends and allies). Sensing himself to be different from those by whom he is surrounded, black and white, his mulatto move may have explained that difference and been his margin of hope or a wedge opening his mind to different possibilities. This is especially true in regard to how he might have made sense of his alienation from Washington Ferguson. But, equally, how he can conceive of making it, while others fail, and thrive owing to his flexibility, where others stick to their guns and are lost.

There is an obvious self-serving quality to such a self-conception, but it is an understandable one and does not have to be taken to mean that he sets himself off against the Negroes. He does not think that way. As a conception of how one might have a leg up in the hard climb of life, even if only an imaginary leg up, it helps him explain the contradiction presented by one's evident ability relative not just to African Americans but to white persons as well. It helps him not to feel bad about black people's sorry plight, but through his distance from them, to gain purchase on a more positive, progressive future for them through his own ministrations. Looked at from another angle: that his difference does not reflect badly on them, but instead he says something like, "I have this advantage by accident of birth; we all work for the good ends for the whole of the Negro people." In that way, his gift is like a ballplayer's lucky relic or the ritual that he does not share with his teammates, but instead guards like the talisman it is—a simple superstition, and even a little bit ridiculous. Abraham Lincoln did not go before the people revealing his sense of hereditary endowment, and neither did he demand their support on that basis. For Washington, it is possibly the same thing: an edge conceived in a private thought, a personal sense. Of course, unlike Lincoln, Washington would not be going before any sort of democratic-minded public that might resent this sense of hereditary endowment; in Washington's case, his supporters, white and proud, were either likely taken by the idea of his white blood telling or were indifferent to it.

Finally, figuring himself in this way—conqueror of his own line—in some more or less profound sense tied him to his mentor, Armstrong; he was affiliated with him, the father found, and now sending the son out into the world to carry on their mutual quest, at once a personal and political mission. But not his original quest, not the one leading the people in a democratic struggle to advance their interests.

Before the building of several scores of schools named for Washington all over the segregated South, and spilling over into the Midwest and Southwest so that Washington is a kind of brand name, not for education, but for the particular sort of underfunded education that is available to African Americans, there was Washington's desire to build a career for himself in the deep South. And before the reign of some thousands of lesser Washingtons, local "Head Negroes in Charge," principals or colored superintendents or honorary "black mayors" who had charge of which people won the favor of a job in schools or post office and lorded it over the community with a haughtiness the belied the narrowness of their fiefdom;[70] before the statue of Washington was build for the Tuskegee campus; before Atlanta made his name and created his national leadership; and before the world would beat a path to Washington's door; before all this and in the absence of the idea of race relations, it is possible to look at Washington and the true problem before him and black people in the South.

If one starts with the propositions that human beings have a specific financial value, and that Negro human beings' financial value is not as high as it should be because of the deficits within their characters but can be raised by contact with white persons of high character, then it is possible, one supposes, to take as an article of faith that "Outfit and apparatus, about which so much fuss is made, are secondary" to the importance of "the personal force of the teacher," as Armstrong asserted.[71] In his first months at the new Tuskegee Institute, Washington would come face to face with the reality that whatever he might have learned from Armstrong about making friends with white people, and whatever he might continually say about the abundance of local white support for his school, this was wholly inadequate to the task. Almost from his first moments there, he began writing a series of letters back to his former teachers and others at Hampton and open letters to the *Southern Workman* describing the fairly desperate situation, the difficulty of raising funds locally, and soliciting loans and other support to sustain the endeavor. "The colored people here are very anxious that the school shall be a success and are willing to do what little they are able to do for it," he wrote to James F. B. Marshall, Hampton's treasurer. Shortly thereafter, he proposed publishing a subscription paper and "getting up an entertainment" to raise funds. Most crucial to Tuskegee's immediate survival, he planned as soon as possible "to get the school on a labor basis, so that the earnest students can help themselves and at the same time learn the true dignity of labor."[72] Because Washington's phrasing toward the end of the sentence is wholly in keeping with Armstrong's lessons about industrial education as a means of teaching the indolent Negro to work it is possible to miss what Washington is actually saying here. What Tuskegee actually does is work its students in order that they might be taught. And taught a course of instruction that trained Tuskegee graduates to be teachers—as befits a normal school—rather than artisans and craftsmen and seamstresses and laundresses that readers falling for the misapprehension cultivated by *Up From Slavery* and other Washingtonian contributions to the Negro problem would believe.

This, along with black self-help and the building up of "pleasant relations between the races," is a pillar of the original Tuskegee experiment, and just as dirty a trick as the second one (in which syphilis patients at the Tuskegee hospital were told their illness was being treated when it was not), but of farther-reaching consequences. For Southern and Northern public consumption, Washington promoted himself and derided African Americans by insisting that their desire for education was a misdirected way of shirking work. He tells of girls who "went to the bad" after "six or eight years of book education had weaned them away from the occupation of their mothers," and other girls who could find "the Desert of Sahara or the capital of China on an artificial globe," but were unable to "locate the proper place for knives and forks on an actual dinner table." Others were only interested big books on "high-sounding subjects"—"the bigger the book and the longer the name . . . the prouder they felt"—or memorizing "long and complicated 'rules' in grammar and mathematics, but had little thought or knowledge of applying these rules to the everyday affairs of their life." He sought "to teach them to study actual things instead of mere books alone," but, he claims, met with resistance from prospective students who "had not fully outgrown the idea that it was hardly the proper thing for them to use their hands, since they had come [to Tuskegee], as one on them expressed it, 'to be educated, and not to work.' " Their parents too often supported them in this, sending along requests that their children be "taught nothing but books."[73]

There are those times when Washington slips up and calls what goes on at Tuskegee "an industrial system"—essentially, a work-study program that redounds to the benefit of Tuskegee's bottom line as well as it helps students from poor families—but the damage has been done. "Industrial education"—teaching the Negro to work, overcoming black fecklessness, stemming the tide that was their flight from field to city; doing all this and thus solving their Negro problem. The collected Washington papers reveal many and not very varied formulations of this kind, as Washington carried his message across the nation seeking support for his Tuskegee Institute. In these we find the public image Washington created for African Americans. But there are other kinds of documents in the Washington papers, including a considerable number of letters from Tuskegee's early years written by or for parents who give little evidence of the sentiment—the uppityness—Washington ascribed to them. There are the letters from a father from Tuscaloosa, Alabama, asking about the price of books, and a mother named Henrietta Bendbow who asked "Dear Professor Washington wont you be kind enough to make my son Robert write me often." Mr. A. Campbell wrote to Washington in 1887, "Kind sir will you take my boy there in your care and educate him and give him a trade such as you think nature has assigned him. I mean for you to take him to your house to wait on you if you need one. If you will, you will greatly oblige me as I am not situated so as to do what I want for him." Or consider the following from Frank Armstead of Greensboro, Alabama, about his boy John:

> he is a boy seemed to be ancious to get a good education and I am ancious to give him a good education but I an not able to furnish money for him to go unless he work to help himself . . . I want you to take charge of him and make him work to help his self through . . . he is a good boy willing to do any thing but he is not very strong. I wish you would please give him such work as he can do anything that is not too heavy I am willing to send yu some money occassionaly to help him I wish you would please [answer] and tell me all about john what books he will study and what kind of work you will give him I heard that you need a good boy in t he printing office and thought that would be a good job for him but I am not particular what kind of work he do but I want you to take charge of him

Armstead closed his letter in two ways ("anxiously waiting your reply" and "respectfully"), but before doing so made this poignant request: "whenever you get ready to send him home notify me before he come I am not particular about him coming hom when the session is out if he can stay there and do anything to help him through school keep him there dont mind what he say but do as I ask you."[74]

There is no Negro problem here, and Washington's responses to parents like Mr. Armstead are similarly above-board and straightforward and respectful. Indeed, the best sort of example of Washington, in his conduct as an educator at least, not participating in the Negro problem comes, ironically, in a letter to the parent of a student being expelled from Tuskegee for theft: "If there was any way in the world for us to retain him in school and spare you the pain we should gladly do so, but we cannot afford to keep dishonest students in schools. We know your feelings in the matter."[75]

What the correspondence describes is people facing real problems, real needs, real aspirations in the salvation education might bring a "not very strong" boy loved and cherished by his father. They are the particular problems of a particular time and place—but recognizable to anyone with children, and, as such, universal problems and surely not "the problem with Negroes."

In the 1880s Washington and his co-workers at Tuskegee did their best against long odds to serve the needs of families like the Armsteads and the "thousands of poor but ambitious young people, far out on the back plantations, and in the woods and hollow, who, if given a chance, would gladly enter school and work there way through."[76]

And the subscription paper and the traveling entertainment were gotten up, and Washington frequently traveled northward to give lectures based on what he called "the science of what is called begging."[77] Tuskegee was built, but the wolves were never far from Washington's door. Commerce with the school was integral to the town of Tuskegee's economy, but contrary to Washington's sayings about good race relations and the miracle of free markets, local merchants charged Washington's school "exorbitant prices," did not hesitate to press hard for payment, and denied Tuskegee credit when it suited their fancy. "We are entirely at their mercy," Tuskegee treasurer Warren Logan wrote Washington in 1888, one of many such letters that passed between the two men.[78] And so Washington beat the hustings, begging for money and inflating his rhetoric as he went, telling Boston Unitarian, for example, about how the mortgage system holds the Negro "in a kind of slavery," but also frightening them with dire warnings about "a dense, degraded and fast increasing Negro population of 15,000" surrounding Tuskegee, and entertaining them with his homily about "dis darkey" being called to preach.[79]

The late 1880s were a difficult time for Washington and Tuskegee, and no time was worse than the first four months of 1889. A fire destroyed his campus home. His brother John Henry (who had joined the Tuskegee faculty) received an anonymous warning of "indignation brewing . . . against the school from the act of the suposed [sic] student; it would be well to look out for fires." And his second wife, Olivia Davidson Washington, died three months after giving birth.[80]

The next year the Mississippi Plan came into existence to disfranchise a majority of the state's voters, and friends of the Negro including Rutherford B. Hayes gathered at Lake Mohonk, and Washington's name came before the gathering thanks to the advocacy of his mentor, Armstrong.

%%%

THERE WILL come a time, after Atlanta and 1895, when all roads will lead to Washington's doorstep; when Washington will have sent out from the Tuskegee print shop flyers directing interested visitors and philanthropists of the most comfortable and convenient routes by which they might make passage to the "experiment" he had undertaken in Alabama. On the page, passenger railroad lines, now defunct and forgotten, are named, connections at stations, long since razed or underused, are delineated: from New York and points northeast, the Pennsylvania Railroad to the Southern Railway to the Atlanta and West Point to the Western Railway of Alabama and then on to the Chehaw station and the Tuskegee Railroad; from Chicago and the Midwest, the Chicago and Eastern Illinois Railroad to the Louisville and Nashville Railroad to the Western.[81] Men of deep pockets will make their way to Tuskegee along the routes so described and, in a broader sense, will be drawn to Washington and Tuskegee by the road map he made of the solution to the Negro problem. The captains of industry and finance will have guides along the way in the form of frequently shallow-pocketed impresarios of good works and noblesse oblige; some of the best of these will be formerly religious men who have given up the cloth to serve new masters and former Confederates who have seen the light of racial and regional reconciliation.[82] But such guides, in comparison to the black man himself waiting at the terminus of the excursion, are but ticket-takers or baggage handlers. It was Washington whom they had come to see on their pilgrimage; their idyll with him in the Alabama countryside providing proof of the rightness of the moral and political order over which they presided, a place that, if not perfect, was in the process of being perfected. It was Washington, his ideas, his vision, who created the setting in which they might engage in two relief efforts: the relief and rescue of the Negro, and the relieving of their own sense that this sort of want and this sort of powerlessness ought not to be made in America; that they are worthy receptacles for our charity because he says we are not responsible for their plight. It was Washington who made the metaphors that provided a way out: he will single-handedly captain the ship heretofore so misguided and misled it cannot find its way to the safe port close at hand; he will raise his black hand and in so doing signal consent—for all Negroes—in the closing off of their part in the political life of the nation.

That having been said, the world within the Tuskegee campus must be just so. The plausibility of his experiment has to be readily apparent to the white patrons and pilgrims who come to see firsthand the doings there and those who partake of the Tuskegee experience through viewing the publicity materials and Institute catalogs Washington has sent out: evident in the photographs of fifteen or twenty male students (rather more, probably, than is strictly necessary) whitewashing a fence; or other young men, clad in vests and shirtsleeves (rather better dressed than is appropriate) and bent not too far over in Tuskegee's crowded classrooms in the fields; or mixed groups of young people, the men in coats and ties and what are clearly store-bought hats, the young ladies in long dresses and bonnets standing in other fields and taking notes on how to steal a march on the low price of cotton; students in lines, sometimes marching and sometimes standing in place, but very definitely ordered. And other photographs: old, dilapidated Negro homes and schools, mean one-room affairs, juxtaposed with brand-new "Washington homes" and "six hundred dollar" schoolhouses; before-and-after photographs marking a transformation as profound as the sort that used to be illustrated in the backs of comic books where the ninety-eight-pound weakling, having had sand kicked in his face and his girlfriend stolen by the bully, takes the Charles Atlas course and becomes a muscleman (except that in the case of the Washington-transformed Negro there is neither the expectation of his winning that girl or being inclined to bash back at his bully).

Washington's vision and the image of Tuskegee he promoted are mutually supporting. But the vision goes first for without it the photographs and stories are readily seen as farcical or absurd—too many shacks remain standing, too many dead Negroes hanging from trees--and he becomes Potemkin to his patrons' Catherine the Great, with Tuskegee the facade concealing an ugly reality of poverty and difficult circumstances. Accepting his vision, his personal story allows him to personify first the gussied up and happy villagers, then Potemkin taking charge of the extreme makeover project, and finally the master of the whole dominion—if you will kindly send him a check.

Frederick Douglass, George Washington, Moses, and even Jesus Christ: these are the figures to whom Washington is compared. Washington's assumption of the mantle Negro leader of a segregated people defies the ready characterizations usually available (this house nigger or that grass-roots militant), but in his being connected to those great men, one gets the sense of just what his time thought of him: a visionary. His rise was the fulfillment of a providential order: the son of a bondswoman driven off and then welcomed back to the fold, wrapped up in the embrace of a part of his father's tribe. He merits, for his filial pietism, a separate inheritance, his own lands, his own fief because of his being more right and true, better than could be expected from any native son, exemplifying the values of those who had scorned him; honoring the rightness and stature of the best in them, especially for those of his supposed or fantasy father's tribe who are sensitive to the possibility that the ways in which the Negro is caused to live might rather tend to suggest a less than exemplary Anglo-Saxon civilization. That reality, in his care, forces not a break with the way white people treat black people, but instead provides an opportunity for charity freely given, for compromise, and the hope of harmony.

And what of Washington's dreams? Zora Neale Hurston once wrote in contemplation of dreams "in the life of men": of their perishability and vulnerability to being "mocked to death by time." "Ships at a distance have every man's wish on board," she felt, "For some they come in with the tide. For others they sail forever on the horizon, never out of sight, never landing until the Watcher turns his eyes away in resignation."[83] Washington once dreamed dreams different from his final dream, but he would never see them realized except in the shadow of power he maintained in his small fiefdom; his delegated authority was useful in defending the battlements from attacks from within, in the form of Negro competition for white attention, but useless against the incursions of outsiders and unable to affect the arrangements that caused African Americans, generally, to lose ground to white Americans, generally, for every moment in which segregation was operative. The fact that this enterprise trained many black people to be teachers, to go forth imparting knowledge and ideas to children, and that it provided employment to some black people is not a part of any grand dream; other schools did the same without the necessity of mobilizing so many extraneous and hyperbolic words in service to progress and solving the Negro problem. Moreover, the provision from Washington's supporters was never enough, always less than what was accorded to others not segregated. But the fundamental problem is not with Tuskegee as an institute of learning.

What of Washington as leader of African America? What of a people placed under the care of his type of imposed leadership and the regime of race relations, where even the most powerful Negro of his time, and, perhaps, of all time, could not act, but could only engage in a series of preludes to real action and pantomimes of real leadership?

It is needless to point out that, whatever else might be true about him, his vision, his final dream of good race relations, ought not to be superimposed upon others as the content of their dreaming, too. That would be absurd, and erroneous. Washington told the people to "Cast down your buckets where you are," but they did not unless silence, imposed or not, is taken as willing obedience. They picked up buckets and departed north. As for those who remained in the South, they picked up buckets, and, in the civil rights era, jammed them into the machinery of Jim Crow, bringing it to a halt; pursuing politics rather than alms, they resolved to be about the upsetting of good race relations. But only a minority answered the call.

Washington's generation declared themselves New Negroes as, seemingly, each leadership cadre of men and women has done up to the time of the 1960s, when the practice caught on more generally. This may well be taken as indicative of a strain of intergenerational conflict running through modern African America history, but more certainly bespeaks an attempt by underfinanced artists and politicos to find the key that will advertise themselves and their group as the one with the way out, whether in the cultural or political arenas. Thus, it is most assuredly a part of the history of the Negro problem. Saying one is a New Negro need not be mean-spirited. In announcing themselves in this way, though, those who do so pay little heed to the insult that is implicit in the declaration. And, it is a funny, perilous dynamic, rife with the potential to breed distrust and, what is worse, there is the consequence of the cynicism of some thousands of little "Booker Ts," knock-off versions of the original, bred of the same dynamic, but smaller because the large deal has gone down; grandees in small dominions, school, church, barber shop, breeding among the people more cynicism and the loss or dissolution of best hopes and common dreams.

And the idea of race relations survives, somehow, not just in conformity to what is reflected in institutions managing personnel matters or schools seeking to inculcate their students to some of the values of a world of legal equality, but, as well, as a synonym for justice or beloved community; that is to say, as a metaphor for current dreams of what might be. This is Washington's legacy even as subsequent history gave the lie to his dreaming.

His idealist rendering of the problem and optimistic solution carried the day. And latter days as well: Washington's metaphors are hard to forget; his homely homilies stick in the mind and become facts of nature and essential truths about black people and their circumstances in the South. As much as it might seem possible to think and speak in a different way about the important matters upon which Washington shaped American opinion, to deploy a larger vocabulary and grammar that that which has been handed down by Washington, one shrinks before the persuasive power of Washington's metaphors—that ship at sea, lost; that hand, raised, fingers spread—and the strength and endurance of the race relations idea. Beloved community falls before it, and Martin King's dream, and the civil rights movement's goal of justice becomes a synonym for merely "optimum race relations" and the beggings of diversity and more racial harmony. The old language remains so current one hundred years distant from the age of Washington and four decades distant from the age of King that it almost seems like the possibility for new metaphors has gone.

And yet one might ask, "What is progress in the anatomy of a hand?" And one might ask, "Was the ship really lost, or didn't we really know precisely its dire position?" And one might see that the resort to those particular metaphors, as powerful as they have been, is itself a means by which American democracy was betrayed by the American people.

※※※

LOOK OUT over the seeming stillness of a river frozen in wintertime. In the darkness at midriver, voices break the silence, asking, "Is this a river we have traveled before? One that fed us and kept us and carried us along?" Impatiently, a voice demands fire to melt the ice, to speed them in their being about their journey. A second, more calmly, calls out that they must leave the river to search for open water elsewhere. A third proposes the felling of trees to build boats and rafts. Still another speaks of other rivers, of streams and brooks, of whitewaters and rapids, eddies and dry beds, and of the requirement that this river, if it is a river, must be traveled like all the other waterways of the world.

Then there is a clamor somewhere up on the banks of the river, and out of it comes a strong, clear, masterful voice, saying, "There is no river but this one. Set down upon the ice where it is thinnest and when the river again flows, you and I will be carried along to what must be our destination."

This he intones through the long night, amid meals prepared and served, children comforted, and songs sung; amid the party's numbers being added to and subtracted from; amid the wind whipping past, and creakings and groanings from the ice.

And when the dawn breaks, warming the ice and ending the echoing reverie of his voice, the surroundings are revealed to their senses and they see they are no longer upstream on the river, but heading deep into the sea. And the ice melts.

Notes

Introduction

1. Langston Hughes, introduction to Booker T. Washington, *Up From Slavery* (New York: Dodd, Mead, 1965).
2. Ralph Ellison, *Invisible Man* (New York: Random House, 1952), 38.
3. The best of the early work is now twenty years old, and it must begin with Aldon D. Morris, *The Origins of the Civil Rights Movement: Black Communities Organizing for Change* (New York: Free Press, 1984). Charles M. Payne offers a powerful account of Mississippians from the 1920s onward struggling bravely for the betterment of their lives in his *I've Got the Light of Freedom: The Organizing Tradition and the Mississippi Freedom Struggle* (Berkeley: University of California Press, 1995). Of seminal importance, too, is Jack M. Bloom's argument about the slipping of the hold on African Americans by the New South agricultural system, abetted by the infusion of capital from the New Deal that allowed for the mechanization of farms and made superfluous some hundreds of thousands of black and white

sharecroppers. Bloom, *Class, Race, and the Civil Rights Movement* (Bloomington: Indiana University Press, 1987).

4. In this, I am motivated by a view of the inadequacies of the two major trends in civil rights studies: the top-down approach, which recapitulates the rendering of contemporary journalism, and the community-studies approach, which focuses on particular or multiple localities (like Morris's) in which the movement played itself out. A main problem with the first is its tendency to rely on a sort of default view that "America" (as opposed to some minority of Americans) responded favorably to King and the movement's moral challenge, which, as Payne points out, "reaffirms what most Americans would like to think of their country," but fails to account for the bitter contestation in the North as well as the South that was a fundamental part of the movement's unfolding. Payne, *I've Got the Light of Freedom*, 413–441. For all their strengths, the problem with the local studies is just that. They might interpret Martin Luther King's coming to their town as a knight arriving on a horse or as a meddler interfering in a heroic struggle or in some other way, but they generally have difficulty in accounting for the relationship between their town or city and the broad-scale political and intellectual wrangling in which King and, to a lesser extent, men like Roy Wilkins and James Baldwin were involved.

5. A number of the contributors to a recent collection of essays on Washington's biography, *Booker T. Washington and Black Progress: Up From Slavery 100 Years Later*, ed. W. Fitzhugh Brundage (Gainesville: University Press of Florida, 2003), cast Washington in a generally favorable light, but such light as makes it unnecessary to evaluate "black progress" in comparison to that of, for example, white Southerners, white Americans generally, or immigrants to America during Washington's time. On a different canvas, Nancy Cohen has powerfully shown modern American liberalism to be founded on the very compromising of democratic values that is my argument here in relation to Washington and his supporters. Cohen, *The Reconstruction of American Liberalism, 1865–1914* (Chapel Hill: University of North Carolina Press, 2002).

6. "Hispanics are the new blacks," I think I once heard a scholar assert, although one supposes this is merely a shuffling for present attention rather than a desire to recapitulate a past struggle through slavery and segregation.

7. Booker T. Washington, *The Future of the American Negro* (Boston: Small, Maynard & Co., 1899), chap. 2.

8. See, for but one of many examples, Jim Sleeper, "Demagoguery in America: Wrong Turns in the Politics of Race," *Tikkun* 6, no. 6 (1991): 43.

9. Arthur M. Schlesinger, *The Disuniting of America: Reflections on a Multicultural Society* (New York: Norton, 1992), chap. 4. In the same vein, Schlesinger also quotes a professor's claim that contemporary campuses have "the cultural diversity of Beirut. There are separate armed camps." The quotation is found on page 104.

10. The percentages come from the following sources. Peter Applebome, "Still a Dream 25 Years After King's Assassination," *New York Times*, April 4, 1993, which I cite only for its typifying the genre; the numbers ebb and flow, but indicate that

at that time 66 percent of African Americans answered "yes" and 58 percent of European Americans answered "no" to the question, "Do you believe that where there has been job discrimination in the past, preference in hiring or promotion should be given to blacks today?" The percentages about job discrimination and fair treatment in public accommodations come from Correspondents of the *New York Times, How Race Is Lived in America: Pulling Together, Pulling Apart* (New York: Times Books, 2001), which includes an appendix entitled "The New York Times Poll on Race: Optimistic Outlook But Enduring Racial Division," and the particular breakdown on page 366. The O. J. Simpson data, from polling by the *New York Times* and CBS News as the trial neared its conclusion, is cited in Robert C. Smith and Richard Seltzer, *Contemporary Controversies and the American Racial Divide* (Lanham, Md.: Rowman & Littlefield, 2000), 127.

11. The primary materials I have used are mainly restricted to the documents from the first four decades of Washington's life that have been collected at the Library of Congress. To ease the way for readers to consult these materials, I have made citations, where possible, to the documents as they appear in the fourteen volumes of the published *Booker T. Washington Papers* (hereinafter, *Papers*), edited by Louis R. Harlan and others and brought out by the University of Illinois Press between 1974 and 1982.

12. Louis R. Harlan, "Booker T. Washington in Biographical Perspective," *American Historical Review* 75 (October 1970): 1581–1599; reprinted in *Booker T. Washington in Perspective*, ed. Raymond W. Smock (Jackson: University Press of Mississippi, 1988), 22.

13. James D. Anderson has made a powerful accounting of the inequities in educational funding and of the deliberate way in which they were reformed into existence in *The Education of Blacks in the South, 1860–1935* (Chapel Hill: University of North Carolina Press, 1988).

14. As examples of the failure to analyze fully the relationship between progressivism and segregation, see Ralph E. Luker, *The Social Gospel in Black and White* (Chapel Hill: University of North Carolina, 1991); Ronald C. White, *Liberty and Justice for All: Racial Reform and the Social Gospel* (New York: Harper & Row, 1990); and Dewey W. Grantham, *Southern Progressivism: The Reconciliation of Progress and Tradition* (Knoxville: University of Tennessee Press, 1983). In *Origins of the New South*, C. Vann Woodward was perhaps too subtle in immediately following his two chapters on the establishment of disfranchisement and segregation ("The Mississippi Plan as the American Way" and "The Atlanta Compromise") with two more on the emergence of "the educational panacea ("Progressivism—For Whites Only" and "Philanthropy and the Forgotten Man"), but the way in which he links these developments makes them all of a piece, particularly so in the last chapter, in which the whole notion of the poor white Southerner as "the forgotten man" is predicated on the notion that enough has been done for the Negro, thus providing a rationale for the inequities Anderson will later describe. Woodward, *Origins of the New South* (Baton Rouge: Louisiana State University Press, 1971 [1951]), chaps.

12–15. Following Woodward and focusing on the more concrete world of politics and legal reform, J. Morgan Kousser entertains no illusions about Southern reformers: their aim was not the spread and strengthening of democratic procedures, and while they may have claimed "the greatest good for the greatest number," (and really, really believed that was what they were accomplishing), their toleration of the continuing, even growing misery of the rural poor rather tends to give the lie to their pretensions. Kousser, *The Shaping of Southern Politics: Suffrage Restriction and the Establishment of the One-Party South, 1880–1910* (New Haven, Conn.: Yale University Press, 1974), 230.

15. It is a commonplace among Washington's biographers and other writers that certain unnamed others in works uncited have called Washington an "Uncle Tom," which they have discovered is wrong and which they will debunk. Typical in this regard is John P. Flynn, "Booker T. Washington: Uncle Tom or Trojan Horse," *Journal of Negro History* 54, no. 3 (July 1969): 262–274. One might imagine that scholars looking to make such a case have turned confidently to the chapter devoted to the city of Tuskegee in Stokely Carmichael and Charles V. Hamilton's *Black Power: The Politics of Liberation in America* (New York: Vintage Books, 1992 [1967]), only to be disappointed by the account found there. Of course, it is possible—likely even—that in the 1960s a "Washington was an Uncle Tom" consensus emerged among, say, civil rights activist encamped in the rural South risking their lives against the racial peace Washington championed, but this has not as yet translated into a historiographical school.

16. John David Smith seeks to make a case for Thomas's relevancy in understanding the age of segregation in his *Black Judas: William Hannibal Thomas and "The American Negro"* (Athens: University of Georgia Press, 2000). The difficulty of proving this proceeds from Thomas's obscurity on one hand and the possibility, on the other hand, that Thomas reached his racist conclusions in more or less the same way as did white racists, and thus is owed no more special attention than is owed to individual bigots generally.

17. Charles A. Lofgren, *The Plessy Case: A Legal-Historical Interpretation* (New York: Oxford University Press, 1987), 5.

18. Booker T. Washington, "Atlanta Exposition Address," September 18, 1895; *Papers*, 3:585.

19. It should be noted that George M. Fredrickson, borrowing the term from Pierre L. van den Berghe, used the term to describe the antebellum situation, but it fits, as well for his interpretation of the post-Reconstruction period. Fredrickson, *The Black Image in the White Mind: The Debate on Afro-American Character and Destiny, 1817–1914* (Middletown, Conn.: Wesleyan University Press, 1987 [1917]), 61, 256–282.

20. Even today, this quality in Washington has the effect of bringing together some ostensibly opposed intelligences. Ishmael Reed's favorable view of Washington's "hard-line practicality" has, at least, a consistency that a number of historians who deem him a pragmatist do not. Reed believes the forces arrayed against African

Americans in the age of Washington were "cruel" and "macabre," which some of them clearly were, but also "genocidal," and he credits Washington for "forestalling an even greater disaster: The extermination of Southern black people by those who had proven that they were capable of such ethnic cleansing." Reed, introduction to *Up From Slavery*, ix–xi. Writing for the *Lincoln Review*, Richard H. Powers, like Reed, wants to defend Washington from the liberal critics who are said to be constantly assailing his accomplishments and memory, but, unlike Reed, holds Washington to be a pragmatist in his diagnosis of black pathology, the "filthy habits, loose sexual behavior, thievery, drinking, lying, fighting, non-performance or slack performance of assigned work, and undisciplined behavior in general" among the students and faculty at Tuskegee. "An American Tragedy: The Transformation of Booker T. Washington From Hero to Whipping Boy," *Lincoln Review* 11, no. 1 (Winter–Spring 1993): 23–24.

21. Morgan Kousser draws attention to the way in which the absence of political power and influence within the courts "crippled" African American efforts to use economic weapons—boycotts and "Don't Buy Where You Can't Work" campaigns—to advance their interests in the age of Jim Crow, "The New Postmodern Southern Political History," *Georgia Historical Quarterly* 87, nos. 3–4 (Fall–Winter 2003), 437.

22. An example of this sort of usage and the obscurantism and confusion it can produce: years ago, Rayford W. Logan called the turn-of-the-century period "the nadir of the Negro's status," which aptly distinguishes that period's disfranchisement, segregation, and lynch law from the vastly more violent Reconstruction era, when African Americans had the vote and political power as a part of their arsenal. A more recent scholar terms the turn of the century "the nadir of race relations," which does not. Logan, *The Betrayal of the Negro: From Rutherford B. Hayes to Woodrow Wilson* (New York: Collier, 1965), 62; Waldo Martin, "In Search of Booker T. Washington: Up From Slavery, History and Legend," in Brundage, *Booker T. Washington and Black Progress*, 39.

23. W. E. B. Du Bois, "The Social Significance of These Three Cases," an address before the Yale University School of Law, January 11, 1950, in *Against Racism: Unpublished Essays, Papers, Addresses, 1887–1961*, ed. Herbert Aptheker (Amherst: University of Massachusetts Press, 1985), 280.

24. King's attack upon the negative peace created by a smoothly efficient system of segregation is an important component of my analysis of the hegemonic function of the race relations idea. He made an early statement of this point in "When Peace Becomes Obnoxious," a sermon delivered at the Dexter Avenue Baptist Church, March 18, 1956, in *The Papers of Martin Luther King, Jr.*, ed. Clayborne Carson, Ralph E. Luker, and Penny A. Russell (Berkeley: University of California Press, 1997), 3:207–208.

25. Basic accounts of the Albany Movement and Birmingham are found in most histories of King and the civil rights movement. The Branch quote is found in *Pillar of Fire: America in the King Years, 1963–65* (New York: Simon & Schuster, 1998), 25.

King's quote is from his "Letter from Birmingham City Jail," first published as a pamphlet by the American Friends Service Committee, and reprinted in *A Testament of Hope: The Essential Writings of Martin Luther King, Jr.*, ed. James M. Washington (San Francisco: HarperSanFrancisco, 1986), 289–302. King's comment is found on page 295.

26. Basil Matthews, *Booker T. Washington: Educator and Interracial Interpreter* (College Park, Md.: McGrath, 1969 [1948]), 335.

1. "The Great and Intricate Problem"

1. "Mr. [W. W.] Campbell's Remarks," "Colonel [Theodore] Roosevelt's Remarks," and "Mr. [Frank] Trumbull's Remarks," in *Memorial Exercises Held Under the Direction of the Board of Trustees in Memory of Dr. Booker T. Washington, Tuskegee Institute, Tuskegee, Alabama, December 12, 1915* (Tuskegee, Ala.: Tuskegee Institute, 1916), 27, 30, 36. Roosevelt spoke of Washington as "one of the men to whose counsel and guidance I frequently turned when I was president" (26).

2. Booker T. Washington, *Up From Slavery* (New York: Viking Penguin, 1986 [1901]), 66.

3. Louis R. Harlan, "Booker T. Washington and the Politics of Accommodation," in *Black Leaders of the Twentieth Century*, ed. John Hope Franklin and August Meier (Urbana: University of Illinois Press, 1982), 9–10.

4. "Mr. Low's Opening Remarks," in *Memorial Exercises*, 9.

5. "Confidential—Not For Publication. Speech of Mr. J. E. Spingarn at Banquet Honoring Dr. W. E. B. Du Bois, Atlanta University, February 25, 1938," NAACP Papers, Special Correspondence, Reel 23, Joel E. Spingarn.

6. Joel Elias Spingarn to Booker T. Washington, December 24, 1909; *Booker T. Washington Papers* (hereinafter, *Papers*), ed. Louis R. Harlan et al. (Urbana: University of Illinois Press, 1974–1982), 10:254.

7. H. G. Wells, "The Tragedy of Color," *Harper's Weekly* 50 (September 15, 1906), 1317–1319; reprinted in *Booker T. Washington*, ed. E. L. Thornbrough (Englewood Cliffs, N.J.: Prentice-Hall, 1969), 102–105. The quotation is found on page 104. Washington biographer Basil Matthews goes further in his investment: "On the basis of textbook principles and abstract syllogisms the critics of Booker Washington can at times make a more convincing statement than his logic would present. But in the setting of history in the Deep South, in the decades that straddled from the nineteenth century to the early years of the twentieth, a careful study of the implacable forces of that time makes it clear that any enterprise based on their logic, would have been doomed to instant and irredeemable futility. In essence the difference between himself and his critics does not lie in principles, but in his realistic study of priorities." Matthews, *Booker T. Washington: Educator and Interracial Interpreter* (College Park, Md.: McGrath, 1969 [1948]), 333.

8. As an example of the contemporary resonance of this vacuous schema, Ishmael Reed in his introduction to a new edition of *Up From Slavery* (New York: Signet, 2000) contrasts Washington's philosophy—based, he writes, "upon common sense and experience"—with that of Du Bois, "the idealist, and visionary," who was among the first of the "Northern elitist intellectuals—the Negro-Saxons," about whom Reed is quite disparaging. Reed does not see the similarities between his view on the matter and those of the liberals, but it does rather suggest that as a tool of historical analysis his particular brand of radical multiculturalism or multicultural radicalism is not so much the break from liberalism that he thinks it is. The quotations are found on pages xiii and xix.

9. Adolph Reed Jr., "Black Consciousness as Petty Bourgeois Invention: Race and Ideology in 20th Century Afro-American Thought," paper delivered at Columbia University, November 8, 1990.

10. William Jeremiah Moses has examined the way in which this system of antinomies is deployed by black people as a folk myth. *Black Messiahs and Uncle Toms: Social and Literary Manipulations of a Religious Myth* (University Park: Pennsylvania State University Press, 1982). Malcolm X's frequent invocation of the supposed differences between house slaves and field slaves as an analogy to distinguish "so-called Negro leaders" from real ones is but one example of the use (if not usefulness) of this scheme.

11. August Meier in his introduction to Booker T. Washington et al., *The Negro Problem: A Series of Articles by Representative American Negroes of To-day* (New York: Arno Press and New York Times, 1969 [1903]). The quotations are from page iii.

12. Louis R. Harlan, *Booker T. Washington: The Making of a Black Leader, 1865–1901* (New York: Oxford University Press, 1973), 117; Harlan, "Booker T. Washington and the Politics of Accommodation," 2, 15; Harlan, *Booker T. Washington: The Wizard of Tuskegee, 1901–1915* (New York: Oxford University Press, 1983), 428.

13. Harlan, *Booker T. Washington: The Wizard of Tuskegee*, 436–437.

14. Meier, introduction, vii. For this general interpretation and the domination of Washingtonian forces in this time, see Meier, *Negro Thought in America, 1880–1915: Racial Ideologies in the Age of Booker T. Washington* (Ann Arbor: University of Michigan Press, 1969 [1963]).

15. King, "When Peace Becomes Obnoxious," sermon delivered at the Dexter Avenue Baptist Church, March 18, 1956; in *The Papers of Martin Luther King, Jr.*, ed. Clayborne Carson, Ralph E. Luker, and Penny A. Russell (Berkeley: University of California Press, 1997), 3:207–208.

16. For the term "ghetto black," see William Julius Wilson, *The Declining Significance of Race*, 2nd ed. (Chicago: University of Chicago Press, 1980), 162.

17. Adolph Reed Jr., "The 'Underclass' as Myth and Symbol: The Poverty of Discourse about Poverty," in *Radical America* 24, no. 1 (Winter 1992): 21–40; reprinted in Reed, *Stirrings in the Jug: Black Politics in the Post-Segregation Era* (Minneapolis: University of Minnesota Press, 1999), 179–196; Stephen Steinberg, *Turning Back: The Retreat From Racial Justice in American Thought and Policy* (Boston: Beacon

234 1. "THE GREAT AND INTRICATE PROBLEM"

Press, 1995), chaps. 2–5. As an instance of this nostalgism, see Wilson's statement that Democratic policy from the 1930s to the 1970s aimed at "integrating the poor and minorities into the mainstream of American economic life" (*The Declining Significance of Race*, 120). Elsewhere, Wilson and others argue that the mid-1960s was a moment of social democratic opportunity wasted by the indulgences of black radicals. See his *The Truly Disadvantaged: The Inner City, the Underclass, and Public Policy* (Chicago: University of Chicago Press, 1987), chap. 6. Wilson's position is based on Bayard Rustin's argument in "From Protest to Politics: The Future of the Civil Rights Movement," *Commentary* 39 (February 1964): 25–31. See also Jim Sleeper, *The Closest of Strangers: Liberalism and the Politics of Race in New York* (New York: Norton, 1990), in which is found the argument that liberal legalisms such as affirmative action policies made King's dream "impossible" (164). And see the statement by two political commentators that "Race is no longer a straightforward, morally unambiguous force in American politics"; Thomas Byrne Edsall with Mary D. Edsall, "The Real Subject Is Race," *Atlantic Monthly* 269 (May 1991): 55–86. The quotation is found on page 53. One might assume the thinking that would allow one to write such a seemingly nonsensical statement is hampered by an inability to distinguish between the words "racism" and "race," but what would seem rather more the case is that the above mentioned instance is really a statement, not about race at all, but about where African American interests and demands fit into a liberal consensus now in flux.

18. Harlan, *Booker T. Washington: The Wizard of Tuskegee*, 244–251, 416–431 (the quotation is from 435); "Booker T. Washington and the Politics of Accommodation," 13; Harlan, "The Secret Life of Booker T. Washington," *Journal of Southern History* 37 (August 1971): 393–416; Matthews, *Booker T. Washington*, 335.

19. Matthews, *Booker T. Washington*, 335.

20. Robert J. Norrell emphasizes the appearance of voter registration efforts and other forms of agitation in Tuskegee in the 1940s as evidence of the unfolding of a design laid down by Washington with the (witting or otherwise) assistance of his national supporters, which enabled him to use or get around the local whites to the extent that Washington can be said to have "sown the wind of racial change." This argument, which needless to say rather narrows the purview of someone whose authority was national in scope, runs aground based on the fact that the local emergence of what scholars have come to call "the early civil rights movement" almost uniformly took place in communities with Negro colleges, along the lines of which the industrial education-oriented Tuskegee Institute had reorganized itself after Washington's death. As well, Norrell is not able to show that the way was made any easier for the movement in Tuskegee, nor its rise accompanied by any less rancor or violence in the 1960s, because of Washington having based operations there. To the contrary, Norrell's own rendering suggests Tuskegee fit the pattern of other Deep South towns affected from within and without by the civil rights movement, with the result that in 1965 Tuskegee students, just like their peers elsewhere, found themselves, of necessity, out picketing "on behalf of the simple right to vote," as Langston Hughes

pointed out in his introduction to the 1965 edition of Washington's autobiography. *Reaping the Whirlwind: The Civil Rights Movement in Tuskegee* (New York: Knopf, 1985), chaps. 1–4; quotation is from page 18; Langston Hughes, introduction to Booker T. Washington, *Up From Slavery* (New York: Dodd, Mead, 1965), x; reprinted in Thornbrough, ed., *Booker T. Washington*, 161. See also Edward L. Ayers, *The Promise of the New South: Life After Reconstruction* (New York: Oxford University Press, 1992), for a similar assertion about how Washington "dug in for a long war on white racism" (326). Adam Fairclough, *Teaching Equality: Black Schools in the Age of Jim Crow* (Athens: University of Georgia Press, 2001) goes farther, arguing that "things might have been even worse" had it not been for Washington's "skillful racial diplomacy." Fairclough reaches this conclusion even as he recognizes the inferior schooling offered African American children based on his apparent premise that years and decades—whole lifetimes—of disadvantage are outweighed by the way this experience of losing ground "heightened blacks' consciousness of their minority status and implicitly challenged Jim Crow." The quotation is from page 18.

21. To adopt the evocative phrase that is the central metaphor of Vincent Harding's *There Is a River: The Black Struggle for Freedom in America* (New York: Vintage Books, 1983), xix.

22. Rayford W. Logan, *The Negro in American Life and Thought: The Nadir, 1877–1901* (New York: Dial Press, 1954). Certainly the relationship of these developments is not impossible to understand. As a starting point, one might reckon with Edwin S. Redkey's statement that Washington was "the most powerful black man in American history" and the price paid—by African Americans rather than by Washington—for this was "the humiliation of Southern blacks in their own eyes and in the eyes of whites in return for telling white businessmen what they wanted to hear about 'happy, docile blacks.'" "The Flowering of Black Nationalism," in *Key Issues in the Afro-American Experience*, ed. Nathan I. Huggins, Martin Kilson, and Daniel M. Fox (New York: Harcourt Brace Jovanovich, 1971), 122.

23. Trotter quoted in Stephen R. Fox, *The Guardian of Boston: William Monroe Trotter* (New York: Atheneum, 1971), 39.

24. In an article on Washington's performance at the Cotton States Exposition, the Chicago *Inter-Ocean* was at some pains to point out the fact that the fruits of the work done by Washington in building the Tuskegee Institute, while impressive, was not nearly so singular as, it seemed, his advocates would have it, and went on to favorably review examples of the good works done by a long list of other schools that have taught "colored youth how to earn their own living by systematic work from trained hands and developed intellects." ("Is He a New Negro?" October 2, 1895, 7). Perhaps this point is as pertinent today as it was then.

25. The characterization of Washington as Moses comes from the *New York World*, September 18, 1895; Washington, *Up From Slavery*, 217.

26. Theodore Roosevelt, "Preface," in Emmett J. Scott and Lyman Beecher Stowe, *Booker T. Washington: Builder of a Civilization* (Garden City, N.Y.: Doubleday, Page & Company, 1916), ix.

27. *A Dictionary of American English on Historical Principles*, ed. William A. Craigie and James R. Hulbert (Chicago: University of Chicago Press, 1942; 1959), vol. 3, offers different definitions for the two terms. "The Negro Problem," first cited in 1920, is said to be "the problem of satisfactory adjustment of Negroes as a race to their social and political environment." "The Negro Question," allegedly first used from 1832, is defined as "the social and political question or problem created by the existence of a Negro population in the United States." The former would seem to put the onus on African Americans to adjust themselves, while the latter might be construed as a matter posed, presumably, to white people. For reasons that will be made clear, I understand them as synonymous and essentially interchangeable. I have not made a systematic study of when the terms were first used, but in 1864 Hollis Read published *The Negro Problem Solved; or, Africa as she was, as she is, and as she shall be. Her curse and her cure* (New York: A. A. Constantine, 1864), so the late date of reference for the Negro problem is surely inaccurate.

28. As an example of the new uses to which a postmodern race are being put, Bryant Simon holds that in the years before the emergence of the modern civil rights movement the white textile workers in South Carolina were put off by liberals like Eleanor Roosevelt and African Americans organizers who, he writes, "attacked their whiteness." Following this logic, what otherwise would be considered political matters—political and labor organizing, voter registration—to advance black people's interests or, even, the common interests of workers, and political problems—how to carry this out—become ways of making race. White mill workers "did not intend to let the whole idea of race and racial privilege evaporate without a fight." But his evidence suggests that they made their stand, not for whiteness, but for the privileges segregation and disfranchisement helped them to tenuously horde. This latter might be their definition of what a white man deserves, but the very fact that they could conceive of the loss of such privileges suggests their consciousness that it was not their definition of what a white man was, is, or inevitably would be. Simon, "Race Reactions: African American Organizing, Liberalism, and White Working-Class Politics in Postwar South Carolina," in *Jumpin' Jim Crow: Southern Politics From Civil War to Civil Rights*, ed. Jane Dailey, Glenda Elizabeth Gilmore, and Bryant Simon (Princeton, N.J.: Princeton University Press, 2000), 239-259. The quotations are from page 255. See also Grace Elizabeth Hale, *Making Whiteness: The Culture of Segregation in the South, 1890–1940* (New York: Pantheon Books, 1998).

29. John David Smith, ed., *Anti-Black Thought, 1863–1925*, vol. 2, pt. 2 (New York: Garland, 1993), xv.

30. J. R. Ralls, *The Negro Problem. An Essay on the Industrial, Political and Moral Aspects of the Negro race in the Southern States as Presented Under the Late Amendments to the Federal Constitution* (Atlanta: James P. Harrison & Co., 1877); reprinted in Smith, *Anti-Black Thought, 1863–1925*, vol. 2, pt. 2, 1–116.

31. Reed, *The Negro Problem Solved*, iii, 319.

32. Charles Murray, *Losing Ground: American Social Policy, 1950–1980* (New York: Basic Books, 1984); Richard Hernstein and Charles Murray, *The Bell Curve: Intelligence and Class Structure in American Life* (New York: Free Press, 1994).

33. Du Bois's hackles were raised by one William Hannibal Thomas, who had undergone some kind of change of heart that caused him to turn an 1890 pamphlet written as a vindication of the freedmen, into a racist screed. Du Bois, "The Storm and Stress in the Black World," review of Thomas, *The American Negro: What He Was, What He Is, and What He May Become: A Critical and Practical Discussion* (New York: Macmillan, 1901), and his earlier "Negro Problems, Land and Education" (Boston: published by the author), reviewed in *The Dial* 30 (April 16, 1901): 262–264. Washington's colleague Charles W. Anderson saw *Up From Slavery* as a fine "rebuttal of the absurd statements" made by Thomas "in that wail of despair." Anderson to Washington, April 7, 1902; *Papers*, 4:438–439. On Thomas's life and career, see John David Smith, *Black Judas: William Hannibal Thomas and "The American Negro"* (Athens: University of Georgia Press, 2000).

34. See, for example, comments by former Senator Bill Bradley, from whose speech before the U.S. Senate on the Los Angeles riots of 1992 the quotations are taken. Bradley's speech is quoted in *Harper's Magazine* (July 10, 1992), 10; Jordan, *White Over Black: American Attitudes Toward the Negro, 1550–1812* (New York: Norton, 1977), 28–29.

35. James Baldwin, "Many Thousand Gone," *Partisan Review* (November–December 1951); reprinted in *Notes of a Native Son* (1955) and in Baldwin, *The Price of the Ticket: Collected Nonfiction, 1948–1985* (New York: St. Martin's, 1985), 66.

36. Christopher Lasch drew attention to this liberal habit of rhetorical inflation in "The Anti-Intellectualism of the Intellectuals," chap. 9 in his *The New Radicalism, 1889–1963* (New York: Norton, 1965).

37. Among historians working before the emergence of the modern civil rights movement, C. Vann Woodward, Vernon L. Wharton, George B. Tindall, Pauli Murray, and Rayford W. Logan, would, each in their own way, turn attention toward the related fate of African Americans and American democracy in the post-Reconstruction time in the South, which, as Logan wrote in 1954, "is one of the neglected periods in American history." This would seem to have much to do with the fact that after Reconstruction was cast as a tragic mistake, it was Washington's story that sufficed as an acceptable narrative of combined Negro and national progress. See Woodward, *Tom Watson: Agrarian Rebel* (New York: Macmillan, 1938); *Origins of the New South, 1877–1913* (Baton Rouge: Louisiana State University Press, 1951); *Reunion and Reaction: The Compromise of 1877 and the End of Reconstruction* (Boston: Little, Brown, 1951); and *The Strange Career of Jim Crow* (New York: Oxford University Press, 1955); Wharton, *The Negro in Mississippi, 1865–1890* (Chapel Hill: University of North Carolina Press, 1947); Tindall, *South Carolina Negroes, 1877–1900* (Columbia: University of South Carolina Press, 1952); Murray, *State Laws on Race and Color* (1952); Logan, *The Negro in American Life and Thought* (from which the quotation above is found on page ix); as well as historical and documentary

works by Carter G. Woodson, Herbert Aptheker, and a few others. On the historical profession's damning of "black Reconstruction" as a large folly, see numerous
articles by John R. Lynch published in the early years of the *Journal of Negro History*
running from "Some Historical Eras of James Ford Rhodes," *Journal of Negro History* 2 (October 1917): 345–368, to his "The Tragic Era," *Journal of Negro History* 16
(January 1931): 103–120; W. E. B. Du Bois, *Black Reconstruction in America: An Essay
Toward a History of the Part Which Black Folk Played in the Attempt to Reconstruct
Democracy in America, 1860–1880* (New York: Atheneum, 1962 [1935]), chap. 17; A.
A. Taylor, "Historians of the Reconstruction," *Journal of Negro History* 23 (Janu-
ary 1938): 16–34; Eric Foner, "Reconstruction Revisited," *Reviews in American His-
tory* 10 (December 1982): 82–100; and Foner, *Reconstruction: America's Unfinished
Revolution, 1863–1877* (New York: Harper & Row, 1988), preface and 608–612.

38. Gunnar Myrdal with the assistance of Richard Sterner and Arnold Rose, *An American Dilemma: The Negro Problem and Modern Democracy*, 2 vols. (New York:
Harper & Row, 1962 [1944]), 1:lxxi. See also David Southern, *Gunnar Myrdal and
Black-White Relations: The Use and Abuse of "An American Dilemma," 1944–1969*
(Baton Rouge: Louisiana State University Press, 1987); and, Walter Jackson, *Gunnar Myrdal and America's Conscience: Social Engineering and Racial Liberalism,
1938–1987* (Chapel Hill: University of North Carolina Press, 1990).

39. One way in which this is done is by finding evidence of moral concern in inac-
tivity. The Southern white ministry keep "aloof from the race problem" and "the
white church in the South has played so inconsequential a part in changing race
relations" because, Myrdal argues, Christian brotherhood is incompatible with
segregation. *An American Dilemma*, 2:868.

40. *An American Dilemma*, 2:785, 786; 1:lxi.

41. See his "Publisher's Introduction," to *What the Negro Wants*, ed. Rayford W. Logan
(Chapel Hill: University of North Carolina Press, 1944), in which Couch avails
himself of the opportunity to engage in an extended polemic against Myrdal's argument.

42. See Richard Kluger, *Simple Justice* (New York: Random House, 1975), chap. 26.

43. See, for example, King's statement in *Where Do We Go From Here: Chaos or
Community?* (Boston: Beacon Press, 1967): "Ever since the birth of our nation,"
he wrote, "white America has had a schizophrenic personality on the question of
race. She has been torn between selves—a self in which she proudly professed the
great principles of democracy and a self in which she practiced the antithesis of
democracy." The quotation is from page 68.

44. Myrdal, *An American Dilemma*, 1:251.

45. F. P. Keppel quoted in Myrdal, *An American Dilemma*, 1:xlviii.

46. Henry Steele Commager, *The American Mind: An Interpretation of American Thought
and Character Since the 1800s* (New Haven, Conn.: Yale University Press, 1950).

47. Ellison's "An American Dilemma: A Review" was written in 1944 for *Antioch Review* but was not published until twenty years later in Ellison's collection *Shadow
and Act* (New York: Random House, 1964). The quotation is from page 315.

48. Alexis de Tocqueville, *Democracy in America*, 2 vols. (New York: Knopf, 1945 [1838]), 1:424.

49. George M. Fredrickson, *The Black Image in the White Mind: The Debate on Afro-American Character and Destiny, 1817–1914* (Middletown, Conn.: Wesleyan University Press, 1987), 332.

50. John P. Diggins discusses the ways in which modern historians follow Jefferson in not being able to unravel the contradictory Enlightenment strains of naturalism and idealism in his thought. "Slavery, Race, and Equality: Jefferson and the Pathos of the Enlightenment," *American Quarterly* 28 (1976): 206–228.

51. Jordan, *White Over Black*, 430.

52. See Andrew Dickson White, "Jefferson and Slavery," *Atlantic Monthly* 9, no. 51 (January 1862): 29–40. The perspective allowing White to reach such a conclusion is suggested by his emphasis on Jefferson's learning "the theories and phrases of Voltaire and Rousseau and Montesquieu. . . . Terrible weapons these,—often searing and scarring frightfully those who brandished them,—yet there was not one chance in a thousand that any man who had once made any considerable number of these ideas his own could ever support slavery. . . . Those French thinkers threw such heat and light into Jefferson's mind, that every filthy weed of tyrannic quibble or pro-slavery paradox must have been shriveled." The quoted passage is found on page 31. The characterization quoted in the text is from David Brion Davis, *The Problem of Slavery in the Age of Revolution, 1770–1823* (Ithaca, N.Y.: Cornell University Press, 1975), 165. Among other early works there is R. E. Swindler, "Thomas Jefferson and Slavery," *Southern Magazine* 1 (February 1935): 6–7, 44, which insists Jefferson was both a good master and antislavery, a complex that one might think would provide opportunities for dialectics. Donald L. Robinson, *Slavery and the Structure of American Politics, 1765–1820* (New York: Harcourt Brace Jovanovich, 1971), 81–97, emphasizes Jefferson's example as the "only political leader of consequence in Revolutionary America who moved openly against Negro slavery." William D. Freehling, "The Founding Fathers and Slavery," *American Historical Review* 77 (1972): 81–93, views Jefferson as antislavery, as does Alexander O. Boulton, "The American Paradox: Jeffersonian Equality and Racial Science," 467–492, who concludes, "Probably no individual before Abraham Lincoln has as much practical success in setting slavery on the course of gradual extinction in the United States" (475). Frank Shuffleton has made a valuable contribution to Jefferson studies with his *Thomas Jefferson: A Comprehensive, Annotated Bibliography of Writings About Him* (New York: Garland, 1983).

53. Jefferson, *Notes on the State of Virginia*, in *The Works of Thomas Jefferson*, ed. Paul Leicester Ford (New York: G. P. Putnam's Sons, 1892–99), 3:266.

54. Edna Glen Williams, "Thomas Jefferson, Slavery and the Negro," M.A. thesis, Howard University, 1938. Benjamin Quarles demonstrates the various ways in which Jefferson was criticized by black abolitionists for his failure to connect forthrightly the plight of the slave to the promise of the American revolutionary spirit in "Antebellum Free Blacks and the Spirit of '76," *Journal of Negro History* 61

(1976): 229–242; David Brion Davis, *Was Thomas Jefferson the Authentic Enemy of Slavery?* (Oxford: Clarendon, 1970), and *The Problem of Slavery in the Age of Revolution* (Ithaca, N.Y.: Cornell University Press, 1975), 169–184.

55. Nathan Schachner, "Jefferson: A Slippery Politician," *American Mercury* 46 (1939): 49–55.

56. Winthrop D. Jordan, *White Over Black*, 455. Richard Hofstadter, with typical insight, wrote that Jefferson developed "an ingrained habit of solicitude for the helpless dependents who supported him." *The American Political Tradition & the Men Who Made It* (New York: Knopf, 1973), 23.

57. See Hofstadter in his introduction to *The American Political Tradition & the Men Who Made It*: "I am here analyzing men of action in their capacity as leaders of popular thought, which is not their most impressive function" (xl); Carroll quoted in Hofstadter, *The American Political Tradition*, 28. In arguing in 1859 for the inapplicability of the Declaration of Independence to the question of slavery, George D. Shortridge insisted, "Mr. Jefferson's doctrine is the dream of an enthusiast or visionary." George D. Shortridge, "Mr. Jefferson—The Declaration of Independence and Freedom," *De Bow's Review* 26 (1859): 547–559.

58. Edmund S. Morgan, *American Slavery, American Freedom: The Ordeal of Colonial Virginia* (New York: Norton, 1975), 385.

59. Adams quoted in Hofstadter, *The American Political Tradition*, 31.

60. "Thomas Jefferson's Thoughts on the Negro," *Journal of Negro History* 3, no. 1 (January 1918): 55–89; Jefferson, *Autobiography* (New York: Putnam, 1959), 35.

61. By 1776 Great Britain had abolished slavery in England by judicial decision in the *Case of James Sommersett v. Stewart*, Lofft. 1, 98 Eng. Rep. 49, 20 How. St. Tr. 1 (1772). Nevertheless, the Crown's colonial policy remained steadfast in rejecting efforts by Jefferson's Virginia to limit the slave trade.

62. Donald L. Robinson, in arguing that Jefferson was the "only leader of consequence in Revolutionary America who moved openly against Negro slavery," cites these rejected passages from the Declaration of Independence. *Slavery and the Structure of American Politics, 1765–1820* (New York: Harcourt Brace Jovanovich, 1971), 81–97.

63. Jefferson, *Works*, 3:267.

64. Ibid., 244–245.

65. One outstanding feature of the controversy over Jefferson's relationship with his slave, Sally Hemings, and his possible paternity of her children, is his defenders' notion, unexamined and trotted out just as if Americans had never modified their views on slavery, that it would be a greater sin for Jefferson to have debased himself with that woman than to debase that woman and scores of others by holding them as slaves. The former may or not make him a cad, but the latter does indeed make him a hypocrite. Thus Douglass Adair writes that a story about Hemings and Jefferson appearing in *Ebony* magazine "is calculated to remind its Negro readers of one of the ugliest features of Negro-white relations in American history," and, quoting Jefferson, stirring up those "ten thousand recollections." Adair, "The Jef-

ferson Scandals," in *Fame and the Founding Fathers: Essays by Douglass Adair*, ed. Trevor Colburn (New York: Norton, 1974), 167. About those who reject out of hand the idea of an intimate relationship between the two of one kind or another, B. R. Burg notes that they would seem to be outraged not by the immorality of Jefferson's putative paternity, but at the possibility of his having sexual relations with a black person. Burg, "The Rhetoric of Miscegenation: Thomas Jefferson, Sally Hemings, and Their Historians," *Phylon* 47 (1986): 128–138. For a discussion of "the Jefferson Scandals," see Scot A. French and Edward L. Ayers, "The Strange Career of Thomas Jefferson: Race and Slavery in American Memory, 1943–1993," in *Jeffersonian Legacies*, ed. Peter S. Onuf (Charlottesville: University Press of Virginia, 1993), 418–456. And for the Jefferson-Hemmings matter, see Annette Gordon-Reed, *Thomas Jefferson and Sally Hemmings: An American Controversy* (Charlottesville: University Press or Virginia, 1997).

66. Jefferson to the Marquis de Condorcet, *Works*, 5:377–379.

67. Jefferson to Fanny Wright, *Works*, 10:344. Jefferson expressed his belief that such experiments were unlikely to succeed because as he said in another connection "to abandon persons whose habits have been formed in slavery is like abandoning children." *Works*, 5:66.

68. Jefferson, *Works*, 3:249.

69. Ibid., 244. The countervailing ideas and the commitments of Jefferson's political, financial, and private life so surpass Myrdal that he is led to think of the Jefferson of this passage merely as a scientist conducting abstract experiments on human subjects. *An American Dilemma*, 90.

70. Jefferson, *Works*, 8:340.

71. Citing Jefferson's *Notes*, J. H. Scruggs Jr. emphasizes how Jefferson saw the capabilities of democratic citizenship, not as a gift, but as a "development of personality." "Thomas Jefferson's Views of Democracy and the Negro," *Missouri Historical Quarterly* 8 (Spring 1946): 95–102.

72. Born in 1785, Walker was the son of a slave father and free mother who settled in Boston, working as a dealer in old clothes and as an agent for *Freedom's Journal*. A militant abolitionist, in 1829 he issued his *Appeal in four articles together with a Preamble to the Colored Citizens of the World, but in particular and very expressly, to those of the United States of America* calling for insurrection against the slave power. He died mysteriously the next year. See Henry Highland Garnet, "A Brief Sketch on the Life and Character of David Walker" (1848), reprinted in *One Continual Cry: David Walker's Appeal to the Colored Citizens of the World*, ed. Herbert Aptheker (New York: Humanities Press, 1965), 40–44. Born about 1800, Nat Turner was a held as a slave in Southampton County, Virginia, until August 22, 1831, at which time he led a band of insurrectionists against the local slaveholders.

73. Lewis P. Simpson argues that in his life and writings Jefferson was consumed by an inherently alienating paradox of the pastoral based on slavery, and figures Jefferson's dream of a pastoral Republican America was more oriented to an audience of non-slaveholders in the North and the South than those of Jefferson's own

slaveholding class in the South. Simpson, "The Garden and the Covenant and the Garden of the Chattel," in *The Dispossessed Garden: Pastoral and History in Southern Literature* (Athens: University of Georgia Press, 1975), 1–33; and Simpson, "The Ideology of Revolution," in *The History of Southern Literature*, ed. Louis D. Rudin, Lewis P. Simpson, and Thomas D. Young (Baton Rouge: Louisiana State University Press, 1985), 57–67. White emphasizes Jefferson's early successful efforts at assisting the yeomanry of colonial Virginia while in the House of Burgesses through support for education and the preventing of "the aristocratic absorption of the soil." White, "Jefferson and Slavery," 31.

74. Jefferson, *Works*, 6:349.

75. Cushing Stout notes Jefferson's strong negative reaction to the Missouri Compromise in his "American Dilemma: Lincoln's Jefferson and the Irony of History," in *Making American Tradition: Visions and Revisions from Benjamin Franklin to Alice Walker* (New Brunswick, N.J.: Rutgers University Press, 1990), 133–151.

76. Jefferson to Jared Sparks, *Works*, 10:293.

77. Richard Hofstadter, *The American Political Tradition*, 31.

78. One is inevitably led to the conclusion that this great breadth also explains his failure to make possible the liberation of his slaves upon his death. There is in this, of course, the matter of his personal indebtedness; that not insignificant fact aside, it may be possible to suppose that Jefferson, unlike Washington whose will did provide for eventual emancipation, having said so much about slavery, human liberty, and the Negro could not bring himself to undertake in his personal affairs an action he would not recommend to the nation. Elizabeth Langhorne tells the story of how Jefferson's private secretary moved to Illinois to free his slaves after Jefferson failed to fight for emancipation in "Edward Coles, Thomas Jefferson and the Rights of Man," *Virginia Cavalcade* 23 (Summer 1973): 30–37.

79. Davis, *The Problem of Slavery in the Age of Revolution, 1770–1823*, 303.

80. See Barbara J. Fields, "Ideology and Race in American History," *in Region, Race, and Reconstruction: Essays in Honor of C. Vann Woodward*, ed. J. Morgan Kousser and James M. McPherson (New York: Oxford University Press, 1982), 161–162.

81. Henry Clay speech at the organizing meeting of the American Society for Colonizing the free people of color of the United States, Dec. 21, 1816; Clay to James Monroe, September 22, 1817; James F. Hopkins et al., eds., *The Papers of Henry Clay* (Lexington: University of Kentucky Press, 1959–92), 2:263–264, 284. See also Robert V. Remini, *Henry Clay: Statesman for the Union* (New York: Norton, 1991).

82. Hammond quoted in Morgan, *American Slavery, American Freedom*, 381. As early as the 1730s, America's colonial rulers were aware of the threat posed to the prospects of poor whites and smallholders by those colonists who had managed to acquire slaves. In 1734, trustees of Georgia colony, resident in England, prohibited the importation and use of "Black Slaves or Negroes" doing so in order to better the chances of the dispossessed white men whom they hoped would make something of themselves without the sharp competition of slaveholding grandees. Even in 1750, when the prohibition was lifted, stern regulations were put in place in

order to maintain a more level playing field by limiting the ratio of the number of slaves to that of white men. *Colonial Records of Georgia*, 1:48–52, 56–62.

83. For example: "If the South must be threatened with the negro question, and with having their throats cut if they attempted to resist, he would ask, on whose side was the bullying?" *Congressional Debates* 2 (April 1832): 2348.

84. An example of the enduring nature of this principle and the difficulty it poses to historians is Peter Novick's discussion of the relative merit of "damage" and "strength" as organizing principles for the study of African American history. Skipping over the question of why this analytic apparatus is employed for black people's history and no one else's, Novick fails to recognize at least two questions at the root of the matter. The first is whether it is appropriate in studying the effects of slavery on African Americans to reach a comparative conclusion—damaged compared to whom?—without specifying the normative party. The second question is whether it is appropriate to explain the poor fate of some black people in the 1960s and later based on what happened to some of their ancestors before 1865. In other words, if a scholar were interested in knowing whether American slaves were damaged by slavery and whether "ghetto blacks"—the term favored by sociologists—were damaged by slavery, who is the control group or groups that provides the implicit referent? If the answer to the first is people who did not experience life as slaves, and the answer to the second is not those who did, the inquiry is likely not really about slavery or "the underclass" at all, but about the nature of the black race or, in the form of race's modern variant, an ahistorical "black culture." Avowing agnosticism on the damage question itself, Novick concludes with a leap from slavery to the breakdown of the modern black family, all the more extraordinary because theoretical unselfconsciousness is his subject. *That Noble Dream: The "Objectivity Question" and the American Historical Profession* (Cambridge: Cambridge University Press, 1988), 480–489; the quotations are found on pages 484 and 489.

85. Paul Finkelman, ed., *Dred Scott v. Sandford: A Brief History with Documents* (Boston: Bedford Books, 1997), 61, 134, 61.

86. Lincoln speaking to Governor Curtin of Pennsylvania, quoted in Francis Bicknell Carpenter, *Six Months at the White House with Abraham Lincoln: The Story of a Picture* (New York: Hurd and Houghton, 1867), 83–84. Lincoln's counterpart, Jefferson Davis, comments "On the Use of Negroes in wartime" before a joint session of the Confederate Congress serve to illustrate the same point. While he was not prepared to arm slaves, he did propose "to liberate the negro on his discharge after service faithfully rendered." The matter, President Davis said, is not just "the mere right of property," which would be easy enough to decide, but also "the social and political question" which "has a far wider and more enduring importance than that of pecuniary interest. In its manifold phases it embraces the stability of our republican institutions, resting on the actual political equality of all its citizens, and includes the fulfillment of the task which has been so happily begun—that of Christianizing and improving the condition of the Africans who have, by the will of Providence, been placed in our charge." *Address to the Confederate Congress*, November 1864.

87. Myrdal writes, "In principal the Negro problem was settled long ago" by the Civil War and the passage of the Reconstruction Amendments. *An American Dilemma*, 2:24.

88. Barbara Jeanne Fields, *Slavery and Freedom on the Middle Ground* (New Haven, Conn.: Yale University Press, 1985), 205–206, 193.

89. "The Slave Who Ran Away," *New York Times*, February 21, 1895.

90. "Death of Frederick Douglass," *Harper's Weekly*, February 23, 1895.

91. "Honors to Frederick Douglass," *New York Times*, February 24, 1895.

92. "Death of Frederick Douglass."

93. "The Most Picturesque Historical Figure in Modern Times," *New York Times*, February 25, 1895; "Death of Fred Douglass," *New York Times*, February 21, 1895.

94. "The Slave Who Ran Away."

95. Booker T. Washington, *My Larger Education: Being Chapters from My Experience* (New York: Doubleday, Page and Company, 1911), 106; *Papers*, 1:424. Washington makes a similar statement in *Frederick Douglass* (Philadelphia: George W. Jacobs, 1906), 349.

96. "The Slave Who Ran Away."

97. Ibid.

98. W. E. B. Du Bois, "Of Mr. Booker T. Washington and Others," in *The Souls of Black Folk*, ed. David W. Blight and Robert Gooding Williams (Boston: Bedford Books, 1997), 62.

99. One interpretation of the function of "representative colored men": Nell Irvin Painter, *Exodusters: Black Migration to Kansas After Reconstruction* (New York: Norton, 1986), 14–16, 22–30.

100. "Death of Frederick Douglass," 198.

101. It is also significant, especially given the way Washington soon came to be the singular Negro leader, that Douglass was erroneously marked a singular African American hero, leaving out all the many other good men and women of accomplishment in the great struggle against slavery.

102. "The Most Picturesque Historical Figure in Modern Times."

103. Quoted in Harlan, *Booker T. Washington: The Making of a Black Leader*, 217.

104. Booker T. Washington, "Atlanta Exposition Address," September 18, 1895; *Papers*, 3:583–587.

105. William Dean Howells, "An Exemplary Citizen," *North American Review* 173 (August 1901): 280–288; *Papers*, 6:191–200.

106. Taking off from this reality, Kelly Miller satirized this sense of the notion of Washington as conservative in telling the story of "a Russian fellow who was informed that some Negroes were conservative while others were radical." This notion, Miller reports, was "more than the Cossack's risibilities could endure. 'What on earth,' he exclaimed with astonishment, 'have they to conserve?'" Miller, "Washington's Policy," Boston *Evening Transcript*, September 18–19, 1903; reprinted in Hawkins, *Booker T. Washington and His Critics*, 49–54. The quotation is found on page 49.

107. Washington, *Up From Slavery*, 230. The interpretation of Washington as a visionary and a progressive goes hand in hand with the argument that his singular contribution to his time and American reform is the notion of "race relations." Although I make some note of the ways in which parts of Washingtonianism are conservative, I do not consider it necessary to tarry too long over that matter. If America had an especial desire to lionize an African American person who was conservative, there were much better representatives of that honorable tradition than Washington in Alexander Crummell, "a towering figure in the black community," who, like Washington, was highly critical of the opportunism of the black political class of the 1890s, an opponent of labor unions, and a critic of the "growing indifference to law and order" in America. Crummell's complete opposition to Washington's materialism was of a piece with his general, religion-based philosophy in opposition to all that was vulgar and decadent in industrializing America, and he believed that African Americans, because of the extent to which they were left out, by the 1890s, of "the savagery and the fanaticism of blatant American democracy," had the opportunity and a moral responsibility to take a different path from the one laid before them by modernism and white people. He was not available for hiring to the post Washington assumed. Crummell, "The Negro as a Source of Conservative Power" (1888), in *Destiny and Race: Selected Writings, 1840–1898*, ed. Wilson Jeremiah Moses (Amherst: University of Massachusetts Press, 1992), 235–244. The quoted part of the characterization of Crummell is by Alfred A. Moss Jr., in *The American Negro Academy: Voice of the Talented Tenth* (Baton Rouge: Louisiana State University Press, 1981), 19.

108. Redkey writes that upon reading *Up From Slavery*, Garvey "suddenly perceived that his own life work was to be a leader of the black race." "The Flowering of Black Nationalism," 117.

109. Washington, "Atlanta Exposition Address," September 18, 1895; *Papers*, 3:586.

110. Consideration of these matters has little or nothing to do with questioning the goodness of this or that feature of Washington's and his followers' dreams. The idea of the building up of business enterprises and the building up of education and the building up of moral character—deficits in all of which Glenn C. Loury calls "the fact of black underdevelopment"—warms the heart and fires the mind for some Americans. Correctly recognizing that Washington's strategy, because of the forces arrayed against it, was quite unlikely to be successful (and indeed it was not), Loury proposes the revival of the "animating *spirit*" of Washington's philosophy because it is today "a sounder guide for the future of blacks than that reflected in the worldview of his critics." Loury, thus, advocates, a policy of "self-help, of good old-fashioned 'uplift . . . to overcome the profound pathology to be found in some quarters of contemporary black life." It will be difficult, he writes, "but one must nevertheless believe that the levels of gang violence, drug abuse, family instability, sexual promiscuity, sloth, indifference to responsibility, and so forth can be changed through concerted effort at the propagation of alternative values." However, his couching of this proposal in terms of ready jibes at, rather than real criti-

cal analysis of, the inadequacies of "today's civil rights orthodoxy," and "Malcolm X and his followers in the urban centers of the 1990s," his failing to explain other sources for that pathology, and his neglecting to explain how the financial capital and moral authority to do this might come into black hands, altogether tends over-much toward the resuscitation of the whole of "the ambiguous but great legacy of Booker T. Washington," as merely another of the species of fantasy inhabiting the history of the Negro problem. Loury, "Two Paths to Black Progress," in *First Things*, October 1992; reprinted *in One By One From the Inside Out: Essays and Reviews on Race and Responsibility in America* (New York: Free Press, 1995). The quotations are found on pages 68–82.

111. Booker T. Washington, "Education Will Solve the Race Problem," *North American Review* 171 (August 1900): 221–232.

112. Howells, "An Exemplary Citizen," 196.

113. Daryl Michael Scott describes this confluence in a systematic and insightful way in his *Contempt and Pity: Social Policy and the Image of the Damaged Black Psyche, 1880–1996* (Chapel Hill: University of North Carolina Press, 1997).

114. Howells, "An Exemplary Citizen," 198.

115. C. Vann Woodward, *Origins of the New South*, 356. Ogden to Washington, October 17, 1895; *Papers*, 4:58–59.

116. Washington, letter in *New York World*, September 20, 1895; *Papers*, 4:15–17.

117. Clark Howell letter in the *New York World*, September 19, 1895.

118. *Atlanta Constitution*, September 20, 1895.

119. William J. Cansler to Washington, September 26, 1895; *Papers*, 4:30–31.

120. *New York World*, September 18, 1895; *Papers*, 4: 3, 8–10.

121. Mary Elizabeth Preston Stearns to Washington, September 19, 1895; *Papers*, 4: 17–18.

122. Still to Washington, September 19, 1895; *Papers*, 4:18.

123. John W. Cochran to Washington, September 21, 1895; *Papers*, 4:20.

124. W. E. B. Du Bois to Washington, September 24, 1895; *Papers*, 4:26.

125. Washington letter in the *New York World*, September 20, 1895.

126. Harlan is rather of a divided mind on this question, at once echoing Washington's stated position that Tuskegee was "an experiment . . . testing whether or not it was possible for Negroes to build up and control the affairs of a large educational in-stitution," while documenting in great detail the pains Washington had to go to raise money from white patrons in order to keep his exercise in black self-suf-ficiency afloat. See Harlan, *Booker T. Washington: The Making of a Black Leader*, chap. 6; Harlan, "Booker T. Washington and the Politics of Accommodation," 1–18; and Harlan, *Booker T. Washington: The Wizard of Tuskegee*. The quotation is from Washington, *Up From Slavery*, 145.

127. Mark Twain and Charles Dudley Warner, *The Gilded Age: A Tale of Today* (New York: Penguin Books, 1994 [1873]), 70.

128. Booker T. Washington, "My View of Segregation Laws," *New Republic* 5 (Decem-ber 4, 1915): 113–114. Inexplicably, Harlan finds it "ironic" that Washington posthu-mously spoke more forthrightly than he had in life." Harlan, *Booker T. Washington:*

The Wizard of Tuskegee, 430. Washington's earlier employment of the rhetorical twist asserting that segregation mainly injures white morals is found in many places in his writings and speeches. The quotation here is from *Up From Slavery*, 165–166.

129. Gramsci distinguishes between "common sense" and "good sense" philosophy in "The Study of Philosophy and of Historical Materialism," in *The Modern Prince and Other Writings* (New York: International Publishers, 1970), 60–75. Elsewhere he defines "common sense" as a received "conception of the world which is uncritically absorbed by the various social and cultural environments in which the moral individuality of the average man is developed." Quoted in Walter L. Adorno, *Hegemony and Revolution: A Study of Antonio Gramsci's Political and Cultural Theory* (Berkeley: University of California Press, 1980), 123.

2. "Negroes Whose Habits You Know"

1. William Monroe Trotter quoted in *Booker T. Washington*, ed. E. L. Thornbrough (Englewood Cliffs: Prentice-Hall, 1969), 118.

2. Georges Altman, "Foreword," in Marc Bloch, *Strange Defeat: A Statement of Evidence Written in 1940* (New York: Norton, 1968), ix.

3. Kelly Miller, "Washington's Policy," *Boston Evening Transcript*, September 18–19, 1903; reprinted in Hugh Hawkins, *Booker T. Washington and His Critics: The Problem of Negro Leadership* (Boston: D. C. Heath, 1962), 49–54. Thornbrough, "Booker T. Washington As Seen by His Contemporaries," *Journal of Negro History* 53, no. 2 (April 1968): 164. Howells played with this notion only to dispel it in his review of *Up From Slavery*, seeing in Washington no evidence of "taint upon the mind and soul of the born thrall." William Dean Howells, "An Exemplary Citizen," *North American Review* 173 (August 1901): 280–288; *Papers*, 6:198.

4. Oliver C. Cox, "The Leadership of Booker T. Washington," *Social Forces* (October 1951): 91, 94–96.

5. Trotter quoted in *Booker T. Washington*, ed. E. L. Thornbrough, 118.

6. Booker T. Washington, *Up From Slavery* (New York: Viking Penguin, 1986 [1901]), 1.

7. This could be said to be equally true in our own time. This persistence is an odd fact, given the scope and wide dispersion of information about black people and African American history. Perhaps it is explained by the ravenous demand for "role models" and the wide dispersion of the notion that "you can do anything" if possessed of a properly sated self-esteem.

8. Washington, *Up From Slavery*, 36.

9. Theodore Roosevelt, "Preface," in Emmett J. Scott and Lyman Beecher Stowe, *Booker T. Washington: Builder of a Civilization* (Garden City, N.Y.: Doubleday, Page & Co., 1918 [1916]), ix, xv.

10. O. K. Armstrong, "Booker T. Washington—Apostle of Good Will," *Reader's Digest*, February 1947, 25–30; reprinted in *Great Lives, Great Deeds* (Pleasantville, N.Y.: Reader's Digest Association, 1964), 284–291. The quotation is found on page 291.

11. Trotter quoted in *Booker T. Washington*, ed. E. L. Thornbrough, 118.

12. This was a quality in Washington, impossible to ignore, but pointed out by the Southern white press only in those situations in which he had aroused their ire. See for example the editorial comment of the *New Orleans States*, quoted in the *Montgomery Journal*, April 20, 1905: Washington has "an eye always on the main chance." This editorial slant is noted by Thornbrough, "Booker T. Washington As Seen by His Contemporaries," 166.

13. Washington's participation in Reconstruction politics is discussed in chapter 4.

14. Louis R. Harlan, *Booker T. Washington: The Making of a Black Leader, 1865–1901* (New York: Oxford University Press, 1973), 169.

15. The characterization of Councill is Washington's; he conveyed it in a letter to Francis J. Garrison, September 23, 1899; quoted in August Meier, *Negro Thought in America, 1880–1915* (Ann Arbor: University of Michigan Press, 1963), 110.

16. Carver was so much a creature of Washington's enterprise at Tuskegee, and his fame so dependent on the publicity machinery Washington and his successors controlled from there, that his life hardly can be seen separately from that of the master of Tuskegee plantation. Linda O. McMurry's biography of Carver—the other African American man of some significant profile in American history textbooks—poses some of the same questions about progress and segregation raised about Washington in this present work. In the same way that Washington was said to be the Negro George Washington, Carver was dubbed the black Thomas Edison, with the implication not only that "Professor Carver is to the peanut industry what Edison is to electricity," but that the benefits Edison brought to the American nation through his inventions and innovative commercial exploitation of electricity had their corollary in the benefits, especially, Jim Crowed African Americans would derive from peanuts. McMurry, *George Washington Carver: Scientist and Symbol* (New York: Oxford University Press, 1981), 176–178, 226. As evidence of black progress in or in spite of segregation, both Carver and Washington remained potent symbols into the 1960s, at least in elementary schools. It is, however, for Washington's exercise of political power and, through that exercise, his greater influence on the Negro problem that he is the essential man in the American embrace of segregation.

17. Perhaps the closest woman to this kind of stature was Ida B. Wells-Barnett, but given her direct manner and principled nature (not to speak of her penetrating criticism of Washington), one thinks she would have resisted the allure of such a position had she been offered it. See her devastation of Washington's advocacy of industrial education—"Booker Washington's hobby"—in her "Booker T. Washington and His Critics," *The World Today*, April 1904, 518–521. And see generally her opposition to Washington's manipulation of African American organizations like the Afro-American League (later the Afro-American Council), the National Negro Business League, his role as patronage chief under President Theodore Roosevelt, and her fear that he would steal away the NAACP from its more earnest purposes in her autobiography, Alfreda M. Duster, ed., *Crusade for Justice: The Autobiography of Ida B. Wells-Barnett* (Chicago: University of Chicago Press, 1970),

40–41, 260–265, 322–324. An argument could be made that in the four decades from Washington's death leading up to the Montgomery bus boycott, the person who best replicated Washington's role in national affairs (as opposed to more local affairs, where there were many smaller versions of the Washington model of Negro leadership) was Mary McLeod Bethune. Bethune was an educator, the founder of the National Council of Negro Women, and a government administrator. The notion of her as a successor to Washington's role comes from her being perhaps the central figure in "the black cabinet" created to sit on the outskirts of the Roosevelt administration in order to give symbolic acknowledgment of African American concerns, while the substance of those concerns was dealt with under the auspices of the regular departments of government. See B. Joyce Ross, "Mary McLeod Bethune and the National Youth Administration: A Case Study of Power Relationships in the Black Cabinet of Franklin D. Roosevelt," in *Black Leaders of the 20th Century*, ed. John Hope Franklin and August Meier (Urbana: University of Illinois Press, 1982), 191–211. See also Raymond Wolters, *Negroes and the Great Depression: The Problem of Economic Recovery* (Westport, Conn.: Greenwood, 1970); John B. Kirby, *Blacks Americans in the Roosevelt Era: Liberalism and Race* (Knoxville: University of Tennessee Press, 1980), especially chap. 6; Nancy J. Weiss, *Farewell to the Party of Lincoln Black Politics in the Age of FDR* (Princeton, N.J.: Princeton University Press, 1983), especially chap. 7; and Patricia Sullivan, *Days of Hope: Race and Democracy in the New Deal Era* (Chapel Hill: University of North Carolina Press, 1996).

18. It is a further indication of the changing nature of things after emancipation that Whittier originally quoted Wright as calling out "Massa, tell 'em we're rising!" The thirteen- or fourteen-year-old Wright wrote to Whittier to say that he liked the poem, but that he had most certainly not called Howard "Massa"—rather, he had "given up that word." Whittier then reedited the poem, replacing the offending term with "General." Wright to Greenleaf, March 9, 1869; *Newburyport Herald*, May 18, 1869; Wright to Whittier, December 8, 1891; and Wright to Roland H. Woodwell, June 13, 1945. Quoted in Woodwell, *John Greenleaf Whittier: A Biography* (Haverhill, Mass.: Trustees of the John Greenleaf Whittier Homestead, 1985), 365–366. See also Elizabeth Ross Haynes, *The Black Boy of Atlanta* (Boston: House of Edinboro, 1952), and Whittier's poem, "Howard at Atlanta," in his *Complete Poetical Works* (Boston: Houghton, Mifflin, 1881), 348–349.

19. One thinks in this connection of Henry Ossian Flipper, born a slave in Thomasville, Georgia, in the same year as Washington. Flipper attended Atlanta University and then the U.S. Military Academy at West Point in 1873, where he was severely hazed by his fellow cadets, but nonetheless graduated in 1877. He was assigned to the Tenth Cavalry, a black regiment, serving at several forts in the Indian territory in Texas. In his position as a commissary officer in charge of food, clothing, and supplies, he was accused in 1881 of embezzlement. He saw that all missing money was returned, and was not convicted but was found guilty of conduct unbecoming an officer and discharged from the army in June 1882. Over the course of the next decades Flipper tried to have this decision set aside through bills in Congress.

Flipper began a second career as a civil engineer and expert in land law in the Southwest and northern Mexico; he was called to Washington by Senator Albert Fall of New Mexico to serve the Senate Foreign Relations Committee during the Mexican Revolution. All the while in the course of his adventurous life, Flipper never seems to have made a statement of any significance on the Negro problem. An individualist and a man of a truly conservative temperament, he, unlike Washington, made his own way through quiet action. In the annals of the hard-striving, Flipper occupies a place second to no one. The relative insignificance of his life compared to Washington's is indicative of the fact that Washington is embraced as a paragon, not mainly for what he did, but for the ideological use to which could be put his formulation of the meaning of that life—in writings and speeches and at Tuskegee. See Flipper, *The Colored Cadet at West Point: The Autobiography of Lieut. Henry Ossian Flipper, first graduate of color from the United States Military Academy* (Lincoln: University of Nebraska Press, 1998 [1878]).

20. It might be added that Washington's career shares features with other of his contemporaries. In some important respect, the course of his life is like that of Thomas Watson, born 1856, for the way in which they both float with the changing winds of politics and then blow hard themselves once segregation is established. And in the way he succeeds by promoting himself and Tuskegee as a nostrum for what ails the country and its people, Washington might well be thought of in the same context as the famous self-promoter and salesman, "Diamond" Jim Brady, also born 1856.

21. Washington, *Up From Slavery*, 1.

22. This story was conveyed in a letter to Eugene D. Genovese by Conor Cruise O'Brien and included in the 1970 revision of Genovese's essay "Slavery and the Roots of Black Nationalism"; in Genovese, *In Red and Black: Marxian Explorations in Southern and Afro-American History* (New York: Pantheon Books, 1971), 154.

23. Du Bois's colloquy with his aunts reminds one of the scene in Ralph Ellison's *Invisible Man* in which the main character is lolling about in the new office provided him by the Brotherhood, only to be interrupted by one "Brother Tarp" bearing a poster featuring the visage of Frederick Douglass. Tarp turns aside the main character's confused thanks, saying only "He belongs to all of us"—a dim reminder to the main character of his grandfather's words: "be more human." Ellison, *Invisible Man* (New York: Vintage Books, 1980), 378.

24. "The Negro in America," An address delivered before the Philosophical Institute of Edinburgh, Scotland, October 16, 1907; reprinted in Carnegie, *Miscellaneous Writings of Andrew Carnegie* (Freeport, N.Y.: Books for Libraries Press, 1968 [1933]), 88–122; the quotation is found on page 119. Baldwin, "The Present Problems of Negro Education," *Journal of Social Sciences* 37 (1899): 53–64.

25. Kenneth O'Reilly, *Nixon's Piano: Presidents and Racial Politics from Washington to Clinton* (New York: Free Press, 1995), 345.

26. Howells, "An Exemplary Citizen," *North American Review* 173 (August 1901): 281–299; *Papers*, 6:192. The Lincoln–Booker Washington connection is taken up in greater depth in chapter 4.

27. T. Thomas Fortune in his introduction to *Black-Belt Diamonds: Gems from the Speeches, Addresses and Talks to Students of Booker T. Washington*, ed. Victoria Earle Matthews (New York: Mnemosyne Publishing, 1969 [1898]), v–xii. A newer edition of this work has been brought out under the new title *Black Diamonds: The Wisdom of Booker T. Washington* (Dearfield Beach, Fla.: Mnemosyne Publishing-Health Communications, 1990), which obliterates the cleverness of the original one.

28. The characterization is Thomas Wentworth Higginson's from his account of the Nat Turner revolt in 1831. Higginson, *Travellers and Outlaws: Episodes in American History* (New York: Arno and New York Times, 1969 [1889]), 277.

29. Confederate General Jubal A. Early was also from Franklin County.

30. Washington, *Up From Slavery*, 1–2, 4.

31. Ibid., 3.

32. Washington, "Negro Homes," *Century Magazine* 76 (May 1908): 71–79; Barry Mackintosh, *Booker T. Washington National Monument: An Administrative History* (Washington, D.C.: National Park Service, 1969); Edwin C. Bears, *The Burroughs Plantation as a Living Historical Farm* (Washington, D.C.: National Park Service, 1969); Correspondence with Booker T. Washington National Monument.

33. Washington, "The Negro's Life in Slavery," *Outlook* 93 (September 11, 1909): 71–78. The quotation is found on page 72.

34. [n.a.], "The Burroughs Plantation as a Living Historical Farm" (National Park Service, May 31, 1969), 27–13–37; Barry Mackintosh, "Agriculture on the Burroughs Plantation, 1856–1865" (National Park Service, 1969), 8, 12, on the different types of tobacco. Barry Mackintosh, "Booker T. Washington National Monument: An Administrative History" (National Park Service, June 18, 1969); Mackintosh, "The Burroughs Family: Owners of Booker T. Washington," in "The Burroughs Plantation: Background Studies" (National Park Service, 1969).

35. Bears, *The Burroughs Plantation as a Living Historical Farm*, 10–11; *Southern Planter* 7, no. 11: 345; Steven Hahn, "Hunting, Fishing, and Foraging: Common Rights and Class Relations in the Postbellum South," *Radical History Review* 26 (1982): 37–64.

36. Mackintosh, "Booker T. Washington National Monument: An Administrative History," 3.

37. Washington, *Up From Slavery*, 1.

38. Robert E. Park, "Tuskegee Principal at His Old Home," *The Tuskegee Student* (October 3, 1908): 3–4; *Papers*, 9:635–640.

39. Booker T. Washington, *The Story of My Life and Work* (Toronto: J. L. Nichols & Co., 1900); *Papers*, 1:12. Anthony Kaye makes a persuasive argument for the neighborhood (in preference to the community) being the key unit in the slaves' collective life in his *The Personality of Power: The Ideology of Slaves in the Natchez District of Mississippi, 1830–1865* (Chapel Hill: University of North Carolina Press, forthcoming).

40. John L. Washington to Asa L. Duncan, August 20, 1913; Harlan, *Booker T. Washington: The Making of a Black Leader*, 17.

41. Washington, *The Story of My Life and Work*; *Papers*, 1:12.

42. Ibid., 12.

43. Washington, *Up From Slavery*, 16.

44. Ibid., 11–12.

45. Ibid., 5.

46. Washington, "The Negro's Life in Slavery," 75.

47. Asa Leland Duncan to Washington, July 23, 1913.

48. Washington, *Up From Slavery*, 5.

49. Harlan, *Booker T. Washington: The Making of a Black Leader*, 24.

50. C. Vann Woodward, *Origins of the New South, 1877–1913* (Baton Rouge: Louisiana State University Press, 1971), 167–168.

51. Washington, "The Negro's Life in Slavery," 75.

52. Booker T. Washington, "Atlanta Exposition Address," September 18, 1895; *Papers* 3:580.

53. Mackintosh, "Booker T. Washington National Monument," 13, quoting the *Roanoke Times*, "Washington Visits Old Home," September 27, 1908; Park, "Tuskegee Principal at His Old Home."

54. George M. Fredrickson, *The Black Image in the White Mind: The Debate on Afro-American Character and Destiny, 1817–1914* (Middletown, Conn.: Wesleyan University Press, 1987), 159–174, 234–255. As Fredrickson has demonstrated, proponents of the racial extinction theory who had taken heart from the evidence of the 1870 census, which seemed to show a slower African American rate of population increase as compared to that of the whites, were brought up short by the evidence of the 1880 census indicating "that the rate of increase of Southern Negroes was substantially greater than that of whites" (239). In Washington's day, experts who had learned nothing from the Reconstruction era's happy Cassandras continued to mine this played-out strain. See, for example, Frederick L. Hoffman, *Race Traits and Tendencies of the American Negro* (1896); John Roach Straton, "Will Education Solve the Negro Problem?" *North American Review* 170 (June 1900): 785–801, to which Washington made an answer with "Education Will Solve the Negro Problem: A Reply," *North American Review* 171 (August 1900): 221–232.

55. Thomas Dixon Jr., "Booker T. Washington and the Negro: Some Dangerous Aspects of the Work of Tuskegee," *Saturday Evening Post* 178 (August 19, 1905): 1–2.

56. Washington, *Up From Slavery*, 133–134, and "Christmas Days in Old Virginia," *Tuskegee Student* 19 (December 21, 1907): 1; also in *Suburban Life* 5 (December 1907). Harlan makes note of how Washington's different audiences determined his message in his introductory comments; *Papers*, 1: xxxvi–vii.

57. Washington, *Up From Slavery*, 14; Washington, "Education Will Solve the Negro Problem," wherein he argued against the notion of "the negro's non-progressiveness." The quotation is found on page 222.

58. Washington, "Industrial Education," in *Minutes of the First Annual Session, Alabama State Teachers' Association, April 6–7, 1882* (Selma, 1882), 22–24; *Papers*, 2:194.

59. Washington, "The Influence of Object-Lessons in the Solution of the Race Problem," an address at the Hollis Street Theater, Boston, Mass., March 21, 1899; *Papers*, 5:55.

60. As an example of this type of Northern disrespect for the sloth they supposed was endemic in the South, see *First Mohonk Conference on the Negro Question held at Lake Mohonk, Ulster County, New York, June 4, 5, 6, 1890*, ed. Isabel C. Barrows (New York: Negro Universities Press, 1969 [1890]); Fredrickson, *The Black Image in the White Mind*; McPherson, *Abolitionist Legacy*.

61. The white South could be moved to righteous indignation when they thought they had caught a whisper of Washington talking not to them, but above their heads to the North. Those most sensitive to his doing this were those who recognized that black and white Southerners were competing for Northern attention and alms and Washington's denigration of the fallen on hard times white man or haphazard disorganization in the Southern way of life gave him and his side a competitive advantage. Washington once told a joke about a convention aimed at increasing white migration to the South. "Uncle Jake," one of many piquant characters of Washington's acquaintance or invention, exclaimed to one of the conventioneers: "For' Gawd, boss, we got as many white folks down hyar now's we c'n support." Washington's purposeful joke, Emma L. Thornbrough discovered, "so offended the Macon *Telegraph* that it demanded that Washington retract it, and several other Southern newspapers wrote editorials about it." The *New Orleans States* editorialized that Washington cunningly sought to capitalize on "the prevailing idea in the North . . . that the whites of the South are indolent and shiftless and the material prosperity of this section is created by the Negroes." Thornbrough, "Booker T. Washington As Seen By His Contemporaries," 166.

62. Washington, "The Influence of Object-Lessons in the Solution of the Race Problem," 55.

63. Washington, "The Negro's Life in Slavery," 71–72.

64. Washington, *Up From Slavery*, 5.

65. Byrd Prillerman, "Booker T. Washington Among His West Virginia Neighbors," *National Magazine* 17 (December 1902): 353–356; Dixon, "Booker T. Washington and the Negro," 1.

66. Washington, Address before the Twentieth Century Club, New York, quoted in *Black-Belt Diamonds*, 3.

67. Washington, "Democracy and Education," speech delivered at the Institute of Arts and Science, Brooklyn, September 30, 1896; also in Ernest Davidson Washington, ed., *Selected Speeches of Booker T. Washington* (New York: Doubleday, Doran & Co., 1932), 60–77; and in *Papers*, 4:214–215.

68. Washington, *The Story of the Negro: The Rise of the Race from Slavery*, 2 vols. (New York: Doubleday, Page & Co., 1909), 1:6–7.

69. It was only after Washington grew to manhood that he did meet "one among my people who knew anything definite, either through personal knowledge or through tradition, of the country or the people from whom my people sprang." Ibid., 8, 4, 6.

70. Ibid., 8.

71. Washington, "The Negro's Life in Slavery," 76; Washington, *The Story of the Negro*, 1:7–8.

72. Washington's comment on the dependence of the slave from "The Emancipator," *Black Belt Diamonds*, 12. Elsewhere, he told a gathering to the African Methodist Episcopal Church: "The crucial test for a race, as for an individual, is its ability to stand upon its own feet." *Black-Belt Diamonds*, 82.

73. Washington quoted in *Black-Belt Diamonds*, 34.

74. Washington, "Stumbling Blocks," quoted in *Black-Belt Diamonds*, 5–6, and 35. This is after he had developed the technique of the pithy anecdote, typically denigrating black people with humor much to the amusement of his various audiences, North and South. These homilies provided much of the entertainment value of his public appearances.

75. Washington, *The Story of the Negro*, 1:5.

76. Washington, *Up From Slavery*, 2.

77. Ibid., 7.

78. Ibid., 45, 70.

79. Washington in an address before the Twentieth Century Club, New York; quoted in *Black-Belt Diamonds*, 82.

80. Washington, *Up From Slavery*, 5.

81. Ibid., 9.

82. Ibid., 2–3.

83. Ibid., 16.

84. In purifying them in this way, Washington conceives himself as the joining up of these two—as some might have it—bloodlines, and the literal embodiment of good race relations. He did not come to this self-conception while in slavery, however, but only later as is discussed in chapters 4 and 5.

85. A problem with the convention of accusing those critical of African American morality of being Victorian is that it misses the very un-Victorian move by someone like Washington to lay bare his mother's sins before the public, inaugurating a convention among black writers and now the general public to reveal intimate details about members of their families or friends, whether for the purpose of amelioration, for attention through appeal to prurient interest, or as an exercise in artistic freedom. This is a sin of which Washington is surely guilty, but this vulgar practice itself becomes so prevalent during the course of the twentieth century that one can hardly find an instance of someone criticizing him for it.

86. Washington, *Up From Slavery*, 16–17. Note further that he need not make a more forthright statement because slavery, being dead, is not the problem before him or black people.

87. Stanley Elkins, *Slavery: A Problem in American Institutional and Intellectual Life* (Chicago: University of Chicago Press, 1959). For the nationalists, see the various writings of Molefi Kete Asanti, including "Racism, Consciousness, and Afrocentricity," in *Lure and Loathing: Essays on Race, Identity, and the Ambivalence of Assimilation*, ed. Gerald Early (New York: Penguin Books, 1993), 127–143.

88. Washington, *Up From Slavery*, 12.

89. Ibid., 13.

90. Ellison, *Invisible Man*, 275.

91. Genovese, "Slavery and the Roots of Black Nationalism."

92. Stowe quoted in William S. McFeely, *Frederick Douglass* (New York: Norton, 1991), 178.

93. Washington, *Up From Slavery*, 13–14, 22.

94. Booker T. Washington, *My Larger Education: Being Chapters From My Experience* (New York: Doubleday, Page & Co., 1911). The Stowe quotation is found on page 178. Washington expands upon his notion in *Frederick Douglass* (Philadelphia: George W. Jacobs & Co., 1906). With more delicately refined tastes than those of Mrs. Stowe, a modern Douglass biographer shares with Washington the conclusion that Douglass, who led a singularly and remarkably accomplished life, was bitter. McFeely, *Frederick Douglass*, 22, 158–159.

95. Washington, *Up From Slavery*, 16–17.

96. Ibid., 18.

97. Ibid., 9, 10; Harlan, *Booker T. Washington: The Making of a Black Leader*, 15.

98. See the letter from her nephew, James A. Burroughs to Booker T. Washington, November 7, 1903; quoted in *Papers*, 2:4 n.7.

99. Harlan, *Booker T. Washington: The Making of a Black Leader*, 13.

100. Quoted in Ibid., 14. Silas C. Burroughs, grandson of James: "I knew John better than I did Booker." "John and I used to play together a great deal. You know we always thought that John was a good deal cleverer than Booker. Booker was rather slow, but John was as bright as a dollar." Quoted in Park, "Tuskegee Principal at His Old Home"; *Papers*, 9:640.

101. In an 1888 address, Washington said, "Hitherto, the education of the Negro has too largely failed to produce special men for special work. The jacks-of-all-trades are too numerous." Instead, the Negro needs "training that will fit him to do one thing well." "Opening Address," April 11, 1888 in *Minutes of the Seventh Annual Session, Alabama State Teachers Association* (Montgomery, 1888); *Papers*, 2:427–434. On John Washington's early role at Tuskegee, see Washington, "One of the Makers of Tuskegee," *Southern Workman* 32 (January 1903): 30–32; *Papers*, 7:25–27; Harlan, *Booker T. Washington: The Making of a Black Leader*, 150, 184; Harlan, *Booker T. Washington: The Wizard of Tuskegee, 1901–1915* (New York: Oxford University Press, 1983), 152; and notations in *Papers*, 1:5–6.

102. Quoted in Harlan, *Booker T. Washington: The Making of a Black Leader*, 14.

103. *Papers*, 2:11; Washington, address at Carnegie Hall, February 23, 1909, *Papers*, 10:47–52.

104. Washington, *The Story of the Negro*, 2:115–116.

105. Indeed, here and elsewhere, Washington's telling of his life follows quite closely Douglass's telling of his life in slavery. This correspondence, to intimate to be a coincidence, will be further illustrated in chapter 3.

106. Washington, Address to the Centennial of the A.M.E. Zion Church; quoted in *Black-Belt Diamonds*, 82.

107. Upon numerous occasions. See Washington, *Up From Slavery*, 128; Washington, "The South as an Opening for a Career," address to the Philosophian Lyceum, Lincoln University, Pennsylvania, April 26, 1888. *Papers*, 2:449.

108. Claude Bowers quotation from Holman Hamilton and Gayle Thornbrough, eds., *Indianapolis in "The Gay 90s": High School Diaries of Claude G. Bowers* (Indianapolis: Indiana Historical Society, 1964), 98–99; reprinted in Thornbrough, ed., *Booker T. Washington*, 84–86. Bowers was the author of *The Tragic Era* (Cambridge, Mass.: Harvard University Press, 1929).

109. Leola Chambers to Booker T. Washington, February 16, 1914.

110. Washington, *Up From Slavery*, preface.

111. Ibid., 12, 19. On the casualties suffered by the Burroughs boys, see: Harlan, *Booker T. Washington: The Making of a Black Leader*, 22–23.

112. Washington, an address to the National Peace Jubilee, October 16, 1898; *Papers*, 4:490–492. The quotation is found on page 491.

113. Spottswood Rice to Kittey Diggs, September 3, 1864, in *Free At Last*, ed. Ira Berlin, Barbara J. Fields, Steven F. Miller, Joseph P. Reidy, and Leslie S. Rowlands (New York: New Press, 1992), 180–182.

114. Washington, an address at the unveiling of the Robert Gould Shaw Monument, Boston, Massachusetts, May 31, 1897, in the *Tuskegee Student* 11 (July 1897): 1, 4; *Papers*, 4:285–288.

115. Washington, *The Story of the Negro*, 2:331–332.

116. Reed, *The Negro Problem Solved; or, Africa as she was, as she is, and as she shall be. Her curse and her cure* (Miami: Mnemosyne, 1969 [1864]), iii.

117. Washington commented favorably on Huckleberry Finn in the *North American Review* 191 (June 1910): 828–830. In a tribute to Twain, he drew attention to the possibility that "the ordinary reader . . . absorbed in the adventures of the two white boys" might miss "the deep sympathy of the author in 'Jim,' who Washington demotes to the status of a boy. I cannot help feeling that in this character Mark Twain has, perhaps unconsciously, exhibited his sympathy and interest in the masses of the negro people."

118. Mary F. Mackie to Washington, November 21, 1900.

119. Park, "Tuskegee Principal at His Old Home"; *Papers*, 9:638–639.

3. "They Will Pull Against You the Load Downward"

1. Washington quoted in an interview with John F. Cowan published as "A Washington of To-day," *Christian Endeavor World* 13 (April 20, 1899): 589–590; *Booker T. Washington Papers* (hereinafter, *Papers*), ed. Louis R. Harlan et al. (Urbana: University of Illinois Press, 1974–1982), 5:83.

2. Booker T. Washington, *Up From Slavery* (New York: Viking Penguin, 1986 [1901]), 19–20, 21.

3. Ibid., 2, 10.

4. Ibid., 21–22.

5. Ibid., 23.

6. Washington deems this story so good he tells it twice in his autobiography. Ibid., 23–24, 123.

7. Quotation from one of Washington's Sunday evening talks to Tuskegee students, excerpted in *Black-Belt Diamonds: Gems from the Speeches, Addresses and Talks to Students of Booker T. Washington*, ed. Victoria Earle Matthews (New York: Mnemosyne Publishing, 1969 [1898]), 5.

8. Washington, *Up From Slavery*, 21–22; Washington, speech before the Brooklyn Institute of Art and Sciences, excerpted in *Black-Belt Diamonds*, 65–66; *Papers*, 4:214.

9. Louis R. Harlan, *Booker T. Washington: The Making of a Black Leader, 1865–1901* (New York: Oxford University Press, 1973), 26.

10. Robert E. Park, "Tuskegee Principal at His Old Home," *The Tuskegee Student* (October 3, 1908): 3–4; *Papers*, 9:636.

11. Washington, *Up From Slavery*, 24–25, 26.

12. Ibid., 26.

13. Harlan, *Booker T. Washington: The Making of a Black Leader*, 30.

14. Washington, *Up From Slavery*, 26.

15. Booker T. Washington, "Work With the Hands," *Everybody's Magazine* 7 (September 1902): 297–300 (the article eventually became the first chapter of Washington, *Working With the Hands*); *Papers*, 6:529–536. The quoted remark is found on page 529.

16. Booker T. Washington, *My Larger Education: Being Chapters From My Experience* (New York: Doubleday, Page & Co., 1911); *Papers*, 1:422.

17. Washington, *Up From Slavery*, 40–41.

18. Booker T. Washington, Sunday evening talk, May 13, 1900; *Papers*, 5:519.

19. In 1911, Washington found himself mired in an ugly affair, still mysterious decades after the fact, when he was accosted and thrashed by a white man outside an apartment building in New York City's seedy and unfashionable Tenderloin district. The controversy over the propriety of his being where he was and for what purpose came to be known as the Ulrich Affair (after Washington's assailant), and cast something of a pall over the last years of his life. See Willard B. Gatewood, "Booker T. Washington and the Ulrich Affair," *Phylon* 55, no. 1 (January 1970): 29–44; Harlan, *Booker T. Washington: The Wizard of Tuskegee, 1901–1915* (New York: Oxford University Press, 1983), 379–404.

20. Washington, Sunday evening talk, May 13, 1900; *Papers*, 5:519, 520.

21. Washington comments in "Two Earnest Addresses Delivered by Prof. Washington and his wife," Charleston *News and Courier*, September 13, 1898, 3; *Papers*, 4:461–469. The reporter's characterization of Washington's remarks is found on page 462.

22. Booker T. Washington, "Education Will Solve the Negro Problem," *North American Review* 171 (August 1900): 221–232; *Papers*, 5:615. This essay makes a reply to

John Roach Straton, a Baptist clergyman on the faculty of Mercer University in Georgia, who previously had written an article ("Will Education Solve the Negro Problem?" *North American Review* 170 [June 1900]: 785–801) championing the application of Social Darwinist ideas to the Negro problem. Following the thesis of Frederick L. Hoffman's *Race Traits and Tendencies of the American Negro* (1896), Straton believed that African Americans would eventually die out in the United States despite all efforts to help. He also was one of Bryan's supporters during the Scopes "Monkey" Trial in 1925.

23. Washington, "Education Will Solve the Negro Problem."

24. As long ago as W. E. B. Du Bois's sociological study *The Philadelphia Negro* (New York: Schocken Books, 1969 [1899]) there has been a record of prostitution and other illegal indulgences with a significant white clientele being situated where black people are concentrated by racist proscription—ghettoized, as it were. In that fact there is an indication of just what racism and segregation deny to African Americans: that is, the means and authority to seal the border of the places where they live from persons up to no good. Roger Lane, in *Roots of Violence in Black Philadelphia, 1860–1900* (Cambridge, Mass.: Harvard University Press, 1986), quite correctly insists that in the high-crime Philadelphia precincts upon which he focuses there is no "black community" that would merit the name, but then misses the point: the insistence on "order" and "predictability" elsewhere tends toward the creation of a fictive "black Philadelphia" that functions as an open sewer and a magnet for all type of vice and all manner of participants in that vice, including a strong host of those in permanent or temporary exile from their own "communities." In this way, "black Philadelphia" does not exist as a definite cultural, much less geographical and political entity, but in the minds of those who enforce limits on black people's movements and those prim reformers who blithely and ignorantly follow their lead.

25. Stephen D. Engle, "Mountaineer Reconstruction: Blacks in the Political Reconstruction of West Virginia," *Journal of Negro History* 78, no. 3 (Summer 1993): 140.

26. Cowan, "A Washington of To-day"; *Papers*, 5:84.

27. Washington, *Up From Slavery*, 30.

28. Washington, "Work With the Hands"; *Papers*, 6:530–531.

29. Washington, *Up From Slavery*, 38.

30. Ibid., 68–69.

31. William T. McKinney to Washington, September 11, 1911.

32. Washington, *Up From Slavery*, 39.

33. Booker T. Washington, "Atlanta Exposition Address," September 18, 1895; *Papers*, 3:578–587.

34. Washington, *Up From Slavery*, 30.

35. Washington, letter to the editor, *Southern Workman*, September 28, 1895; *Papers*, 1:389.

36. Booker T. Washington, *The Story of My Life and Work* (Toronto: J. L. Nichols & Co., 1900); *Papers*, 1:17.

37. Washington, *Up From Slavery*, 38.

38. Ibid., 30. The "dark and discouraging" quotation is from Booker T. Washington, "What I Am Trying to Do," *World's Work* 27 (November 1913): 101–107; *Papers*, 13:352–353.

39. Thus, as an example, there is the treatment Ferguson receives from Basil Matthews in *Booker T. Washington: Educator and Interracial Interpreter* (College Park, Md.: McGrath, 1969 [1948]), 32, 33–36, 52–54.

40. Harlan, *Booker T. Washington: The Making of a Black Leader*, 45.

41. Gary Scharnhorst and Jack Bales, *The Lost Life of Horatio Alger, Jr.,* (Bloomington: Indiana University Press, 1985), x, 152; Horatio Alger, *The Lost Tales of Horatio Alger*, ed. Gary Scharnhorst (Bar Harbor, Maine: Acadia, 1989), xii.

42. Scharnhorst with Bales, *The Lost Life of Horatio Alger, Jr.*, 129. The authors cite Malcolm Cowley, who as long ago as 1945 showed how this image of Alger came as a product of invocations of "the Alger pattern" a decade after Americans had stopped reading tales of "Ragged Dick" and other such offerings (149–150).

43. The "industrial education" system Washington would come to advocate may be understood as just such an intervention, although less than miraculous, responding to a readily apparent flaw in the revolutionary forces of industrial capitalism: the market's inability to call up in a timely fashion and discipline a sufficiently pliant work force of skilled and unskilled workers. What actually went on at Tuskegee, on the other hand, was more like a work-study program, a point touched upon in chapter 5.

44. Hasia B. Diner has noted that the *Jewish Daily Forward* was quite taken by Washington's story, even despite the fact that the paper "did not believe in the American dream of 'rags to riches,' nor did it generally ascribe to the notion that individual achievement would help the masses out of poverty." *In the Almost Promised Land: American Jews and Blacks, 1915–1935* (Baltimore: Johns Hopkins University Press, 1995), 57–58.

45. These words may never have passed between the two, but it is a part of the lore of Stowe's family. See Catherine P. Gilbertson, *Harriet Beecher Stowe* (New York: D. Appleton-Century, 1937), 273.

46. Washington, *Up From Slavery*, 35.

47. Washington, "What I Am Trying To Do," 1913; *Papers*, 12:354, 353.

48. Washington, "Atlanta Exposition Address."

49. Washington, "What I Am Trying To Do," 1913; *Papers*, 13:353–354. This account combined with elements of another version of this story found in a Washington address given two months after the above article to the First National Conference on Race Betterment, Battle Creek, Michigan, January 8, 1914; reprinted in *Selected Speeches of Booker T. Washington*, ed. Ernest Davidson Washington (Garden City, N.Y.: Doubleday, Doran & Co., 1932), 218–234; *Papers*, 12:406–417, which offers Washington's telling of slightly different details of the story. *Papers*, 12:414–415.

50. Washington, Sunday evening talk at Tuskegee labeled "Strength in Simplicity," January 10, 1909, in *Tuskegee Student* 20 (January 23, 1909): 1, 2; *Papers*, 10:9–12. The quoted passage is found on page 11.

51. Washington, *Up From Slavery*, 33–34.

52. Washington quotation from *Black-Belt Diamonds*, 41.

53. Washington, "What I Am Trying To Do," 1913; *Papers*, 12:352–353.

54. Harlan, *Booker T. Washington: The Making of a Black Leader*, 17; Washington, *Up From Slavery*, 26–27.

55. Douglass, *Narrative of the Life of Frederick Douglass, an American Slave, written by himself*, ed. David W. Blight (Boston: Bedford Books, 1993), 74–75.

56. Washington, *Up From Slavery*, 44. Details on the Ruffners' lives are from Harlan, *Booker T. Washington: The Making of a Black Leader*, 38–41.

57. Harlan, *Booker T. Washington: The Making of a Black Leader*, 40.

58. Washington, *The Story of My Life and Work*; *Papers*, 1:19.

59. Harlan, *Booker T. Washington: The Making of a Black Leader*, 43; Washington, *Up From Slavery*, 45.

60. Washington, *The Story of My Life and Work*; *Papers*, 1:18.

61. Washington also lent his name to advertisements for various products such as cigars. He would not allow his image to be used in conjunction with the marketing of liquor, however. See Emmett J. Scott to A. Eichelburger, July 24, 1915, and Washington to Schiller Brothers Distilling Company, October 25, 1911.

62. Washington, address at the Burlew Opera House, published in the *Colored American*, September 9, 1899; *Papers*, 5:189.

63. Harlan, *Booker T. Washington: The Making of a Black Leader*, 44.

64. Dixon quoted in Daniel W. Cryer, "Mary White Ovington and the Rise of the National Association for the Advancement of Colored People," Ph.D. dissertation, University of Minnesota, 1977.

65. Washington's role in undermining an earlier gathering in 1908 cannot be definitively established. Charles Flint Kellogg, *NAACP: A History of the National Association for the Advancement of Colored People* (Baltimore: Johns Hopkins University Press, 1967), 71–72; Louis R. Harlan, "The Secret Life of Booker T. Washington," *Journal of Southern History* 37 (August 1971): 413–415. An indication of the adverse publicity that dinner provoked or had provoked for it is suggested by the title of one account: "White Girls at an 'Equality Feast' With Negroes," *New York American*, April 28, 1908. When the 1911 dinner was being organized, Washington wrote to one of his New York colleagues instructing him to "be sure to get hold of same reporter who reported for America year or two ago [*sic*]." Washington to Charles William Anderson, January 21, 1911. Anderson replied indicating he would "leave no stone unturned." Anderson to Washington, January 23, 1911. After doing so, he sent along clippings of the press coverage. Anderson to Washington, January 25, 1911. The sub-headlines are from "Three Races Sit At Banquet for Mixed Marriage," *New York Press*, January 25, 1911. See also Mary White Ovington, *Black and White*

Sat Down Together: The Reminiscences of an NAACP Founder (New York: Feminist Press, 1995), 32–36.

66. Common sense would suggest that the blunt question about amalgamation, and its barely more subtle successors—"Would you want your daughter to marry one?"—are actually not likely to enter into the minds of most white Americans in the normal course of their lives in the age of segregation. Dixon and those of a more practical ilk do not seek or expect a perfected white unity—their arms are too short to embrace totalitarianism—but only sufficient numbers to be aghast at the publicized exceptions, the "white Juliets" (as Ida B. Wells-Barnett called them), who provide occasion for example to be made of their "black Romeos" through gruesome rituals of public violence. When the worthiness of that warning fails to hold the line or begins to sound to harsh to the enlightened, it is then supplanted by the cautious humanitarianism of more recent vintage: "think of how difficult it will be for the children" stated freely to any and all who would dare "cross the color line," including not only expectant parents and affianced couples but also teenagers contemplating crushes or preparing for first dates.

67. Booker T. Washington, *Frederick Douglass* (Philadelphia: George W. Jacobs & Co., 1906), 15.

68. Douglass, *Narrative*, 57.

69. Ruffner to Gilson Willetts, May 29, 1899, in Willetts, "Slave Boy and Leader of His Race," *New Voice* 16 (June 24, 1899): 3; quoted in Harlan, *Booker T. Washington: The Making of a Black Leader*, 42; Washington, *The Story of My Life and Work*; *Papers*, 1:17, 50.

70. Washington, *The Story of My Life and Work*; *Papers*, 1:17.

71. Washington, *Up From Slavery*, 44; Washington, *The Story of My Life and Work*; *Papers*, 1:17; *Up From Slavery*, 44.

72. Harlan, *Booker T. Washington: The Making of a Black Leader*, 43.

73. Washington, *The Story of My Life and Work*; *Papers*, 1:24.

74. Washington, *Up From Slavery*, 175. "Absolute cleanliness of the body has been insisted upon from the first." He continues: "often we had to teach them how to sleep at night; that is, whether between two sheets . . . or under them. . . . The importance of the use of the nightgown received the same attention." Students were "inspected" daily to insure that they were clean and properly clothed, with nary a button missing. The quotation is found on page 176.

75. Washington, address to the White Rose and Industrial Association, New York quoted in *Black-Belt Diamonds*, 63.

76. Washington, "Increased Wants," quoted in *Black-Belt Diamonds*, 25.

77. Booker T. Washington, *The Future of the American Negro* (Boston: Small, Maynard & Co., 1899); *Papers*, 5:301–392. The quotation is from page 314.

78. Leola Chambers to Washington, February 16, 1914; Washington to Chambers, February 25, 1914. The editors of the Washington papers indicate that this letter was signed in Washington's assistant Emmett J. Scott's hand. *Papers*, 12:451.

79. Washington, address to the First National Conference on Race Betterment, Battle Creek, Michigan, January 8, 1914; reprinted in Washington, ed., *Selected Speeches of Booker T. Washington*, 218–234; *Papers*, 12:414.

80. Washington, "Our Duty in the South," an address at the Unitarian Club of New York ca. January 1899, *Christian Register* 78 (February 2, 1899): 121–122; *Papers*, 13:496–498.

81. Washington, "Democracy and Education," speech before the Brooklyn Institute of Arts and Sciences, September 30, 1896; *Papers*, 4:214, also excerpted in *Black-Belt Diamonds*, 65–66.

82. Washington, "The Educational and Industrial Emancipation of the Negro," address before the Brooklyn Institute of Arts and Sciences, February 22, 1903; *Papers*, 7:92.

83. Washington, "Negro Advance," quoted in *Black-Belt Diamonds*, 67.

84. Washington, *Up From Slavery*, 35–36.

85. Ibid., 86.

86. Du Bois, "Of Mr. Booker T. Washington and Others," *Souls of Black Folk*, 393.

87. Ida B. Wells-Barnett, "Booker T. Washington and His Critics," *World Today*, April 1904; reprinted in *Booker T. Washington and His Critics*, ed. Emma Lou Thornbrough (Englewood Cliffs, N.J.: Prentice-Hall, 1969), 120–122.

88. Washington, *Black-Belt Diamonds*, 15.

89. Washington, "The Educational and Industrial Emancipation of the Negro," in *Selected Speeches of Booker T. Washington*, 100–117; also in *Papers*, 7:91.

90. Washington, Sunday evening talk at Tuskegee, excerpted in *Black-Belt Diamonds*, 28.

91. Harlan, *Booker T. Washington: The Making of a Black Leader*, 45.

92. Harlan, *Booker T. Washington: The Wizard of Tuskegee*, ix.

93. William H. Ruffner to Harriet Ruffner, January 7, 1866; quoted in Harlan, *Booker T. Washington: The Making of a Black Leader*, 41.

94. Viola Knapp Ruffner to Washington, February 27, 1899. That same month, Washington composed a Lincoln Day Address in which his formulation of the matter bore more than a little resemblance to his friend and former employer's. See his Lincoln Memorial Address, delivered February 14, 1899, in Philadelphia.

95. Ruffner quoted in Willetts, "Slave Boy and Leader of His Race," 3; Harlan, *Booker T. Washington: The Making of a Black Leader*, 45.

96. Washington, Sunday evening talk, excerpted in *Black-Belt Diamonds*, 75–76.

97. Viola Ruffner to Gilson Willetts, May 29, 1899, in Willetts, "Slave Boy and Leader of His Race," 3.

98. Washington, *Up From Slavery*, 54.

99. Ibid., 52.

100. Washington, *The Story of My Life and Work*; *Papers*, 1:18.

101. Washington, *The Future of the American Negro*; *Papers*, 5:301–392; the quotation is from 365.

102. Washington, "Atlanta Exposition Address"; *Papers*, 3:583–584.

103. Washington, *Up From Slavery*, 33.

104. Ibid., 78.

105. Ibid.

106. Washington, "Our Duty in the South," 121–122.

107. Washington, "Atlanta Exposition Address"; *Papers* 3:585.

108. Washington, "Our Duty in the South," 121–122.

109. Washington, *The Future of the American Negro*; *Papers*, 5:308.

110. Washington, *Up From Slavery*, 83–84.

111. Washington, "Our Duty in the South," 121–122.

112. Washington, *Up From Slavery*, 84–85.

113. Ibid., 80–81.

114. Washington, *Black-Belt Diamonds*, 82.

115. Washington, *Up From Slavery*, 36–37.

116. Washington, "Work With the Hands," 1902; *Papers*, 6:529–530.

117. The illustration is found in Steven Hahn, *A Nation Under Our Feet: Black Political Struggle in the Rural South from Slavery to the Great Migration* (Cambridge, Mass.: Harvard University Press, 2003), which describes the promise of freedom and its playing out in a powerful way.

118. Washington, *The Story of the Negro: The Rise of the Race from Slavery*, 2 vols. (New York: Doubleday, Page & Co., 1909), 2:8.

119. Max Bennett Thrasher, "Booker T. Washington's First Sunday-School Teacher," August 20, 1904; *Papers*, 8:53.

120. Washington, address at the Burlew Opera House; *Papers*, 5:189–193.

4. "Gathered From Miscellaneous Sources"

1. Richard Wright, *Black Boy: A Record of Childhood and Youth* (New York: Harper & Brothers, 1945).

2. Booker T. Washington, "Education Will Solve the Race Problem—A Reply," *North American Review* 171 (August 1900): 221–232; *Booker T. Washington Papers* (hereinafter, *Papers*), ed. Louis R. Harlan et al. (Urbana: University of Illinois Press, 1974–1982), 5:614.

3. Booker T. Washington, *Up From Slavery* (New York: Viking Penguin, 1986 [1901]), 30. See also Washington, letter to the editor of the *Southern Workman*, September 28, 1895.

4. Washington, *Up From Slavery*, 113, 114–115.

5. Ibid., 37.

6. This is not to say that this proves Washington a hypocrite. The evidence of the contradiction between what he wanted for himself and what he felt was attainable for African Americans was not used by his opponents as ammunition against him, most likely because he was, just as much as they were, a charter member of the post-emancipation leadership class of African America. Recognizing this, his enemies may have had too much grace to point out that this most stark of con-

tradition because they fully well knew why a black boy of ability would not and ought not to have to see his abilities wasted through consignment to the blighting mines.

7. Louis R. Harlan, *Booker T. Washington: The Making of a Black Leader, 1865–1901* (New York: Oxford University Press, 1973), 32, 33.

8. Washington, *Up From Slavery*, 35.

9. It is interesting in this connection that Washington is largely silent on the exploitation of child labor. His opposition to having to engage in one type of child labor, but claiming to have derived special benefits from his engagement in another type rather tends to point toward the conclusion W. J. Cash reached about Washington's New South colleagues, the reformers who were against the abusing of children as workers, but not against their being gainfully employed. Endeavoring "toward conciliating the frown of the world," they pushed forward "reasonable" child labor laws without teeth or provisions for real enforcement. Cash, *The Mind of the South* (New York: Vintage Books, 1991 [1941]), 225–226.

10. Ibid., 34–35. In different accounts the teacher is a man, as here (possibly William Davis, born free in Ohio and a veteran of Lincoln's bodyguard, who Washington will later praise); elsewhere the teacher is a woman.

11. Robert E. Park, "Tuskegee's Principal at His Old Home," *Tuskegee Student* 20 (October 3, 1908): 3–4, reprint from the *New York Evening Post*, n.d.; *Papers*, 9:635–640.

12. O. K. Armstrong, "Booker T. Washington—Apostle of Good Will," *Reader's Digest* (February 1947), 25. See also Mary F. Mackie to Washington, November 21, 1900; *Papers*, 5:675.

13. Included among those who comment on the George Washington–Booker Washington connection is John F. Cowan, who interviewed Washington in 1899. Cowan, "A Washington of To-day," *Christian Endeavor World* 13 (April 20, 1899): 589–590; *Papers*, 5:83–88. Mackie to Washington, November 21, 1900; *Papers*, 5:675. Pyne to Washington, October 3, 1902; *Papers*, 6:567–571.

14. Booker T. Washington, *The Story of My Life and Work* (Toronto: J. L. Nichols & Co., 1900); *Papers*, 1:16.

15. Washington, *Up From Slavery*, 35.

16. Washington quoted in Cowan, "A Washington of To-day," 589–590; *Papers*, 5:84.

17. Ibid.

18. Harlan, *Booker T. Washington: The Making of a Black Leader*, 36.

19. Ibid., 324.

20. Louis R. Harlan, "Booker T. Washington and the Politics of Accommodation," in *Black Leaders of the Twentieth Century*, ed. John Hope Franklin and August Meier (Urbana: University of Illinois Press, 1982), 2, 14.

21. Booker T. Washington, *The Story of the Negro: The Rise of the Race from Slavery*, 2 vols. (New York: Doubleday, Page & Co., 1909), 1:57.

22. Ibid.; *Papers*, 1:414.

23. Washington, *Up From Slavery*, 24.

24. Washington, *The Story of the Negro*, 1:57–58.

25. Park, "Tuskegee's Principal at His Old Home," 3–4; *Papers*, 9:636; Washington, *The Story of My Life and Work*, reprinted in *Papers*, 1:13.

26. Park, "Tuskegee's Principal at His Old Home."

27. Byrd Prillerman, "Booker T. Washington Among His West Virginia Neighbors," *National Magazine* 17 (December 1902): 353–356; *Papers*, 6:617–618.

28. Thrasher, "Booker T. Washington's First Sunday-School Teacher," August 20, 1904; *Papers*, 8:53–56.

29. W. T. McKinney to Washington, September 11, 1911; *Papers*, 11:307.

30. Prillerman, "Booker T. Washington Among His West Virginia Neighbors"; *Papers*, 6:618.

31. Booker T. Washington, *My Larger Education: Being Chapters From My Experience* (New York: Doubleday, Page & Co., 1911); in *Papers*, 1:422–423.

32. A report appearing in the Charleston *West Virginia Journal*, July 24, 1872; *Papers*, 2:21.

33. Booker T. Washington, "Atlanta Exposition Address," September 18, 1895; *Papers*, 3:583–584.

34. See Eric Foner, *Reconstruction: America's Unfinished Revolution, 1863–1877* (New York: Harper & Row, 1988), especially chap. 7.

35. Washington, *Up From Slavery*, 39.

36. Foner, *Reconstruction*, 410.

37. Harlan steps wrongly here in failing to consider how black men elected to high political office in Reconstruction may have influenced Washington, insisting in one essay that the absence of "black models in his life with the charisma of power" caused Washington to "become inordinately attached to a succession of fatherly white men." Harlan, "Booker T. Washington in Biographical Perspective," *American Historical Review* 75 (October 1970): 1581–1599; reprinted in *Booker T. Washington in Perspective*, ed. Raymond W. Smock (Jackson: University of Mississippi Press, 1988), 21. This perspective causes him to diminish the scale of Washington's aspiration by presenting only local white politicians of the paternalistic Republican variety and the Ruffners as sparks for his ambition. He writes, "Booker's ambition had been kindled by the contract with the Ruffners, and it lighted his way through work in the mines," and names only a sole local white Republican politician, Romeo Freer, as an inspiration for Washington. Later, he suggests that Washington's experience at Hampton caused him "for the first time to realize what it means to be a man instead of a piece of property." Harlan, *Booker T. Washington: The Making of a Black Leader*, 48, 72. See also August Meier, *Negro Thought in America, 1880–1915* (Ann Arbor: University of Michigan Press, 1963), 100–103.

38. The quoted words are those of the Unionist former governor of South Carolina, Benjamin F. Perry, in Foner, *Reconstruction*, 292.

39. Washington, *Up From Slavery*, 47–48.

40. Washington, address to the First National Conference on Race Betterment, Battle Creek, Michigan, January 8, 1914; reprinted in Ernest Davidson Washington, ed.,

Selected Speeches of Booker T. Washington (New York: Doubleday, Doran & Co., 1932), 218–234; and in *Papers*, 12:413.

41. The point is not that being a minister or lawyer was the only means by which Washington could enter politics, but rather that they were the ones most likely to him. In general, those in the law and religion, along with teachers and planters, made up only a substantial minority of the 1,500 or so black men elected to office from 1865 to 1877; the majority was drawn from the ranks of artisans and craftsmen, men in the trades, and laborers of various stripes, from country as well as from town. Eric Foner, ed., *Freedom's Lawmakers: A Directory of Black Office-holders During Reconstruction* (New York: Oxford University Press, 1993), 253–261. And, of course, extending the net to include those more or less actively involved in politics but neither winning nor seeking elective office would further broaden the base of Reconstruction politics. The suspicion is, however, that Washington was not seeking a position at the lower reaches of the base of someone else's ascendance.

42. Harlan, *Booker T. Washington: The Making of a Black Leader*, 47.

43. Ibid., 47. On the Klan in West Virginia battling white authority up to and including the governor of the state, see H. E. Metheny, *Wood County, West Virginia in Civil War Times* (Parkersburg, W.Va.: Trans-Alleghany Books, 1987), 454–462; Steven D. Engle, "Mountaineer Reconstruction: Blacks in the Political Reconstruction of West Virginia," *Journal of Negro History* 78, no. 3 (Summer 1993): 145–146.

44. Washington, address to the Unitarian Club of New York, c. January 1899, published as "Our Duty in the South," in the *Christian Register* 78 (February 2, 1899): 121–122; *Papers*, 13:497.

45. Washington, *Story of the Negro*, 1:8, 10. "It seemed to me at that time a mark of degradation that people should go about with almost no clothes upon their backs. It did not occur to me that, possibly, the difference in the customs of wearing clothes in African and in America, and the difference in the feeling that people in Europe and in Africa have about clothes, was largely a matter of climate." See also Washington quoted in R. E. Park, "Principal Washington's Campaign," in the Springfield *Republican*, November 24, 1909; *Papers*, 10:229–230.

46. Washington, *The Story of the Negro*, 1:10.

47. Ibid., 11–12.

48. Ibid., 13.

49. Ibid., 11.

50. Cash, *The Mind of the South*, 122–123.

51. Robert Charles was a Mississippi-born advocate of African emigration who responded to what he perceived to be as racist police coercion by killing seven white persons—four policemen and three civilians—in New Orleans in 1900. See Ida B. Wells, "Mob Rule in New Orleans," in *Southern Horrors and Other Writings: The Anti-Lynching Campaign of Ida B. Wells, 1892–1900*, ed. Jacqueline Jones-Royster (Boston: Bedford Books, 1997); Huey Newton and J. Herman Blake, *Revolutionary Suicide* (New York: Harcourt Brace Jovanovich, 1973); Chester Himes, *Plan B*,

ed. Michel Fabre and Robert E. Skinner (Jackson: University Press of Mississippi, 1993); Suffren Griggs, *Imperium in Imperio: A Study of the Negro Race Problem—A Novel* (Miami: Mnemosyne Publishing, 1969 [1899]); Eldridge Cleaver, "Soul on Ice," in *Soul on Ice* (New York: Dell, 1992 [1968]), 31.

52. William Dean Howells, "An Exemplary Citizen," *North American Review* 173 (August 1901): 281–299; *Papers*, 6:196.

53. Washington, *The Story of the Negro*, 1:13.

54. Engle, "Mountaineer Reconstruction," 142–147; Woodson, "Early Negro Education in West Virginia," *Journal of Negro History* 7 (January 1922): 23–63.

55. Washington, "Atlanta Exposition Address," *Papers*, 3:584.

56. Washington, "Education Will Solve the Race Problem."

57. Booker T. Washington, "The Educational and Industrial Emancipation of the Negro," in Washington, *Selected Speeches*, 100–117; *Papers*, 7:91.

58. Washington, *Up From Slavery*, 86.

59. Washington, "Our Duty in the South," 1899; *Papers*, 13:497.

60. In this connection, one is reminded of the Malcolm Little of 1943, not figuratively fatherless but literally orphaned owing, he supposed, to the depredations of white persons and the state of Michigan, and deep in the depths of his gangster phase, "skipping and tipping" his zoot-suited, hair-conked self into the psychiatrist's office at the Army induction center, where he whispered *sotto voce* to the man there that he wanted into the Army: "I want to get sent down South. Organize them nigger soldiers, you dig? Steal us some guns, and kill up crackers!" Far from thinking this politics, as his later interpreters will suggest, this incident is of interest in showing how the boy who will become Malcolm X tells himself that what he is doing is only a scam to get out of serving and nothing more because he cannot, at eighteen, admit to himself (or perhaps really go mad) that treading the hard road of actually fighting the bigots is what he really ought to do. He had a long way ahead before he would stand up to the sterner requirements of politics. Malcolm X and Alex Haley, *The Autobiography of Malcolm X* (New York: Random House, 1984 [1965]), 104–107. The quotations are found on pages 105 and 106.

61. Washington, *Story of My Life and Work*; *Papers*, 1:16.

62. Emmett J. Scott and Lyman Beecher Stowe, *Booker T. Washington: Builder of a Civilization* (Garden City, N.Y.: Doubleday, Page & Co., 1918 [1916]), 29; Howells, "An Exemplary Citizen," 1901; *Papers*, 6:194. Emma L. Thornbrough, "Booker T. Washington as Seen by His White Contemporaries," *Journal of Negro History* 53, no. 2 (April 1968): 165.

63. Harlan, *Booker T. Washington: The Making of a Black Leader*, 36; Harlan, *Booker T. Washington: The Wizard of Tuskegee, 1901–1915* (New York: Oxford University Press, 1983), 122–123. Matthews, *Booker T. Washington: Educator and Interracial Interpreter* (College Park, Md.: McGrath, 1969 [1948]), 32, 33–34.

64. See Booker T. Washington, N. B. Wood, and Fannie Barrier Williams, *A New Negro for a New Century* (Chicago: American Publishing House, [1900]).

65. Lincoln said this to John L. Scripps, a newspaperman writing his campaign auto-

biography, who in turn passed it on to Lincoln's law partner, William H. Herndon. Quoted in David Herbert Donald, *Lincoln* (London: Jonathan Cape, 1995), 19.

66. Ibid., 20. The Lincoln quotation is from *Collected Works of Abraham Lincoln*, ed. Roy P. Basler (New Brunswick, N.J.: Rutgers University Press, 1953). Quoted in Donald, *Lincoln*, 19.

67. Donald, *Lincoln*, 20, 32.

68. Tacitly following this line of reasoning, David L. Dudley figures Washington as paterfamilias to a line of succeeding black writers struggling to overthrow *Up From Slavery* in order to establish their own authority over the black narrative in freedom. Washington Ferguson does not appear in the study. To the extent that Washington is a son at all it is in relationship to Frederick Douglass, whom Dudley quite correctly views Washington as endeavoring to supplant so as to situate himself as "rightful heir in the line of African American leadership." See Dudley, *My Father's Shadow: Intergenerational Conflict in African American Men's Autobiography* (Philadelphia: University of Pennsylvania Press, 1991), chaps. 2–3. The quotation is found on page 50.

69. Donald, *Lincoln*, 605n.

70. Washington. *Up From Slavery*, 2. In his *Story of My Life and Work*, Washington simply says, "I only know that he was a white man." *Papers*, 1:10.

71. Washington, *The Story of the Negro*, 1:24.

72. Samuel Chapman Armstrong to George Washington Campbell, May 31, 1881; *Papers*, 2:127.

73. Howells, "An Exemplary Citizen," 1901; *Papers*, 6:194.

74. Archer added his judgment that Du Bois, on the other hand, has little "of the negro" in him. William Archer, *Through Afro-America: An English Reading of the Race Problem* (London: Chapman and Hall, 1910), 45–47.

75. Howells, "An Exemplary Citizen," 1901; *Papers*, 6:192.

76. The comment on Washington's appearance is in Harlan's annotation of the 1860 Census report on the Burroughs farm; *Papers*, 2:7n.; Harlan, *Booker T. Washington: The Making of a Black Leader*, 3–5. In his annotation of the 1870 Census report on the Ferguson family, however, Harlan overrules the evaluation of the census taker in marking down Washington's brother and sister as respectively "Black" and "Mulatto."

77. Bruce found so much to agree with in Washington's Atlanta speech that he concluded that Washington had to be a full-out Negro. The full line is: "The negro (?) of mixed blood and the white men of the north with more zeal than judgment or sagacity, have conspired by their interminable twaddle about Negro equality in the South to intensify the feeling against the black race and to retard its progress." *Papers*, 4:55–56.

78. Washington, *Up From Slavery*, 47.

79. Washington, address at the Burlew Opera House, Charleston, West Virginia, 1899; *Papers*, 5:190.

80. Samuel Chapman Armstrong to George Washington Campbell, May 31, 1881; Armstrong to Dudley Allen Sargent, May 5, 1887; *Papers*, 2:347. (Harlan quotes the

phrase from the letter to Sargent as "no ordinary darkey." *Booker T. Washington: The Making of a Black Leader*, 152.) Seeking to gain Washington's entrance in a course in physical culture and "gymnastic drill" at the Hemenway Gymnasium of Harvard University, Armstrong was at some pains to make sure both that Harvard would be inclined to accept Washington and fully forewarned as to who they were accepting into their midst. The quotation is from Armstrong to Washington, May 5, 1887.

5. "Prepared for the Exercise of These Privileges"

1. Adams quoted in Eric Foner, *Reconstruction: America's Unfinished Revolution, 1863–1877* (New York: Harper & Row, 1988), 567.
2. Speech of Rutherford B. Hayes, delivered at Virginia Hall, Hampton, Virginia, May 20, 1880. R. B. Hayes Papers, Library of The Rutherford B. Hayes Presidential Center (microfilm edition, roll 293, frame 406.) Credit for apparently being the first to bring forward this connection belongs to George Sinkler in his prosaically titled but valuable work, *The Racial Attitudes of American Presidents: From Abraham Lincoln to Theodore Roosevelt* (New York: Doubleday, 1971), 168.
3. Booker T. Washington, *Up From Slavery* (New York: Viking Penguin, 1986 [1901]), 51.
4. W. E. B. Du Bois, *Black Reconstruction in America: An Essay Toward a History of the Part Which Black Folk Played in the Attempt to Reconstruct Democracy in America, 1860–1880* (New York: Atheneum, 1962 [1935]), 478.
5. Booker T. Washington, "Report on the Triennial Meeting of the Hampton Institute Alumni Association," *Southern Workman* 13 (June 1884): 75; *Booker T. Washington Papers* (hereinafter, *Papers*), ed. Louis R. Harlan et al. (Urbana: University of Illinois Press, 1974–1982), 2:252.
6. Washington, *Up From Slavery*, 52–53. In a March 24, 1882, *Philadelphia Inquirer* article, "The Nation's Wards," Washington (misnamed Mr. G. Booker Washington) indicated that he swept the room five times; *Papers*, 2:181.
7. Hollis B. Frissel, chaplain of Hampton while Washington was there and Samuel Chapman Armstrong's successor as president of the school, quoted in a review of Francis G. Peabody, *Education for Life: The Story of Hampton Institute* (New York: Doubleday, Page & Co., 1918), in *Journal of Negro History* 3, no. 4 (October 1918): 449.
8. Wesley Brown, *Boogie Woogie and Booker T.*, performed at the New Federal Theatre, New York, February 12, 1987; reprinted in *Plays in Process* 8, no. 3 (New York: Theatre Communications Group, 1988). Washington advertised this meeting, sometimes called the New York Conference, as an effort to unite African American leaders, as he wrote to Du Bois, "to try to agree upon certain fundamental principles." Washington to Du Bois, November 8, 1903, in *The Correspondence of W. E. B. Du Bois* (Amherst: University of Massachusetts Press, 1973), 1:53–54. Washington's ulterior motive, as Louis R. Harlan sees it, was "to outmaneuver and overwhelm"

some of his critics (Washington's most adamant critic, William Monroe Trotter, among others, was excluded from attendance), and thus to limit the damage they might do to his standing with the patrons whose interest he had a solid lock upon. Harlan, *Booker T. Washington: The Wizard of Tuskegee*, chap. 3. The quotation is found on page 63. There is an additional level to Washington's machinations that involves his inviting of several of his most important supporters from the worlds of philanthropy and journalism including Andrew Carnegie and Oswald Garrison Villard. This was surely, as Harlan suggests, to overawe the gathering (which, anyway, he had packed with Washingtonians). But, one thinks, it was also to impress Washington's white guests with his mastery of the occasion; that is to say, Washington saw this summit of important Negroes as a pageant—like the Tuskegee Institute itself—within which he could demonstrate to white people, rather than persuade African Americans of, the greater efficacy of his ideas.

9. Washington, *Up From Slavery*, 53.

10. Washington, letter to the editor of the *Southern Workman*, September 28, 1895; *Papers*, 1:389–391; Washington, *Up From Slavery*, 54–55.

11. Smiley and Armstrong comments in Isabel C. Barrows, ed., *The First Mohonk Conference on the Negro Question Held At Lake Mohonk, Ulster County, New York, June 4, 5, 6, 1890* (New York: Negro Universities Press, 1969 [1890]), 21–22, 13–14.

12. Indeed, Washington invoked the same rude calculus later in his career, but to make a quite different point than Armstrong, arguing that "from the very day that Lincoln emancipated us we have taken care of ourselves, so far as our bodily and personal needs are concerned, except in the case of some special or local calamity." Untitled address at Carnegie Hall delivered February 23, 1909; *Papers*, 10:47–52. The quoted remarks are found on page 52.

13. The outline of the Armstrong family's life in Hawaii and the quotations above are from Robert Francis Engs, *Educating the Disfranchised and Disinherited: Samuel Chapman Armstrong and Hampton Institute, 1839–1893* (Knoxville: University of Tennessee Press, 1999), chap. 1.

14. Louis R. Harlan, *Booker T. Washington: The Making of a Black Leader, 1865–1901* (New York: Oxford University Press, 1973), 61, 64.

15. Washington, *Up From Slavery*, 73–75.

16. Armstrong in the *Southern Workman* 6 (February 1877): 10; Harlan, *Booker T. Washington: The Making of a Black Leader*, 74.

17. Louis R. Harlan, *Booker T. Washington: The Wizard of Tuskegee, 1901–1915* (New York: Oxford University Press, 1983), 72.

18. Armstrong quoted in Engs, *Educating the Disfranchised and Disinherited*, 149.

19. Harlan, *Booker T. Washington: The Wizard of Tuskegee*, 75.

20. [n.a.], "The Seventh Annual Commencement," *Hartford Courant*, June 14, 1875, 1; [n.a.], "Commencement Day with the Colored Students," *New-York Times*, June 15, 1875, 5; and [n.a.], "Colored Youth on the Commencement Stage," Springfield *Daily Republican*, June 26, 1875, 8; reprinted in *Papers*, 2:51, 58.

21. The characterization of Armstrong's attitude is Harlan's in *Booker T. Washington: The Making of a Black Leader*, 60.

22. King won second place in the Webb Oratorical contest in his second year. The individual who won first place is not mentioned in the literature of the civil rights movement. Stephen B. Oates, *Let The Trumpet Sound: The Life of Martin Luther King, Jr.* (New York: Harper & Row, 1982), 19.

23. Mary Mosely Lucy to Washington, November 3, 1903, quoted in Harlan, *Booker T. Washington: The Making of a Black Leader*, 76.

24. Washington, *Up From Slavery*, 66.

25. Ibid., 76.

26. Booker T. Washington, *The Story of My Life and Work* (Toronto: J. L. Nichols & Co., 1900); *Papers*, 1:24.

27. Quoted in Byrd Prillerman, "Booker T. Washington Among His West Virginia Neighbors," *National Magazine* 17 (December 1902): 353–356; *Papers*, 6:618.

28. Washington, *Up From Slavery*, 75.

29. Lewisburg *Greenbrier Independent*, August 4, 1877, 2; *Papers*, 2:72.

30. Malcolm X and Alex Haley, *The Autobiography of Malcolm X* (New York: Random House, 1984 [1965]), 36.

31. Washington, *Up From Slavery*, 16.

32. Washington, "What I Am Trying to Do," *World's Work* 27 (November 1913): 101–107; *Papers*, 12:354–355.

33. Washington, "Atlanta Exposition Speech," *Papers*, 3:584, 586.

34. Washington, 'What I Am Trying To Do"; *Papers*, 12:352.

35. Ibid., 353, 354.

36. Booker T. Washington, *The Future of the American Negro*; *Papers*, 5:307–308.

37. Washington, *Up From Slavery*, 149, 153, 145.

38. Quoted in August Meier, *Negro Thought in America, 1880–1915* (Ann Arbor: University of Michigan Press, 1963), 4.

39. Howells, "An Exemplary Citizen," *North American Review* 173 (August 1901): 280–288.

40. Booker T. Washington, *The Future of the American Negro* (Boston: Small, Maynard & Co., 1899); *Papers*, 5:308.

41. Ibid., 307–308, 313.

42. In completing his thought, even Washington recognizes this truth about singular black accomplishment and the rule of exceptions, and so takes pains to add, "This I have said here, not to call attention to myself as an individual, but to the race to which I am proud to belong." *Up From Slavery*, 41.

43. Booker T. Washington, "The Negro's Life in Slavery," *Outlook* 93 (September 11, 1909): 71–78; *Papers*, 10:174.

44. Foner, *Reconstruction*, 577.

45. Guy M. Bryan to Rutherford B. Hayes, December 19, 1874; Rutherford B. Hayes to Guy M. Bryan, January 2, 1875; Hayes to Bryan, July 27, 1875; all in Sinkler, *Racial Attitudes*. The characterization of Bryan's role is found on page 162.

46. Carl Schurz to Hayes, June 21, 1876; Sinkler, *Racial Attitudes*, 175.

47. Hayes to Schurz, June 27, 1876; Sinkler, *Racial Attitudes*, 175–176.

48. Hayes letter of acceptance, July 18, 1876; in James Quay Howard, *The Life, Public Services and Selected Speeches of Rutherford B. Hayes* (Cincinnati: R. Clark & Co., 1876).

49. Cox to Hayes, January 31, 1877; Hayes to Cox, February 2, 1877; Sinkler, *Racial Attitudes*, 178–180.

50. Hayes diary entry of February 9, 1877; Hayes diary entry of February 18, 1877; "Inaugural Address of President Hayes, March 4, 1877," in Sinkler, *Racial Attitudes*, 181–182.

51. See John W. Burgess, *The Administration of President Hayes* (New York: Charles Scribner's Sons, 1916), and, especially, Louis D. Rubin Jr., *Teach the Freeman: The Correspondence of Rutherford B. Hayes and the Slater Fund for Negro Education, 1881–1887 & 1888–1893* (Baton Rouge: Louisiana State University Press, 1959), vols. 1 and 2. On the other hand, Rayford W. Logan, *The Negro in American Life and Thought*, chap. 1, disagrees sharply with this argument.

52. On the planning of the conference and the effort to attain an ideological consensus, see comments by organizer Albert K. Smiley and by Hayes in Barrows, *First Mohonk*, 7–12.

53. Armstrong comments, ibid., 66.

54. See: Abbott, "Letters to Unknown Friends," *Outlook* 100 (January 20, 1912): 115–116. The characterization is Du Bois's from "Dr. Abbott and the Good Samaritan," *Crisis* 3 (May 1912): 18–19; see also "An Unswerving Friend," *Crisis* 7 (March 1914): 224.

55. Tourgee comments in Barrows, *First Mohonk*, 115–116.

56. Ibid., 106.

57. Ibid., 67.

58. Armstrong to Washington, February 10, 1879, *Papers*, 2:75; Washington, *Up From Slavery*, 65; *Congregationalist* 31 (May 28, 1879), 169 in *Papers*, 2:76n.

59. Booker T. Washington, "Incidents of Indian Life at Hampton," *Southern Workman* 9 (December 1880): 125; *Papers*, 2:95.

60. Booker T. Washington, "Incidents of Indian Life at Hampton," *Southern Workman* 10 (January 1881): 7; *Papers*, 2:103-104; Washington, "Incidents of Indian Life at Hampton," *Southern Workman* 10 (April 1881): 43; *Papers*, 2:124–125.

61. Washington, "Incidents of Indian Life at Hampton," (April 1881); "Incidents of Indian Life at Hampton," *Southern Workman* 9 (October 1880): 103; *Papers*, 2:86.

62. Washington, "Incidents of Indian Life at Hampton" (October 1880).

63. Washington, "Incidents of Indian Life at Hampton," *Southern Workman* 10 (May 1881): 55; *Papers*, 2:128–130, 131n.

64. Armstrong to George Washington Campbell and Trustees of the Tuskegee Institute, May 31, 1881; *Papers*, 2:127.

65. Washington, *Up From Slavery*, 100–101.

66. Washington, *The Story of My Life and Work*; Papers, 1:24.

67. Stone to Washington, July 2, 1903; *Papers*, 7:192–193; [n.a.],"Changing the Angle of the Forehead: That is the Problem that Confronts the Negro," San Francisco *Examiner* (June 1903), quoted in Emma L. Thornborough, "Booker T. Washington As Seen by His White Contemporaries," *Journal of Negro History* 53, no. 2 (April 1968): 164–165.

68. George Washington Taylor to Washington, June 27, 1904; Washington to George Washington Taylor, July 5, 1904; *Papers*, 8:5.

69. Washington, *Up From Slavery*, 41. The burden of Joel Williamson's argument is that the origins of the civil rights movement may be found in the "rivalry between mulatto and black perspectives," and that the former, personified by Washington as a part of the "mulatto elite," held sway until the rising of the 1950s led by Martin King, who Williamson takes to be an exemplar of the "black elite." One need not embrace or even be conscious of one's membership in the "mulatto elite," but rather has only to fail to inaugurate a social movement and, perforce, be properly enlisted by the historian. *New People: Miscegenation and Mulattoes in the United States* (New York: Free Press, 1980), 180.

70. Mamie Garvin Fields describes one of this type, a man known as the "black mayor of Charleston" because he worked as a factotum for the actual mayor of the South Carolina city and was supposed to "do for the black what the mayor did for the white." Fields thought this not so, although he was allowed "to hand out jobs that you couldn't get otherwise." His real function, as she saw it, was to keep a handle on Negro doings for the white city fathers. Mamie Garvin Fields with Karen Fields, *Lemon Swamp and Other Places: A Carolina Memoir* (New York: Free Press, 1983), 108–109.

71. Armstrong quoted in L. P. Jackson, "The Origins of Hampton Institute," *Journal of Negro History* 10, no. 2 (April 1925): 149. On covering up about the economics of industrial education, Engs writes, "A basic fallacy in Armstrong's argument for Hampton was his oft-repeated claim that manual labor 'could support itself.' It could not. Armstrong knew that and had admitted as much during Hampton's formative years. It was true that most students were able to defray the costs of room and board through their labor, but they could not earn enough to pay tuition and other expenses. To keep Hampton afloat, the general had to raise enormous amounts of money" (151). This , too, was an example Washington would follow at Tuskegee. Sociologist Charles S. Johnson pointed out years ago that Tuskegee and other citadels of industrial education were "handicapped by lack of facilities." *A Preface to Racial Understanding* (New York: Friendship Press, 1936), 78.

72. Washington to the Editor, December 18, 1881, in *Southern Workman*, 11 (January 1882): 9; Washington to James Fowle Baldwin Marshall, June 25, July 5, July 7, July 9, July 16, July 18, and July 23, 1881; Washington to Francis Chickering Briggs, June 28 and July 16, 1881; Washington to Marshall, June 29, 1881; Washington to Marshall, November (?) 3, 1881; Washington to the Editor, July 14, 1881, in *Southern Workman*, 10 (September 1881): 94. This correspondence may be found in *Papers*, 2:132–152.

73. Washington, *Up From Slavery*, 154, 90–91, 123, 122, 126, 143, and 155–156.

74. Jeremiah Barnes to Washington, September 14, 1887, Reel 95, 113–114; Henrietta Benbow to Washington, September 19, 1887, Reel 95, 115–116; A. Campbell to Washington, September 27, 1887, Reel 95, 509; Frank Armstead to Washington, September 18, 1885, Reel 95, 14–15; Washington to Littleton Cobb, October 13, 1887; Washington Papers, Library of Congress, Reel 93, 122–123.

75. Washington to Littleton Cobb, October 13, 1887; Washington Papers, Library of Congress, Reel 93, 122–123.

76. Booker T. Washington, "Industrial Education," speech before the Alabama State Teachers Association, April 7, 1882, in *Minutes of the First Annual Session, Alabama State Teachers' Association, April 6–7, 1882* (Selma, 1882); *Papers*, 2:192.

77. Washington, *Up From Slavery*, 83.

78. Logan to Washington, July 12, 1888; *Papers*, 2:468.

79. Washington, untitled speech before the Boston Unitarian Club, 1888; *Papers*, 2:498, 503.

80. Harlan, *Booker T. Washington: The Making of a Black Leader*, 155; Anonymous to John Henry Washington, April 23, 1889; *Papers*, 2:526.

81. Flyer entitled "Convenient Routes To and From Tuskegee, Institute, Alabama," in Washington Papers, Library of Congress, Reel 425, 620.

82. C. Vann Woodward describes the business variant of this fetish for ex-Confederates, writing, "It was a poor subsidiary of an Eastern railroad that could not find some impoverished brigadier general to lend his name to a letterhead." *Origins of the New South, 1877–1913* (Baton Rouge: Louisiana State University Press, 1971), 14.

83. Hurston, *Their Eyes Were Watching God* (New York: HarperCollins, 1990 [1937]), 1.

Index